WAR OF THE WORDS

WAR OF THE WORDS

EDITED BY JOY PRESS

 THREE RIVERS PRESS · NEW YORK

A complete list of permissions appears on pages 315–318.

Published by Three Rivers Press, New York, New York.
Member of the Crown Publishing Group.

Random House, Inc.
New York, Toronto, London, Sydney, Auckland
www.randomhouse.com

THREE RIVERS PRESS is a registered trademark and
the Three Rivers Press colophon is a trademark of
Random House, Inc.

Printed in the United States of America

Library of Congress Cataloging-in-Publication Data is
available upon request.

ISBN 0-609-80853-2

10 9 8 7 6 5 4 3 2 1

First Edition

Contents

Introduction by Joy Press . . . . **vii**
A Short but Sweet Oral History of The VLS . . . . **x**

O N E Writers Reconsidered: New Takes on the Old Guard **1**

Albert Mobilio **on** *Gertrude Stein* **3**
David Foster Wallace **on** *Feodor Dostoevsky* **17**
Henry Louis Gates, Jr., **on** *Langston Hughes* **30**
Blanche McCrary Boyd **on** *Katherine Anne Porter* **43**
Paul Elie **on** *John Cheever* **50**
Bharati Mukherjee **on** *Salman Rushdie* **53**
Andrew O'Hagan **on** *Don DeLillo* **64**

T W O Rescue Me: Snatching Writers from the Dustbin of History **71**

Michele Wallace **on** *Zora Neale Hurston* **73**
Erik Davis **on** *Philip K. Dick* **84**
Gary Indiana **on** *Thomas Bernhard* **89**
Greg Tate **on** *Samuel Delany* **96**
Edmund White **on** *Djuna Barnes* **103**
Darcey Steinke **on** *William Goyen* **110**
Joe Wood **on** *Albert Murray* **113**
Rick Moody **on** *Angela Carter* **129**

T H R E E Signs of the Times: Capturing a Cultural Moment **135**

Walter Kendrick **on** *the Freud Backlash* **137**
Ellen Willis **on** *Angela Davis, bell hooks, and*
   Black Feminism **152**
Richard Goldstein **on** *Plague Literature in the*
   Age of AIDS **166**

Thulani Davis **on** *Buppie Writers* **176**
Michael Bérubé **on** *Postmodernism* **186**
Michael Warner **on** *Queer Theory* **200**
Scott L. Malcomson **on** *Whiteness and Anthropology* **208**
Lynne Tillman **on** *the Future of Fiction* **220**

🄵🄾🄾🅁 **Pulp Friction:**
Obsessing over Pop Culture **223**

Dorothy Allison **on** *Anne Rice* **225**
Lisa Jones **on** *Black Romance Novels* **232**
Geoffrey O'Brien **on** Classics *Comics* **236**
Hilton Als **on** *Sammy Davis, Jr.* **240**
Greil Marcus **on** *Situationism* **242**
Guy Trebay **on** The Andy Warhol Diaries **259**
Vince Aletti **on** *Physique Magazines* **266**
Jonathan Lethem **on** *Science Fiction's Lost Promise* **268**
Paul Berman **on** The Pentagon Catalog **274**
Mark Dery **on** *Apocalypse Culture* **276**

🄵🄸🅅🄴 **Brave New Wave:**
Spotlight on Emerging Writers **279**

Peter Schjeldahl **on** *Dennis Cooper* **281**
C. Carr **on** *Kathy Acker* **285**
Stacey D'Erasmo **on** *Mary Gaitskill* **292**
David Shields **on** *Nicholson Baker* **296**
Katherine Dieckmann **on** *Lorrie Moore* **300**
Jeff Yang **on** *Chang-Rae Lee* **302**
Richard B. Woodward **on** *Jonathan Lethem* **307**

Acknowledgments **311**
About the Contributors **312**
Permissions **315**

■ntroduction

I confess: *VLS* warped my young mind. Stumbling upon it as a teenager in the mid-'80s, I found a space in which you could be an intellectual and a punk; where it was okay to love Kafka and comic books, Anne Sexton and the Sex Pistols, Mary McCarthy and Mary Gaitskill. Back then, lit-crit institutions like the *Partisan Review* and *The New York Review of Books*—once breeding grounds for original minds—had settled into a stiff, stuffy worldview. Swapping highbrow snobbery for a seductive mix of downtown cool and zealot fervor, *The Voice Literary Supplement* discovered a new audience—readers like me who loved books but felt alienated by the way the established magazines treated literature as a sanctuary from the funky mess of the modern world.

When I was offered the chance to edit *The VLS* in 1997, it was my dream job. The intoxicating level of editorial freedom means that *VLS* can be esoteric or accessible—preferably both. There's no pressure to run positive reviews of "important" books, and conversely no one to disapprove if we rave about an uncool mainstream book. Its placement in *The Village Voice* (read by about 700,000 people) and its very reasonable cost (free) makes it possible to imagine converting the unconverted, or serendipitously nabbing some readers who pick it up out of curiosity, piqued by a striking cover image or compelled by the prospect of a long subway journey. *VLS* may have started as a New York institution, but by now its national reach (and its online presence) allows us to expose new voices to a broad, eclectic audience. The annual Writers on the Verge issue, which I inaugurated four years ago for that very reason, spotlights writers we think have the talent to shake up the literary landscape. And every month, *VLS* allows me to bring on board livewire, opinionated writers and let them surprise me.

A dream job, but also a heady challenge—building on *The VLS's* legacy while making sure it evolves with the times. Founded by *Village Voice* arts editor M. Mark in 1981 as an extension of the *Voice's* book review section, *The VLS* rapidly became a forum for the most adventurous critical writing of the day. Its mission statement might have been: Locate the cutting edge, rethink the canon, resurrect the unjustly forgotten. *The VLS* fostered new talent by publishing short stories from emerging writers like Dorothy Allison, Russell Banks, Sandra Cisneros, and Michelle Cliff. And it became a sort of homebase for a New York coterie of writers—Kathy Acker, Gary Indiana, Dennis Cooper, Eileen Myles, Lynne Tillman—whose work was dubbed "transgressive" or "downtown" fiction. Alongside this support for contemporary renegade writers, *The VLS* also forged its own loose and unruly countertradition of mavericks, misfits, and ahead-of-their-time visionaries—a sort of anticanon in which Feodor Dostoevsky rubbed shoulders with Dawn Powell, and Herman Melville jostled for space with Philip K. Dick.

VLS was never "just" a book review, though. It treats literature as something intimately entangled with the conflicts and confusions raging outside the realm of paper and ink. *VLS* emerged against a Reagan-era backdrop of cultural retreat, a reaction against the previous decades' radicalism and hedonism. But this apparent placidity was just a thin membrane concealing all kinds of turmoil. Throughout the '80s and '90s, crusades for and against multiculturalism, postmodernism, and dozens of other -isms convulsed American public life. *The VLS* leaped into the fray with a series of landmark essays and thinkpieces that grappled with the era's most provocative debates and literary movements: women's and gay studies, AIDS, pornography, the rise of Asian-American writers, the mainstreaming of black fiction, religious fundamentalism, and the fragmenting of the American left.

But what made *The VLS* stand out from the pack was the way it simultaneously had fun being serious and took fun seriously. So Greil Marcus wrote about Elvis back in 1981, J. Hoberman covered film lit, and C. Carr dissected all kinds of marginal ephemera, from stamp art to zines and weirdo pamphlets. Pulp genres that highbrow journals shunned—comics, science fiction, romance novels, potboilers—found a home in *VLS*, as our writers gleefully traced their cultural significance, aesthetic power, and cheap thrills.

Today, of course, it's much less clear what "bohemia" or "underground" signifies than when the supplement was founded. From music to films to the literary scene, left-field ideas cross over with disconcerting speed, a process that depletes them of content while sapping the community that originally nourished them. And business culture permeates the book world like never before; borders between criticism and commerce blur as magazines play merchant by selling books online, and retailers disguise themselves as reviewers. Elsewhere, editorial and advertising increasingly collapse into one, as if book reviews were just consumer guides or a handy source of blurbs for the back cover. In the face of all this, *VLS* maintains its independent editorial spirit, sifting through cultural flotsam and jetsam—whether an obsession with freak literature or Internet diaries—and mining them for significance. *VLS* has morphed with several generations of writers and readers because it encourages its critics to keep open to cultural change. Above all, *The VLS* remains a place somewhere between a playground and a training camp for emerging critics; we encourage them to stretch out and take risks, and then set them loose on an unsuspecting world.

S canning the yellowing pages of *VLS*'s dusty, bound archives last fall, I was staggered by the consistent quality of the writing over the years, as well as the caliber of writers and editors who've come through the ranks. In my initial excitement about putting together an anthology with such a vast selection of good material to choose from, I overlooked the down side: what a vast selection of good material to choose from! At least three completely different and equally fine collections could be compiled from the material I've left out, and it does pain me to think of some of the brilliant essays not included here. This anthology is not a collection of the Top 40 pieces of writing that ever appeared in *The VLS* (an impossible thing to judge, and anyway, *VLS* was never about simplistic decrees of superiority). Instead, it is one editor's attempt to convey the magazine's multiple facets and to tell its story.

Journalism is a funny, fleeting thing. Some of the articles I remembered most fondly from the past didn't hold up to contemporary scrutiny; dozens of others I didn't recollect have gained enormous resonance with the passage of time. Some are included in this collection precisely because they are dated. I mean that in a good way: They reflect their cultural moment with a vividness and precision that could never be re-created retrospectively. Others, particularly the profiles of individual writers, have the quality of ageless classics. Regardless of when they were written, all of the pieces chosen for this book feel alive today.

JOY PRESS
Literary Editor, *The Village Voice*
January 2001

A Short but Sweet
Oral History of *The* Ⓥ Ⓛ Ⓢ

David Schneiderman (*Village Voice* editor-in-chief, 1978–1985, now CEO of *Village Voice* Media): One of the things I remembered well from the '70s as a *Voice* reader was this thing in the book section that happened maybe once a quarter—a couple of pages of books called *VLS*, like a takeoff on *TLS*. So I had this name, *VLS*, in the back of my head. When I became the *Voice*'s editor, I made M. Mark arts editor. We loved books and tried to figure out what we could do, but kept getting discouraging news from the ad department.

M. Mark (*VLS* editor, 1981–1994, now teaches at Bard College and edits *PEN America*.): In spring 1981, I was down in the advertising department complaining that our books section was tiny. There were so many wonderful writers who weren't getting the attention they deserved because we didn't sell enough ads. [Ad rep] Sally Cohen conferred and came back to me and said, "You're not going to believe this—we have trouble selling a three-page book section, but we might be able to sell a monthly magazine. Do a prospectus we can take to the ABA [American Booksellers' Association convention]." I sat down and brainstormed with a bunch of my friends, then I went off and did the prospectus. I felt so free because I didn't think anything would come of it, and I basically put down my dream magazine.

David Schneiderman: So they came back from ABA and said, "A lot of people like this idea."

M. Mark: I reacted to this by having a full-blown anxiety attack. I used to wake up early in the morning kind of sweaty. Because David said, "Your prospectus sold it. You do what you think is right." In terms of my editorial autonomy he was remarkable. He was there when we'd have brainstorming sessions and he had a lot of good ideas. I used to joke that it was like Mickey Rooney and Judy Garland— "Hey, my dad has a barn and I'll make the costumes"—yet it was true. There was this sort of "Wow, we're kids, but they let us have a magazine."

The cover piece for the first issue in October '81 was by Walter Kendrick—I think the headline was "What Do Shrinks Really Want?" Walter was an accomplished essayist, and he was always early with his copy. But his deadline passed, and he was in a panic and I was in a panic. . . . It was Thursday, and we had to have all the edited copy to the printer by Monday night. I said, "Bring me what you've got." Walter was usually extremely neat, but I remember him standing at the door of my apartment looking so tragic, clutching this grimy, slightly balled-up manuscript. And it was awful, truly awful. I really wanted an expansive essay in which books made an appearance, and the later ones we did without much effort, but doing that first one was really hard. Those were the days before computers, and the only thing I could think to do was to cut up this 15-page essay into little strips. We just put it on the floor—maybe 75 to 80 pieces of paper—and I moved the pieces around, and then we stapled them to pieces of a yellow legal pad. Here's the remarkable thing: Walter took it home, slept for a few hours, worked for another 24, and then he came back 28 hours later with a beautiful essay.

David Schneiderman: I put the first issue on the cover of the *Voice* and it sold really well; it was one of the best sellers of the year. As long as I was editor virtually every *VLS* we did was the cover story.

M. Mark: The first several issues, the staff was really me, the unflappable Judy Hottensen, and a young editor who left New York many years ago named Debra Rae Cohen. We were a skeletal staff, working round the clock, but we didn't regret a moment of it, it was so much fun. . . . As we grew and got more ads, David gave the okay to hire more staff, so Ellen Willis—an old friend of mine—came for a while. Then she went off to have a baby and Walter Kendrick came. He gave up his teaching job for two years in order to come and partner me—it really did feel like a dance we were doing.

Geoffrey O'Brien (writer): When I met Walter I thought he was one of those characters in the movies who would be played by George Sanders or Clifton Webb who effortlessly uttered these beautifully shaped aphorisms while sipping on his cocktail. When his book on pornography, *The Secret Museum,* came out they had him on TV up against some Christian-right guy. There was Walter, cool as a cucumber, imperturbable, just uttering his little bon mots.

Dorothy Allison (writer): Walter Kendrick was determined to teach me to get over saying "I." He believed that you couldn't be a real journalist unless you learned to give up the first person pronoun and become an impartial distant observer. You gotta break the bones and reset 'em, he told me at one point. The hours to train me out of the habit of saying "I" were just astronomical, but after that I had the choice. By the time I passed Walter's standards I could pass almost anybody's standards.

**Polly Shulman (editorial assistant/senior editor 1984–1994, now reviews books for *Newsday*): One of the things we did was encourage really young people. We had an unspoken rule that we'd let anyone write a Brief Encounter [review]. If it didn't work, so we wasted one Brief. But if it worked out we might find some new sensibility. That let in a lot of people—they grew up a little in our pages, then more mainstream places would pick up on them. Scott Malcomson, Colson Whitehead, Jane Mendelsohn, Hilton Als . . . Dwight Garner started out with us and ended up at the *Times,* so did William Grimes.

M. Mark: Wes Anderson, my art director, heard me give a speech once where someone asked me about my editing philosophy. I said, "Well, embarrassing as it seems, I just wanted to publish articles I think are interesting." And Wes said, "Oh yes, the masturbatory approach to editing!" He had a point. The staff grew in the same way: I would meet someone whose mind interested me.

Gary Indiana (writer): I think *The VLS* was a great vehicle for a lot of people, particularly for the kind of writers who were stigmatized as "downtown writers"—Kathy Acker, Lynne Tillman, Dennis Cooper, me. . . . I was just one of a number of writers who worked very hard and tried to do adventurous things, and yet would have this reputation as being some sort of sordid drug-addicted whatever. . . . These were writers who were out of the mainstream—the mainstream literary world in the United States is so ghastly anyway. It's a club. At least with *VLS* people who were not in the club had their own club.

Geoffrey O'Brien: From a writer's point of view, the beauty of it was that there was tremendous freedom both in terms of subject matter and length. I did this piece on Melville, which took up a major chunk of that issue of *The VLS,* and it took months to write. We were very nearly on food stamps as a result of the length of time it took to finish. But I was just really excited about the fact that there was a desire at *VLS* to do what other people weren't doing— anything from an arcane scholarly monograph to an underground comic or a reassessment of Ovid.

M. Mark: It was important to me to talk about books and authors who weren't being treated with respect elsewhere. It was also really important to have idiosyncratic writerly voices. I wanted us to be able to write about the most scholarly book, but in a conversational tone. Intellectually and philosophically rigorous, but vivid and colloquial in tone. So that we would open up the discussion of literature to a lot of people who were smart and interested but who wouldn't read the sort of scholarly writing that is jargon-ridden and only aimed at fifty of the writer's colleagues.

Laurie Muchnick (associate editor 1990–1992, now books editor of *Newsday*): Mainstream was M.'s biggest derogatory word. She would talk about a writer she didn't like too much and she would say they're "too mainstream." So we saw our mission as reviewing the books that no one else was reviewing. Whereas [*Village Voice* editor] John Larsen saw our mission differently: as reviewing the books everybody else is reviewing but giving the *Voice* perspective on them.

David Schneiderman: It was a really great place to attract new writers and allow them to write about sociopolitical issues they wouldn't necessarily get to tackle elsewhere in the *Voice*, then allegedly dominated by what we called "the white boys." It was one of the charming political splits in the paper: The front and back of the book eventually became the white boys versus the Stalinist feminists, which is what M. and [editors] Karen Durbin and Ellen Willis were dubbed.

Dorothy Allison: I was always hearing rumors about bloodbaths in the halls in the *Voice*, people turning bookcases over. It was always, you should've been here! I did go to the bathroom once and heard people having sex in the next stall. I never got over that. I ran out of there as fast as I could—heterosexuals sound different having sex!

Polly Shulman: My first day at *VLS* there was a fistfight behind my desk. There was a lot of noise and I turned around and there were two large men socking each other, and David had to come out of his office and break them up. . . .

M. Mark: When we moved to the Cooper Square office *The VLS* was on a different floor from the rest of the *Voice*, which I suspect caused some ill feeling at the paper because we had beautiful big offices up there—as big as some people's apartments—all lined with bookshelves.

Dorothy Allison: In the office, books were stacked hip and shoulder high. You'd try to pull out something eight books from the bottom, and M. would say, "Ohmigod, not that one!" and snatch another one from the top. Then you'd have to go later and shift books until you got the one you wanted, and if you had a good argument she'd probably let you try it. Out of chaos came some wonderful stuff.

M. Mark: I was always pushing for bigger and better and more. And what made it all possible was, not only did readers seem hungry for alternatives to the *New York Times* and *The New York Review* but publishers did as well. They had lots of books that didn't seem appropriate to advertise elsewhere, so the response was amazing.

David Schneiderman: *VLS* was doing well, it was bringing readership in, it was good for the paper editorially, the staff liked writing for it, it had a nice reputation. And then in 1988 a new publisher came in and convinced us that if we went national this thing would really take off. We figured, we're going to compete with the *New York Review of Books.*

Stacey D'Erasmo (associate editor/senior editor 1988–1996, now writer): *The New York Review of Books* and the *Partisan Review* were like our parents' or even our grandparents' intellectual generation. *The VLS* addressed a new intellectual generation who needed a voice. And of course, we were going to speak about the pop culture, the gender politics, the gay stuff—that's our time.

Scott Malcomson (senior editor 1989–1996, now writer): *The New York Review* had a set of writers and a way of thinking that had been, if not radical, oppositional for quite a while. But by the '80s it was no longer oppositional. Just about everything we focused on happened to be things the *Review* didn't—anything explicitly by women, gay people, nonwhite people, and concerning trends within academia was not published there. That was the space we came to fill.

Geoffrey O'Brien: A lot of us were looking for a different tone of voice for literary writing. Not that kind of scholar-peering-out-from-within-this-academic-fortress. At the same time, we did not want to be cheerleaders for pop culture. We wanted this kind of balance somewhere in the middle of all of those things. It seemed important to find a different way of talking that would allow you to entertain complex and maybe ambiguous arguments, without necessarily taking a militant stand on one side or another.

Stacey D'Erasmo: It was literary journalism, which no one does anymore. There was a time when you could say, "I do literary journalism." Now it now sounds like, "I draw specimens of birds," something really important in the 19th century. *VLS* really took everything as living text that you could roll around in. Who was it who said metaphor is the yoking together of unlike things? You could continually yoke together unlike things and think about them with equal weight. Now I guess we would call it "postmodern."

Laurie Muchnick: Stacey and Scott were plugged in to what was going on in the Academy, so we had an issue on queer theory long before anyone else covered it. We had a really early issue on cultural studies, and an Internet issue in 1993!

Stacey D'Erasmo: These were the days when theory was really, really hot and really contested, and *The VLS* made all of that very sexy. I'd been doing my master's in English lit and was not happy in academia. When I got to *The VLS* it was like I could take all the stuff I had been doing and completely turn it around—be irreverent, write about it now in the present moment. This headline "Yo, Hermeneutics!" really summed up that spirit. In one issue, you could have Walter writing about Vanna White, Scott writing about Slavoj Žižek, someone else writing about Dr. Seuss. It took the walls down in a way that was, for book reviews, like rock and roll.

Scott Malcomson: When you're in your early 20s and ambitious, almost anything you do feels like you're in the middle of a cultural explosion, even if no one else knows it. The connection between multiculturalism and theory was that both were devoted to opposing a single dominant view of history and culture. Multiculturalism argued for the necessity of paying attention to a variety of cultural groups. Theory undermined Eurocentrism in a more philosophical manner, by dismantling the grand narratives. But they were very connected because they were both different ways of opposing a monolithic Western worldview.

Geoffrey O'Brien: The '80s were like the hangover after this great intoxicated period of political commitment. It was the morning after, and lots more contrary impulses were at work. The unspoken theme of a lot of our writing was, "Well where are we now? What is the legacy of everything we went through these last 15 years? Are we still going somewhere or are we just drifting through the wreckage of this great enterprise?" But still with a lot of good humor about it, not this overwrought apocalyptic tone.

Stacey D'Erasmo: There was a Monty Python aspect of *VLS* that I really loved. It recognized that yes, smart people read trash. In book reviews, this had not been done before. In other kinds of journalism, the upending of high and low, and everything that we think about as New Journalism, had obviously been done. But book reviews were these very earnest, staid publications that were very cautious and reserved in tone. So I'm not saying we were the first people to talk about pop culture, but in terms of book reviews, it was a big deal.

Geoffrey O'Brien: There was a sense that it's the quality of the attention that is the issue here, so whether one is writing about Hegel or a comic book is not important. It's what they are making out of it.

Lee Smith (editor 1995–1996, now literary editor of *Talk* magazine): Before I took over as editor of *The VLS*, I'd written a piece for it, so I knew *VLS* well. There were things that infuriated me about it. I remember once I was with a friend, walking up and down screaming about some pieces in *The VLS*. I was so enraged I was going to write a letter. There are few publications that can get you that mad.

My sense was that *The VLS*, like the *Voice*, had already won the battle it set out to win. A lot of their writers are now published in mainstream places, and everyone was totally influenced by the *Voice*. Like the *Voice*, the *VLS* seemed to have won pretty decisively.

They had managed to make these books people cared about. So I wanted to change the tone a bit. There were a number of novelists I'd known for a while starting to publish their books—like David Foster Wallace, Rick Moody, A. M. Homes—whom I really believed in, so I wanted to get behind them. With the nonfiction stuff I was actually more mad at *The New York Review of Books* than at *VLS*. *NYRB* was so old, and they were missing so much stuff, it was insane. So I was sort of responding to what they'd missed. We had a nice cover piece on Rem Koolhaas by Frederic Jamison. And I said, Frederic Jamison is a real heavyweight—who cares if it's legible? . . . I was probably wrong to have moved as far off from pop culture as I did. But it's not really my thing. I wanted to avoid anthologies, because they seemed to me to be just about identity politics. I was much more interested in intellectual attack than celebration. That's a great *Voice* tradition, getting people incensed. . . . Tom Frank wrote a piece on Andrew Ross and Ross wrote a letter. It said something like, "In the same pages you attack bell hooks, me, Cornell West. . . . What has happened to the *Voice*?" Tom wanted to write a long response but I said, no, no, no. Just say, "Mr. Ross forgot to mention that I compared him to Kevin Bacon in the movie *Footloose*." I liked taking it down to that level sometimes. I think it's a good thing if people have lively debates in this community.

Hugh Garvey (editorial assistant/associate editor 1993–1997, now senior editor at *The Industry Standard*): I wrote this article about how Ethan Hawke had written a novel, and my reporting suggested that he was holding the film rights so he could make a movie based on his own book. So I had this really mean kicker, something like, "As Divine Brown knows, you can get $50,000 for fellating a movie star. Ethan Hawke seems to have learned that if you're a movie star you can get five times that amount for fellating yourself." Some months later at the ABA, I was at a party and this publicist says, "Hugh, do you want to meet Ethan Hawke? Ethan, this is Hugh." At first he averted his eyes and drank Bloody Marys. Eventually I fessed up that I'd written that article. He turned and looked me in the eye and said, "*You're* Hugh Garvey? Well, *fuck you man*. Fuck you!" He said, "Of all the pieces ever written about me, that one affected me most. I was writing in my journal over and over again, 'I'm sucking my own dick, I'm sucking my own dick!'"

Jonathan Lethem (writer): Yeah, people did recognize me on the street [after *VLS* published a profile and the review that appears in this collection]. That was a real watershed moment, getting that spread in *VLS*. But also it was such an incredible thrill to be photographed by [longtime *VLS* photographer] Sylvia Plachy. She's this strange, amazing character. All her lights are these handmade objects, pre-war things modified with tin foil and pipe cleaners. She'd say, "I don't know if this will work. Be warned, sometimes I fail." It was an experience.

M. Mark: *VLS* is established now. It's not an establishment publication, but it's been there for as long as many of the young writers can remember and when we were starting it was ipso facto more open because it hadn't been built yet. We were just building it, a board at a time.

Jonathan Lethem: I worked at bookstores in San Francisco and we always were reading *VLS*. It was the alternative to the *Times*, and at that point—7 or 8 years ago—it seemed like there were fewer attempts being made at that kind of authority. What strikes me about recent years is the way you've been freed and freed yourself to grow beyond being the antidote voice, not being too bound into that relationship of the sole alternative against the mainstream. There's a lot more assurance and flexibility to the current *VLS*. I think *VLS* became a model and helped widen the conversation. It's like a finger pointing to the underground, the zines and graphic novel community. Graphic novels—that's an area where it's so clear that you guys were nailing down the bridge board by board, creating the possibility to talk about them as books. Now it's done and it seems so obvious.

Lenora Todaro (associate/senior editor 1997–present): I came to the *VLS* from book publishing, where I'd just finished editing Emer Martin, whose novel was being described as the female *Trainspotting*. I remember in my interview for this job being asked how I found Emer, and I said, "I hunted her down." I was worried that sounded hubristic, but I later realized that was what *VLS* was looking for—someone who would hunt down authors, whether by plowing through manuscripts, going to readings in bars, or chasing down writers to see what they wanted to write about. And that's still what it feels like. The Writers on the Verge issue is an extension of that, and it's a perfect format for a book editor turned literary review editor, because we read manuscripts in various stages of rawness and readiness. It's like flirting with all of this potential in these pages, and you get to hone your instincts and sensibilities. The Verge writers keep in touch with us, some do readings together, some become our reviewers. A number of them have been *VLS* readers for years, so to find themselves profiled or splattered across the cover feels right. Verge has created a kind of mini-literary community—which is what *VLS* has been doing for 20 years.

O N E

Writers Reconsidered:
New Takes on the Old Guard

*V*LS has always believed that canons are for blasting. While the literary establishment cherishes its tightly policed pantheon, our writers love nothing more than taking a sledgehammer to a hallowed icon, defiling the sacred cow. Walter Kendrick set the tone with his 1984 piece, "Genius: Who Needs It? The Long, Boring Canonization of T. S. Eliot."

It's not all about assault and battery (although the Paul Elie essay included in this section does feel like a poison dart aimed at the stolid flesh of John Cheever). *VLS* writers have penned provocative and imaginative re-evaluations of the established literary greats: David Foster Wallace dives into Dostoevsky's lurid world and returns with a sprawling survey (complete with trademark footnotes) that puts the Russian writer in terms the modern reader "gets." Gertrude Stein emerges from Albert Mobilio's essay not just as an eccentric, square-headed salonista but as a radical writer who has exerted a subterranean impact on subsequent generations of experimentalists. And Bharati

Mukherjee's fatwa-era piece heralds Salman Rushdie as the creator of a new language supple enough to depict the mutating identities and uprooted lives of a postcolonial generation.

Other essays read like love letters, albeit ambivalent ones: Blanche McCrary Boyd's luminous paean to Katherine Anne Porter argues that her personal failings made her work about "good, evil, and complicity" all the more resonant. Andrew O'Hagan thrills to Don DeLillo's sentences and defends him from critics who oversimplify him as a post-Pynchon bard of paranoia. And Henry Louis Gates, Jr., confesses to falling in love with the complexities of Langston Hughes, loosening him from the strangling limitations of the "public negro" role.

THE LOST GENERATOR
Gertrude Stein Builds a Better Reader

By Albert Mobilio

We first know her as an icon: the sharply sculpted, masklike face hovering above the piled-upon folds of her body. Her head tilts slightly forward to catch an unnaturally harsh light. Her eyes are askew; one is indifferently wide, the other squints in judgment. Depicting an unsettled Buddha who seems both at rest and about to rise from her overstuffed chair, Picasso's portrait of Gertrude Stein is, perhaps, the most familiar emblem of the Modernist epoch. We can hardly look at this painting and not imagine, standing just outside the frame, Braque, Apollinaire, Matisse, Pound, Hemingway, assorted Futurists, Dadaists, and Cubists—all those who made the art that made this century. Stein appears enthroned, a high priestess presiding over her charmed circle at 27 Rue de Fleurus. Inevitably, the grand scene the portrait conjures—Paris in the teens and '20s, the Lost Generation—obscures its subject. While we view her as a pivotal, even essential, participant in the artistic turmoil of her times, it is always in relation to her legendary salon, her role as hostess. Yet it was Stein, among all her guests, who truly executed the letter of the Modernist law to "make it new." She did this in some 40 books that leave no genre untouched. Whether as librettist, poet, novelist, or essayist, Stein consistently produced work so radical it remains so today. Sadly, this achievement too little informs what we see when we see Stein. Regarded more as icon than artist, more aphorist than author, she is our century's most famous unread writer.

Stein lacks readers not merely because the writing is difficult but because it is, at times, literally unreadable; that is, she cannot be read the way we've been taught, the way we want to read. She sought to reinvent the relationship between reader and page. Arriving in New York to lecture in 1934, she made her intent plain to a group of inquiring newsmen. Surprised by the clarity of her responses, one asked, "Why don't you write the way you talk?" "Why don't you read the way I write?" she replied. Doing that means unlearning the fluid rapidity and instantaneous assimilation we automatically bring to bear. We are sent back to our earliest experiences with written words, when their size, shape, and sound were as consequential as the information they conveyed. By tearing at the seams between sentences, between words, Stein invites readers to join in an almost physical act; she forces the eye to retrace, the mind to rethink. Unraveling one of her commaless run-on sentences can resemble a tug-of-war in which Stein pulls you heedlessly forward while you dig in your heels with imagined commas, colons, and periods. Stein unnerves us; she contorts what we think is the natural flow. The violation of so many conventions upends the implicit contract between writer and reader. In place of that neatly struck bargain, Stein insists her readers read recklessly, with no hands on the wheel and a busy eye on the words ahead:

> *I want readers so strangers must do it. Mostly no one knowing me can like it that I love it that every one is of a kind of men and women, that always I am looking and comparing and classifying of them, always I am seeing their repeating. Always more and more I love repeating, it may be irritating to hear from them but always more and more I love it of them.*

The going can be, by turns, tedious, tiring, or a heady thrill. Much in the way that Schoenberg's unchromatic 12-tone compositions disturb listeners, Stein jangles our ears. Too often her reputation for difficulty has cut short attempts to turn some actual pages. The notion that reading Stein is an unrewarding chore abides, curiously enough, even among her most likely audience—fans of women's and avant literature. The notoriety dates back to the early teens, when Stein published *Portrait of Mabel Dodge* and *Tender Buttons*. These experiments in nonrepresentational prose inspired satirists and provoked critics to extravagant condemnations. (As Stein struggled to find publishers, *Tender Buttons* was parodied in *Life*.) Believed to be something of a great Sphinx writing solely in repetitive riddles and double-talk, Stein seemed to epitomize the Post-Romantic author's dilemma of recreating an intensely private language as public voice. The consensus held that she didn't turn the trick, and she became a byword for Modernist and avant-garde excess.

True enough, Stein flouted grammatical convention, reveled in obscure personal reference, and produced books of daunting length, but how did she differ from Joyce and Pound? Modernist monuments like *Finnegans Wake* and the *Cantos*, never candidates for beach reading, have been treated, since their publication, to exhaustive (and exhausting) attention. Stein, on the other hand, has been ridiculed or ignored for the same sins. (Witness the recent flap over editing errors in the new edition of *Ulysses* while *The Making of Americans* remains out of print.) Stein's eccentricities appeared to be willful and self-indulgent, the products of a wealthy dilettante's proximity to real genius. Of course, her male counterparts wielded a purposeful obscurity and bent the rules for only the best of reasons—as a woman, Stein couldn't muster quite the same tolerance from critics. But there's a more telling difference. For as much as innovators like Joyce and Pound wore the mantle of the new, they played a game as old as the Talmud. If you have the right education and access to a good library, reading their "difficult" books amounts to solving an elaborate crossword puzzle. The allusions may be complex, but the hierarchical roles of author as master locksmith and reader as forger of keys remains unchanged. Stein stood resolutely outside this comfy arrangement. She presented the reader an open-ended game in which interpretations were presumed to be private and always in flux. In the absence of fixed symbols writ large, she devised truly free-form texts that converted readers into writers.

The blurred distinction between reader and writer follows from Stein's belief that writing is simply a way of knowing. In the essay "Sentences," she locates the source of what's written: "A sentence can be in one. A sentence in one sentence has been in one. It has been one." Translation—logos is within; in fact, it defines your being. The writer uncovers what's already penned. To call Stein's broken-stride style idiosyncratic is to misjudge its decidedly universal aims. She wanted to capture the rhythms of thinking, an Ur-beat that could be found in "the everlasting feeling of sentences as they diagram themselves." Stein's spiraling sentences mimic the unstoppable quality of thought; she means to draw us deeply in. Her intentionally abbreviated line—"A sentence made slowly"—suggests by its very condensation that the time it takes to write a sentence should equal the time it takes to comprehend it. Consequently, her ideal reader inhabits her sentences' production and reenacts the summing of their parts. This reader surrenders to the jagged pulse of a record being played at variable speeds and is eventually surprised at how right it sounds. If there is a deep grammar, Stein tapped the vein. By stripping the habitual from our sentence-making and reading, she revealed a circularly logical, lucidly incantatory speech, an atavistic tongue flowing just beneath the finely built phrases. Its grammar is the grammar of first speech, the motion and sound are those of human thought.

B y agreement, Stein's German-Jewish parents had five children, but two deaths in infancy permitted the births of Leo and Gertrude. A sense of precariousness and unease over owing their lives to the deaths of their siblings would always trouble them both. The family's wanderings did little to encourage feelings of security. By the time Gertrude was seven, the Steins had lived in Pennsylvania, Vienna, Paris, and Baltimore before settling in Oakland.

These uprootings made keener the isolation she experienced as the family's youngest. Although pampered and indulged, she was often left to herself or in the company of Leo. She weathered the chaotic procession of languages—acquiring a child's smattering of French and German— but found in the use of English a private pleasure, as if it were her true home. Her choice to live in Europe among foreign languages would replicate the childhood world in which she was "all alone with english and myself."

Neither parent did much to temper her estrangement. Her mother, who died when Stein was 14, was a marginal presence, "never important to her children excepting to begin them." Her father loomed large as an impatient, argumentative, sometimes tyrannical figure. While mothers appear infrequently in Stein's writing, domineering fathers proliferate. Indeed, Daniel Stein, fictionalized as David Hersland in *The Making of Americans*, is the most vivid and passionately drawn of all her characters. Certainly he soured her on fathers for good, so much so that she could later link Hitler, Stalin, Roosevelt, and Mussolini through the common denominator of patriarchy: "There is too much fathering going on just now and there is no doubt about it fathers are depressing." Instead, she cleaved to Leo. Bound by the similar circumstances of their conception, they also shared an attitude of superiority toward the rest of the family. She followed him to Harvard, Johns Hopkins, and Europe, hewing to each of his many turns of mind. Snobbishly brilliant and self-obsessed, Leo Stein thrived on the intensity of intellectual pursuit as well as his own neuroses. He was in thrall to one mentor after another— William James, Matisse, Freud—always measuring himself against them, only to be found wanting. What he called his "pariah complex" condemned him to a cycle of hero-worship and frustration. Eventually, in despair over his continued failure and her first successes, he turned his withering condescension on his sister, destroying a bond that had endured for 30 years. Nonetheless, Gertrude was undoubtedly enriched by his aggressive curiosity. Leo furnished her with his style of imperious conviction (which she would leaven with wit) and introduced her to the people who would help supply the convictions.

Stein entered Radcliffe in the mid-1890s and, like Leo, enlisted as one of William James's most avid students. James admitted her to his graduate seminar, where she studied the nature of consciousness and its relation to human behavior. Not just James but many professors and fellow students were impressed by her intellect and frank charm. A much-told anecdote, in which she walks out of James's final exam after writing across the blue book, "Really I do not feel like an examination paper in philosophy today," lays claim to a precocious degree of self-possession. In fact, Stein felt sorely out of place in Cambridge. She was a Westerner with a European glaze among prim New Englanders. Her college essays—first-person confessionals steeped in romanticism—are artifacts of struggle. The grammar is shaky, and kernels of her mature prose—"The eternal feminine is nice to be sure but its painfully illogical"—seem less a matter of intent than of verbal inadequacy. The essays portray anxious, strong-willed young women uncertain and frightened of their sexuality. Earnestly melodramatic, replete with hints of incest and sadomasochism, these characterizations were an attempt to control the many selves and voices that had risen up in the years of quiet isolation. Writing, like her interest in psychology, became a means of sorting through the mind's many choruses.

On James's recommendation, she attended Johns Hopkins Medical School to prepare for a career as a psychologist. After four years of study she grew bored and failed to graduate. Instead, she joined Leo in Europe, eventually settling in Paris on the Rue de Fleurus. There she completed her first novel, *Things As They Are*, a Henry James–like analysis of the emotional entanglements among three well-educated women. Based on Stein's thwarted affair with a Baltimore woman, the novel marked her acceptance of her sexual identity and confirmed her vocation as an author. In 1906, while working on her second book, she met Alice Toklas. Upper-class, Jewish, and a San Franciscan, she was comfortingly familiar to Stein. Toklas became both lover and eternally approving audience, devoting herself to domestic details which included typing each day the pages Stein would produce in all-night writing sessions. The evenings were reserved for callers, the days for picture-buying and tramping about Montmartre. In her salon and in her intimate relations with painters like Matisse, and especially Picasso, a surer, more forthright but decidedly aloof personality emerged—the Gertrude Stein of legend. Although her atelier was common ground for the many pre-war artistic rebels, Stein was too bourgeois to endorse their less than proper antics. Yet she drew selectively on the ideas she heard debated nightly. Not a ringmaster but a cryptically wry observer, she preferred a crossroad to a cabal.

After the first world war, Rue de Fleurus became a shrine. It spread Stein's name around the world. Her public persona was clearly the product of deliberate design; she craved fame. Perhaps because of her solitary vantage and abiding sense of aloneness, she greatly desired acceptance; perhaps her experiments and the rejection she risked compelled her to declare her own genius. In any event, the decades following the war were dedicated to self-promotion, which culminated in the charming but nakedly egotistical *Autobiography of Alice B. Toklas*. Much like her friend and onetime student Hemingway, Stein labored hard at her myth, bringing forth an outsized creature that ranged beyond her control. As caricatures and jokes turned up in movies, comic strips, and musicals, the Bohemian *doyenne* superseded the author. She delighted in the celebrity, yet even within the ample confines of her fame she remained an island. Although she had served as midwife to the new century—studying psychology with James, abstract art with Picasso—Stein retained her roots in the 19th century. Distant and overwhelmed by propriety, part of her would not respond to the demands of modern fame. When *Four Saints in Three Acts* premiered in New York in 1934, her name was in lights on Broadway; she declined to attend and instead sent a note: "I rarely believe in anything because at the time of believing I am not really there to believe." Stein would hold fast to her apartness, a wise child among foreign tongues.

T hinking, for Stein, was not merely a prelude to composition but both its subject and method. In *Three Lives* she explored this notion. Especially in the "Melanctha" section, she created characters whose substance derived from an exacting transcription of their consciousness. They came to life in prose that circled at great remove from a bare-bones narrative, touching down only to jog it forward, then flying off. Published in 1909, the novel, her second, decisively announced her uniqueness. There was little precedent for *Three Lives*'s fidelity to the workings of human psychology. Only Henry James, at about the same time, pursued a similar goal. James took pleasure in the mind's propensity for hairsplitting refinements; he traced the balancing act in card-house sentences, sliding clause upon sub-clause. The elegance of his deftly constructed syntax suggests he may have conceived of the mind as an instrument powered by light and air to produce the music of a tuning fork's hum. Stein heard a rougher noise. Throughout *Three Lives* the rendering of the thinking mind suggests machinery hard at the task, clanking and catching, relentless. Her use of working-class and black-American dialects acquainted her with the expressive power of staggered rhythm and repetition. From these she fashioned a truer sound, something closer to the core of consciousness.

Having recently arrived in Paris when she started *Three Lives*, Stein found her inspiration in Flaubert and Cézanne. Both were foremost among brother Leo's obsessions at the time. She worked at a translation of Flaubert's *Trois Contes* and absorbed the broad outline of the character Félicité from the story "Un Coeur Simple." Félicité, a dying woman who has suffered quietly through a life of service to others, reminded Stein of the immigrant and black housekeepers and midwives she had known as a medical student in Baltimore. In their bruised, emotionally cramped lives she found a reflection of her own sexual and creative frustration. From Cézanne's paintings she took instruction in a method of depiction. Those paintings emphasized presence, the palpability of a face or vase. She wished to invest her trio of women—Anna, Lena, and Melanctha—with the undeniable reality of Cézanne's washwomen and card-players. She disdained biographical details and narrative plot and assembled her women in the "continuous present." In this newly created tense, "there was a constant recurring and beginning there was a marked direction of being in the present . . ."

The characters manifest themselves at every point in the telling as a painting offers its subject completely from any particular view. Verbal tics like Melanctha's tireless repetition of the word "certainly" serve as apertures through which she is apprehended whole. Thus the speaker's rhythms become indistinguishable from the speaker; in fact, they express an essence: "Melanctha Herbert was always losing what she had in wanting all the things she saw. Melanctha was always being left when she was not leaving others. Melanctha Herbert always loved too hard and much too often." Stein used language as an impressionist painter used color, to catch what William James called the "vague and inarticulate" dimension of conscious life. This is not the artful stream of consciousness of Joyce. In the ebb and flow of Melanctha's thought, there is a music unique and quotidian as a signature; Stein wrote the mind the way she heard it.

If, as Stein proclaimed, *Three Lives* was literature's first step into the new century, *The Making of Americans* may find a home in the next. Intractable, interminable, yet strangely mesmerizing, the novel resides in the black hole of literary history. In the 75 years since its completion, *Americans* has been in print only sporadically, most often in abridged editions. Rarely seen, more rarely read, its 925 densely printed pages offer some of the knottiest prose in the language. Few have the stamina (myself included) to plow from cover to cover. Lacking any formal organization, narrative logic, or even a place to rest, the writing proceeds at full pitch, battering through the notion of the well-made novel. Stein believed *Americans* to be her masterpiece. She regarded it with great affection and kept faith with its most egregious flaws. When she proofed the galleys, few changes were made: "I always found myself forced back into its incorrectness." She knew those flaws—the bottomless sentences, badly joined narrative, and ragged pacing—constituted the voice she had struggled to achieve. Writing at a time of emotional isolation, she battled the deep suspicion that her unorthodox method was consigned to failure. She both doubted and wished to embrace her "incorrectness": "I have been very glad to have been wrong. It is sometimes a very hard thing to win myself to having been wrong about something. I do a great deal of suffering." The admissions of uncertainty recur throughout *Americans*. Her "big book," as she called it, was very much about the making of Gertrude Stein. It served as the laboratory of her own self-discovery, in which she sought the "great author inside one."

The quest for greatness explains the immense sprawl. *Americans* is overcrowded by Stein's many ambitions. With Olympian naïveté, she said her intent was to "describe really describe every kind of human being that ever was or is or would be." She also wanted to indulge an autobiographical impulse and tell the story of her German-Jewish immigrant family, then draw from their experience—"the old people in a new world, the new people made out of the old"—a transcendent national archetype. Even the novel would take on a representative function as "an essentially American book." Stein plunged ahead on all fronts but failed to keep step. Her rich ideation outraced her ability to shape a coherently multidimensional fiction. The same unvaried single-mindedness that flexed strangely in her prose made for a crude reductionism in the realm of conception. Preferring stark opposition to shading and ambiguity, Stein lacked the intellectual cast to balance the conflicting demands of so many goals. In the end, mythmaking and family history run poor seconds to the psychologist's urge to describe and classify.

Americans's fictional family, the Herslands, are recognizable as the Steins, and their daughter Martha as the author, yet there is little of the specificity of detail we expect from an autobiographical novel. Relations between characters are broadly sketched and narrative development is bound by the continuous present; everyone is in a state of becoming. The extensive use of pronouns—he, she, one, some, they—helps contain the characters' reality within the scope of clinical report. The flatness is deliberate; the characters appear like many different masks behind which Stein makes the case that everyone is different but the same. The Herslands sit in as typological specimens for an extended meditation on behavioral patterns and patterns of description: "There are many ways of making kinds of men and women. In each way of making kinds of them there is a different system of finding them resembling. Sometime there will be here every way there can be of seeing kinds of men and women." As in *Three Lives*, the rhythms of speech embody what Stein termed a character's "bottom nature": "Slowly, more and more, one gets to know them as repeating comes out in them. In the middle of their living they are always repeating . . ." However, the novel is less about "kinds," "ones," and Americans than it is about the mind obsessed with these distinctions. *The Making of Americans* is a driven book, as relentless as many of its dithyrambic, train-length sentences. Stein set herself the task of thinking on paper for a thousand pages until she had "not many things but one thing." What she had was an artifact of consciousness, a mind's true life played out as the "steady pound of repeating."

A mericans liberated Stein from tentativeness and self-doubt and confirmed her break from any fealty to conventional structure and syntax. She had pushed past telling into a new arrangement with the reader, one in which the reader felt the text become itself. In *Tender Buttons* and her portraits, she pushed even further. Struck by the composition of Picasso's cubist collages, she noted that "to have brought the objects together already changed them to other things, not to another picture but to something else, to things as Picasso saw them." In her middle, or *Tender Buttons*, period Stein pursued the same effect. Like the Cubists, she would avoid literal representation in depicting objects and people. She found a compositional equivalent to cubist recombination in "the ridding myself of nouns." *Tender Buttons* describes things without mentioning them, without metaphoric comparison. Instead, Stein adopted the cubist approach of looking at an object from many perspectives, then collapsing the impression into a single expressive image:

CARELESS WATER
No cup is broken in more places and mended, that is to say a plate is broken and mending does do that it shows that culture is Japanese. It shows the whole element of angels and orders. It does more to choosing and it does more to that ministering counting. It does, it does change in more water.

Although *Tender Buttons* was written in 1911, the boldness of the experiment remains unmuted. We have grown accustomed enough to cubist and abstract visuals that they can be used in advertisements, but a line like "The change in that is that red weakens an hour" still unsettles us. Yet these prose poems were not meant to shock; they were launched from familiar ground. Stein chose household items—*A Carafe, A Red Hat,* or *A Seltzer Bottle*—along with abstract but homey commonplaces like *In Between, A Time To Eat,* and *A Centre in a Table.* To each she responded with a subjectivity so unyielding that the relationship between text and object is indecipherable. *Malachite*: "The sudden spoon is the same in no size. The sudden spoon is the wound in the decision." *Cold Climate* abstracts abstraction: "A Season in yellow sold extra strings makes lying places." What is a "lying place"? The usage and grammar are still so fresh we have the impression we are reading a distorted translation from another language, or maybe the ramblings of an aphasiac. The logic of the connections, whether hallucinatory or mundane, is rigorously private. Stein rendered interpretation futile; she preferred her reader to enter the synesthetic domain of the poem and respond as subjectively as the author had.

"Language as a real thing," Stein wrote in "Poetry and Grammar," "is not imitation either of sounds or colors or emotions it is an intellectual recreation . . ." In *Toklas* she credits her work with "the destruction of the associational emotion in poetry and prose." She was adamant about disconnecting texts from predictable reactions. She believed in the use of language as an end in itself, not as a medium of expression but as a vital expressive element. It's clear that language lacks the plasticity of color or a musical note; it is inescapably tied to a denotative intent. Stein chafed at this limit but recognized it; she simply wanted to lengthen the leash. By placing words in unworn sequences, the dislocated sentences in *Tender Buttons* restored substantiality, a thinginess, to desiccated syllables. This was the thinking behind her notorious "rose is a rose is a rose." In that line, Stein remarked, "the rose is red for the first time in English poetry for a hundred years."

Her attraction to painting and its suggestive capacity also led to a series of word portraits in which she attempted to depict with "exactitude" her subject's "inner and outer reality." Usually made for close friends—Matisse, Picasso, Sherwood Anderson—the portraits continued exploring the relation between description and types: "In doing a portrait of any one, the repetition consists in knowing that that one is a kind of a one, that the things he does have been done by others like him that the things he says have been said by others like him . . ." After having "talked and listened" to her subject, she re-created what struck her as essential. The *Portrait of Mabel Dodge*, written in 1911, introduced Stein's textual cubism to the literary world. Dodge was so flattered by the piece she had 300 copies printed and bound in Florentine wallpaper (an inspired stroke on her part) and distributed them to the New York literati, who were confused by "So much breathing has not the same place when there is that much beginning. . . . So much breathing has the same place and there must not be so much suggestion. There can be there the habit that there is if there is no need of resting. The absence is not alternative." Because it felt arbitrary it was deemed gibberish. Stein's composition relied less on randomness as a method than on creating the effect of randomness for the reader. No doubt, Stein rummaged freely in shaping her impressions, but her vocabulary was carefully circumscribed by the demands of each piece, and the internal rhythmic and imagistic consistency rarely wavered. She manipulated a sense of semantic chaos so that her reader might find new points of entry into old words or discover a delicious strangeness in an ordinary notion. Her "gibberish" slowed the eye and allowed the words to be pronounced on the tongue and in the ear.

The randomness irked many readers. In 1934 B. F. Skinner publicized experiments Stein had helped conduct at Harvard investigating the possibility of automatic writing. He charged that *Tender Buttons* was the product of just such a process, and his claim became a convenient reason for dismissing her work. Stein denied, in several contradictory statements, any connection, and her partisans have been at pains to echo her denials. The skill in Stein's wordplay and linguistic technique is too obvious to attribute to chance, but that doesn't preclude some role for the principles behind automatic writing. She wrote each day for a specific amount of time (occasionally sitting in her Ford while Toklas ran errands) and tended to revise very little. The immediacy she sought was diluted by revision and heightened by the need to fill the page. Stein's craftsmanship appears keener when its improvisatory component is understood: her incremental variations on a single phrase are closer in spirit to a musician like Charlie Parker than they are to any other writer.

I n her poems and librettos, Stein openly aspired to the persistent music of lyric verse. The repetitions are carefully layered so they accumulate into melodic, rolling tones. Some phrases in *Four Saints in Three Acts* mimic tribal chant: "Saints settled saints settled all in all saints. All saints. Saints in all saints. Saint Settlement." There is a litter of mantra-like bits of nonsense—"windows and windows and ones"—that infiltrate the mind to stay. The long poems—"Lifting Belly," "Patriarchal Poetry," and "Stanzas in Meditation"—thrive on swung measure and song. The availability of line breaks and verse's more open page encouraged Stein to parse out her compound run-on sentences, as if she needed the clutterless white expanse to keep track of their unpackaged parts. The line breaks in "Stanzas in Meditation" create breathing room the prose lacks and demonstrate just how she built sentences from clauses:

> *Full well I know that she is there*
> *Much as she will she can be there*
> *But which I know which I know when*
> *Which is my way to be there then*
> *Which she will know as I know here*
> *That it is now that it is there*

The metrics are as basic as the meaning is opaque. Typically, abstract words like "which," "when," and "there" have been placed to connote some tangible representation, teasing our expectation that the poem might refer to a reality outside itself. For Stein the text can be an autonomous thing, its references bound within its actual occurrence, within the continuous present. Meaning isn't a matter of referring but rather of becoming. In contrast, "Lifting Belly," an erotic hymn to Toklas, is rich in specific details about their daily life together:

> *Can you can you.*
> *Can you buy a Ford.*
> *Did you expect that.*
> *Lifting belly hungrily.*
> *Not lonesomely.*
> *But enthusiastically.*
> *Lifting belly altogether.*
> *Were you wise.*
> *Were you wise to do so.*

The coy bits of personal trivia—what car Stein owned—don't require exegesis; a better clue to their intimate lives might be found in the poem's odd mix of nursery-rhyme singsong and the language of passion. Regardless of whether her writing skirts second- and third-tier abstraction or turns on a sexual pun, Stein's subject is always herself. By purging language of its stock associations, she claimed she could invest words with a new reality. In fact, what she did was shape a language that is wholly her own. At a time when many writers pressed to expand the self to include a world, Stein drew the world in upon herself. She devised a system of relations, a grammar of reference, that posited her at its center.

During her lifetime, Stein served as her own best critic. The job was not sought by many. Her writing was too extraordinary to attract a ready crew of village explainers. Having stirred so much curiosity about her life and work, she took to explicating herself. And she enjoyed the work. The strong element of public performance in her essays (even those she never delivered as lectures) indicates she relished the opportunity to instruct. An invitation to speak at Oxford in 1926 provided the occasion for her first critical essay. Appearing before a standing-room audience, she treated them to the uncompromisingly knotty "Composition As Explanation." What the dons made of roundabout dictates like "Romanticism is then when everything being alike everything is naturally simply different" is anyone's guess. She did make clear that her difficult style was not a clever conceit to be put off when it was time to talk shop. Her method of exploring characters in fiction should be as useful and legitimate for explaining that method in an essay. She insisted her writing be of one piece. For example, the assembling and disassembling paragraphs and sentences in *How To Write* discuss her techniques while employing them. Consequently, when she talks about specific works, it becomes unclear where the fiction leaves off and the explanation begins: "The Gradual Making of the Making of Americans," a blueprint made in retrospect, could blend imperceptibly into the novel.

The closed circuit of this critical exchange—Stein analyzing Stein—suggests an unabashed solipsism, which she most enthusiastically practiced. But it also gives some measure of her originality and its isolating effect. She could cite no literary forebears for her mature style, and comparisons with contemporaries were limited to those whom she'd influenced. Stein built, occupied, and still dwells in a room truly of her own. Her early publications were self-subsidized; she was 59 and had been writing for over 30 years when an American publisher finally accepted a book of hers; much of her writing was published posthumously, some not at all; today her presence in American bookstores and universities is sporadic, always qualified. It is ironic that a writer whose aesthetic enterprise was so tied to the reader and the experience of reading should find an audience hard to come by.

Nevertheless, she is without doubt one of the most influential writers of the century. Her list of debtors, direct and indirect, is uncountably long. Sherwood Anderson proudly acknowledged the impact of *Three Lives*; Hemingway, who typed sizable portions of *Americans*, was less candid, but his bluntly clipped sentences and notions of suggestive detail are obviously Stein's. ("The worst, he said, were the women with dead babies. You couldn't get the women to give up their dead babies. They'd have babies dead for six days. Wouldn't give them up.") Her stark rhythms and repetitions were absorbed by writers as diverse as Beckett and Chandler; the "steady pound of repeating" embodied this century's rebellion against the florid arabesques of the Victorian era. Like Picasso's recovery of the primitive eye through his use of masks, Stein restored to language its connection to the spoken. Her demolition of grammatical constraint stirred almost every American author and practically spawned a homegrown (not European-inspired) tradition of experimental writing. She proved that sentences needn't stop when the rules said so, but could roll on till they exhausted themselves; Faulkner and Kerouac took note. Her painterly approach, the power she sprang from the performance of words as words, launched the Language poets, one of the most vital movements in postwar American writing. In a broader sense, the example of her life, her Yankee stubbornness and subversive vigor, cut the cloth for the American avant-garde style in all the arts. Indeed, she is the mother of us all.

"Think of anything," Stein wrote, "of cowboys, of movies, of detective stories, of anybody who goes anywhere or stays at home and is an American and you will realize that it is something strictly American to conceive a space that is filled with moving, a space of time that is filled always filled with moving . . ." She brought the continuous movement of the mind, with its churned and unresting music, to the page. She conjured an immediacy that made reading new. "I am writing for myself and strangers," she announced in *The Making of Americans*. Yet she brings those strangers close to the act of written creation, so close inside her struggle with the sayable that we cannot remain strangers very long. To read Stein is to relinquish our place outside the text and to begin with her to make the words make sense.

November 1988

FEODOR'S GUIDE

By David Foster Wallace

> DOSTOEVSKY
> VOLUME I: THE SEEDS OF REVOLT, 1821–1849
> VOLUME II: THE YEARS OF ORDEAL, 1850–1859
> VOLUME III: THE STIR OF LIBERATION, 1860–1865
> VOLUME IV: THE MIRACULOUS YEARS, 1865–1871
> *By Joseph Frank*

The citizen secures himself against genius by icon worship. By the touch of Circe's wand, the divine troublemakers are translated into porcine embroidery.
> —Edward Dahlberg, "Can These Bones Live?"

"At the present time, negation is the most useful of all—and we deny—"
   "Everything?"
   "Everything!"
   "What, not only art and poetry . . . but even . . . horrible to say . . ."
   "Everything," repeated Bazarov, with indescribable composure.
   —Turgenev, *Fathers and Sons*

Dostoevsky's *Notes from Underground* and its narrator are just about impossible really to understand without some knowledge of the intellectual climate of Russia in the 1860s, particularly the frisson of utopian socialism and atheistic utilitarianism then in vogue among the radical Russian intelligentsia, an ideology that Dostoevsky loathed with the sort of passion only Dostoevsky could loathe with.

In 1957, Joseph Frank, as he was wading through some of this particular-context background so that he could give his Princeton complit students a halfway comprehensive reading of *Notes,* started to get interested in the fiction of Dostoevsky as a kind of bridge between two distinct ways of coming at text, a purely formal aesthetic approach v. a social-dash-ideological criticism that cares only about thematics and the philosophical assumptions that lie behind them. That interest—plus 40 years of what must have been skull-crunching scholarly labor—has yielded the first four volumes of a projected five-book study of Dostoevsky's life and times and writing. Probably all serious scholars of Dostoevsky are waiting bated to see if Frank can hang on long enough to bring his encyclopedic study all the way up to the early 1880s, when Dostoevsky finished the fourth of his great novels, gave his famous Pushkin speech, and died. Even if the fifth volume doesn't get written, though, the appearance now of the fourth ensures Frank's own status as the definitive biographer of one of the best fiction writers ever.

Am I a good person? Do I even, deep down, really wish to be a good person? Or do I only want to seem like a good person so that people will approve me? Is there a difference?

Frank persuades us that Dostoevsky's mature works were fundamentally ideological novels and simply cannot be read unless one understands the polemical agendas that inform them and to which they were directed. Thus the concatenation of universal and particular that characterizes *Notes from Underground*[1] in fact characterizes all of the best work of FMD, a writer whose "evident desire," Frank says, is "to dramatize his moral-spiritual themes against the background of Russian history."

A nonstandard feature of Frank's project is the amount of straightforward critical attention he pays to the actual books Dostoevsky wrote. "It is the production of such masterpieces that makes Dostoevsky's life worth recounting at all," his preface to *The Miraculous Years* goes, "and my purpose, as in the previous volumes, is to keep them constantly in the foreground rather than treating them as accessory to the life per se." At least a third of this latest volume is given over to close readings of the stuff Dostoevsky produced in this amazing six years— *Crime and Punishment, The Gambler, The Idiot, The Eternal Husband,* and *Demons.* These readings aim to be explicative rather than argumentative or theory-driven—i.e., their aim is to articulate as fully as possible what exactly Dostoevsky himself wanted the books to mean. While this approach seems to act as if there's no such thing as the Intentional Fallacy,[2] it seems prima facie justified by Frank's own project, which is always to trace and explain the novels' genesis out of Dostoevsky's own ideological engagement with Russian culture.

**What does "faith" mean? Isn't it crazy to believe in something there's no hard proof of? Is there any difference between "faith" and a bunch of nose-pierced natives sacrificing virgins to volcanos because they believe

it'll produce good weather? How can somebody have faith before they're presented with a sufficient reason to have faith? Is somehow needing to have faith a sufficient reason for having faith?**

To appreciate Joseph Frank's achievement, it seems important to emphasize how many different approaches to biography and criticism he's trying to marry. Standard literary biographies spotlight an author and his personal life—especially the seamy or neurotic stuff—and pretty much ignore the specific historical context in which he wrote. Other studies—especially those with a theoretical agenda—focus almost exclusively on context and treat an author and his books as mathematical exponents of the prejudices, power dynamics, and metaphysical delusions of his age. Some biographies act as if their subject's own works have already been all figured out, and they treat a personal life's relation to meanings the biographers assume are already fixed and inarguable; whereas most of this century's "critical studies" treat an author's books hermetically, ignoring facts about the writer's circumstances and beliefs that can help explain not only what the work is about but why it has the particular individual magic of a certain writer's own unique voice and vision.[3]

But if I decide to decide there's a different, less selfish, less lonely point to my life, isn't the reason for this decision my desire to be less lonely, meaning to suffer less pain? So can the decision to be less selfish be anything other than a selfish decision?

Frank's four volumes compose an extremely detailed and demanding work on an extremely complex and demanding author, a fiction writer whose time and culture and language are alien to us. Russian, a non-Latinate language, is extraordinarily hard to translate into English, and when you add to this the archaism of a language 100-plus years old,[4] Dostoevsky's prose and dialogue can come off stilted and pleonastic and silly.[5] Then there's the kind of soppy-seeming formality of the 19th-century culture Dostoevsky's characters inhabit. These are characters who, e.g., when they're absolutely furious at each other, do stuff like "shake their fists" and call each other "scoundrels" and "fly at" each other.[6] Speakers use exclamation points in quantities now seen only in comic strips. Social etiquette is stiff to the point of absurdity. People are always "calling" on each other and either "being received" or "not being received" and obeying rococo conventions of politeness even when they're insulting each other.[7] Plus obscure military ranks and bureaucratic hierarchies abound; plus rigid and totally weird class distinctions that are hard to keep straight and understand the implications of, especially because the economic realities of old Russian society are so strange (see, e.g., the way even a destitute "former student" like Raskolnikov or an unemployed bureaucrat like the Underground Man can somehow afford a servant and a cook).

The point is that there is real and alienating stuff besides just the death-by-canonization that stands in the way. But Dostoevsky is worth the work despite his place astride the Western canon. One thing that canonization and course assignments[8] obscure is that Dostoevsky isn't just great, he's *fun*. His novels almost always have just ripping good plots, lurid and involved and thoroughly dramatic. There are murders and attempted murders and police and dysfunctional-family feuding and spies and tough guys and beautiful fallen women and unctuous con men and inheritances and silky villains and scheming and whores. Of course the fact that Dostoevsky can tell a really good story isn't alone enough to make him great—if it were, Judith Krantz and John Grisham would be great fiction writers, and as matters stand they're not even very good. What keeps them and lots of other seriously gifted plot-weavers from being very good is that they don't have much talent for (or interest in) characterization—their plots are usually inhabited by undeveloped or broadly drawn stick figures. (In fairness, too, there are writers who are great at making complex and fully realized human characters but who don't seem able to insert those characters into a believable and interesting dramatic plot. Plus others—usually the type regarded as most "literary"—who seem able/interested in neither plot nor character, whose books' movement and appeal depends entirely on rarified aesthetic or meta-aesthetic agendas.)

The thing about Dostoevsky's characters is that they *live*. And by this I don't mean just that they're successfully realized and believable and "round." The best of them live inside us, forever, once we've met them. Recall, e.g., the proud and pathetic Raskolnikov, the naive Devushkin, the beautiful and damned Nastasya of *The Idiot*,[9] the unctuous Lebedyev and spiderish Ippolit of the same novel; Stavrogin; *C&P*'s ingenious maverick detective Porfiry Petrovich (without whom there would be no commercial detective stories and eccentrically brilliant cops); Marmeladov, the hideous and pitiful alcoholic; or the vain and noble roulette addict Aleksey Ivanovich of *The Gambler*; the gold-hearted whores Sonya and Liza; the beautiful stone-hearted Aglaya; or the unbelievably repellent Smerdyakov, that living engine of slimy resentment in whom I see parts of myself I can barely stand to look at; or the child- and Christ-like, idealized and all-too-human Myshkin and Alyosha (the doomed human Christ and triumphant child-pilgrim, respectively). These—many more—live, and not because they're just accurately drawn types or facets of human beings, but because, acting within plausible and ripping good plots, they dramatize the profoundest parts of all human beings, the parts most conflicted, most serious: the ones with the most at stake. Dostoevsky's characters also—and without ever ceasing to be human and real—represent ideologies and philosophies of life: Raskolnikov the "rational egoism" of the 1860s left, Myshkin mystical Christian love, the Underground Man the influence of European positivism on the Russian character, Ippolit the raging human will confronted by death, Aleksey the perversion of Slavophilic pride in the face of European perfidy . . . on and on.

FMD's concern was always *what it is to be a human being*—i.e., how a person, in the particular social and philosophical circumstances of 19th-century Russia, could be a real human being, a person whose life was informed by love and values and principles, instead of being just a very shrewd species of self-preserving animal.

Is it possible really to love somebody? If I'm lonely, empty inside, everybody outside me is potential relief: I need them. But is it possible to love what you need? Does love have to be voluntary to be love? Does it have to not even be in my own best interests, the love, to count as love?

It's a famous irony that Dostoevsky, whose fiction is famous for its wisdom and compassion and moral rigor, was in many ways kind of a prick in real life—vain, self-absorbed, arrogant, spiteful, selfish. A fellow with a pretty serious gambling problem, he was almost always broke, whined constantly about his poverty, was always badgering his friends and colleagues for emergency loans that he never repaid, held grudges, and pawned his young wife's coat in cold weather so he could gamble, etc.[10] But it's also well-known that Dostoevsky's own life was full of incredible suffering and tragedy. His Moscow childhood was so miserable that never once in any of his books does Dostoevsky set or even mention any action in Moscow.[11] His remote and neurasthenic father was murdered by his own serfs when FMD was 17. Seven years later, the publication of his first novel,[12] and its endorsement by critics like Belinsky and Herzen, made Dostoevsky an instant superstar at the same time that he was starting to get involved with the Petrashevsky circle, a group of revolutionary intellectuals who plotted to incite a peasant uprising against the tsar. In 1849 FMD, the McInerney of his era, was arrested as a conspirator, convicted, sentenced to death, and underwent the "mock execution of the Petrashevsky," in which the conspirators were blindfolded and tied to stakes and at the *"Aim!"* stage of the firing-squad process when an imperial messenger rode up with a supposed "last-minute" reprieve from the merciful tsar.

His sentence commuted to imprisonment and exile, the epileptic

Dostoevsky ended up spending almost a decade in balmy Siberia, returning to St. Petersburg in 1859 to find that the Russian literary world had all but forgotten him. Then his wife died—unpleasantly—then his beloved brother Mikhail died, then his literary journal *Epoch* went under, then his epilepsy started getting so much worse that he was constantly terrified that he'd die or go permanently crazy from the seizures.[13] Hiring a 22-year-old stenographer to help him complete *The Gambler* in time to satisfy a publisher with whom he'd signed an insane deliver-or-forfeit-all-royalties-for-everything-you-ever-wrote contract, Dostoevsky married his amanuensis four months later, just in time to flee *Epoch*'s creditors with her, wander unhappily through a Europe whose influence on Russia he despised,[14] have a daughter who died of pneumonia almost right away, writing constantly, penniless, often literally hungry, often clinically depressed in the aftermath of tooth-rattling grand mal seizures, going through cycles of roulette binges and then crushing self-hatred. Volume IV details a lot of Dostoevsky's European tribulations via the journals of his young new wife, Anna Snitkin,[15] by all accounts a really nice and patient person whose emotional martyrdom as the spouse of this guy ought to qualify her as patron saint of the codependency recovery movement or something.[16]

> ****What is** "an American"? *Do we have something in common, as Americans? Or do we all just happen to live inside the same arbitrary boundaries? How is America different from other countries? Is there something special about it? Forget about special privileges that go with being an American—are there special responsibilities that go with being an American? If so, responsibilities to whom?***

Frank doesn't try to whitewash the icky parts,[17] but he takes great care to relate Dostoevsky's personal and psychological life to his fictions and the ideologies that inform them. That FMD is first and finally an *ideological* writer[18] makes him an especially congenial subject for Frank's contextual approach to biography. And the four volumes of *Dostoevsky* make it clear that no personal event was as important to the genesis of the "mature" FMD than the mock execution, a period of several minutes when the frail and neurotic 28-year-old aesthete believed his life was over. The result was some sort of very deep "conversion experience," though it gets complicated, because the Christian convictions that inform Dostoevsky's writings thereafter are not those of any organized church, really, and are also bound up with a kind of mystical Russian nationalism and a political conservatism[19] that led the next century's Soviets to suppress FMD's work and any evidence of its influence.[20]

Does this guy Jesus Christ's life have anything to teach me even if he wasn't "divine"? What are the implications that somebody who was supposed to be God's relative and so could have turned the cross into a planter or something with just a look still voluntarily let them nail him up there, and died? And did he know? Did he know he could break the cross with just a look?—Speaking of knowing: did he know in advance that the death'd just be temporary? Had God clued him in? I bet I could climb up there, too, if I knew an eternity of right-handed bliss lay on the other side of six hours of pain—Does any of this even matter? Can I still believe in J.C. or Muhammed or Buddha or whoever even if I don't "believe" they were relatives of God? Plus what would that even mean, anyway: "believe in"?

What seems most important is that FMD's near-death experience changed a typically vain and trendy young writer—a very talented one, true, but still somebody whose basic ambitions were for his own literary glory[21]—into somebody who believed deeply in moral/spiritual values[22], more, into somebody who believed that a life lived without moral/spiritual values was not just incomplete but depraved.[23]

So, for me anyway, what makes Dostoevsky invaluable is that he possessed a passion, conviction, and engagement with deep moral issues that we, here, today, cannot or do not allow ourselves. And on finishing Frank's books, I think any serious American reader/writer will find himself driven to think hard about what exactly it is that makes so many of the novelists of our own time look so thematically shallow and lightweight, so impoverished in comparison to Gogol, Dostoevsky, even lesser lights like Lermontov and Turgenev. To inquire of ourselves why we—under our own nihilist spell—seem to require of our writers an ironic distance from deep convictions or desperate questions, so that contemporary writers have to either make jokes of profound issues or else try somehow to work them in under cover of some formal trick like intertextual quotation or incongruous juxtaposition, sticking them inside asterisks as part of some surreal, defamiliarization-of-the-reading-experience flourish.

Part of the answer to questions about our own art's thematic poverty obviously involves our era's postindustrial condition and postmodern culture. The Modernists, among other accomplishments, elevated aesthetics to the level of metaphysics, and "Great Novels" since Joyce tend to be judged largely on their formal ingenuity; we presume as a matter of course that serious literature will be aesthetically distanced from real lived life. Add to this the requirement of textual self-consciousness imposed by postmodernism, and it's fair to say that Dostoevsky et al. were free from certain cultural expectations that constrain our own novelists' freedom to be "serious."

But it's just as fair to observe that Dostoevsky operated under some serious cultural constraints of his own: a repressive government, state censorship, and above all the popularity of post-Enlightenment European thought, much of which went directly against beliefs he held dear and wanted to write about. The thing is that Dostoevsky wasn't just a genius—he was, finally, *brave*. He never stopped worrying about his literary reputation, but he also never stopped promulgating ideas in which he believed. And he did so not by ignoring the unfriendly cultural circumstances in which he was writing, but by confronting them, engaging them, specifically and by name.[24]

Maybe it's not true that we today are nihilists. At the very least we have devils we believe in. These include sentimentality, naivety, archaism, fanaticism. Maybe it'd be better to call our art's culture one of congenital skepticism. Our intelligentsia (us) distrust strong belief, open conviction. Material passion is one thing, but ideological passion disgusts us. We believe that ideology is now the province of the rival SIGs and PACs all trying to get its slice of the big green pie—and, looking around us, we see that it is indeed so. But the Dostoevsky one sees in Frank's biography would point out—more like hop up and down and shake his fist and fly at us and scream—that if this is so it is because we have abandoned the field.

Take a look at just a snippet from the famous "Necessary Explanation" of Ippolit in *The Idiot*:

> *"Anyone who attacks individual charity," I began, "attacks human nature and casts contempt on personal dignity. But the organization of 'public charity' and the problem of individual freedom are two distinct questions, and not mutually exclusive. Individual kindness will always remain, because it is an individual impulse, the living impulse of one personality to exert a direct influence upon another. . . . How can you tell, Bahmutov, what significance such an association of one personality with another may have on the destiny of those associated?"*

Can you imagine any of our important contemporary novelists allowing a character to say things like this?—not, mind you, just as hypocritical bombast so that some ironic hero can put a pin in it, but as part of a 10-page monologue by somebody trying to decide whether to commit suicide. The obvious response to the question is also a true one: Such a contemporary novelist would be ridiculous. Such a speech in our art would provoke, not outrage or invective, but worse: one raised eyebrow and a very slight smile. (Maybe—if it was a really *major* novelist—a very subtle deadpan line in a Letterman monologue.) The novelist would be—and this is our own age's truest vision of hell—laughed out of town.

So he—we, fiction writers—won't—ever—dare try to use serious art to advance ideologies.[25] The project would be as culturally inappropriate as Menard's *Quixote*. We'd be laughed out of town. Given this—and it is a given—who is to blame for the philosophical passionlessness of our own Dostoevskys? The culture, the laughers? But they wouldn't—could not—laugh if a piece of passionately serious ideological contemporary fiction was also ingenious and radiantly transcendent fiction. But how to do that—how even, for a writer, even a very talented writer, to get up the guts to even try? There are no formulae or guarantees. But there are models. Frank's books present a hologram of one of them.

FOOTNOTES

1. Volume III, *The Stir of Liberation*, contains I bet as fine an explicative reading of *Notes* as has ever been done, tracing its genesis as a reply to the "rational egoism" made fashionable in Chernyshevsky's 1863 novel *What Is to Be Done?*, and identifying the Underground Man's intended function for Dostoevsky as basically a parodic caricature. Frank's persuasive explanation for the frequent misreading of *Notes* (a lot of critics don't read the book as a *conte philosophique* and assume Dostoevsky designed the U.M. as a serious Hamlet-grade archetype) also helps explain why Dostoevsky's masterpieces are often read and admired even without any real appreciation of their ideological agendas: "the parodistic function of [the Underground Man's] character has always been obscured by the immense vitality of its artistic embodiment"—that is, in certain ways, Dostoevsky was too good for his own good.

2. Frank never in four volumes mentions the Intentional Fallacy or tries to head off the objection that his biography commits it all over the place. This is real interesting to me. In a way it's understandable, because the tone Frank maintains through all his readings is one of maximum restraint and objectivity: He's not about imposing a certain theory or way of decoding Dostoevsky, and he steers way clear of arguing with other critics who've applied various axes' edges to FMD's stuff. When Frank does want to criticize or refute a certain reading (as in occasional attacks on Bakhtin's *Problems of Dostoevsky's Poetics*, or in a really brilliant refutation of Freud's 1928 "Dostoevsky and Patricide" in the Appendix to Volume I), he always does so simply by pointing out that the historical facts and/or Dostoevsky's own notes and letters contradict certain assumptions a critic has made. His argument is never that somebody else is wrong, just that they don't have all the facts ... which again gives implicit authority to Frank's agenda of providing completely exhaustive and comprehensive context, The Whole Story.

3. It is the loss of an ability to countenance and discuss the *particularity* of works of literary genius that is maybe most to be loathed about the theory industry's rise to power in contemporary fiction-criticism. A lot of poststructural theory is fascinating in its own right, but when it comes to actually reading some piece of fiction, most theoretical readings consist in just running it through a kind of powerful philosophical machine. This is in all meaningful ways equivalent to dissecting a flower instead of looking at it or smelling it. Dissection has its place, as do systems and general applications of method; but so does appreciation, and so does countenancing the singularity of something beautiful. It is

Professor Frank's determination to treat *both* the ideological forces at work around Dostoevsky's fictions *and* the completely distinctive and unabstractable way in which FMD transforms those forces that makes his biography so valuable, I think.

4. How familiar—I mean *emotionally* familiar, resonant—does the syntax of Hawthorne and Poe and Bierce seem to you?

5. Especially in the excruciatingly Victorianish translations of Ms. Constance Garnett, who in the '30s and '40s cornered the FMD/Tolstoy translation market, and whose 1935 rendering of *The Idiot* has stuff like (I'm scanning almost at random):

> *"Nastasya Filippovna!" General Epanchin articulated reproachfully. "I am very glad I've met you here, Kolya," said Myshkin to him. "Can't you help me? I must be at Nastasya Filippovna's. I asked Ardelion Alexandrovitch to take me there, but you see he is asleep. Will you take me there, for I don't know the streets, nor the way?"*
>
> *"The phrase flattered and touched and greatly pleased General Ivolgin: he suddenly melted, instantly changed his tone, and went off into a long, enthusiastic explanation."*

And even in the acclaimed new Knopf translations by Richard Pevear and Larissa Volokhonsky, the prose (in, e.g., *Crime and Punishment*) is still like:

> *"Enough!" he said resolutely and solemnly. "Away with mirages, away with false fears, away with spectres! . . . There is life! Was I not alive just now? My life hasn't died with the old crone! May the Lord remember her in His kingdom and—enough, my dear, it's time to go! Now is the kingdom of reason and light and . . . and will and strength . . . and now we shall see! Now we shall cross swords!" he added presumptuously, as if addressing some dark force and challenging it. . . .*

Umm, why not just *"as if addresing some dark force"*? Umm, can you challenge a dark force without addressing it? Or is there, in the Russian, something that keeps the above from being redundant, stilted, *bad*? If so, why not recognize that in English it's bad, and clean it *up* in an acclaimed new Knopf translation? I just don't get it.

6. What on earth does it mean to "fly at" somebody? It happens dozens of times in every FMD novel. What, "fly at" them in order to beat them up? To get in their face? Why not say that, if you're translating?

7. Q.v., from Pevear and Volokhonsky's acclaimed rendering of *Notes*:

> *"Mr. Ferfichkin, tomorrow you will give me satisfaction for your present words!" I said loudly, pompously addressing Ferfichkin.*
>
> *"You mean a duel, sir? At your pleasure," the man answered. . . .*

8. Somebody has only to spend one term trying to teach literature in school to realize that the quickest way to kill a writer's vitality for potential readers is to present that writer ahead of time as "great" or "classic." Because then the author becomes for the students like medicine or vegetables, something that the authorities have declared "good for them" that they "ought to like," and then the students' nictitating membranes come down, and everybody's dead. Should this surprise anybody? We could learn a lot from bored students who hate to read, in my opinion.

9. Who was, like Faulkner's Caddie, "doomed and knew it," and whose heroism consists in her haughty defiance of a doom she also courts—FMD seems like the

first fiction writer really to understand that some people love their own suffering. Nietzsche would take Dostoevsky's insight and make it a cornerstone of his own devastating attack on Christianity, and this is vastly ironic: In our own age and culture of enlightened atheism we are very much Nietzsche's children, his ideological heirs; and without Dostoevsky there would have been no Nietzsche; and yet Dostoevsky is among the most deeply religious of all writers. . . .

10. Frank doesn't blink this sort of stuff, but in his account we learn that Dostoevsky's character was paradoxical: insufferably vain about his literary reputation, FMD was also tormented his whole life by what he saw as his inadequacies as a writer; a leech and a spendthrift, he also did stuff like voluntarily assume financial responsibility for his stepson, for the unbelievably nasty family of his dead brother, and for the debts of the famous journal *Epoch* that he and that brother had coedited. Frank's fourth volume makes it clear that it was these honorable debts, not general deadbeatism, that sent Mr. and Mrs. FMD into exile in Europe to avoid debtor's prison, and that it was only at the gambling spas of Europe that Dostoevsky's gambling mania kicked in.

11. Sometimes this allergy to Moscow is awkwardly striking: q.v. the start of Part Two of *The Idiot*, when Prince Myshkin—the novel's protagonist—has left St. Petersburg for six full months in Moscow: "Of Myshkin's adventures during his absence from Petersburg we can give little information." Frank doesn't mention much about this Moscophobia that I could find.

12. *Poor Folk*, a regulation "social novel" that frames kind of a goopy little love story with depicitions of urban poverty sufficiently ghastly to elicit the approval of a socialist Left that in 1840s Russia more or less equalled the literary episcopate.

13. It's true that FMD's epilepsy, including the mystical illuminations that attended his preseizure auras, gets no more than cursory attention from Frank, and a reviewer like the *Times* of London's James L. Rice (himself the author of a weird book on epilepsy and Dostoevsky) complains that Frank "gives no idea of the malady's chronic impact" on Dostoevsky's religious ideals and representation in his books. Other critics who complain that Frank doesn't pay enough attention to FMD's pathology include Stephen Jan Parker of the *NYTBR*, who spends a third of his review of Volume III making arguments like "It seems to me that Dostoevsky's behavior does conform fully to the diagnostic criteria for pathological gambling as set forth in the American Psychiatric Association's diagnostic manual." As much as anything, it's reviews like this that ought to make us appreciate Frank's own evenhanded breadth and absence of specific axes to grind.

14. I don't want to neglect the observation that Frank's biography often provides good and interesting dirt. W/r/t FMD's adventures in Europe, we learn in Volume IV that his famous 1867 fight with Turgenev, which was mostly over the fact that Turgenev (whom Frank clearly doesn't like, and portrays as a kind of yuppie with a monocle) had offended Dostoevsky's passionate nationalism by attacking Russia in print and moving to Germany and declaring himself a German, was also partly over the fact that Dostoevsky had years earlier borrowed 50 thalers from Turgenev and promised to pay him back right away and never did. Frank is too restrained to point out that it's much easier to live with stiffing somebody if you decide that person's an asshole.

15. An unexpected bonus is that Frank's volumes are full of marvelous and funny and tongue-rolling names—Snitkin, Dubolyobov, Appolinaria, Strakhov, Golubov, von Voght, Katkov, Nekrasov, Pisarev. You can see why Russian writers

like Gogol and Dostoevsky raised to fine art the employment of epithetic names.

16. Q.v.: *"Poor Feodor, he does suffer so much . . . and is always so irritable, and liable to fly out about trifles . . . It's of no consequence, because the other days are very good, when he is so sweet and gentle. Besides, I can see that when he screams at me it is from illness, not from bad temper."* Frank quotes large amounts of this sort of stuff without much evident awareness that the Dostoevskys' relationship was in certain ways pretty sick, at least by 1996 standards: "Anna's forbearance, whatever prodigies of self-command it may have cost her, was amply compensated for (at least in her eyes) by Dostoevsky's immense gratitude and growing sense of attachment." Beattie, Bradshaw, et al. would have a field day with this sort of stuff.

17. See also, e.g., Dostoevsky's disastrous passion for the utter bitch-goddess Appolinaria Suslova, or the mental gymnastics he performs to justify his roulette, or the fact, amply documented by Frank, that FMD really was an active part of the Petrashevsky circle and as a matter of fact *did* deserve to be arrested, *pace* a lot of biographers who've tried to claim that FMD was just at the wrong radical meeting at the wrong time.

18. I guess you could argue that Tolstoy and Hugo and Zola and the 19th-century titans were ideological writers. But the thing about Dostoevsky's gift for character and for rendering the psychological and moral and spiritual conflicts within (not just *between*) people is that it let him dramatize extremely heavy and serious moral themes without ever seeming preachy or reductive, that is, without ever blinking the difficulties of moral and spiritual conflicts or making goodness or redemption seem simpler than they really are. You need only compare the protagonists' final conversions in Tolstoy's *The Death of Ivan Ilych* and FMD's *Crime and Punishment* to appreciate Dostoevsky's ability to be moral without being moralistic.

19. Here's another thing Frank discusses brilliantly in Vol. III's chapter on *House of the Dead*—part of the reason why FMD abandoned the fashionable socialist principles of his twenties is that years of imprisonment in Siberia with the absolute bottom-feeders of society taught him that the peasants and urban poor of Russia totally hated the upper-class intellectuals who wanted to "liberate" them, and that they were kind of right for hating them. If you want to get some idea of how Dostoevskyian irony might translate into modern U.S. culture, try reading *House of the Dead* and Tom Wolfe's "Mau-Mauing the Flak Catchers" at the same time.

20. This state of affairs is one reason why Bakhtin's *Problems of Dostoevsky's Poetics,* published under Stalin, had to seriously downplay FMD's ideological involvement with his own characters: A lot of Bakhtin's praise for Dostoevsky's "polyphonic" characterizations and the "dialogic imagination" that allowed Dostoevsky to refrain from injecting his own values into his books is the natural result of a Soviet critic trying to discuss an author whose reactionary views the State wanted forgotten. Frank, who takes out after Bakhtin at a number of points, doesn't really make clear the constraints Bakhtin was operating under.

21. Should I find it depressing that the young Dostoevsky was just like young U.S. writers today, or kind of a relief? Does anything ever change?

22. Not surprisingly, FMD's exact beliefs are idiosyncratic and complicated, and Frank does a good job of tracing them out as they're dramatized in the novels (the effect of egoistic atheism on the Russian character in *Notes* and *C&P;* the deformation of Russian passion by worldly Europe in *The Gambler;* and, in *The*

Idiot's Myshkin and *The Brothers Karamazov*'s Zosima, the implications of a Christ literally subjected to nature's scientific forces, an idea central to everything Dostoevsky wrote after he saw Holbein the Younger's *Dead Christ* at the Basel Museum in 1867).

But what Frank has done phenomenally well is to distill the enormous amounts of archival material that exist by and about FMD, helping make it comprehensive instead of just using parts of it to bolster a particular critical stance. E.g., near the end of Vol. III, Frank finds and cites obscure notes for "Socialism and Christianity," an unfinished essay, that give a reasonably succinct picture of Dostoevsky's beliefs. Q.v.:

> *Christ's incarnation . . . provided a new ideal for mankind, one that has retained its validity ever since: "NB. Not one atheist who has disputed the divine origin of Christ has denied the fact that He is the ideal of humanity. The latest on this—Renan. This is very remarkable." And the law of this new ideal, according to Dostoevsky, consists of the return to spontaneity, to the masses, but freely. . . . Not forcibly, but on the contrary, in the highest degree willfully and consciously. It is clear that this higher willfulness is at the same time a higher renunciation of the will.*

23. FMD's particular foes were the Nihilists, the radical progeny of the '40s socialists, whose name comes from a speech in Turgenev's *Fathers and Sons*. But the real battle was wider. It is no accident that Joseph Frank's big epigram for Vol. IV is from Kolakowski's classic *Modernity on Endless Trial*, for Dostoevsky's abandonment of utilitarian socialism for an idiosyncratic moral conservatism can be seen in the same light as Kant's awakening from "dogmatic slumber" into a radical Pietist deontology nearly a century earlier: "By turning against the popular utilitarianism of the Enlightenment, [Kant] also knew exactly that what was at stake was not any particular moral code, but rather a question of the existence or nonexistence of the distinction between good and evil and, consequently, a question of the fate of mankind."

24. Ploughing through the historical and linguistic impediments actually to *read* this author makes it very clear why Dostoevsky deserves his canonical spot. In his novels, great and profound issues simultaneously transcend and are rooted in the particularities of place, time, history, character. The irony of his now being abstracted by canonization is that he is almost unequalled in his ability to make abstractions concrete and bare ideas alive and vital.

25. We will, of course, without hesitation use art to parody, ridicule, debunk or protest ideologies. But there is a difference.

April 1996

THE HUNGRY ICON

Langston Hughes Rides a Blue Note

By Henry Louis Gates, Jr.

THE LIFE OF LANGSTON HUGHES: I, TOO, SING AMERICA,
VOLUME I: 1902–1941
By Arnold Rampersad

THE LIFE OF LANGSTON HUGHES: I DREAM A WORLD,
VOLUME II: 1941–1967
By Arnold Rampersad

SELECTED POEMS OF LANGSTON HUGHES

The burden of the past plays itself out rather differently in the white and black literary traditions. For the scholar of Western literature, the authority of canonized texts and interpretations can hobble creativity. How many years would it take just to *read* all the commentaries on Shakespeare, let alone make the corpus one's own—and then to transcend it through a novel interpretation? The scholar of mainstream Western culture quickly collides with an enshrined collective memory that can confine just as surely as it preserves continuity and enables the extension of tradition.

The curse that the scholar of African and African-American studies bears, by contrast, is the *absence* of a printed, catalogued, collective cultural memory. Despite the interest in Black Studies since the late '60s, we still have relatively few reference works—biographical dictionaries, annotated bibliographies, disciplinary histories, and especially encyclopedias, concordances, and dictionaries of black language use. The absence of these tools almost always forces one to re-create from degree zero the historical and critical contexts that mainstream scholars can take for granted (imagine a critic of Shakespeare having to do primary research just to identify the poet's allusions and his historical contemporaries). The terrible excitement that scholars of Black Studies feel stems from the knowledge that virtually everything they see or write can be new—free of the burden of the canonical past, the prison house of tradition. To publish criticism still feels like making a fresh inscription on a large tabula rasa. Too often, African-Americanists must reinvent the wheel, their work forever trapped in the paradox of "repeating themselves for the first time."

The stories of individual African-American lives are not exempted from this dearth of basic information. As Arnold Rampersad demonstrated in the *Yale Review* a few years ago, very few blacks have written full-length biographies of black subjects. This is particularly curious because *remembering* is one of the cardinal virtues of black culture—from subtle narrative devices like repetition of line and rhythm (the sermon, black music, oral narration) to more public commemorations such as the observation of "black" holidays ("Juneteenth," Black History Month, Kwaanza) or eating Hoppin' John on New Year's Day or reinterpreting the Fourth of July to make it analogous to Good Friday rather than Easter ... from Founder's Day ceremonies and family reunions to the naming of institutions and places—Wheatley, Carver, Dunbar, and Washington public schools, Martin Luther King boulevards—to repeated historical concepts or metaphors, such as the African Methodist Episcopal Church.

Remembering characterizes African-American culture because blacks have been systematically denied access to their history, both during and after slavery. Under slavery, of course, they were forbidden the tools of formal memory—reading and writing. They were also denied their native languages and even the drum itself (deemed subversive by many masters, and correctly so, as it was the "home" of repetition and contained a Pan-African language many blacks could understand). The intent was to deprive blacks of their memory, and their history—for without history, as Hegel said, there could be no memory, and without memory there could be no self. An abolitionist described in his memoirs this encounter: He asked after one slave's "self," and the man responded, "I ain't got no self." Without hesitation the abolitionist asked, "Slave are you?" "That's what I is."

This connection among language, memory, and the self has been crucial to African-Americans, intent as they have had to be upon demonstrating both that they had common humanity with whites and that their own "selves" were as whole, "integral," educable, and noble as those of any other ethnic group (including, among the historical twists and turns, sundry "white ethnics"). Deprived of formal recognition of their subjectivity in Western arts and letters, in jurisprudence, and in all that signals full citizenship, African-Americans sought the permanence of the book to write their rhetorical selves into language. I write therefore I am. The perilous journey from object to subject is strewn with black autobiographies; *Unscathed by Slavery* could very well be the subtitle of the hundreds of memoirs published by ex-slaves between 1760 and Booker T. Washington's *Up from Slavery* in 1901.

This passionate concern with the self makes Rampersad's discovery— the lack of an individual biographical impulse in the black tradition— especially fascinating. Although over 300 *collective* black biographies were published between the late 18th century and the middle of the 20th, and despite the fact that ours is one of the very few traditions in which writers can establish themselves as authors and spokespersons by publishing their autobiographies as *first* books (autobiography remains the dominant genre in the African-American tradition), only a handful of black writers have re-created the lives and times of other blacks.

It is as if the very vitality of autobiography produced a concomitant nonvitality of black biography; the energy necessary to proclaim "I am" could not be dissipated in making that claim for another. One's public initiation was a most private act; one crossed, alone, the abyss between nothingness and being—positing humanity, selfhood, and citizenship with the stroke of one's own pen. Only in biographical dictionaries was this isolation overcome; biography was collective, a testament to the existence of "the Negro" from A to Z, alphabetically ordered parts amounting to an African-American whole. Nurses and churchmen, club women and members of fraternal orders, freemasons and free citizens of Cincinnati—each group had its own collective testimony.

Arnold Rampersad's biography of Langston Hughes has ended this trend. For Rampersad, in elegant but understated prose, has rendered the world that Langston Hughes made and the world that made him.

The re-creation of *detail* is Rampersad's most stunning achievement. He has arranged volume II in 16 chapters, each of which addresses one, two, or three years between February 1, 1941, Hughes's 39th birthday, and May 25, 1967, the day of his memorial service at Benta's funeral home in Harlem. The book opens with a description of Hughes's gonorrhea and its painful cure, and ends with a meticulously re-created account of his prostate surgery, brief recovery, then ultimate deterioration. Between these rather intimate frames we learn who Hughes is, reading over his shoulder as he reveals his likes and dislikes, whom he admires and envies, when he is brave and when not so brave, when he is petty and jealous and when he is noble, when he writes for art and writes to eat, and his concerns and anxieties about his own immortality, the place of his icon in African-American letters.

Of the several rhetorical techniques Rampersad employs, none is more effective than his use of "free indirect discourse."

Emotionally more content, Langston also spoke now with a clearer voice on politics. Attending a Carnegie Hall memorial to W. E. B. Du Bois,

undeterred by the fact that Du Bois had died a communist, he also pub-
lished a tribute to him in the New York Post *and in black newspapers*
through the Associated Negro Press. To interviewers from Italian televi-
sion and the Voice of America, and in an appearance for CORE at
Barnard College, he spoke confidently, but in the interests of modera-
tion, about the freedom movement. The present turmoil was a good thing,
because it was making people think. Those who did not think, but wailed
apocalyptically, were doing little good.

The "voice" in those last two lines reveals thoughts that are those of both
Hughes and Rampersad, and, strictly speaking, of neither. Rampersad
merges, to great effect, the third-person narrative voice of the biographer with the first-person voice of his subject. He is able to tell us what
Hughes thought and felt without resorting unduly to direct quotations
from Hughes's notes or letters. The technique is effective precisely
because it is scarcely noticeable amid so much detail.

I have to confess that in reading this book I fell in love with Hughes,
the person, for the first time. The more I learned of his complex emotions about his peers and rivals (Du Bois, Baldwin, Wright, Ellison,
Gwendolyn Brooks, a mad Ezra Pound sending him fan letters from the
asylum), the more I admired him. My respect and affection for Hughes
grew so much that I found it difficult to finish the book because I knew
he was going to die. I mention these feelings because I think they're
symptomatic of a literary-critical generation that recognized Hughes as
icon and little else—failing, among other things, to read his poetry
closely, a mistake that led to glib assertions about a body of work that
was actually unfamiliar. Rampersad has removed Hughes's cardboard
cutout from the Black Hall of Fame, and replaced it with a three-
dimensional figure who *created* a specific, vernacular idiom in African-
American poetry, one informed by the blues and jazz—by both the
classic and the urban blues and early jazz in his two masterpieces, *The
Weary Blues* (1926) and *Fine Clothes to the Jew* (1927), and by bebop, the
cool, and even postmodern, poststructural, early/transitional Coltrane
in *Ask Your Mama: Twelve Moods for Jazz* (1961). *Ask Your Mama* is to
Hughes's canon as Duke Ellington's longer compositions are to his earlier,
shorter, popular pieces—that is, either maligned or ignored. Hughes's
experiments with vernacular music and speech, and their combination
into a new idiom of American and African-American verse, ensure for
him a permanent place in both canons.

Just as important was Hughes's role in mediating among African
cultures in the old world and the new. Only Du Bois, as both covener of
the Pan-African congresses and epitome of African intellection, can
possibly rival Hughes in being *the* conduit between black poets and their

poetry in Spanish, French, and English. Aimé Césaire and Léopold Senghor read Hughes; Hughes translated them into English, just as he did Jacques Roumain's *Masters of the Dew* (with Mercer Cook). He also translated Nicolás Guillén and García Lorca's *Gypsy Ballads* from the Spanish. Hughes's role in creating a Pan-African literary *culture*, where poems by black authors in French, Spanish, Portuguese, and English directly inform the shape of other poems by other black authors, has no rival in our intellectual history. Hughes's poetry and his translations forged a direct line between the new Negroes in Harlem and the Pan-Africans in Paris, Havana, Rio, Lagos, Dakar, Kingston, and Port-au-Prince. He worked to create a Pan-African intellectual culture just as Latin and the Church forged a Pan-European culture in the Middle Ages, even when peasants in what is now Germany or France knew not one jot about a "European" anything.

Hughes preserved his letters and memorabilia as if he were his own historian or archivist, with one eye on his correspondent, and the other on the James Weldon Johnson Collection at Yale, where Carl Van Vechten had arranged for Hughes's papers to be housed. Over almost a decade, Rampersad patiently pored over and sifted through the voluminous documentation, supplementing the testimony of the correspondence with thousands of hours of taped interviews. The result of such diligent labor, rendered in a highly readable narrative style, is a splendid thing to behold: Rampersad has published the most sophisticated biography of a black subject, and set the example by which all other biographies of black subjects will be judged. He has, in other words, defined a standard of excellence and simultaneously created a field: The success of these books, as measured in sales, accolades, and well-deserved prizes, will certainly make biography a central field in African-American literary studies. Meeting the standard he has established, however, will be extraordinarily difficult.

Rampersad's two volumes have been reviewed extensively, from Greg Tate's fascinating essay in these pages (*VLS*, July 1988) and Darryl Pinckney's meditation in *The New York Review* (February 16, 1989), to two full-length reviews in the *Times Book Review* by *two* black women Pulitzer Prize–winning poets, Gwendolyn Brooks and Rita Dove— surely a coup of sorts in the history of black literary criticism. It is a tribute to Rampersad's skill that each of these reviews has become a basis for discussing the implications of Hughes's life and art, as if the biographer's own work could be taken for granted or was, somehow, transparent. Of course, one measure of successful biography as Rampersad practices it is just this "transparency," this absence of methodological discussion in favor of a full-scale engagement with Langston

Hughes, or rather with "Langston Hughes" as lovingly re-created by this subtle biographer.

Rampersad brings us into Hughes's world, feeling as he feels, seeing as he sees. Not once do we feel the hand of the author on our shoulder, pushing us to interpret this way or that:

> *The day was cool, the sky above the Monterey Peninsula murky with rain and winter mists when Langston rode from the hospital to the grounds of his friend and patron Noël Sullivan's estate, Hollow Hills Farm, some five miles away in Carmel Valley. Since September, he had been living there as a guest of Sullivan's in a one-room cottage built especially for him, where he could write and sleep free from most distractions. Now, however, he unpacked in an upstairs room in the main house where, over the next two weeks or so, he would nurse himself back to health. The room was comfortable, and soothingly decorated entirely in blue. On a side table was a gift sent from New York by his loyal friend Carl Van Vechten—a flowering plant, "a kind of glowing little tree growing out of white pebbles in a white pot . . ."*

Imagine how much research was necessary to re-create these scenes; the lines read like passages from a novel. Rampersad *shows* us what it was like to be Hughes as a human being, a human being who smells and breathes and hurts, who dreams and is ambitious, who can be loving and peevish and jealous, who laughs rather too much when he is most anxious or full of dread, and who cares enormously about maintaining a love affair with the entire race.

If ever a loving concern for "the race," and a concomitant concern with its regard for him, defined what it means to be a "race man," then Hughes was *the* example of it. Hughes cared passionately about regular Negroes, and about the importance of not appearing distant from them; as Rampersad says, "Langston psychologically needed the race in order to survive and flourish." What's more, he was "one of the few black writers of any consequence to champion racial consciousness as a source of inspiration for black artists." Hughes earned the right to call himself the poet laureate of the Negro race. And Rampersad's art as a biographer lets us understand why.

Rampersad explains how the "depth of [Hughes's] identification with the race" helped free him

> *not only to understand that the profession of writing was distinct from its "subject," but also to see his race in a rounded, humane way, rather than mainly as a deformed product of white racism. To Langston, Bald-*

win was tortured by a sense of an "all but irreconcilable" tension (in Baldwin's words) between race and art because he lacked confidence in his own people and certainly did not love them, as Langston did. To Hughes, only a deep confidence in blacks and a love of them (two qualities that could not be divorced) would allow a black writer to reach the objectivity toward art that Hughes saw as indispensable. Baldwin was undoubtedly more troubled by race than he was, but Langston was far more what blacks regarded approvingly as a race man, far more involved with other blacks on a daily basis as a citizen and an artist, far less willing to estrange or exile himself from the culture, as Baldwin had done in going to live abroad.

R ampersad treats Hughes's attitudes toward Baldwin, Wright, Ellison, and other black peers at fascinating length. For example, in 1953 a young Ralph Ellison, whom Hughes had befriended early on, emerged almost overnight as the dominant black voice in American letters:

Ellison's triumph with Invisible Man *was crowned when he accepted the National Book Award in fiction. Present at the ceremony but obviously alienated in spirit, Langston reported to Arna Bontemps* [a black novelist and Hughes's closest friend since the Renaissance] *that the proceedings were "mildly interesting," dull really, with all the speeches stuffily delivered from prepared texts. Not long afterwards, at a cocktail party at the Algonquin Hotel in mid-Manhattan to welcome Ellison as a new member of PEN, he begged the new star of Afro-American writing not to read a long, dull paper when he visited Fisk University soon— long papers were so dull. As he had with Wright almost fifteen years before, Langston was feeling the chill of his own eclipse.*

But it was Baldwin with whom Hughes had the most difficult relations:

He shivered again early in February when an advance copy reached him of the latest sensation in black literature, James Baldwin's dramatic first novel, Go Tell It on the Mountain, *about a black boy's troubled passage to manhood in the face of raw conflicts with his domineering father and the terrifying pressures of black "storefront" religious fundamentalism. Worse yet, from Hughes's point of view, the book was being published by Knopf, who for all practical purposes had dropped him (the reception of* Montage of a Dream Deferred *had gutted its interest in his volume of selected poems). Criticizing Baldwin's sometimes unstable blending of gritty realism and refined rhetoric in the novel, Hughes judged that if Zora Neale Hurston, "with her feeling for the folk idiom," had been its author, "it would probably be a* quite *wonderful book." Baldwin, however, "over-writes and over-poeticizes in images way over the heads of the folks supposedly thinking them," in what finally was "an 'art' book about folks who aren't 'art' folks."* Go Tell It on the Mountain, *he concluded, was "a low-down story in a velvet bag—and a Knopf binding."*

In spite of this criticism, Langston dutifully mailed a blurb for the novel to Knopf.

Nine years later Baldwin still troubled him.

To Langston, there was little that was truly creative, much less visionary, about Another Country. *Privately to Arna Bontemps, he described Baldwin as aiming for a best-seller in "trying to out-Henry Henry Miller in the use of bad BAD bad words, or run [Harold Robbins's]* The Carpetbaggers *one better on sex in bed and out, left and right, plus a description of a latrine with all the little-boy words reproduced in the telling." In the same letter, Langston linked what he saw as Baldwin's excesses to the trend of integration sapping the strength of black youth. Paying a stiff price for the modicum of integration allowed them, young blacks were abandoning the old values and practices in the rush to be like whites. "Cullud is doing everything white folks are doing these days!" Langston mocked. . . . "Integration is going to RUIN Negro business," he predicted—as it apparently threatened to ruin the finest young writer of fiction in the race.*

Rarely have we been privy to the real feelings of black creative artists and intellectuals toward one another. The disagreement with Baldwin, was, to be sure, one of many. Indeed, Hughes's reactions to Melvin Tolson, Robert Hayden, and LeRoi Jones/Amiri Baraka—in addition to Wright, Baldwin, and Ellison—reveal how fraught with rivalry life "behind the veil" is, just as Jessie Fauset's comments to him ("I've suffered a good deal from colored men writers from Locke down to Bontemps—you know") begin to suggest the degree of sexism that also has characterized African-American literary relations.

I had never realized that Hughes interacted with so many major figures in the artistic world between 1925 and his death in 1967. Hughes knew *everybody,* if almost no one knew him, or was able to penetrate the veils and masks that the truly vulnerable fabricate to present public personas to the world. Leafing through Rampersad's index, one finds a veritable Who's Who of 20th-century art, from Stella Adler and Toshiko Akiyoshi, Tomas Mann and Dorothy Maynor, to Ezra Pound and Allen Tate, Mark Van Doren, Kurt Weill, Max Yergan, and Yevgeny Yevtushenko. In so many ways and to so many people, Hughes was "the Negro," or at least "Negro literature," its public face, its spoken voice and cocktail-party embodiment as well as the source of its printed texts. Reading Rampersad's volumes makes it clear how deeply ingrained American Negro literature was in the larger American tradition, even if scholars, until very, very recently, bracketed it into a ghetto apart, the Harlem of the American canon.

In rendering Hughes's reactions to and interactions with his equally famous contemporaries, Rampersad's biography chronicles almost half a century in the history of both American art and the life and times of one of its most important figures. Through him we see and feel exactly how the great events in black history—the Harlem Renaissance, the Depression, World War II, McCarthyite repression, the civil rights movement, the emergence of Africa and the larger process of decolonization as the Age of Europe came to a close with the lifting of "the color curtain," and the rebirth of black nationalism in the Black Power era—how all of these large forces simultaneously delimit and open up individual choices in the daily events that, taken together, define a life. Never has an account of a black human being revealed more vividly the particularities of a life within the context of large, public forces and events. No life, no matter how great, can possibly escape its context, its historical moment. For all his political ambivalences, Hughes saw this clearly, saying in one unpublished reflection:

> *Politics in any country in the world is dangerous. For the poet, politics in any country in the world had better be disguised as poetry. . . . Politics can be the graveyard of the poet. And only poetry can be his resurrection.*
>
> *What is poetry? It is the human soul entire, squeezed like a lemon or a lime, drop by drop, into atomic words. The ethnic language does not matter. Ask Aimé Césaire. He knows. . . . Perhaps not consciously—but in the soul of his writing, he knows. . . . The Negritudinous Senghor, the Caribbeanesque Guillén, the American me, are regional poets of genuine realities and authentic values. Césaire . . . takes all that we have, Senghor, Guillén and Hughes, and flings it at the moon, to make of it a spaceship of the dreams of all the dreamers in the world.*
>
> *As a footnote I must add that, concerning Césaire, all I have said I deeply feel is for me true. Concerning politics, nothing I have said is true. A poet is a human being. Each human being must live within his time, with and for his people, and within the boundaries of his country. Therefore, how can a poet keep out of politics?*
>
> *Hang yourself, poet, in your own words. Otherwise, you are dead.*

Rampersad deftly creates a sense of the social, the political, and the historical as these are locked in a dialectical relationship with individual choices, determining their range of response yet determined by such responses as well. Nowhere in black biography has this relation between "text" and context been rendered as sensitively and truly.

F or most of his professional life, Hughes lived hand to mouth, his choices circumscribed perhaps even more by economics than by racism. He was supported by patrons like Noël Sullivan, a dependence necessitated by the insulting treatment he received from publishers and the pittance he earned for his writings and readings.

Hughes's books were widely reviewed in mainstream journals by mainstream writers, even if few understood his experiments with black vernacular forms. His newspaper character, Jesse B. Semple (a/k/a "Simple"), who appeared in a regular column Hughes wrote for the *Chicago Defender*, was remarkably popular; he was the vox populi persona of Hughes the "race man." Simple once spoke eloquently to an obtuse friend on the meaning of bebop music:

> *That is where Bop comes from, . . . out of them dark days we have seen. That is why Be-Bop is so mad, wild, frantic, crazy. And not to be dug unless you have seen dark days, too. That's why folks who ain't suffered much cannot play Bop, and do not understand it. They think it's nonsense—like you. They think it's just crazy crazy. They do not know it is also MAD crazy, SAD crazy, FRANTIC WILD CRAZY—beat right out of some bloody black head! That's what Bop is. These young kids who play it best, they know.*

Simple's discussion of bebop shows how rich the *Defender* columns were, and how crucial jazz was to Hughes. Accordingly, we must learn to read him in new ways, "through" or "against" the African-American vernacular.

As Rampersad puts it:

> *At varying, unpredictable times witty, sardonic, ironic, expository, whimsical, documentary, and tragic, "Montage of a Dream Deferred" is an expansive poetic statement on the fate of blacks in the modern, urban world. The manuscript was Hughes's answer in 1948 to the overwhelming question of the day in Harlem and communities like it, and possibly, prophetically, of the Afro-American future: "What happens to a dream deferred? / Does it dry up / like a raisin in the sun?" "This poem on contemporary Harlem," Langston wrote as a preface, "is marked by conflicting changes, sudden nuances, sharp and impudent interjections, broken rhythms, and passages sometimes in the manner of the jam session, sometimes the popular song, punctuated by the riffs, runs, breaks,*

*and disc-tortions of the music of a community in transition." The poet's
love for the community is paramount, but his brooding intelligence is such
that the wooden phrase "community in transition" is really portentous.*

In "Jazztet Muted," for example, the 11th section of *Ask Your
Mama*, Hughes introduced the poem with a musical cue that called for
"bop blues into very modern jazz burning the air eerie like a neon
swamp-fire cooled by dry ice":

> *IN THE NEGROES OF THE QUARTER*
> *PRESSURE OF THE BLOOD IS SLIGHTLY HIGHER*
> *IN THE QUARTER OF THE NEGROES*
> *WHERE BLACK SHADOWS MOVE LIKE SHADOWS*
> *CUT FROM SHADOWS CUT FROM SHADE*
> *IN THE QUARTER OF THE NEGROES*
> *SUDDENLY CATCHING FIRE*
> *FROM THE WING TIP OF A MATCH TIP*
> *ON THE BREATH OF ORNETTE COLEMAN.*
> *IN NEGRO TOMBS THE MUSIC*
> *FROM JUKEBOX JOINS IS LAID*
> *AND FREE-DELIVERY TV SETS*
> *ON GRAVESTONES DATES ARE PLAYED.*
> *EXTRA-LARGE THE KINGS AND QUEENS*
> *AT EITHER SIDE ARRAYED*
> *HAVE DOORS THAT OPEN OUTWARD*
> *TO THE QUARTER OF THE NEGROES*
> *WHERE THE PRESSURE OF THE BLOOD*
> *IS SLIGHTLY HIGHER—*
> *DUE TO SMOLDERING SHADOWS*
> *THAT SOMETIMES TURN TO FIRE.*
>
> > HELP ME, YARDBIRD!
> > HELP ME!

Rampersad's assessments of Hughes's poetry are always judicious; he
never claims more for Hughes the poet than the poetry can deliver, yet his
sensitive analyses of the poems should dispel forever the whisper among
our critical generation that Hughes's poetry does not withstand the rigors
of formal analysis. Quite the contrary, Rampersad's readings of Hughes's
best work—his vernacular poetry, cast in "the idiom of the black folk"
and found especially in *The Weary Blues, Fine Clothes to the Jew,* and *Ask
Your Mama*—should go a long way toward generating interest in rereading, *closely,* Hughes's work, since as Hughes himself recognized, "only
poetry can be [the poet's] resurrection." As Senghor wrote, Hughes excels
in the creation of "images, analogical, melodious, and rhythmical, with

assonance and alliteration. You will find this rhythm in French poetry; you will find it in Péguy, you will find it in Claudel, you will find this rhythm in St. John Perse. . . . And it is this that Langston Hughes has left us with, this model of the perfect work of art."

Hughes was wrong when he wrote that only his poetry could possibly resurrect him, for it is also true that a great biographer resurrects the poet *and* the poetry, a life and a body of work—the latter "as fragile as pottery," as Hughes put it. One of Arnold Rampersad's great gifts to Hughes, and to all of us who love literature, is that never again shall the poetry or the poet be silenced.

R ampersad's other great gift is that he has made biography a glamorous pursuit within the new black criticism, which has been dominated recently by feminist and poststructural theorizing. This two-volume biography will go a long way toward generating other biographies and thereby building up an African-American cultural memory. We need good biographies of so many figures, from Phyllis Wheatley and Harriet Jacobs to Du Bois and Alain Locke, James Baldwin and Lorraine Hansberry—virtually everyone who was anyone in the tradition remains to be written about, *honestly.*

For far too long, each of us has been imprisoned by peer pressure, forced to represent only certain images of the Negro in order to avoid inadvertent reinforcement of racist stereotypes. This sort of tortured logic has surfaced most glaringly in misguided protests against key black feminist texts: Michele Wallace's *Black Macho and the Myth of the Superwoman,* Ntozake Shange's *For Colored Girls . . . ,* Alice Walker's *The Color Purple.* "What will white racists *think* of black men?" the protesters asked, barely managing to keep a straight face. (Since when does a racist read *The Color Purple*—or anything at all, for that matter?)

No, we no longer need to sanitize the black past as we set about the complex business of generating our own African-American icons of the near and distant past. For it is our generation of African-Americanists that, at last, has the wherewithal to encode the cultural memory in print, in video, on compact disc and online, freed at last from forever reinventing the wheel.

Rampersad has made a breathtaking start in treating Langston Hughes, who suffered more than most from the cramped solitude of iconography. Hughes's public face(s)—and although he sought and found refuge in his beloved Harlem, he was certainly our most public poet, speaking in one week alone to some 10,000 people—were crafted such that his true human substance could not be seen among his carefully manufactured shadows. He was a lonely man, and he suffered this isolation in the most private ways, almost never voicing it. The irony did not escape him; he fondly quoted Dickinson's famous lines—"How public—like a Frog—/ To tell your name—the livelong June—/ To an admiring Bog!"

The ironies hardly end there. Hughes protected—censored—himself as a racial icon; Black Studies scholars have censored their treatment of many figures in the interest of positive images; and black artists today, indeed most any black public figure, must contend with the tradition of self-censorship. Consider the impact this had on Langston Hughes's sexuality. As Rampersad judges, with great sensitivity:

> *The truth about his sexuality will probably never be discovered. If Hughes indeed had homosexual lovers, what may be asserted incontrovertibly is that he did so with almost fanatical discretion. On this question, every person curious about him and also apparently in a position to know the truth was left finally in the dark. He laughed and joked and gossiped with apparent abandon but somehow contrived to remain a mystery on this score even to his intimates. His ability to appear to be at ease and defenseless, and at the same time to deny certain kinds of knowledge to those with him, was extraordinary. All his life he prized control far too highly for him to surrender it in his most mature years. Control above all meant to him the preservation of his position as the most admired and beloved poet of his race. That position, which he saw as a moral trust, and which intimately connected his deepest emotional needs to his function as an artist, may have meant too much for him to risk it for illicit sex.*

Rampersad was unable to prove our assumption about Hughes's homosexuality, despite his impressive research skills. Had it been provable, Rampersad would have done so. His bolder conclusion is that this most basic "fact" about Hughes remains elusive after two volumes precisely *because* of Hughes's determination to be a racial icon, to be presentable as the public face of the race. "Don't go to that swimming pool," my mother used to say, "without that moisturizing cream. I don't want you to embarrass the race by turning ashy." That's one part of black history we need to bury, the urge to produce a public Negro somehow more palatable to white people than the real thing. In defining the standard by which literary biography in our tradition, and in every tradition, shall be measured, Rampersad has helped to do just that. As Hughes and his alter ego, Arna Bontemps, liked to say, Rampersad has "done himself *brown.*"

THE BAD MOTHER

Katherine Anne Porter and How I Grew

By Blanche McCrary Boyd

My friend Fletcher, who had a stroke several years ago, does not speak easily, but when he found out I was going to write about Katherine Anne Porter, he managed to say, "Bad person."

Katherine Anne Porter was a coquettish, dissembling woman, a lady in the worst sense of the word; she was arguably racist and anti-Semitic, a liar who made up chunks of her past, and she was capable of great personal betrayal. There was, apparently, little nurturance in her makeup. Married five times, she had trouble remembering all of her husbands. She was physically beautiful, childless, a hard drinker, and a great conversationalist. Flawed and mythical, she was also one of the finest stylists ever to write the American language. The best of her fiction is among the best of ours.

Porter's output was small. The collected stories fit into one not-very-large volume, and the collected essays and occasional writings are even slimmer. There is a meager offering about the Sacco-Vanzetti case, *The Never Ending Wrong,* and there is one novel, *Ship of Fools.* A collection of her letters was published last year by Atlantic Monthly Press. All of it is worth reading, but her literary importance rests mainly upon a half dozen stories: "Flowering Judas," "The Jilting of Granny Weatherall," "Theft," "The Old Order," "Holiday," and "Pale Horse, Pale Rider."

Born in Texas in 1890, Porter, who was called Callie as a child, was raised in unstable, impoverished circumstances, a history she gradually revised into being born Katherine Anne Porter, part of a "white pillared" society where, she told Barbara Thompson in her *Paris Review* interview, "Everyone was literate as a matter of course," and "All the old houses . . . were full of books, bought generation after generation. . . ."

Porter did not publish until she was in her thirties ("I think it is the most curious lack of judgment to publish before you are ready") and her first collection, *Flowering Judas,* was printed in a limited edition of 600. She prided herself on being an artist, called herself one often, spoke of her art as her "vocation," and literally went hungry at times, piecing together grants and writing reviews to survive. She had a lot of nerve. "One of the marks of a gift," she said, "is to have the courage of it."

For much of her life, Porter remained the quintessential writer's writer, arrogant, broke, and influential, dragging around the world with her—to Mexico, Germany, Paris—trunks of unfinished manuscripts. Two of these projects became well known in literary circles, a biography of Cotton Mather, which she never completed, and her novel, *Ship of Fools*, which she did. After working on *Ship of Fools* for 20 years, she published it when she was 72.

Ship of Fools was, inexplicably, a bestseller, and Porter, in her seventies, became famous and rich. Her first large purchase was a 12-carat emerald; later she bought a home in College Park, Maryland. When *The Collected Stores of Katherine Anne Porter* was published in 1965, she won two of the big prizes: the National Book Award and the Pulitzer.

A blackout drinker by this point and still arrogant (she was offended not to win the Nobel), Porter became a combination of pathetic and grande dame. After a stroke, she developed textbook paranoia and was convinced that everyone was trying to steal from her. The courts eventually had to appoint a guardian; nurses cared for her around the clock. She died in a nursing home at the age of 90, soothed, apparently, by the confessions of Catholicism. Given her history and the tough disconsolations of her writing, it seems doubtful that she ever developed the kind of faith someone like Flannery O'Connor had.

Twenty-five years ago, while I was still in college, I was introduced to the writings of Katherine Anne Porter, Flannery O'Connor, and Eudora Welty. I was a young Southerner with an uncomfortable itch, and these women were offered to me as models by my first writing teacher. All three eventually became important influences, but when I read Porter's "Pale Horse, Pale Rider" I had a formative experience; for several days I cried and laughed and could not leave my apartment. This reaction was not sorrow. It was not like anything that had happened to me before. It was, well, literature. I hadn't known until then that anything could reach into the core of me, touch me where Porter's story had. In later years I would find this experience in other ways—through drugs, sex, meditation, even other works of literature—but I lost my artistic virginity to KAP.

When Porter died 11 years ago I attempted to write about her, but the grief that rose in me was too puzzling and ultimately sentimentalizing. Presumably I'm maturer now, and I've been toughened toward Porter by two careful readings of Joan Givner's *Katherine Anne Porter:*

A Life, originally published by Simon & Schuster in 1982 and recently reissued, with a revised prologue and epilogue, by the University of Georgia Press. Givner painstakingly exposes Porter's deceptiveness, her loose relationship with facts, and her extraordinary self-centeredness. She also offers original, compelling insights into Porter's writing.

Among literary folks, there is currently a distaste for Porter and a tendency to discredit her as an artist in light of both Givner's revelations and the shocking evidence presented in Elinor Langer's biography of Josephine Herbst that Porter had betrayed Herbst, who was her close friend, to the FBI. This tendency to reject Porter on moral grounds (which Givner herself does not fall into) is unfortunate, not only because there is a great deal to be learned from Porter's mistakes as well as her successes, but because there remains, inescapably, the stunning experience of her writing.

The argument over whether bad people can be good artists is an old one and not worth rehashing here, but in Katherine Anne Porter's case, I think her moral complexity, even her failings, actually contributed to her accomplishments.

For Porter, art had to address moral issues as certainly as for Flannery O'Connor art had to address the question of grace. O'Connor, obsessed with God, wrote from an omniscient point of view; Porter, concerned with good, evil, and complicity, usually wrote from a limited third person point of view, a technique that allowed her to enter a main character's mind while drawing a larger picture. In O'Connor's work, humble people are put into extreme situations in which they may receive grace: At the end of "A Good Man Is Hard To Find," when the grandmother is shot by the killer who calls himself the Misfit, she dies with a smile on her face because she has seen the Misfit as "one of my own children." The Misfit's comment, "She would of been a good woman if it had been somebody there to shoot her every minute of her life," is an expression of O'Connor's own view.

In Porter's stories, as Givner demonstrates, there are good guys, bad guys, and, in the main role, someone maneuvered by indifference or confusion or merely circumstances into terrible mistakes and responsibilities. In "Theft," the main character, who has been rejected by a lover, has her purse stolen by the woman janitor in her building. The janitor blames the narrator for her own transgression, attacking her looks and her values. The story ends with the narrator realizing she need not "be afraid of any thief but myself, who will end by leaving me nothing."

In "Flowering Judas," the protagonist, Laura, is unable to stand up to the corrupt revolutionary Braggioni, and she is, moreover, implicated in the death of the innocent Eugenio, who, in prison, has taken all of the pills she brought him for sleeping. Although Laura knows Eugenio will die, she does not insist on calling the doctor. There is a flowering judas tree outside Laura's window, and when she sleeps she dreams of the moral consequences of her failure to act: "Then eat these flowers, poor prisoner, said Eugenio . . . and from the Judas tree he stripped the warm bleeding flowers, and held them to her lips. She saw that his hand was fleshless, a cluster of small white petrified branches, and his eye sockets were without light, but she ate the flowers greedily, for they satisfied both hunger and thirst. Murderer! said Eugenio, and Cannibal! This is my body and my blood. . . . she awoke trembling, and was afraid to sleep again."

If Porter at times seemed unable to face the consequences of her own behavior, she was nevertheless incapable of deceiving herself about her characters. She never let them off the hook. She told Barbara Thompson, "That is where the artist begins to work: With the consequences of acts, not the acts themselves."

Porter was, in her life, capable of careless cruelty, and Givner raises the possibility that she may have been in an alcoholic blackout or gray-out when she informed on—actually lied about—Herbst, especially in light of the fact that she kept up their friendship. It is also quite possible that she merely minimized to herself the importance of what she had done. When she married Albert Erskine he was 26 years old and she was 50, a fact he did not find out until their wedding day; Porter, rather than feeling that she had deceived him implicitly or explicitly, was furious that he showed his dismay.

She was also a woman capable of careful cruelty. Her piece on Gertrude Stein, "The Wooden Umbrella," is a masterful character assassination, portraying Stein as "really sluggish, like something eating its way through a leaf." And Porter was careless with herself, taking a number of alcohol-induced falls that left her with broken ribs or serious cuts. At a party that got out of control, six of her ribs were broken in a sexual altercation. It does not seem particularly surprising that she would be careless with a friend's life as well.

Issues of guilt and betrayal were in Katherine Anne Porter's heart, and even in a failed novel like *Ship of Fools*, her struggle with these issues served her. Herr Lowenthal may be a caricatured Jew selling rosaries and almost every character in this novel may be repellent, but the reader still feels the growing weight of small complicities as the ship heads toward Germany and the world heads toward Nazism and death camps.

"Nothing is pointless, and nothing is meaningless if the artist will face it," Porter told Thompson. It is Porter's direct engagement with ultimate questions that helps create the sense of distillation, of compression in her stories, just as it does in O'Connor's. Both of these women were urgent, obsessive, cut-to-the-chase writers, and it is interesting to contrast their work with Eudora Welty's, since Welty lacks this ferocious sense of focus.

Welty's stories aim for mood, nuance, for pictures composed beautifully for their own sakes. Welty always takes her time, and she is ladylike in the best sense of the word, modest, discreet, sunny—better adjusted, a shrink might say. It is impossible to imagine Porter or O'Connor producing something like Welty's *The Robber Bridegroom* with its combination of history and myth, its sense of exuberance, even joy. If Porter or O'Connor felt joy, they kept it out of their work.

Welty's language can become water-colored, overly pretty, getting *between* the reader and the subject; reading her novel *Losing Battles* is like trying to see through a haze of organdy. With Porter and O'Connor, language is subordinated entirely to story, and the style is precise and clean.

O'Connor's favorite device is irony, not only imbedded structurally—in "Good Country People," Hulga, who thinks she knows something about meaninglessness, has her wooden leg stolen by a Bible salesman—but also laced through the language: "Why, that looks like that nice dull young man," Hulga's mother remarks, watching the Bible salesman walk across the field with his suitcase, not knowing it contains her daughter's leg.

Porter's use of irony is sparing but harsh. In "Pale Horse, Pale Rider," Miranda, a Denver newspaper reporter during WWI, is falling in love with a soldier about to be sent to the trenches, and she is certain he will die in the war. "'I don't want to love,' she would think in spite of herself, 'not Adam, there is no time . . .'" Miranda contracts influenza in the plague-like epidemic that killed so many in 1918–1919, and Adam nurses her through the first hallucinatory night. When she wakes up after weeks of unconsciousness, the war has ended, but Adam has not been saved by the armistice. He caught the flu from her and died of it. The story ends with the line, "Now there would be time for everything."

But the exquisiteness of Porter's style lies in more than its clean lines and occasional ironies. "I've been called a stylist until I really could tear my hair out," she told Thompson. "I simply don't believe in style. The style is you." Yet Porter did have well-formulated stylistic theories: "You have to speak clearly and simply and purely in a language that a six-year-old child can understand; and yet have the meanings and the overtones of language, and the implications, that appeal to the highest intelligence . . ." This is as good advice about writing as I've ever heard.

Perhaps the following passage from "The Jilting of Granny

Weatherall" will illustrate some of the special qualities of Porter's prose. Granny Weatherall is lying in bed drifting in and out of consciousness; she is dying, though the reader knows this much sooner than Granny does:

> *Lighting the lamps had been beautiful. The children huddled up to her and breathed like little calves waiting at the bars in the twilight. Their eyes followed the match and watched the flame rise and settle in a blue curve, then they moved away from her. The lamp was lit, they didn't have to be scared and hang on to mother any more. Never, never never more. God, for all my life I thank Thee.*

There is much to appreciate in this passage, aside from its lovely sound. The words feel like stones that have been carved and fitted against each other with great care, so that although the surface remains smooth, the sense of weight and depth and solidity is unmistakable. The echo of Poe ("Quoth the Raven, 'nevermore'") is effective, as is the religious reference, and the analogy of children to calves is elegantly made. The match and its flame lighting the lamp conjure life as a light which is literally passed from mother to child. But the most brilliant stroke in this passage is the word blue. Striking a match does cause a blueness in the flame (for Porter, the realistic level of an image must always be present), but it is what she manages to do with this blueness by the end of the story that is remarkable.

She grounds her transition to the bitterly transcendent ending by having Granny complain about her daughter Cornelia's lampshade. (Granny is always complaining about this daughter, who is charged with the difficult task of caring for her.) "The light was blue from Cornelia's silk lampshades. No sort of light at all, just frippery . . ."

Granny Weatherall has, all of her life, avoided her anger at the man who jilted her on her wedding day. It is only in the weakness of dying that she can no longer avoid the anguish that has run beneath her seemingly happy life: "I want you to find George. Find him and be sure to tell him I forgot him. I want him to know that I had my husband just the same and my children and my house like any other woman. . . . Tell him I was given back everything he took away and more. Oh no, oh, God, no, there was something else. . . . something not given back . . ." An abstraction like innocence doesn't quite describe what was not given back to Granny Weatherall; trust, belief, romance don't cover it either.

Porter believed that "we exist on half a dozen planes in at least six dimensions and inhabit all periods of time at once"—by memory, racial experience, dreams, and fantasy—and that "a first rate work of art somehow succeeds in pulling all these things together and reconciling them." So, at the very end of the story, when Granny is dying, Porter carries the match lighting the lamp through the blueness of the lamp-shade right into the experience of death itself. In this passage, death is seen as the ultimate jilting. Granny is not only jilted by George, she is jilted by death:

> *The blue light from Cornelia's lampshade drew into a tiny point in the center of her brain, it flickered and winked like an eye, quietly it fluttered and dwindled. Granny lay curled down within herself, amazed and watch-ful, staring at the point of light that was herself; her body was now only a deeper mass of shadow in an endless darkness . . . God give a sign!*
>
> *For the second time there was no sign. Again no bridegroom and the priest in the house. . . . Oh, no, there's nothing more cruel than this—I'll never forgive it. She stretched herself with a deep breath and blew out the light.*

In an essay entitled "Katherine Anne Porter: The Eye of the Story," Eudora Welty points out that Porter is a writer "who does not give us the pictures and bring us the sounds of a story. . . . What Miss Porter makes us see are those subjective worlds of hallucination, obsessions, fever, guilt."

Porter's landscape was internal, and part of her brilliance lay in the fact that she took language right into death, where it didn't belong. Porter made fiction operate on many levels, and in doing this elevated her best stories to the intensity of poetry. She was, as Alfred Kazin said of Flannery O'Connor, a genius.

n 1978 Tillie Olsen, who had recently seen Porter, wrote me a note. She said Porter was bedridden, frightened, and bitter. Knowing of my admiration, Olsen suggested I write Porter a letter. "She feels isolated, forgotten, and to younger writers, unknown."

I sat with this request for a long time, finally deciding it would be presumptuous of me to think I could have any role in consoling Kather-ine Anne Porter. If death is the ultimate jilting, Porter had faced that in her work. "Oh, no, there's nothing more cruel than this. I'll never for-give it." Who was I to intrude on her reckoning?

In retrospect, I know my decision was wrong. I've learned, in the last decade, to be less intransigent, and to value all forms of comfort, even partial ones; certainly Katherine Anne Porter appreciated the kindness of strangers. If I had it to do over I would write to her and tell her that she was my mentor, and that she taught me more than any other writer. Like her, I understand regret.

May 1991

FIRED FROM THE CANON:
JOHN CHEEVER

Suburban Blight: The Stories of John Cheever

By Paul Elie

I wince whenever I come upon the word, and I have come upon it an awful lot lately. It is meant to suggest stylish high quality. Instead it calls to mind the burlesque.

The word is *Cheeveresque*. Not only is it a pat piece of journalistic shorthand. It is also based on a mistaken idea, which is that John Cheever's work is worthy of imitation.

John Cheever is the most overrated American writer there is. That is a plain English sentence. With the addition of only a few words, it becomes Cheeveresque. "John Cheever was one of those overrated American writers who nervously stuffed his paper napkin into his coat pocket whenever his editor raised a glass to him in an East Side roof garden as the sky darkened overhead."

Cheever hammered out stereotypes of men and women and called them *we* and *us*. He stated his particular observations as general truths and called it art. Yet Cheever's stories have beguiled the very people their author seems to have despised. By now, to criticize Cheever is to find fault with falling leaves and clapboard houses and vacations by the sea. It is to lack a beating heart.

In graduate school, I read the big red book of Cheever stories and was astonished by how clumsy and fatuous they were. Astonished because it is the stories that made his reputation, that won him the Pulitzer Prize.

Recently, I decided to give Cheever's stories another chance. They are as I remembered them, like the apple core left in an ashtray in one of his stories, turning brown and beginning to smell bad.

"If there is anybody I detest," Cheever wrote, "it is weak-minded sentimentalists—all those melancholy people who, out of an excess of sympathy for others, miss the thrill of their own essence and drift through life without identity, like a human fog." Cheever marinated in his bitter conviction that the lives of the American bourgeois are sad and false. He thought this would inoculate him from the sentimentality of what is now called "Cheever country."

He was wrong.

Cheever is supposed to be the laureate of suburbia, employing a native's knowledge with an anthropologist's precision. But most of his stories are rigged on observations so obvious a desert anchorite could make them. There's That Kind of Person: "Jim and Irene Westcott were the kind of people who seem to strike that satisfactory average of income, endeavor, and respectability that is reached by the statistical reports in college alumni bulletins." And there is That Kind of Day: "It was one of those midsummer Sundays when everyone sits around saying 'I *drank* too much last night.'"

Supposedly Cheever was the last of the great *New Yorker* story-tellers before the minimalists took over. But his stories are rarely stories, in which people act and are acted upon and are left changed. They are little melodramas, or situations set up and then abandoned, as in "The Chaste Clarissa," in which a man tries to seduce a woman even duller than he is. Or they are episodes clumped together magnetically like postcards on the fridge, as in "The Trouble of Marcie Flint," where the husband's adventures in Rome are backlit by his wife's affair in Shady Hill.

Cheever's characters are supposed to be people we recognize. What's more, they are supposed to be people in whom we recognize ourselves. Unfortunately, there is no *they* there. In "The Five Forty-Eight," a man's former secretary follows him home and puts a gun to his head—but the story never comes to life because Cheever can't be bothered to describe the woman specifically ("Her hair was dark, her eyes were dark; she left with him a pleasant impression of darkness"). Rabbit Angstrom looms as large as Raskolnikov in comparison.

Cheever ventured away from the generalization at his peril. "The Brigadier and the Golf Widow" begins like this: "I would not want to be one of those writers who begin each morning by exclaiming, 'O Gogol, O Chekhov, O Thackeray and Dickens, what would you have made of a bomb shelter ornamented with four plaster-of-Paris ducks, a birdbath, and three composition gnomes with long beards and red mobcaps?'" It is hard to imagine any writer but Cheever exclaiming such a thing.

That said, the most promising Cheever stories are those that begin with fanciful conceits. Take "The Country Husband." A businessman survives a plane crash, but when he gets home his family has no idea what has happened to him. "He had traveled faster than the newspapers or the rain, and the weather in New York was sunny and mild. It was a day in late September, as fragrant and shapely as an apple." But the story itself soon crashes like the plane, as the man's marriage predictably comes apart in a matter of pages.

Or take "The Enormous Radio." The Westcotts are a conventional Sutton Place couple, except for "an interest they shared in serious music." When their radio malfunctions, Jim buys Irene a new one. But instead of music, she hears the neighbors quarreling. She begs Jim to reassure her that they aren't like that—but soon they are at it too, and the radio hears them.

When they aren't quarreling, they are bored. "Jim was too tired to make even a pretense of sociability, and there was nothing about the dinner to hold Irene's interest, so her attention wandered. . . ." The story—written when Cheever was in his early twenties—is an adolescent exposé of the hypocritical grown-up world. Bored with these grown-ups and impatient for the next radio scene, Cheever pins his boredom and impatience on Jim and Irene.

At the other end of his career, Cheever wrote "The Swimmer," another surrealish story. Standing poolside at the Westerhazys, Neddy Merrill realizes that there is a nearly unbroken chain of swimming pools across the county. So he decides to swim home. He dives into one pool and climbs out of the next. Neighbors hand him drinks. Friends wonder where he is going. Lifeguards shout at him: "'Hey you, you without the identification disk, get outa the water.' He did, but they had no way of pursuing him and he went through the reek of suntan oil and chlorine."

"The Swimmer" is the only good Cheever story I have read. In it Cheever found a way to work within the limitations of his boredom and contempt. On the run, nearly naked, passing through his friends' backyards, Neddy Merrill is free. Likewise Cheever is free of the storyteller's usual obligations—free from having to create convincing characters or scenes, set free into a world where an extended metaphor will get you home before dark.

In his journals, too, Cheever set himself free from the conventions of the short story, and the result is authentic and moving. The journals suggest that the short-story form was as stifling to him as his marriage and his suburban address and the "family magazine" standards of *The New Yorker* of the period.

I can imagine the journals being read long after the stories are retired—read the way we now read the daily jottings of Renaissance men, published under some bland title like *Diary of a Man* or *The Courtier's Day-Book*. Perhaps then, when he is anonymous and unremarkable, just a man in his undershorts tapping away at his typewriter in the basement, their author will be home at last in Cheever country.

April 1998

PROPHET AND LOSS

Salman Rushdie's Migration of Souls

By Bharati Mukherjee

THE SATANIC VERSES
MIDNIGHT'S CHILDREN
SHAME

If I seem a little bizarre, remember the wild profusion of my inheritance . . . perhaps, if one wishes to remain an individual in the midst of the teeming multitudes, one must make oneself grotesque.
    —Salman Rushdie, *Midnight's Children*

I, too, like all migrants am a fantasist. I build imaginary countries and try to impose them on the ones that exist. I, too, face the problem of history: what to retain, what to dump, how to hold on to what memory insists on relinquishing, how to deal with change.
    —Salman Rushdie, *Shame*

The great writers of our time are apocalyptic farceurs, comic voices unraveling an elaborate tapestry of the sheerest horror: Grass, García Márquez, Appelfeld, Beckett. Of the recent past: Nabokov, Primo Levi, and Flannery O'Connor; on the sidelines, temporarily one trusts, Thomas Pynchon. Fantasists and blasphemers all, carrying their dispute with God to a final, collective grave. I think there is only one other English-language author who belongs in their company, and his name is Salman Rushdie.

Let us call Rushdie's three novels of the 1980s—*Midnight's Children, Shame,* and *The Satanic Verses*—a trilogy, a vast, comic, morbid masterpiece of conceptual and architectural brilliance. About what? About (in no particular hierarchy) Hindu and Islamic myth; the post-Independence political history of India, Pakistan, and Bangladesh; the tarnishing of the bright ideals of Indian independence *(Midnight's Children)* and Pakistani godliness *(Shame);* the origins of Islam, the metamorphoses of the immigrant, and the death of British decency *(The Satanic Verses)*. Its time span is roughly 40 years. Its axis is London-Bombay/Karachi. Its style is a fevered fusion of appropriate and appropriated nativisms, Britishisms, puns, and coinages. Its subject is a restless movement: the *vast* movement of people, not just within the historical Raj but outward to Britain, and their subsequent transformations. Secular Bombay Muslims into impious Pakistanis. Muslims into Hindu gods. Indians into Englishmen. Men into djinns. And always, of course, the psychogenetic aftershocks of colonialism. For Rushdie, a fallen culture inhabited by ghosts and grotesques is the proper setting for postcolonial tragicomedy.

Rushdie's novels identify psychodramatic conditions previously undiagnosed: *sperectomy,* or the draining of hope, as India's founding ideals, her claim to the world's higher moral ground, are trampled in Mrs. Gandhi's "Emergency"; *shame,* in Pakistan's murderous nostalgia, the conversion of "Moghul" culture and history into a pawnshop for shabby tyrants. In *The Satanic Verses,* the condition is distortion: the shape-changing djinn-hood of immigration, the literal loss of one's unique identity in the rush to translate oneself into a properly acceptable Englishman.

Rushdie's is the voice of postcolonial man. He remembers a nearly tribal past that he cannot return to; he mimics and masters the culture of his erstwhile colonizer. His soul is always at risk, from his past and his present, in wondrous ways that only an intricate and outrageous epic can reveal.

aken together, Rushdie's books tell one vast story: autobiographical, mythic, political. In *Midnight's Children* the consciousness is born in 1947 in Bombay to a well-off, "relaxed Muslim" family and spends a pampered childhood exercising his extraordinary gifts (they are the special historical gifts of being born simultaneously with the country; born, that is, in a moment of idealistic frenzy, and raised in an orgy of blamelessness). The contradictions eventually claim him: a Muslim in a Hindu country; an idealist in a corrupt state. He carries his gifts and hopes reluctantly to the next-door theocracy, Pakistan, there to end up a soldier against his erstwhile country. He is witness to the breakup of Pakistan, the butcheries in Bangladesh, the venality of modern India (personified by "The Widow" as prime minister); he loses his hopes and his talents. The generation of 1947, those born with a dream of casteless secularism, those with special sensitivities to each other's individual gifts, are systematically murdered or disbanded. The setting is a richly conceived modern India, but politically the stage is the entire Third World—all those Chinas, Ghanas,

Cubas, Israels, Egypts, Jamaicas, Nigerias, Indonesias where socialist ideals were meant to thrive, where brotherhood would reign, and where bloodshed, corruption, and heartbreaking poverty have created grotesque parodies of free peoples, made coolies, thugs, and criminals out of the children and grandchildren of freedom fighters.

Shame, too, is a meditation on postcolonial consciousness. Shame (and its shadowself, shamelessness) is the primitive form of self-consciousness, the only freedom left to a people whose souls are whipped by mullahs, and whose bodies were once the property of resident viceroys, now replaced, seamlessly, by a corrupt train of native generalissimos. *Shame* tells a grotesque fairytale of palace intrigues in a "not quite" Pakistan where a "not quite" Zia eventually ousts, and hangs, a "not quite" Bhutto, leaving a "not quite" Benazir, known as "The Virgin Ironpants," to pick up the pieces. As befits a country ruled by 20 families, all intermarried, *Shame* is grand political guignol, statecraft as a soap opera.

Shame's structure is quite remarkable, shaped by irony and division. An overtly autobiographical author, all but named Salman Rushdie, resident of London, infrequent visitor to his family in Pakistan, narrates, bullies, and manipulates his political *Arabian Nights* about modern "Peccavistan" from the controlling metaphorical high ground of shame. He sees evidence of this shame all around him in London, in his own family, in newspaper clippings. He reads of a Pakistani father murdering his daughter out of suspicion that she has shamed family honor, of a Pakistani girl (perhaps his own sister) molested in a London subway; she is too ashamed to tell anyone. And he sees, finally, how shame—a principle of submission—erupts into shameless violence, so-called "race riots," how satisfaction grows from the demonstration of raw, crude, self-defeating, unreasoning violence. All of those awarenesses are projected not onto London but back to a fictionalized Pakistan. Rushdie wants to understand origins, not their accidental consequences. Authorial control, ironic distance, direct passion and address coexist here in proportions rarely seen in the modern, post-Jamesian novel. You'd have to go back to the origins of the novel, or outside the Western tradition altogether, to find their equal.

Rushdie's imagination is cyclically Hindu and dualistically Muslim, with an extravagant inventiveness that seems pan-Indian. Certainly the Hindu and Islamic cosmogonies are richer, fictionally speaking, than the Jewish Genesis, and Rushdie uses them both for modern fictional purposes. According to Islam, humanity was brought into a world already seething with dangers, displacing the angels, who remain jealous, yet still subject to corruption by the subhuman, shape-changing djinns. *The Satanic Verses*, in spite of its much-reported brush with Islamic orthodoxy, is a *very* Muslim book.

The novel is a blatant fantasy, a reenactment (as I understand it) of an Islamic myth of creation, fall, and redemption. The focus this time is on London, or "Ellowen Deeowen." There is, again, a split narrative, with two central characters: Gibreel Farishta, a Bombay actor specializing in Hindu religious roles—he impersonates gods—and Saladin Chamcha, "the man of a thousand voices," a successful, transcendentally British immigrant. Both are Bombay natives.

Gibreel and Saladin meet in a cataclysm. Their Air-India jumbo jet is blown out of the skies by Canadian Sikh terrorists at 29,002 feet, the height of Everest. (Speaking as the coauthor of a book on the actual Canadian-Sikh bombing of an Air-India flight in which all 329 passengers were killed, I can't help wondering why, in Rushdie's version of the disaster, the women, children, and Sikhs are allowed to disembark before the plane takes off. In real life, they were not. Real life shouldn't be starker, more horrible, more unflinching than fiction.) Miraculously, the two men float to a snow-covered British beach, without parachutes or oxygen, there to begin altered lives. They have fallen, after the burst of light. Chamcha, during the fall, becomes a goat: hairy legs, horns, veinous balls. He gets Gibreel's famously ghastly mouth odor. Gibreel remains, outwardly, unchanged. Inwardly, he now believes his own press kit: No longer is he the low-born Bombay tiffincarrier turned superstar. Now he is the actual Archangel Gibreel who delivered the Quran to Mohammed. His bursts of megalomania (eventually controlled with medication) inevitably result in riots and destruction.

In his new-found arrogance, Gibreel makes a fatal mistake. He denies knowing Chamcha, the goat-man, who, lacking identification or a credible story, is herded away by the British police. Thus is born the enmity, as Chamcha struggles to regain his human form and Gibreel is brought down from his unmerited godliness. Djinn and archangel, struggling to become human. (In realistic terms, of course, they had already lost their humanity in the bloated corruptions of Hindi films or in the abject conformity of immigration.) Iago and Othello, Shakespeare's Moor: one a machine of vengeance, the other a repository of suggestiveness.

The "through-line," as they say in scriptwriting, is rather clear: what it means to be a human being. How varied are the distractions from humanity, how rare and simple are its pleasures. Rushdie is a humanist in very familiar Western terms, but the story he delivers is enormously convoluted, a Persian carpet bloated with symbols and subplots, twisted and turned on its head by every manner of splitting and replication. The subplots—concerning Gibreel's last true love, Alleluia Cone, the one-woman conqueror of Everest; his former love, Rekha

Merchant, now a djinn following her suicide over his abandonment of her; his hilarious experiences as an elephant-headed god of Hindi films; his (perhaps) fantasized existence as the Archangel Gibreel—are comic adumbrations of a plot with a serious purpose. (Rushdie, like Grass and García Márquez, is always *playing*.) Gibreel Farishta the lightweight clown *is* Gibreel the archangel, who is (perhaps) his brother archangel, Shaitan (Satan), who is Chamcha. Just as Shaitan (perhaps) delivered the Quran to a credulous Mahound (Mohammed) who took it as the word of Allah, so does, this time, Gibreel take the word of Chamcha (in his Iago-phase of poisoning his love with Alleluia/Desdemona) as truth, leading to murder and suicide.

Like Grass's improbable narrators—Oskar, or his later dogs and flounders—or like the bewildered citizens of García Márquez's Macondo, like O'Connor's redneck simpletons and Beckett's tramps, Rushdie's Third Worlders are witnesses to the miraculous. The miraculous speaks through them; they are larger than life. The subplots reinforce their stature; the authorial inventions are Scheherazadean, biblical, protean, symphonic. When the clear, fairly simple, "human" story finally emerges—in *The Satanic Verses*, Saladin Chamcha regains his full humanity when he returns to Bombay to nurse his dying father—we feel we have been treated to the full vision of what humanity means. Rushdie puts us through it, squeezes his characters for all the life they're capable of giving.

There is, of course, a downside to Rushdie's narrative exuberance. His designs inevitably get messy; his plots race ahead like a span of ponies under loose control. Even the 547 pages of *The Satanic Verses* are cramped space for the history he has to tell. Subplots scurry for shelter like tropical insects. Undramatized material lies inert on the page— paid-for props that couldn't be filmed. I admire this book, but I didn't always enjoy it. That is, I respect the design without necessarily connecting with all of the contents. Reading it is like touring room after room in the Versailles Palace or the Taj Mahal: One sometimes wants to get out and just *look* at it, from a long way off.

> **T**he book would have been banned, dumped in the rubbish bin, burned. All that effort for nothing! Realism can break a writer's heart!
>
> Fortunately, however, I am only telling a sort of modern fairy-tale, so that's all right; nobody need get upset, or take anything I say too seriously. No drastic action need be taken, either.
>
> What a relief!
>
> —Shame

Consider for a moment the unique plight of Salman Rushdie. (Yes, he's a major world author, a very rich man, and universally honored. This automatically makes his uncomfortable situation a plight.) Whatever his legal status at the moment, he is a citizen, a cultural resource and repository, of three countries: his native India (born Bombay, 1947), his family's Pakistan, and his adoptive Britain. His latest novel comes to us precanonized by a hat-trick of bannings in India, South Africa, and the Muslim world. There have even been attempts by some Muslims to flush it from the British Isles. Censorship on religious grounds is cruel to Rushdie not because it denies him an audience but because it trivializes his message. As a satirist he must be doing something right: He faces literary deportation from all three of his homelands.

"Fantasy or Blasphemy?" asked *The New York Times* last October, reporting on the Indian government's predictable but still outrageous ban on its greatest author's latest book. The easy answer is: both. Most great books, by any imaginative definition of "great," are blasphemies ("showing irreverence to anything regarded as sacred"). To change perceptions—the distinction between greatness and mere excellence—some pieties must be destroyed. But the mullahs and the mullah-minded have historically mandated the obliteration of *any* contradictory or competitive image or idea in their path. Though it's really a minor part of his book, Rushdie makes the charge of blasphemy easy to support. Where Islam holds sway, uncomplimentary mention of the Prophet is blasphemy.

Rushdie's Prophet is admittedly something of a mess. He fears, but cannot express it, that his Quran might be a hoax. The Archangel Gibreel, who delivered the words, might really have been his brother angel, Shaitan. That is, in Rushdie's dualistic universe, Gibreel might be both devil and angel. The all-too-human Mahound (whom the mullahs assume to be Rushdie's rendering of the historical Prophet) has founded a successful religion, even though it teaches some dubious truths and behaves in cruel and arbitrary ways. The religion is quite possibly a joke, but it's too late to change it. (Mahound can't believe the faithful will go along with *five* prayers a day. They insist the number can't be altered.) When he rides his camel out to Yathrib (Medina), the camel looks suspiciously like a tiger.

Rushdie's Mahound is Mohammed the same way his Peccavistan is Pakistan and Ellowen Deeowen is London. Rushdie is an allegorist: His Archangel Gibreel becomes a Bombay film actor, playing Hindu religious roles behind elephant masks and using his god-drag to please his girlfriends; Mount Cone, a sacred hill in Mecca, becomes the blond English mountain climber Alleluia Cone (née Cohen). In Rushdie's fiction, it is always 1400 A.H. (After Hegira). A 20th-century sensibility with modern and medieval material. A 600-year-old-man—no wonder he writes with such range.

Rushdie humanizes Mohammed—whose nondivinity is one of the pillars of the faith—but in decidedly contemporary terms. Rushdie's Mahound patronizes whores, tolerates a few Arabian tribal gods, and splits the territory with the local competition, Jews and Christians, who've been expanding their franchises on Arabian turf. It's not Mohammed who comes out badly; it's his traditional interpreters, the mullahs, those who've institutionalized Mahound's own fear of self-scrutiny into an aggressive, fortressed denial of all criticism.

Orthodox, intolerant Islam is long overdue for a kick in the pants. Ridicule works on fanatics like salt on a leech, and Rushdie is to the mullahs what Philip Roth as Tarnopol/Zuckerman only fantasizes himself being to suburban rabbis. As a great disillusioned hater, Rushdie plays in a different league from anyone in America; he's up there with Joyce and Solzhenitsyn, an educated, implacable, remorseless dissenter from deep inside the family.

Rushdie's novels are allegorical, mythical, allusive, pop, topical, and satirical, but they are also an autobiographical recording—usually highly realistic—of the postcolonial and immigrant experience. And always on tap are the vulgar energy, high parodic comedy, and many of the archetypes of the Bombay film. Rushdie's voice is that of Bombay, India's brashest city. He is still a rarity, a big-city man from the Third World, a Bombay Augie March. He is topically, even parochially, political—British, Pakistani, or Indian. Take, for example, these riffs on Indian prime minister Indira Gandhi, Pakistan's General Zia, and the latest incarnation of malicious vapidness, Margaret Thatcher:

> *It was Picture Singh who revealed to me that the country's corrupt "black" economy had grown as large as the official, "white" variety, which he did by showing me a newspaper photograph of Mrs. Gandhi. Her hair, parted in the centre, was snow-white on one side and blackasnight on the other, so that, depending on which profile she presented, she resembled either a stoat or an ermine.*
>
> *—Midnight's Children*

So much for Gandhi. Of Zia and his bizarre strategy for restoring Pakistan's "honor" after the Bangladesh defeat, Rushdie writes:

> *General Raza Hyder fought with one hundred and eleven soldiers and was thrashed by them all. He made no attempt to win, concentrating, instead, on the far more difficult business of losing against opponents who had forgotten that it was possible to win; of losing, moreover, while giving the impression of struggling for victory with all his might . . .*

The wrestling strategy of Raza Hyder gained him a double victory. It helped the Army to accept his leadership, because now he was united with his men in that macabre fellowship of shame. As Old Razor Guts was drop-kicked in the jaw, dumped on canvas with the ankles knotted round his neck, throttled by an infantryman's arm; as his ribs snapped and his arms left their sockets, the old popularity of the hero of Aansu was reborn . . . it shone once again, like new.

—Shame

And of Margaret Thatcher:

She's radical, all right. What she wants—what she actually thinks she can fucking achieve—is literally to invent a whole goddamn new middle class in this country. Get rid of the old woolly incompetent buggers from fucking Surrey and Hampshire, and bring in the new. People without background, without history. Hungry people. People who really want and who know that with her, they can bloody well get. Nobody's ever tried to replace a whole fucking class before, and the amazing thing is she might just do it if they don't get her first. The old class. The dead men. . . . And it's not just the businessmen. . . . The intellectuals, too. Out with the whole faggoty crew. In with the hungry guys with the wrong education. New professors, new painters, the lot. It's a bloody revolution. Newness coming into this country that's stuffed full of fucking old corpses. It's going to be something to see. It already is.

—The Satanic Verses

One wonders why eight years of Reaganism haven't activated the same visceral reactions among American writers. It's Maggie, not Mohammed, in the Darth Vader role behind *The Satanic Verses,* just as she lingers with a sulfur smell over the films of Hanif Kureishi and Stephen Frears.

"**F** act is," *he said without any of his usual bonhomie, "religious fafaith, which encodes the highest ass ass aspirations of the human race, is now, in our cocountry, the servant of lowest instincts, and gogo God is the creature of evil. . . . Bad days," Sisodia went on. "For the moomoo movies also TV and economics have Delhi Delhi deleterious effects."*

—S. S. Sisodia, moviemaker
The Satanic Verses

The late Terrence Des Pres, writing on Milosz, identified a common denominator for those we might wish to term great: They bear the burden of historical consciousness without despair. And he set a collateral requirement: that they create a language equal to the pressures upon us.

Complex visions, in other words, generate a density of structure and expression to carry them. *Dog Years* and *Midnight's Children* and *Autumn of the Patriarch* are like superchips, holding more information and conveying it more rapidly than standard language in conventional forms. Only by inventing a style as rich and eccentric as his plotting and characters could Rushdie express the passion of his indictments. Style announces theme: cool, temperate English is subverted by fevered, subtropical India. The result is transformation: of character, of language, of consciousness. Take, for example, this account of a venal film colony responding to the reported (faked) death of Gibreel Farishta:

> *On one of Rama Studios' seven impotent stages, Miss Pimple Billimoria, the latest chilli-and-spices bombshell*—she's no flibberti-gibberti mamzell, but a whir-stir-get-lost-sir bundla dynamite—*clad in temple-dancer veiled undress and positioned beneath writhing cardboard representations of copulating Tantric figures from the Chandela period . . . offered up a spiteful farewell before an audience of sound recordists and electricians smoking their cynical beedis. Attended by a dumbly distressed ayah, all elbows, Pimple attempted scorn. "God, what a stroke of luck, for Pete's sake," she cried. "I mean today it was the love scene, chhi chhi, I was just dying inside, thinking how to go near to that fatmouth with his breath of rotting cockroach dung." Bell-heavy anklets jingled as she stamped.*

There really is a Dimple Kapadia in the Hindi film world, and she really does have an actor-sister named Simple. The more you know of India, the less fantastic, the more charming, Rushdie's inventions become. In *Midnight's Children*, the narrator evokes the interior of a run-down Bombay cafe:

> *The Pioneer Cafe was not much when compared to the Gaylords and Kwalitys of the city's more glamorous parts; a real rutputty joint, with painted boards proclaiming* LOVELY LASSI *and* FUNTABULOUS FALOODA *and* BHEL-PURI BOMBAY FASHION, *with filmi playback music blaring out from a cheap radio by the cash-till, a long narrow greeny room lit by flickering neon, a forbidding world in which broken-toothed men sat at reccine-covered tables with crumpled cards and expressionless eyes.*

We of the Third World who grew up in the shadow of a retreating colonialism and the emerging light of independence are all, in essence, "midnight's children." We were born, like Rushdie's Saleem Sinai, with certain gifts of mimicry, talents for empathy across borders and genders. Fifteen or more years into our Indian, Caribbean, or African independence, we were still taking our Overseas Cambridge exams, still writing odes on never-seen nightingales in passable imitation of Shelley and Keats.

Our collective experience is mirrored in the works of two magnificent writers: V. S. Naipaul and Salman Rushdie. Either—following Naipaul—we are less than fully human, pathetic trained monkeys, mimic men; or we are miraculous translations, Lamarckian mutations, single lives that have acquired new characteristics and recapitulated the entire cultural history of our genotype. Naipaul's prose is a model of poise and exclusion, as pure a literary English as can be written, its rhythms and its desiccation as insistent as T. S. Eliot's. Rushdie's is a fusion of master and slave, imported and native; jangly, harsh, punning, allusive, windy, and grandiloquent.

One of Rushdie's more appealing notions (which I hope is not an unfounded flattery) is that immigration, despite losses and confusions, its sheer absurdities, is a net *gain*, a form of levitation, as opposed to Naipaul's loss and mimicry. Of course, the gain is equivocal. Many of us, Rushdie included, traded top-dog status in the homeland for the loss-of-face meltdown of immigration. He dramatizes that pain, that confusion, with a thousand inventions and some very shrewd, dead-on observations. Rushdie's language is a mask, a way of projecting all the forms of Indian speech at once (bombastic, babu, bureaucratic, Vedantic, vehement, servile, and Sellersish, without mocking or condescending) while remaining true to the essentially damaged, ego-deficient, postcolonial psyche.

Look through Rushdie: Distortion is everywhere. Saleem's great nose and his built-in radio transmitter in *Midnight's Children*; "rubescent" Sufiya Zinobia of *Shame*, who absorbs the shame of others around her; the ruttish breath and tumescent goat-body of Saladin Chamcha, inverting all the distortions and repressions he'd gone through to marry his Pamela and become a perfect Englishman. And distortion takes us back to Rushdie's earlier quote: "I, too, face the problem of history: what to retain, what to dump, how to hold on to what memory insists on relinquishing, how to deal with change."

In the modern world of jet travel and multiple rerootings, millions of Chamchas face this problem every day. Immigrants change their clothes, their accents, their ancient ways of seeing and believing. Death and rebirth are natural. Many have multiple parents. Many pay an occult price. Many turn red with invented shame, slinking when they should have fought—or pull a knife when they should have written their member of Parliament.

Antiblasphemy laws assert that history is immutable, that a truism once learned need never be amended. *The Satanic Verses* is precisely what Rushdie says it is: a novel that faces the problem of history. Not isolated problems *in* history, and not "historical" problems. The problem is not in history; the problem *of* history is in ourselves. History remains stationary. We are changing. We will get nowhere (except on *Masterpiece Theatre*) by re-creating history in our likeness, by deforming the past to compliment the present. To understand *how* much we change, how distorted *we* are against the backdrop of history requires grotesque imagery. Grass's dogs, dwarfs, and flounders are just a beginning. García Márquez's patriarch, Appelfeld's zombie-Jews of Badenheim—they all are blasphemies, they all change our perceptions.

Excellent books must be perfect; great books can stumble. *The Satanic Verses* has too many tangential subplots, too much undramatized narration, and too many pages where the major characters simply are not present ever to be confused with workshop excellence. Inevitably, the book will be characterized as bloated; I prefer to think of it as swollen with irritated life. This book completes a trilogy that must be swallowed whole, python-style, hair, horns, and hooves intact.

March 1989

NATIONAL ENQUIRER

Don DeLillo Gets Under America's Skin

By Andrew O'Hagan

UNDERWORLD

Don DeLillo is now the best writer of sentences in America. Once or twice a year you might happen across some radiant and quite unexpected verbal event, some divine turn in the common words, coming from an archangel such as Joan Didion, or from some new guy who is tight with his own foreignness. But from Don DeLillo you can count on good sentences by the yard. Like Salman Rushdie—another former advertising man—DeLillo knows how to place an idea at the heart of every line, and he can command those sentences to live a life both pretty and profound.

English novelists used to tour their grand sentences around the world. There was no escaping the complex society they conjured up, with felicity of language and depth of concern. But nowadays the English writers are most often bent with nostalgia and the need for reassurance. It has been left to Indian and Irish writers, to Scottish novelists and American essayists, to put some of this right. In England, you could count on one hand the examples of living writers who possess a good combination of tenderness and gravity and who show an interest in imagining the relationship between local individuals and the forces of the state, or in distilling the workings of the market, or the effects of the Cold War, the tragedy of nuclear waste, the absurd comedy of modern planning, or the way in which media images so madly intrude on the inner life. Where is the English novelist with the imaginative gumption to enter, subcutaneously, as DeLillo does, into the world of supermarkets, all-night gas stations, denatured submarine bases, hinterland housing projects, food-processing plants, the secret history of the soil beneath you, and the whole underworld of public and private affairs, all wired from the breathing perspective of the new family?

Lionel Trilling once referred to the "habitual music of Scott Fitzgerald's seriousness." Don DeLillo's seriousness is no less habitual, and no less musical, although nowadays a novelist's deeper concentration can seldom enjoy the free empathy that goes with the word *serious*. People prefer to say paranoid, and the unrelenting weight of DeLillo's preoccupations has caused him to be dubbed "the chief shaman of the paranoid school of American fiction."

DeLillo has always been a student of American derangement. Very early in his career he demonstrated the ability to see madness inherent in contemporary ideas of communication and entertainment, and like nobody else, he has detected and followed the weird shadows passing over everyday life in the United States. In his first novel, *Americana,* he turned a cold eye on the world of advertising. In that arena of excellent lies he saw how far a country might be steered from itself—from its decent heart—if commercial energies went wild and free. In the world's most populist country, DeLillo has always been the writer who understands the downside of mass democratic craving; he has written novels about the rock scene *(Great Jones Street)* and has upended the common apprehension of glory that feeds the great American sports *(End Zone)*. Mass popularity, the rough hysteria of the common grain, has always fascinated DeLillo, and in most of his books he has led readers back, again and again, to the presence of threat in large groups of people who seem to believe in the same things. Like Elias Canetti or Sinclair Lewis, DeLillo has long drawn on the notion that crowds are often not good together, or that they are vulnerable to forces—some within, some without—that are not good for them. In his 1977 novel *Players,* he wrote about the terrorist as a figure who understands the way modern people move, and he examined the manner in which unnoticed lives can be subject to interventions they never suspected. *Libra,* his fictional account of the John F. Kennedy assassination, gave an unbelievably acute sense of how this kind of power had somehow moved from the center of corporate agencies into the minds of individuals and into the living rooms of every one of us. By the time of DeLillo's last book, *Mao II,* the terrorist had arrived at the place where he could replace the novelist: The man with the bomb, not the pen, was the one who could alter the consciousness of his times in an instant. But as if to contradict this, DeLillo's vision has gathered force with each of his novels, and all his finer senses of America's talent for both massive secrecy and mass belief have come together in his latest novel, *Underworld*.

Mao II opened with a crowd at Yankee Stadium, and the idea of crowds never left that book alone: "the future belongs to crowds." This new one opens on a stadium too, but the sinister sway of the crowd here quickly gives way to the slow movements of several individuals, and soon we are wrapped up in the matter of their interconnected yearnings and sufferings. The whole novel is a journey into the repositories of personal memory, on the one hand, and the grave machinations of global threat, on the other.

Never before, on the page, have we been led to consider so deeply our spiritual reliance on the threat of nuclear destruction. Not in this way—with the smallness of lives so appended to the greatness—and not with such grand melody and sadness for the age we have lived through. DeLillo has come up with a Cold War lament, a sore song with which to close down the century, but all in all it is a work of magical rescue. His novel is like a flying carpet, beneath it Breughel's *The Triumph of Death*. One art work standing inside another. And given this, we might come to feel, if only for the length of a long novel, that we now know the meaning of the term "mutually assured destruction." The meaning of art and the meaning of weapons systems are seen to mingle and change places. DeLillo is interested in what art has to say about our vast dying.

But it all starts with Bobby Thomson hitting his great home run— "the shot heard round the world"—that gives the Giants the pennant. It is 1951, and J. Edgar Hoover shares a box at the New York Polo Grounds with Frank Sinatra, Jackie Gleason, and Toots Shor. The crowd is beneath them, begging for entertainment and its share in a day's triumph. "All these people," DeLillo writes, "formed by language and climate and popular songs and breakfast foods . . . have never had anything in common so much as this, that they are sitting in the furrow of destruction." And the shrill promise of destruction is whispered into Hoover's ear at the game: An aide comes with the news that the Russians have just tested their first atom bomb. The Director sees skeletons dancing about the field. You get the impression this is the news Hoover has waited for all his life. It means his time has been well spent, the Soviets are indeed a threat, and you can almost imagine him sleeping better at night for the realization. "It's not enough," he reckons, "to hate your enemy. You have to understand how the two of you bring each other to deep completion."

*U**nderworld* is vastly episodic: locations change from part to part, and so does time, and point of view. But the alternations only add to our sense of how time plays out in the average mind, and they might offer a lesson in how memory lives its own life, coming and going, bringing new stuff in a new way every time. DeLillo also has the virtues attendant upon a very consistent tone. It is the tone which keeps the novel together: a voice of reason and dismay lies behind all that we encounter.

The central figure in the book is a 57-year-old called Nick Shay. He is from the Bronx, he once had an affair with the wife of his chemistry teacher, who is now an artist, and he goes off to see some sort of installation she has created in the desert. "The past brings out our patriotism, you know?" she tells him. "We want to feel an allegiance. It's the one undivided allegiance, to all those people and things." Her name is Klara Sax. She is working in an area where America once tested its big bombs. She is famous. Nick and Klara, we might imagine, are the love interest, two more-or-less messed-up figures who once tried for love in a Cold War climate. Their love was deceitful and curious and a long time ago, yet it is a small moment of frozen urgency in both their lives. You get the feeling they know how their secret love happened to counterpoint a secret rage in the world around them. But they might also represent something else. He works in Waste; she works in Art. They are both concerned about the machinations of Defense. DeLillo gives you the feeling that the intimacy shared by these people—a long-ago intimacy of the hot Bronx afternoon—is not only gone from them, it has become impossible for them. And so we see how local emotion is overwhelmed by global concerns and the largeness of time.

The work she is doing in the desert entails painting old B-52 bombers, and she is given to describing what she does in the following way:

> She said, "See, we're painting, hand-painting in some cases, putting our puny hands to great weapons systems, to systems that came out of the factories and assembly halls as near alike as possible, millions of components stamped out, repeated endlessly, and we're trying to unrepeat, to find an element of felt life, and maybe there's a sort of survival instinct here, a graffiti instinct—to trespass and declare ourselves, show who we are."

Klara is an amalgam of New York '60s conceptualist art types, the sort of artist who is into found objects and who makes statements about waste and recycling. Her art and her speech and her memory are very much of a time: They rely on overexcited juxtaposition. Some of this excitement is clearly DeLillo's own. She went to Truman Capote's Black & White Ball and knew she might have stood next to J. Edgar Hoover, and later we hear, from Hoover's point of view, that the antiwar protesters were gathered in force outside the Plaza. DeLillo, like all the most likable conspiracy theorists, is never one to miss a twist.

The Thomson home run is viewed as a moment of innocence, and all around it that day had gathered the portents of doom. And the baseball itself (or a notion of the actual ball) is what beats us back ceaselessly into the past of this novel. The ball disappears, and the boy who caught it and the father he gave it to become characters in this account of contemporary American time. In those days before instant replays, the strike and the home run could only be seen to happen once, and then the event became part of the memory of the crowd. It could only be reproduced in the clear imagination. This is what I mean by innocence; the reader knows that beyond Thomson's unrepeatable moment of joy lies the dark, endlessly repeating horror of Zapruder's home movie of JFK's assassination, every frame of which now lies inside the head of most people with a television set. Across the century, particularly in America, it became the case that everything would happen again and again until it lost its shock. The Thomson homer just happened *once*.

For DeLillo, technology forever offers a challenge to our fleshly reality: it makes our lives unlifelike; it muddles our respect for truth and for cause and effect. One of the more ominous elements of *Underworld* (and with DeLillo that does not rule out funny) is the narrative of the Texas Highway Killer, who speaks in the book, and whose murderous actions are watched by regular families on a television loop. They watch it like a favorite commercial. In DeLillo's *White Noise* it is this use of television which lies behind the notion of "brain fade." Murray is arguing against the use of human disaster as TV entertainment: "People get brain fade," he says. "This is because they've forgotten how to listen and look as children. They've forgotten how to collect data. In the psychic sense a forest fire on TV is on a lower plane than a ten-second spot for Automatic Dishwasher All. The commercial has deeper waves, deeper emanations. But we have reversed the relative significance of these things."

ick's father is missing. He went out to buy cigarettes one day and he never returned. This is one of the central estrangements of the boy's life. His brother Matt is a chess lover, and a weaponsmaker who knows in his bones that "the game is location, situation and memory." And the shadow of the bomb passes over everything.

DeLillo's Cold War childhood—the Bronx of those days, the immigrant scene—might be thought to lie buried at the palpitating heart of *Underworld*. The image of the baseball might bring him all the way to the center of his childhood fevers. For Nick Shay, as for millions of American boys and girls, the unfolding *detente* imposed order on his early life, and the rules of survival, the threat of ruin, offered a structure for living in those days of the bomb. A childhood of "duck and cover" under the school desk.

Nick's colleague Brian has a conversation in the book with a guy called Marvin, who is a dedicated collector of baseball memorabilia. He is more than just a collector, though; he speaks like a trailer-park wizard. He is a seeker of meaning in the people's century, and baseball, the everything of baseball, gives him his big way in.

Brian said, "I went to a car show and it did something to me."
"What did it do?"

"Cars from the nineteen-fifties. I don't know."

"You feel sorry for yourself. You think you're missing something and you don't know what it is. You're lonely inside your life. You have a job and a family and a full executed will, already, at your age, because the whole idea is to die prepared, die legal, with all the papers signed. Die liquid, so they can convert to cash. You used to have the same dimensions as the observable universe. Now you're a lost speck. You look at old cars and you recall a purpose, a destination."

"It's ridiculous, isn't it? But probably harmless too."

"Nothing is harmless," Marvin said. "You're worried and scared. You see the cold war winding down. This makes it hard for you to breathe."

Brian pushed through a turnstile from an old ballpark. It creaked sort of lovingly.

Without the dependable threat of the bomb, Brian, and Nick too, is simply and individually "the lost man of history." Nick and Brian have a fin de siècle vibe about them. Each of them is packed with all the last-minute notions of the society to which they belong. They are waste experts. On a visit to the Fresh Kills landfill site on Staten Island, Brian is overwhelmed by the monumental look of the dump, like the pyramids at Giza, and he knows that among the great contemporary questions is how to "keep this mass metabolism from overwhelming us." We have a fine sense of Shay's emotional sickness: He is full of dread and bad information. As an employee of the Waste Containment Company he is privy, for example, to the news that a great amount of toxic waste is routinely dumped in LDCs (Less Developed Countries) in return for a fee which is often four times their GNP. Don DeLillo is like Ezra Pound: He thinks that civilization is built on garbage. But in DeLillo's case, our relationship to rubbish is mainly one of self-defense: "Consume or die. . . . Garbage comes first, then we build a system to deal with it." One of the most disastrous ironies of our age is that we may in the end use nuclear weapons for one purpose only—to help in the killing of nuclear waste.

Nick Shay is a man in pursuit of himself. He is presented to us as was Lee Harvey Oswald in the conspiracy novel *Libra*, as a man who is no accidental American, a man who is charged with the ominous energies of the age, and who can feel history seeping through the walls of his every room. Despite all this appropriate darkness, *Underworld* contains some of the funniest of DeLillo's writing. He really gets under the jangled skin of the '60s counterculture thing. Meet Jesse Detwiler, "a fringe figure in the sixties, a garbage guerrilla who stole and analyzed the household trash of a number of famous people. He issued mock-comintern manifestos about the contents, with personal asides, and the underground press was quick to print this stuff. His activities had a crisp climax when he was arrested for snatching the garbage of J. Edgar Hoover from the rear of the Director's house in North Washington." In a manner we might recognize, Detwiler became sort of famous himself, "part of a strolling band of tambourine girls and bomb makers, levitators and acid droppers and lost children."

DeLillo grasps at the counterculture as a tale of America told by an idiot, full not only of sound and fury but also of a special kind of sense, and the kind of sense that would not go down well in a police state. They are a carnivalesque troupe who seek the higher truths, a generation who feel failed by their parents' cars and houses and TVs, and who set out to open up their minds and to run from brutality. The spirit of wrecked shamanism is everywhere evident in *Underworld*—Lenny Bruce appears now and then—and the common, mainstream love of baseball is contrasted with that '60s generation, who sought a new commonality, and who often looked for it in painting and rock music and films.

At one point in the book Klara Sax goes to see a new Eisenstein movie called *Unterwelt*. Long suppressed by the Soviets and the Germans, it is a portrait of strangely gray mutant figures scurrying around in some nether region, living in secret, fighting some powerful unknown quantity. From here DeLillo's narrative itself goes underground, and we find a world there of apocalyptic graffiti artists, young Americans on the verge of something big, fame or destruction. "You can't tell the difference between a soup can and a car bomb," thinks Nick's brother Matt, adrift in his own weirdness, "because they are made by the same people in the same way and ultimately refer to the same thing."

DeLillo's book is a furious and gentle montage in itself; an exercise in the uncovering of power-fantasy. The author has long been a good traveler over the landscape of America's huge secrets. This time he has gone farther, and gone deeper, and has delivered himself of something quite touched with human pity and honor. *Underworld* has a uniquely warm glow at its center—the color of a life's experience, the noble gleam of decent inquiry properly met. DeLillo unwinds some of the more dark and mysterious configurations at the heart of American life during the Cold War. He takes us toward an understanding of how popular culture, across the century, has played into our dreams and our yearnings and our deepest fears, and he makes newly explicit the ties that bind art and ruin. For all this, and other things too, *Underworld* could be the most interesting American novel since *Catch-22*.

Fall 1997

T W O

Rescue Me: Snatching Writers from the Dustbin of History

Most avid bibliophiles nurture an obscure obsession or three— books that, for whatever reason, tickle you to the core yet have somehow written themselves out of literary history. Dusting off these neglected tomes, digging for buried treasure: These have always been crucial components of the *VLS* mission. From the start, the regular *VLS* feature "Save This Book," which later mutated into a similar column called "Lost Classic," was a favorite of writers and readers alike.

The beauty of writing about one of these long-cherished books is that it's so personal—there's no point hiding behind the scrim of objectivity, since these pieces represent special pleading of the most partisan sort in the face of mass indifference. Darcey Steinke's "Lost Classic" piece, for example, interweaves William Goyen's novel about a hermaphrodite with her own memories of dancing with a drag queen named Connie Girl. And Gary Indiana's essay on his hero Thomas Bernhard's final novel is a masterpiece of digression. Resisting the very idea of trying to judge the maestro of melancholy, Indiana circuitously captures Bernhard's essence.

Other essays up the stakes and make a forceful case for a marginalized or genre-bound writer's canonical status, like Erik Davis's 1989 salvaging of "master mindfucker" and paranoid visionary Philip K. Dick from the sci-fi dumpster, or Greg Tate's celebration of Samuel Delany's polymorphously perverse Afro-futurist fiction. Michele Wallace's expansive 1988 essay on Zora Neale Hurston doesn't so much rescue a once-denigrated writer as examine the way in which a series of well-intentioned reha-bilitators—Alice Walker, Henry Louis Gates, Harold Bloom—have gotten Hurston so wrong. Edmund White's nimble reckoning of Djuna Barnes fashions her as an important Modernist innovator perpetually detained in the canon's anteroom. And in his por-trait of African-American critic Albert Murray—"the last of an endangered breed of literary-political thinkers"—Joe Wood dares to critique his hero's work, in the process taking on an entire African-American intellectual world.

Angela Carter has probably been the subject of more *VLS* pieces than any other writer; Rick Moody's posthumous review of her short stories offers a final glimpse of her wicked sensibility and eerie intelligence. Despite our unflagging devotion and sup-port, Carter made nary a dent in the American literary scene. But hey, aren't lost causes the most glorious kind?

WHO DAT SAY WHO DAT WHEN I SAY WHO DAT?

Zora Neale Hurston Then and Now

By Michele Wallace

Habitually, Afro-American literary criticism has kept a strict lookout for backsliding to, say, the antebellum days when some free blacks wrote Southern state legislatures asking to be re-enslaved because their living conditions were so tenuous. The fear has been that because black writers had to please white audiences, editors, and publishers, a grotesque minstrelsy—discursively equivalent to Stepin Fetchit's shuffle—would surface in works of Afro-American literature, deadening the inevitable polemical sting. The prime exhibit for the prosecution was once Zora Neale Hurston, whose fiction and folklore collections have in the past been repeatedly dismissed by the black male literary establishment on the grounds that she was simply "cutting the fool" for white folks' benefit.

But as a pioneer of the Harlem Renaissance's literary translation of the Afro-American oral tradition (blues and bebop, folklore, street language and Black English, toasts, jive, and the dozens), Hurston dared to laugh at racist stereotypes—even to risk verifying them—in order to make a point on behalf of "the folk farthest down." At a time when the Ku Klux Klan was still lynching blacks en masse, and the tone of racial wisdom, à la W. E. B. Du Bois and Richard Wright, was dignified and dramatic, Hurston rejected the racial uplift agenda of the Talented Tenth on the premise that ordinary bloods had something to say, too. As she wrote in her autobiography in 1942, among blacks "there was a general acceptance of the monkey as kinfolks. Perhaps it was some distant memory of tribal monkey reverence from Africa. . . . Perhaps it was an acknowledgment of our talent for mimicry with the monkey as a symbol." How black intellectuals must have cringed. Then.

Now Afro-Americanist extraordinaire Henry Louis Gates calls Hurston's rebellion "signifying" or "critical signification" and proposes the Signifying Monkey—preeminent trickster of the Afro-American oral tradition—as a figure to evoke the patterns of imitation and reversal that enable black narrative to respond to and defy an exclusionary white culture. Gates describes the way Hurston's figure works as "the ironic reversal of a received racist image in the Western imagination of the black as simianlike, the Signifying Monkey—he who dwells at the margin of discourse, ever punning, ever troping, ever embodying the ambiguities of language." Gates readily concedes that no writer before Ishmael Reed better demonstrated the range of signifying strategies than Zora Neale Hurston.

As folklorist, anthropologist, and novelist, she was vigilant in her quest to render the Afro-American oral tradition and its characteristic "signifying" a permanent feature in the museum of American culture. And Gates suggests that in *Their Eyes Were Watching God*, Hurston was "the first author of the tradition to represent signifying itself as a vehicle of liberation for an oppressed woman, and as a rhetorical strategy in the narration of fiction." Which is why, despite the sexism that once clouded Afro-Americanists' view of Hurston's assets, Gates now leads a gang of black male Afro-Americanists who make pivotal use of Hurston's work in their most recent critical speculations.

They follow the lead of black feminist critics and novelists—Alice Walker, Sherley Anne Williams, Toni Cade Bambara, Mary Helen Washington, Barbara Christian—who first proclaimed Hurston, with the help of Robert Hemenway's biography. The change in her reputation is due, in part, to feminist enlightenment but also to a general easing up: It's time to reassess Hurston's self-conscious manipulation of a kind of dialectical minstrelsy that may be the crucial mark of Afro-American cultural and artistic productivity.

Since slavery, Afro-Americans have produced culture in a peculiar limbo between languages, between nationalities. The integrity of the signifier (the Law of the Father or the Sacred Word) was always a scandal from the Afro-American point of view—as unobtainable as American justice. The resultant narrative funkiness, which can also look like political evasiveness, is what Ralph Ellison may have meant by "invisibility" in 1952. Remember in the beginning of *Invisible Man*, the grandson is instructed to "overcome'm with yesses, undermine'm with grins, agree'm to death and destruction . . ." Afro-American literary criticism has finally drawn substantial insight into the subtleties of race business from the literature itself.

Still, that Afro-American critics should be interested in an Afro-American writer, though she is female, seems to require no backbreaking explanation, even if it's never happened before, which it *never* has. Yet how do we explain the interest of Yale's Harold Bloom, godfather of a white, patriarchy-obsessed literary theory? Bloom, who is editing Chelsea House's vast series of critical anthologies, ominously entitled "Modern Critical Views," has devoted one of the early volumes to

Hurston. How do we explain the work of Marxist critic Susan Willis, who has written *Specifying*, a book on black women writers that takes its name from Hurston's use of the term in her autobiography, *Dust Tracks on a Road*. Or the two articles on Hurston in deconstructionist Barbara Johnson's new book, *A World of Difference*. Or even the emergence of a pseudo-black feminist criticism practiced by white feminists, the outstanding example of which is the introduction to *Conjuring: Black Women, Fiction and Literature*, where Marjorie Pryse appears to be attempting a codification of Alice Walker's "womanist" method. Last year's annual meeting of the National Women's Studies Association, which focused on "Women of Color," leads me to think that a host of other "modern critical views" will soon follow.

All well and good, you may say. About time. Literature needs a rainbow coalition—black, white, male, female, artists and academics, historicists and deconstructionists joining together to insure the preservation of Hurston's work and reputation. Except that canon formation has little to do with such benign cultural practice. Rather, Hurston's extraordinary textual ambivalence about race, class, nationality, sex, religion, and family, her cryptic, inscrutable subjectivity, offers a crucial vantage point on the crisis in signification which fuels postmodernism and haunts Western self-esteem—and which, not coincidentally, lies at the core of the Afro-American experience. So, like groupies descending on Elvis Presley's estate, critics are engaged in a mostly ill-mannered stampede to have some memento of the black woman who could mock the 1954 Supreme Court decision desegregating the schools, who simultaneously insisted upon substantive racial difference and no difference at all, who epitomizes our inability to revise the text of American racism, or to acknowledge its sexism. For what is at stake is the integrity and vitality of language, literature, and American thought, from the bottom up.

Remember how this whole Zora Neale Hurston thing got off the ground. Not how it started, which was when Hurston made the best move of her literary career by dying of stroke, poverty, and a profound lack of literary appreciation in a welfare home in Saint Lucie County, Florida, in 1960. Focus on Alice Walker's mystical attempt (documented in her essay "Looking for Zora") to locate Hurston's body in an abandoned cemetery overgrown with weeds by calling out to her, "Zora . . . I'm here. Are you?" When Walker's foot sank into a hole, she took it as a sign. In that spot, she installed a granite stone reading, "Zora Neale Hurston 'A Genius of The South' [she borrowed Jean Toomer's poetic use of the phrase], 1901–1960, Novelist, Folklorist, Anthropologist." From 1960 to 1973, Hurston had been buried in an unmarked grave in a segregated cemetery in Fort

Pierce, Florida, a place Hemenway calls "symbolic of the black writer's historical fate in America."

The current unceremonious exhuming of the Hurston corpse should be considered in the reflected glory of these two distinctly different memorials—the erasure, anonymity, and degradation of the unmarked pauper's grave and the double-whammy of canonization as signified by the gravestone that may have missed the mark, and that employs the term *genius* ambivalently and in quotes. Not only may we be canonizing a Hurston who never existed, or the wrong corpse, but it may simply be intrinsic to the process of canonization (think mummification) to lay waste to the symbolic and intellectual urgency of this or any other cultural object of our affections.

The efforts of Washington, Walker, Williams, Bambara, and Hemenway to resurrect and republish Hurston have certainly been useful (although I privately wonder about so much reverential awe for a woman who scorned the stuff), but what if their unwillingness to submit Hurston's signifying to rigorous examination invites others, who are not of the faith, to misuse her and derail the future of black women in literature and literary criticism? The time to consider such questions is upon us, for Hurston's cultural use has clearly passed beyond the control of black feminists/womanists.

Even when the opportunity obviously exists to describe and define the black woman in her own terms, her own voice, white male and female and black male expertise may persist in silencing her by unwanted sexual/textual acts. Take Harold Bloom's book on Hurston. Bloom means well, I suppose, but in an introduction almost too short to bother reading, he sweeps aside those critical challenges to the canon that first recovered Hurston's achievements from the dust heap of marginality: "Her sense of power has nothing in common with politics of any persuasion, with contemporary modes of feminism, or even with those questers who search for a black aesthetic."

Rather, he makes a case for Hurston's protagonist Janie, firmly locating her in the only tradition that matters to him—the one that began with Samuel Richardson's Clarissa and peaked with Dreiser's Carrie and Lawrence's Ursula and Gudrun. Predictably, he recasts *Their Eyes Were Watching God* as the story of a woman's struggle with repression. The blackness of virtually everybody in the book takes a backseat to the issue of Janie's beleaguered sexuality. Further, according to Bloom, it's another woman, the grandmother, who offers the largest obstacle to Janie's sexual fulfillment and self-articulation. Grandma's pretext, that she was raped in slavery and that her daughter, Janie's mother, fared not much better, is utterly ignored in Bloom's elegant but slapdash revision. He wraps it up by proposing that we see Hurston as the Wife of Bath, that antifeminist mouthpiece proposed in the 14th century as a cure for priests who would choose marriage over celibacy. Cute, huh?

What follows in the book, you might wonder. Precisely the Afro-Americanist and feminist interpretations Bloom has just erased—the prefaces, introductions, and articles by Darwin Turner, Larry Neale, Hemenway, Walker, Williams, and Washington that have accompanied Hurston's republication these past 14 years.

The cumulative effect is of some kind of cosmic blunder: Bloom's introduction doesn't introduce but rather supersedes the text that follows. He morbidly objectifies Hurston in a sexually charged image of Western culture's embedded antifeminism. Hurston's silent black body floats to the surface of a systemic dilemma. The irony is that Afro-American studies and women's studies courses will constitute a captive audience for this book.

I t was in my first narrative writing class at the City College of New York that I first encountered Hurston. In 1971, that twilight year of Black Power, on a campus at the margins of open enrollment and my native Harlem, I felt buried alive by the self-regard of black males and the blindness of the faculty's typical white male, who could not imagine a black feminist writer. Then my writing teacher, Mark Mirsky, pressed upon me a hardcover copy of *Mules and Men*, Hurston's deceptively simple presentation of black story-telling, the oral tradition, and voodoo in the '30s in the rural South.

Her unequivocal presentation of "rustic folk" as speaking subjects whose race was not compromised but informed by their sexuality was music to my ears. *Mules and Men* portrayed Afro-American oral tradition in three settings. In Hurston's hometown, all-black Eatonville, old friends treat her like long-lost family. Twice she makes extended visits to an impoverished sawmill camp in Loughman, Florida. The women in Loughman often engage in knife fights, and Hurston requires the constant protection of the roughest of them all, Big Sweet, who is described admiringly by one of Hurston's male informants as "uh whole woman and half uh man." Finally, there's the quasi-European, quasi-African New Orleans, where Hurston pursues several apprenticeships as a voodoo priestess.

Her archly heretical tone about such sacred cows as racial pride, skin color, slavery, the eating of watermelon, the singing of the blues, and conjure—her skillful narrative flow into and out of dialect, and the multiple rhetorical strategies of her "native" informants—was a revelation to me. Not because I'd never heard such linguistic antics before—in Harlem, the crossroads of the African diaspora, such a medley of voices was not unfamiliar—but I'd never seen the attempt to write it down.

Soon after that, I read *Their Eyes Were Watching God* in connection with a newly inaugurated women's studies program at CCNY and was thoroughly enchanted, although alarmed. On one hand, in a community deeply split over the appropriate use of black English, Hurston's confident handling of dialect gave this story the rigor and readability of a black *Alice in Wonderland*. On the other hand, I was disappointed that Janie didn't pursue intellectual curiosity, as Zora playing herself did in *Mules and Men*, barreling down the backroads of Florida in her Chevrolet in search of stories old and new, borrowed and blue. Instead of a career, Janie pursues the right kind of marriage and finally finds it with Tea Cake, who teaches her how to play checkers and beats her, then brags to his friends about how ladylike she is and how easily she scars.

Black feminists Alice Walker, Mary Helen Washington, and Sherley Anne Williams have suggested that it's wisest to see such moments in the plot as subsidiary to Janie's triumph of voice when she virtually loud-talks her second husband to death and achieves mastery in the telling of her own tale at the end of the book. It's true that concentrating on this symbolic resolution is more satisfying than dealing with how Hurston ultimately faced the conflict and left it unresolved. But Harold Bloom also defends the evolution of Janie in his ritual canonization of *Their Eyes*. In the process, he further consolidates the black female absence in a white male literary establishment—which suggests to me that other "critical views" more subversive than "modern" must be ventured.

The book I've read since 1971 that helped me to see both *Their Eyes Were Watching God* and Hurston's career in another light is *Dust Tracks on a Road*. Here is Hurston's recapitulation of the blues wisdom concerning black women, as opposed to "brown" women like Janie:

> *They brought bad luck for a week if they came to your house of a Monday morning. They were evil. They slept with their fists balled up ready to fight and squabble even while they were asleep. They even had evil dreams. White, yellow and brown girls dreamed about roses and perfumes and kisses. Black gals dreamed about guns, razors, ice picks, hatchets and hot lye. I heard men swear they had seen women dreaming and knew these things to be true.*

Here Hurston is at her signifying best. These remarks constitute a major transitional moment in a chapter called "My People! My People!" that discusses, or rather juggles, competing notions of "race." In a seductively entertaining way that makes you first think you're reading fluff, Hurston repeatedly assaults the concept of racial essence, revealing its basis as absurd and fundamentally rhetorical. She does this by exploring a series of rhetorical relations—between blacks and whites, the black middle class and the black poor, males and females, blacks and tans—what each says about the other in the process of defining the superior self. Hurston gives the impression of a constantly shifting perspective (much like Virginia Woolf's in *A Room of One's Own*) until it becomes clear that race is a game played with mirrors called words. While she's at it, she gives W. E. B. Dubois's celebrated "colorline," as in "the problem of the twentieth century is the problem of the colorline," a good working over.

Although she draws the rather obvious conclusion that blacks, therefore, are individuals, what's more important is the polyvocal and multidirectional terms in which the argument is made. Here's how she ends this chapter in her autobiography:

> *I maintain that I have been a Negro three times—a Negro baby, a Negro girl and a Negro woman. Still, if you have received no clear-cut impression of what* The Negro in America *is like, then you are in the same place with me. There is no* The Negro *here.*

Politics is less the issue than the amazing audacity of this woman who dared to challenge the rhetoric and posturing of a race. Hurston's work—the nonfiction writing on oral tradition in *Tell My Horse, The Sanctified Church, Mules and Men,* and *Dust Tracks on a Road,* as well as the fiction of *Their Eyes Were Watching God, Jonah's Gourd Vine, Mose, Man of the Mountain,* and the short stories—forms an essential complement to the occasional tunnel vision of Booker T. Washington, Jean Toomer, James Weldon Johnson, Alain Locke, Langston Hughes, Sterling Brown, and Richard Wright. Dubois, Hughes, Brown, and Wright all expressed grave doubts about the viability of Hurston's writing—and that's precisely why we ought to read her and them in tandem. She provides a funky footbridge between the lofty pronouncements of a public racial self-consciousness and a private (ordinarily anonymous) collective black sensibility, a sense that somebody/women had another view of things.

How peculiar that Hurston should be taught, read, and written about as though the context of Afro-American cultural and intellectual history did not exist. For one thing, Hurston was always signifying. If you don't know the boys, how do you know what she was signifying on?

In *Specifying,* Susan Willis announces the intention of historicizing the literature of contemporary black women writers. But not unlike Bloom's crypto-deconstructionism, Willis's "historicism" inserts "Hurston" where one might expect to read history. Her analysis of Hurston's rhetoric suffers the consequences. For instance, Willis takes the title of her book from a passage in *Dust Tracks on a Road* in which

Hurston describes her first encounter with Big Sweet, who was in the process of "specifying" somebody:

> *Big Sweet broke the news to him, in one of her mildest bulletins that his pa was a double humpted camel and his ma was a grass gut cow, but even so, he tore her wide open in the act of getting born, and so on and so forth . . .*

Bypassing more complex explanations of the use of figurative language in the Afro-American oral tradition, some of which Hurston herself helped to supply, Willis settles upon "name-calling" to denote "specifying" and concludes that it "represents a form of narrative integrity. Historically, it speaks for a noncommodified relationship to language, a time when the slippage between words and meaning would not have obtained or been tolerated."

The translation of "specifying" that Hurston offers within the text is "putting your foot up" on somebody, which Big Sweet promptly does when a troublemaker in camp threatens Hurston with a knife. "Specifying," more like Gates's "Signifying," is a fluid, relational process unconcerned with original intent. If the slippage between signifier and signified is the problem, the writing of Zora Neale Hurston is not the cure, except to the degree that the cure is making the unconscious judgment apparent, re-establishing the severed links between "linguistic undecidability" and economic and political fact. Hurston often did this in her writing, not by forcing meaning to heel, but rather by tracking its proliferation/demise.

Willis makes valid observations, but her interpretation bears the unmistakable stamp of the tourist because of her failure to read Hurston in the context of Afro-American letters and her determination to cast black women's writing in polar opposition to the alienation and reification of white middle-class culture.

I don't mean to imply that you have to be a black feminist to do Zora Neale Hurston justice. A fine example of a way to tackle the territory is provided by Barbara Johnson in *A World of Difference.* Her approach is forthright from the beginning: "It was not clear to me what I, a white deconstructor, was doing talking about Zora Neale Hurston, a black novelist and anthropologist, or to *whom* I was talking. . . . Was I talking to white critics, black critics, or myself?" Johnson decides that the answer is "all of the above" and that her interest in Hurston's "strategies and structures of problematic address" does not have a single motivation. "I had a lot to learn then," she writes, "from Hurston's way of dealing with multiple agendas and heterogeneous implied readers."

Johnson recalls the double-voicing of the Afro-American literary tradition in terms of Dubois's famous veil metaphor, which divides the

Afro-American citizen, automatically assumed to be male, between contending allegiances to race and country. She illustrates Hurston's location in that discourse by quoting from Richard Wright's review of *Their Eyes Were Watching God*, in which he wrote that "the sensory sweep of her novel carries no theme, no message, no thought." Johnson says of this statement, "the full range of questions and experiences of Janie's life are as invisible to a mind steeped in maleness as Ellison's *Invisible Man* is to minds steeped in whiteness."

Following black feminist readings, Johnson suggests that Janie's display of rhetorical mastery in the male-dominated world of an all-black town constructs a symbolic resolution of the dilemma that plagued Hurston's career. But she proposes, as well, that discussions of race or gender invariably rely upon an oppositional or dualistic logic that forces the black woman writer into a virtually untenable position in critical discourse.

As Johnson finally puts it, "The black woman is both invisible and ubiquitous; never seen in her own right but forever appropriated by the others for their own ends." Yet even in Hurston's nonfiction writing, ultimate resolution of the dilemma is always displaced, for as Johnson insists, "unification and simplification are fantasies of domination, not understanding" and "the task of the writer" is "to narrate both the appeal and the injustice of universalization, in a voice that assumes and articulates its own, ever-differing self-difference."

In Hurston's nonfiction writing, she insists that Afro-American oral tradition is unique and irreplaceable, thereby seeming to confirm the notion of an irreducible racial essence. At the same time, she makes the counterclaim that "race" as a way of categorizing and limiting a writer's domain simply shouldn't and doesn't exist. Although generalizations about Hurston are probably useless, her life offers a possible explanation of this apparent contradiction.

While Hurston's anchor in New York was her scholarship with Franz Boas in anthropology at Columbia, the road was rocky still. Besides the criticism of her male peers, constant financial troubles, and the increasing inaccessibility of publication, Hurston had bad luck with husbands, didn't get along with her family, and couldn't keep a teaching job. Invariably, her response to "worriation" was to go on another folklore hunting trip in the South, or South America or the Caribbean. Financial and professional security were strangers to her all her life, which may explain why she never seemed to recover from the shock of the headlines in the *Afro-American*, a black Baltimore paper, reporting a morals charge in 1948 that accused her of sodomizing the teenage son of her Harlem landlady while she was, in fact, out of the city. Though she soon fled the North for the South's "heart of darkness," never to return, her writing became more politically conservative and color blind: She was clearly disillusioned with the racial politics of a Northern black bourgeoisie that had never offered her anything but torment anyway.

The biographical approach has its uses, but I like Johnson's take on Hurston's self-contradiction. Fur Hurston, she says, "Difference is a misreading of sameness, but it must be represented in order to be erased. The resistance to finding out that the other is the same springs out of the reluctance to admit that the same is other." The point here, it seems to me, is both political and literary: Black and white, and male and female exist in asymmetrical relation to one another; they are not neat little opposites to be drawn and quartered. We recognize the persistence of such measures in our narratives in order to dismantle them in our lives.

Forceful black female critical voices are needed to verify the crucial assault on the logic of binary oppositions of race, class, and sex already launched by contemporary black women novelists, poets, and playwrights. Scrutiny of Hurston's nonfiction writing could inspire us to take on this task. Instead, the thrust of black feminist writing on Hurston implicitly proposes her life and work as a role model for contemporary black female scholarship, intellectual curiosity, and literary production. The model is too narrow.

Black feminist criticism on Hurston may already be changing its tune, or so *Invented Lives: Narratives of Black Women 1860–1960*, edited and annotated by Mary Helen Washington, would seem to indicate. Washington's introduction to excerpts from Hurston's novels questions the viability of Janie as a heroic voice and suggests that Hurston's real sympathies lay with John Pearson, the protagonist of *Jonah's Gourd Vine*. Hurston depicts the oral tradition in the all-black town of *Their Eyes* as sex-segregated and male-dominated: Janie doesn't stand a chance. Is Washington's analysis a step in the right direction, or is it the inevitable swing of the pendulum back to a position dismissive of Hurston's work?

We need a re-evaluation of Hurston's re-evaluation, a running blow-by-blow commentary on the progress and health of the black female literary/critical voice and its relationship to the mainstream. As for role models, we might do ourselves greater service to choose among that school of black women writers flourishing now—Paule Marshall, Toni Morrison, Alice Walker, Audre Lorde, Toni Cade Bambara, Sonia Sanchez, June Jordan, Ntozake Shange, Gloria Naylor, Thulani Davis, Lucille Clifton, Sherley Anne Williams, Maya Angelou, critics Barbara Christian, Barbara Smith, May Helen Washington, Gloria Hull, bell hooks. It is now that black women are "writing themselves into history," as black feminist critic Hortense Spillers aptly puts it in her afterword to *Conjuring*.

Yet there are those of us who fear the proliferation of continental theory. Audre Lorde and Barbara Christian have said as much, on the grounds that "the master's tools cannot be used to dismantle the master's house," which makes me think the reluctance of black women writers to rise to the challenge of critical self-definition may not be only the fault of male and/or white intimidation. As bell hooks suggested recently, in an essay called "Talking Back," critical writing may hold a special terror for black women as a result of an anti-intellectual bias that is automatic, unconscious, and defensive in our upbringing.

To be more specific, little black girls are not encouraged at home or at school to value their own thoughts. To articulate them is often labeled "talking back" and even punished. The sense that black females should be either supportive or silent is carried over into adulthood. So, like Jane Austen hiding her novel-writing under blotting paper in the family room, black women, too, have been forced to conceal their best contemporary articulations of self under the cloak of fiction. Even our endless respectful tributes to our mothers' courage and endurance in the face of slavery and racial oppression may actually interfere with our intellectual growing up as daughters.

It's time to consider that the process of concealment, which was once essential to our collective survival, has outlived its usefulness. Although I'll grant you that talking back is a risky business, the alternative is that Afro-American women will continue to be objects, not subjects, in the global production of knowledge. So, hagiography is fine if you have the time, but more urgent matters call. It probably won't do any of us any good to make that childless trickster Zora Hurston into a madonna figure, whose arms we can lie in and be safe. Black women have written numerous autobiographies, among which *Dust Tracks on a Road* takes the prize for inscrutability. We do well to remember that when dust tracks blow away, they are impossible to follow.

April 1988

TECHNOMANCER

Philip K. Dick's Signal Achievements

By Erik Davis

THE THREE STIGMATA OF PALMER ELDRITCH

A SCANNER DARKLY

THE DIVINE INVASION

BLADE RUNNER (DO ANDROIDS DREAM OF
ELECTRIC SHEEP?)

TIME OUT OF JOINT

VALIS

When Philip K. Dick died after a stroke in 1982, he left behind almost 40 science fiction novels, over a hundred short stories, a few remarkable essays, and the "Exegesis," a crazed document that attempted to interpret the divine intelligence which he claimed invaded his mind in 1974. Though Dick remains partially buried in the mildewed heap of yesterday's pop trash (best known as "the guy who wrote the book they based *Blade Runner* on"), his dedicated following has grown since his death. Some of his best books are out of print in the States, but a steady trickle of unpublished (and mostly non-SF) work has been released in the last few years. Whether or not Dick hacked out the most brilliant American science fiction ever is debatable; that his work remains the most brilliantly fucked-up SF is beyond doubt.

Though he uses generic devices like androids, spaceships, Martians, and moon colonies, Dick's worlds are usually bummers just around the corner, near-futures characterized by rampant overpopulation, surveillance, urban decay, repressive state apparatuses, ubiquitous ads, and invasive technology. As far back as the '50s, Dick saw the dark, paranoid side of McLuhan's global village. The animism that primitive humankind projected onto Nature was for him reborn in our technological environment, where ominous spiritual forces merged with the instruments of late capitalism. Dick's machines are black jokes rather than believable imaginings: the portable computerized psychiatrist, Dr. Smile, in *The Three Stigmata of Palmer Eldritch;* the empathy machine in "The Little Black Box," which fuses the users' consciousness with a televised savior; *The Divine Invasion*'s holographic multicolored Bible.

Driven by what he called "divine discontent," Dick howled in his dystopic wilderness against the powers that be. His characters are ordinary schlemiels, bumbling Joes and Janes struggling with small moral dilemmas, poverty, politics, and psychic breakdowns in worlds where entropy reigns and communication breakdowns are inevitable. Unlike Pynchon—whose obsessions resemble his in many ways—Dick maintained little ironic distance from his characters, and his empathy for them and their hopeless struggles is palpable as well as odd. Not that Dick didn't undercut the pathos with comic gags. In *A Scanner Darkly,* Charles Freck tries to kill himself by consuming wine and a handful of reds: "However, he had been burned. The capsules were not barbiturates, as represented. They were some kind of kinky psychedelics.... Well, he thought philosophically, this is the story of my life. Always ripped off.... The next thing he knew, a creature from between dimensions was standing beside his bed looking down on him disapprovingly."

Dick's characters battle not only themselves, but also the second law of thermodynamics. Entropy is a major trope in SF, but in Dick's hands it's a dark god. *Do Androids Dream of Electric Sheep?* features the semi-retarded John Isidore living "alone in this deteriorating, blind building of a thousand uninhabited apartments, which like all its counterparts, fell, day by day, into greater entropic ruin. Eventually everything within the building would merge, would be faceless and identical ... buried under the ubiquity of the dust. By then, naturally, he himself would be dead, another interesting event to anticipate as he stood here alone with the lungless, penetrating, masterful world-silence.... Better, perhaps, to turn the TV back on."

This move towards the TV was characteristic, because Dick was obsessed with communications technology—radio, records, tapes, television, phones, computers—using it as a metaphor for the social web people build from their individual signals to keep entropy at bay. Technology only re-inscribed for Dick the signals, noise, distortion, and overlapping frequencies that we are already simultaneously trapped in and estranged from.

He usually wrote in the subjective third person, jumping among the variable perspectives of the characters that made up his narratives. By switching viewpoints, Dick formalized and toyed with his contention that objective reality is both synthetic and fragile, a "hypothetical universalization of a multitude of subjective realities." Most of his tales contain false worlds, spurious environments simulated and controlled by nefarious powers using drugs, technology, and psychic power. In *The Three Stigmata of Palmer Eldritch*, the eponymous figure returns from space and markets Chew-Z, a drug which projects users into a world he controls. As Dick's creations discover off-kilter clues in their environment, their paranoia and sense of irreality grow, until their suspicions are not only fulfilled but often grossly exceeded. Dick was a narrative trickster, a master mindfucker. He pulled the whodunit inside out: Decoding small meaningful details doesn't put the picture together so much as rip it apart. By twisting the page-turning groove of pulp into a Möbius strip, Dick attempted to undermine the political, social, technological, and psychic structures of "reality." He wanted a pulp guerrilla ontology that deconstructed everyone's power trip—Nixon's, IBM's, God's, the author's.

Dick's first fully fake world appeared in *Time Out of Joint* (1959), which shivered with the Cold War. In it, Ragle Gumm spends his days drinking beer in '50s suburbia, supporting himself through his unusual skill at playing a newspaper puzzle called "Where Will the Little Green Man Be Next?" Strange slippages in the normal order occur—he finds a phone book with unfamiliar exchanges, picks up unlisted programs on his ham radio—and Gumm becomes increasingly paranoid, convinced his world is spurious. We eventually find out that it's 1996, the Earth is at war with lunar colonists, and the puzzle takes advantage of Gumm's uncanny ability to predict the next hostile bombing. It turns out that Gumm had become sympathetic with the colonists and refused to continue aiding Earth, so the military-industrial complex created the false environment and drugged him into useful forgetfulness.

Dick engaged the mutant logic of late capitalism and the technological simulacrum before Baudrillard knew a megabyte from a baguette, coming to the conclusion that only an antagonistic relationship with reality—even to the point of madness—is sane. In a world of crystal-clear transmission, Dick tuned to the static between channels, turned up the volume, and listened for hidden messages. His skepticism constitutes an increasingly fervent metaphysics. He was obsessed with the Gnostic concept of a demiurge, a false god who obscured the true world with illusory time and space. Part of the authorial fragmentation that pervades Dick's work arises because, though he clearly identified with his flailing characters and their metaphysical morality plays, he remained the demiurge of his own narratives.

In *Valis*, Dick made the provocative statement that "the symbols of the divine show up in our world initially at the trash stratum." While the fragments of schizo vision scattered throughout Dick's work may not have been holy, he certainly got the trash part right. By almost every standard of literary quality, Philip K. Dick was a hack. Most of his work is clunky, uneven, and occasionally awful. Having first published SF in 1951, he never lost touch with the gaudy mechanics of earlier SF pulpsters like A. E. van Vogt. Though one develops an affection for his characters, their dialogue is often forced and obvious. Both the science and the plots strain credulity. The hasty feel of many of his books is no accident. Driven by poverty, obsession, and frequently by amphetamines, he wrote like the madman he probably was. In 1965, he published four novels; two a year, plus numerous short stories, was his standard rate.

Dick's schizophrenia turns him into many authors: a poor-man's Pynchon, an oracular postmodern, a rich product of the changing counterculture, a lunatic. As Thomas Disch said, he was a "science fiction writer's science fiction writer," respected in the SF community even though his U.S. sales were mostly mediocre (he was much more popular in Britain and France). He's a particular favorite among scuzzy underground rock bands like Sonic Youth and the Reverb Motherfuckers, as well as scuzzy underground rock critics like Byron Coley. Diehards chronicle and compile his every word and deed, blurring the distinction between literary love and cult. And some academics of the leftist poststructuralist bent, most notably Fredric Jameson, love his political metafictions, his gaudy feel for the process of reification, his hack Kafka humor. On the other hand, Harold Bloom—an eternal advocate of imagination over reality—finds Dick vastly overrated, but that's probably because, as anyone who's read Bloom's *Flight to Lucifer* knows, Dick can write Gnostic science fiction and Bloom can't.

Part of the appeal of Dick's *oeuvre* is that, despite its futuristic setting and outlandish events, it functions as autobiography. Most of the recent reissues of his novels feature his bearded visage on the cover, in part because fans recognize that the real subject of his texts was his own frail, intense, and fragmented self. Because he didn't distance himself from his novels, they read as both Freudian confessions and Jungian dream journals. Dick himself had numerous wives and young girlfriends, and the relationships he described are invariably screwed up, sad affairs of misunderstandings, adulteries, and recriminations. But Dick's psychological obsessions go beyond the erotic and personal into the archetypal. Patterns and motifs reappear throughout his novels with the archaic and gaudy power of symbols: broken pots, the Black Prison, policemen, toys, jewelry, books which are read randomly (based on the *I Ching*), miniature figures, simulacra. These two confessional aspects of Dick are well represented in *The Dark-Haired Girl*, a collection of letters and dreams about the teenage girls he was obsessed with. One letter will be depressingly naïve and pathetically sentimental; the next will describe some fascinating overloaded dream, then an equally strange interpretation of the symbolism involved.

Dick's most overblown reading of an event occurred in 1974, when the sight of a delivery woman's Christian fish necklace triggered his psychic contact with the "divine intelligence" he called VALIS, or Vast Active Living Intelligence System. Among other things, he communicated with a persecuted Christian living in ancient Rome, who warned him through a Beatles song that his son Christopher would die unless he was taken to a hospital. Dick also became convinced that the universe was a hologram and that VALIS was a camouflaged parasite which entered human beings through subliminal messages. The information lurked everywhere, especially in trashy artifacts of pop culture, so that in the end Dick must have believed himself to be less a writer than a pulp contagion, a pirate transmitter in a world jammed with increasingly vivid and increasingly delirious signals.

August 1989

SAINT BERNHARD
Preface to a Multi-Volume Suicide Note

By Gary Indiana

I looked forward to Thomas Bernhard's final novel with morbid antici-
pation. It arrived six years after his death, for which it seemed every
book was an elaborate, nattering, malcontented, euphoric, excoriating
rehearsal, a last gasp of disgust at the modern world, Austria, National
Socialism, the Catholic Church, received ideas, capitalism, socialism,
the middle class, the upper class, the proletariat, nature, urbanism, pas-
toralism, philistinism, artists, and first and foremost himself. Along
with Witold Gombrowicz, after whom he named the mad Prince's gar-
dener in *Gargoyles*, Bernhard had been my decisive aesthetic and mental
influence among 20th-century writers. He revealed the shrunken, petty,
deformed condition of human beings as the modern world transformed
them into things.

I always read this Bernhard with relief. Even though he was in Austria and not America, even though he wrote of Austria's hideousness
instead of America's hideousness, even though he continually provoked
and ridiculed the so-called cultural elite of Austria and not the so-called
cultural elite of America, I felt grateful that someone, somewhere, could
write exactly as he pleased with impunity, fearlessly, and that his reputation grew and grew as he became more and more disagreeable, more
contrary, more intolerant of hypocrites and imbeciles. That his hatred
of the state and the Catholic Church remained unassuaged, no matter
how many prizes and awards were thrown at him. "No money *and* being
pissed on," he wrote about receiving the Grillparzer Prize, "that was
intolerable." "I let them piss on me in all these city halls and assembly
rooms," he wrote in *Wittgenstein's Nephew*, "for to award someone a
prize is no different from pissing on him."

I wondered, months before *Extinction* arrived, if it would still be
possible to write something interesting about this Bernhard, whom
some believed to be the greatest writer in the world, and whom others
believed to be an obscure and irritating misanthrope, having made two
previous attempts, once in *Details*, of all ridiculous places, and once in

The Village Voice, because whenever I attempted to write something about Bernhard I found myself in the predicament of Rudolf, the narrator of *Concrete,* whose attempts to begin an essay on Mendelssohn Bartholdy have been thwarted and crushed for 20 years, by the importunate visits of his sister, for example, and then by his sudden loneliness when his sister returns to Vienna after visiting him in the country, or by his longing for the city while he's in the country, then his conviction, in the city, that he can only write in the country. "I believed *fervently,*" Rudolf writes, "that I needed my sister in order to be able to start my work on Mendelssohn Bartholdy. And then, when she was there, I knew that I didn't need her, that I could start work only if she wasn't there. But now she's gone and I'm *really* unable to start. At first it was because she was there, and now it's because she isn't. On the one hand we overrate other people, on the other we underrate them; and we constantly overrate and underrate ourselves; when we ought to overrate ourselves we underrate ourselves, and in the same way we underrate ourselves when we ought to overrate ourselves."

Rudolf ends by saying very little about Mendelssohn Bartholdy in *Concrete,* though perhaps he says more than he really needs to, just as Reger, in *Old Masters,* says very little about Tintoretto's *White Bearded Man,* the painting he's studied every other day for 20 years in the Kunsthistorisches Museum, just as Konrad, in *The Lime Works,* never gets around to writing his all-important treatise on the sense of hearing, despite endless acoustical experiments on his wife, whom he finally kills with a Mannlicher carbine she kept behind her old-fashioned invalid chair in the desolation of the lime works. "Only two years ago," Konrad says, "I was still of the opinion that the lime works would be good for my work, but now I no longer think so, now I can see that the lime works robbed me of my last chance to get my book actually written. I mean that sometimes I think, he is supposed to have told Wieser, that the lime works is precisely why I can't write it all down, and then at other times I think that I still have a chance to get my book written down precisely because I am living at the lime works."

Whenever a new Bernhard book appeared, I remembered that the first Bernhard novel to fall into my hands was the English edition of *Concrete,* for which I traded the English edition of Gombrowicz's *Operetta,* a book that has vanished. I now have the French edition of *Operetta,* but whenever I am in England I ransack Foyle's and all the other bookshops looking for that English version, with no luck, and of course I also recall that the person with whom I traded *Operetta* for *Concrete* is a woman I no longer talk to. A new Bernhard novel invariably reminds me of this failed relationship, so similar to Bernhard's relationship to the so-called poet Jeannie Billroth in *Woodcutters:* "To think that I once loved this woman Jeannie Billroth, whom I have hated for the last twenty years, and who, also, hates me. People come together and form a friendship, and for years they not only endure this friendship, but allow it to become more and more intense until it finally snaps, and from then on they hate each other for decades, sometimes for the rest of their lives."

As these Bernhard novels appeared one by one, I also remembered my long visits to Alter Pfarrhof, winter and summer, only a few miles across the German border from the village where Bernhard lived, not far from Wels, and Attnang-Puchheim, and the other Bavarian towns "where Catholicism waves its brainless sceptre," as Bernhard's grandfather put it. At that time I had many friends in Germany, and now all but a handful have committed suicide.

These suicide deaths are never far from my thoughts, especially when the books Bernhard was writing during those very years when my friends were killing themselves appear. *Wittgenstein's Nephew,* for example, and *The Loser,* books that describe the impossibility of life, that describe the cost of living, the mental and physical toll of a few decades of disappointment, disappointment with oneself and one's failures first of all, accompanied by the horror that is other people, the true extent of which is the only enduring surprise life has to offer, as Bernhard demonstrates, for the truth is that we always seek some acceptable level of endurable horror only to find that each time we accommodate ourselves to what we believe to be the worst that can happen this level of horror reveals itself as a temporary reprieve from an even greater horror, and so on, right up to the ultimate horror of death, which supposedly releases us but is actually the biggest horror of all. We think we can dilute the horror of life by pursuing some activity, by writing books or composing music, yet everything conspires to make this activity impossible, everything stops us in our tracks, until even our wish to continue becomes an absurdity. I have always thought that Faulkner's Nobel lecture, with its godawful valediction that man will not only endure but prevail, is actually a sinister wish, a bit of cant unworthy of Faulkner. "I had jotted down a few sentences," Bernhard writes of accepting the State Prize for Literature, "amounting to a small philosophical digression, the upshot of which was that man was a wretched creature and death a certainty."

In those years when Bernhard was writing *The Loser, Old Masters, Woodcutters,* and finally *Extinction,* I lived in a country where the obvious truth of Bernhard's writing was intolerable, a country where a writer like Bernhard or Sartre or Gombrowicz would only be reviled as a nest-fouler, a raging disease of a country bent on becoming Disney World, a country of advanced senility, a malignant nation of putrid happy endings, a country ruled by malevolent dwarfs, a country intoxicated by technology, a country crawling with desperate hypocrites, spiritually no different than Austria. "After I had delivered my speech," writes Bernhard, "which lasted altogether no more than three minutes, the minister, who had understood nothing of what I had said, indignantly jumped up from his seat and shook his fist in my face. Snorting with rage, he called me a cur in front of the whole assembly and then left the chamber, slamming the glass door behind him with such force that it shattered into a thousand fragments." It doesn't matter even slightly, I thought, if Nazis call themselves Christians, or National Socialist Catholics call themselves Episcopalian Republicans, or fascists call themselves leftists or what have you, the object remains the same, the whole movement of life in the modern world is to turn people into things and jam life into death. The Austrians have National Socialism in their past and have never recovered, and we have National Socialism in our future. Instead of facing life's realities, we bury ourselves in mysticism and sex, both of which, and certainly in combination, any pig with the will to power can manipulate for his own purposes.

Bearing in mind all the thoughts that Bernhard had made available to me, and not simply Bernhard, of course, but the writers he returned to again and again, Dostoevsky and Tolstoy, for example, and Kafka, always Kafka, and Schopenhauer, who is more important to me than Nietzsche, though I have never really understood a word of either Nietzsche or Schopenhauer, I opened the loose galleys of *Extinction*, expecting to read through the book at one sitting, but the idea that this was the "final novel" stopped me, just as the idea that *small g* was the final novel of Patricia Highsmith stopped me from finishing it for months and months. Once I've read *Extinction*, I thought, I will have read everything by Thomas Bernhard, except a few untranslated plays, which of course made me wonder why, throughout the many years that I traveled back and forth to Germany, I never learned German, all my efforts to learn German came to nothing, even when Schroeter offered me a major part in a Shakespeare play at the Freie Volksbuhne, if only I would learn the lines of the Schlegel translation of *The Comedy of Errors*. There are so many books by Ingeborg Bachmann and Christian Enzensberger that I could read if only I knew German, yet even when encouraged to learn German by one of Germany's eminent stage and film directors I failed miserably in my efforts, resenting Schroeter the whole time for casting me in a play translated from my native language, which made the job of learning it in German seem perverse and sinister. If I knew and could read German, I could read all of Bernhard, yet even when Schroeter hired a daily coach to rehearse my lines with me, I could never get them out of my mouth. Furthermore my coach, a television actor in a moronic crime series, resented Schroeter for giving a German role to an American, and therefore resented me, practically guaranteeing my inability to learn my lines. The same thing happened with the Ottinger film and the Schlingensief film; in the end all my lines had to be dubbed, and of course in the Ottinger film it was really only one line, which I have forgotten now and in any case never could speak. Faced with *Extinction*, I was also faced with my miserable botched job of learning German, as well as the sad thought that this was the "final novel," and also with the sudden apprehension that I might very well not be in the mood for Bernhard and so might put off, even indefinitely, the new book, *Extinction*, because for years I had ingested every word published by this author, as soon as it appeared, for years I couldn't get enough of Bernhard, my Bernhard mania, so-called, was well known to the people around me, for years I would read long passages of Bernhard to my friends on the telephone, whether they wanted to hear Bernhard or not.

"Swallowing and gulping down the body of Christ every day," I would read into the telephone, "was essentially no different from rendering daily homage to Adolf Hitler. While the two figures are totally different, I had the impression that at any rate the ceremonial was the same in intent and effect. And I was soon confirmed in my suspicions that our relations with Jesus Christ were in reality no different from those we had had with Adolf Hitler six months or a year earlier. When we consider the songs and choruses that are sung to the honour and glory of any so-called extraordinary personality, no matter whom— songs and choruses like those we used to sing at the boardinghouse during the Nazi period and later—we are bound to admit that, with slight differences in the wording, the texts are always the same and always sung to the same music. All in all these songs and choruses," I would read, "are simply an expression of stupidity, baseness, and lack of character on the part of those who sing them. The voice one hears in these songs and choruses is the voice of inanity—universal, worldwide inanity. All the educational crimes perpetrated against the young in educational establishments the world over," I would read, "are perpetrated in the name of some extraordinary personality, whether his name is Hitler or Jesus or whatever."

I could never get enough of Bernhard, yet I worried that perhaps by this time, faced with a final or ultimate Bernhard, I had had too much, that another long plunge into Bernhard's mind would leave me depressed and empty, which I already was, and Bernhard must have known, I thought, that he would die soon after finishing this novel, or even while writing it. I have noticed that after a certain moment in writing a novel even a healthy writer begins to suspect that he will die before finishing his book, and Bernhard's health was never good. Here he describes, in the words of his alter persona, receiving a telegram informing him of his parents' and his brother's death in a car accident, "unexpectedly outliving" these people he was supposed to predecease, and then all the complex feelings that go along with the "sudden deaths" of people you have hated for decades because everything you did in life disappointed and alienated them, people whom, nevertheless, you are obliged to love, or, rather, to carry some memory of love for with you from cradle to grave, and the incredibly sad history of these terrible families, where they have hated you and you have hated them for years and years, and now you have to lay them out and stick them in the ground, with all the ghastly so-called survivors in attendance. "Though my parents had been pathetic in every way," writes Bernhard, "I had always regarded them as demons, and now suddenly, overnight, they had shrunk to the ridiculous, grotesque photo that I had in front of me and was studying with the most shameless intensity."

It takes a superior honesty to write about such things, an honesty practically unheard of in contemporary writing, since contemporary writing avoids all necessary cruelty and specializes in gratuitous cruelty, especially where this topic of one's family is concerned. And this is especially true of American writing. I have read so many lying, utterly deceitful novels by Americans about their families, especially by the so-called black sheep of these families. "All the time they have nothing in their heads but portraying themselves," Bernhard writes, "in the most distasteful manner, though they are quite oblivious of this." So many utterly deceitful novels whose writers invent ghastly families that are actually more glamorous than the ghastly families they really had. Utterly deceitful novels that are camera-ready for some wretched motion picture. "Photography," Bernhard writes, "is a base passion that has taken hold of every continent and every section of the population, a sickness that afflicts the whole of humanity and is no longer curable." Of his mother he writes, "To my mother, with her craze for dolls, my sisters were actually talking dolls that could be made to laugh or cry when she wished and dressed and undressed when she wished, while her husband and son were puppets, whose strings she pulled whenever the mood took her." Of his father he writes, "My father joined the Nazi party at my mother's instigation, and it has to be added that he was not ashamed to wear his party badge quite openly on all occasions. . . . On Uncle Georg's last visit . . . he reminded my father that he had once been a member of the Nazi party, and not just briefly. Whereupon my father leaped up, smashed his soup plate on the table, and stormed out of the room."

One is fortunate if one's father was not a Nazi, I thought, but that's as far as it goes. One is driven away from these horrible families at the earliest age possible, and with luck they will never have the slightest idea what you do in life, will never read a word you write, since anything you write and anything you do is bound to disgust them. "Wherever you go in Austria today you're surrounded by lies," Bernhard writes, and, I thought, the same goes for here. "Wherever you look, you find only mendacity," Bernhard writes, and, I thought, the same goes for here. "Whoever you talk to, you're talking to a liar," writes Bernhard, truthfully. "This ridiculous country and this ridiculous state are basically not worth talking about, and to think about them is just a waste of time." And what American, unless he has a heart of stone, could not say the same about his own ridiculous country, his own ridiculous state: an utter waste of time.

"A literary event of the first magnitude," some editor has written on the flyleaf of *Extinction*, knowing perfectly well that literary events have no magnitude whatsoever anymore, that this unparalleled Thomas Bernhard is far too good a writer to occasion any sort of literary event in America, except perhaps a public bonfire in front of the town library, though he might see such a fire as yet another ignorant prize or award, or even an homage, this Thomas Bernhard who wrote, "Time destroys everything we do, whatever it is," and who certainly knew what he was talking about.

March 1996

GHETTO IN THE SKY

Samuel Delany's Black Whole

By Greg Tate

STARS IN MY POCKET LIKE GRAINS OF SAND

*Semiotics attempts to make explicit the implicit knowledge which
enables signs to have meaning, so it needs the reader not as a person
but as a function: the repository of the codes which account for the
intelligibility of the text. The reader becomes the name of the place
where the various codes can be located: a virtual site.*

—Jonathan Culler
The Pursuit of Signs: Semiotics,
Literature, Deconstruction

Yes, this is the ghetto.
—Donny Hathaway

Everybody's hip to what a B-Boy is, right? Well, one night I'm out with
my friend Pam from Los Angeles, part-time starlet and TV newswriter
on leave from her slave (read: gig) with ABC News. When I relate to her
that these two Negroes barreling up Sixth Avenue like to knock somebody down are called B-Boys, she cracks that out in El Lay, B-Boy is a
Sunset Boulevard drag queen. Then she claims her B-Boys are as deep
into hiphop as ours. The moral of this tale is: Pan across what seems to
be a world of difference and you'll find as many connections as disjunc-
tions. This in turn leads us to the subject at hand: the science fiction of
Samuel R. Delany, which for a quarter century now has explored what
happens when alien worldviews intersect, collide, or mesh. Take *Stars in
My Pocket Like Grains of Sand*, homeboy's new novel (him being black
and Harlem-born, mind you), in which humans share a society with an
alien race known as the evelm. Scaled, six-legged, taloned, winged, and
blessed with multiple tongues, the evelm live alongside cloned descendants of a human settler colony. In this social system, termed a nurtur-
ing stream culture, human and evelm children are brought up by a
mixture of human and evelm mothers.

I asked Delany if this conception of cooperative childrearing was based on an African communal model. Turns out instead it was inspired by the Harlem he grew up in, and his own extended family. Sure enough, any number of dialogues between the protagonist Marq Dyeth and his mothers seem full of the kind of warmhearted upbraiding feisty old black grandmothers and aunts like to hand out. Not coincidentally, almost all the major characters in this intergalactic epic are black. Delany told me, rather devilishly, that there's only one white character in the book and that the trick is to spot whitey. How much of a smile this conceit brings to your lips depends on your sensitivity to SF universes full of a zillion species of extraterrestrials and only caucasoid humans. Delany plays with this convention even more explicitly when Dyeth reflects on the strange-looking boy who turned up one day in his stream's sandbox: "At that age, I did not know that at one time perhaps a fifth of the human race had such pale skins and such colored and textured hair—and were called caucasian . . ." Thinking back on that scene from a perspective deeper in the text, you have to wonder whether Dyeth's fascination with this boy had to do with his race or with his nail biting, a trait Dyeth finds arousing in potential sexual partners—who in his constellation are always male.

Besides being black Delany is gay, and in his books sexual preference figures as prominently as racial identity, if not more so. Dyeth's love interest in the new novel is Rat Korga, former slave and lone survivor of a mysteriously annihilated world, who has been computed by the Web to be Dyeth's perfect erotic object out to a few decimal places. The Web, by the way, is one of three political factions waging the Information Wars over the 6000 planets in the novel's galaxy. The Family and the Sygn are the other two. Their enmity stems from a long-standing dispute: "The Family trying to establish the dream of a classic past . . . on a world that may never even have existed in order to achieve cultural stability, . . . the Sygn committed to the living interaction and difference between each woman and each world from which the right stability and play may flower." And the Web, an arm of the Sygn, being the interstellar agency in charge of the general flow of information about the universe. The Web manages this flow through a technique called GI—General Information—which maps and circuits synapses, then accesses them to a vast galactic computer library. Among the features of this system are instantaneous reading and comprehension of poetry and the option of calling up data to fill in the gaps when communication bogs down between you and an alien.

That all this makes the book seem less like some futuristic homo-erotica, or Toni Morrison in the 28th century, and more like the science-fiction novel as semiotics enterprise will come as no surprise to those readers who know that besides being black, gay, and a feminist to boot, Delany is a structuralist critic. He speaks of science fiction not as a genre but as a form of *paraliterature,* and has written a book, *The American Shore,* that's a 300-page exegesis on a 20-page short story by Thomas Disch. (When I told him his various philosophies convey the sense that he's out to become the ultimate ghetto writer, he replied that his mother was always saying he had a ghetto mentality.) Delany uses the cold war between the Family and the Sygn to signify on two systems of dictatorship—one authoritarian, one libertarian—and how they structure human and alien possibility. Asked if he felt a kinship with Eastern European writers because of their treatment of cultural alienation, Delany said he was more intrigued by their depiction of how social engineering inevitably leads to social decay. He felt this brought a sense of reality to their fiction missing from traditionally utopian American SFs.

Given his concern for the dialectics of social organization, a case can be made for Delany the Marxist. His work has always seemed to play with one of Uncle Karl's more famous dicta—to wit, the future of woman will be a future of class struggle. My favorite Delany novel, *Nova,* besides being a space-opera reworking of *Moby-Dick* and the quest for the Holy Grail, presents future societies full of class divisions and class antagonisms. Following his own belief that SF doesn't so much represent reality as misrepresent it, Delany makes cultural rather than economic oppression the cause of those antagonisms. He envisions a 31st century where the inequities and alienation brought on by class division of labor and relative work-value have been handily dispensed with:

> *The entire sense of self-control and self-responsibility that man acquired during the Neolithic Revolution when he first learned to plant grain and domesticate animals was seriously threatened. The threat had been coming since the Industrial Revolution and many people had pointed it out before Ashton Clark. But Ashton Clark went one step further. If the situation of a technological society was such that there could be no direct relation between a man's work and his* modus vivendi, *other than money, at least he must feel he is directly changing things by his work . . . technology had reached the point where it could do something about what Ashton Clark was saying. Souquet invented his plugs and sockets, and neural-response circuits, and the whole basic technology by which a machine could be controlled by direct nervous impulse, the same impulses that cause your hand or foot to move. And there was a revolution in the concept of work. All major industrial work began to be broken down into jobs that could be machined "directly" by man. . . . Now a man went to a factory, plugged himself in, and he could push the raw materials into the factory with his left foot, shape thousands on thousands of precise parts with one hand, assemble them with the other, and shove out a line of finished products with his right foot, having inspected them all with his own eyes. And he was a*

*much more satisfied worker ... Ashton Clark, it has been said, was the
philosopher who returned humanity to the working man. Under this system, much of the endemic mental illness caused by feelings of alienation
left society. The transformation turned war from a rarity to an impossibility and—after the initial upset—stabilized the economic web of worlds
for the last eight hundred years.*

The flipside of this futuristic Marxist kingdom come is revealed when
the gypsy minstrel, Mouse (kind of a cross between Jimi Hendrix and
Huck Finn), tells how on Earth gypsies were hunted and slaughtered for refusing to literally plug in to the homogenizing cultural mainstream. Which
you can read if you choose (and I do) as Delany's way of saying that even
in the 31st century it'll be open season on niggers of one kind or another.

Considerations of work, race, and place in society don't take a backseat in Delany's new novel either. The bulk of it is Dyeth's first-person
narrative about his work as an Industrial Diplomat (someone who facil-
itates exportation of industrial materials between alien cultures). Dyeth
gets to travel to other worlds and meet interesting new extraterrestrials in
a universe where fewer than 3 per cent of the inhabitants of one world ever
set foot on another because both the Family and the Web frown on interstellar travel. (Otherworldly curiosity has to be satisfied by a technique
known as vaurine projection, which functions as a kind of interactive trav-
elogue experience.) Dyeth's favorite rumination is on how alienating an
alien culture remains no matter how much GI you got going for you. He
discourses on things like how on one world it's taboo not to accept a gift
offering yet tantamount to asking for a death sentence to accept the *gift*, or
how humans in the Family-controlled part of his world are involved in
violent conflict with the evelm because they don't care to make genetic
distinctions between them and the low-order flying dragons and therefore consider relations between evelm and humans bestiality. Family
members also consider relations between humans of the same gender to
be a form of perversion. The evelm, by the way, have three sexual types—
male, female, and neuter—all of whom are capable of bearing children,
though for the males this reproductive rarity often proves fatal. The
humans in Dyeth's stream aren't products of direct egg-sperm relations
but of cloning. Stream culture is matriarchal and personal pronouns
refer to both males and females in the feminine gender. (Human/evelm
mutation has not been experimented with, case you were wondering.)

The specter of racism rears up in the book's third-person prologue,
which describes Rat Korga's years as a slave on Rhyonon before the
planet was immolated. One of the intriguing things about this chapter
is how similar Delany's satirical handling of slavery and slave mentality
is to Ishmael Reed's and Ralph Ellison's. Just check the book's open-

ing—"Of course, you will be a slave . . . but you will be happy with who you are and with the tasks the world sets before you." Korga hears this from the doctor who gives him the synapse-snipping operation known as Radical Anxiety Termination, which not only makes for happy slaves but slaves incapable of reasoning, information processing, or self-preservation. Korga nearly incinerates himself walking across the hot side of his planet when one of his masters misdirects him there. He also lets two other slaves fester and die because RATs can't handle inductive reasoning or emotional identification with other slaves. For his negligence he's beaten unmercifully with a steel pipe by one of his female masters, while sympathetic males cower in revulsion. A scene which ain't exactly what you'd call an endorsement of the sexually liberated female—but then one of the subtexts of the novel is that black women are going to be the folk who conquer the stars and gonna bust some balls along the way to doing it. (Hence on Rhyonon the terms "bitch" and "dog" are reversed, women deploying bitch as a trope of sexual power, men wearing the dog collar as a mark of impotence and shame.)

These extrapolations on postfeminism move from the high dramatic to the high satirical when Korga is "liberated" by a bohemian who has designs on him. She frees the seven-foot, herpes-scarred Korga to stud for her but doesn't realize that he's gay. This turns out to be of minor consequence since she doesn't really desire a sex slave; what she wants is mastery of a man who's read everything she's read—"I want to control such a man, make him lie down in the sand and suck my toes." She gives Korga a glove which imprints reams of interstellar texts on his brain (we're talking apocryphal and Borgesian volumes of the stuff here, like *The Mantichorio* with its 137,000 lines of alternating heptameters and hexameters and "the complete extant work of the twenty-two-year-old prodigy Steble, her five multicharacter dialogues, the handful of papers on algebraic algrammaticalities, the surviving fragments of her journal for the '88-'89 concert season, and the final impassioned letters sent from her deathbed in the disease-infested Jabahia Prison complex . . .") and for a brief time allows Korga a cosmic sense of his mind and the universe. When his liberator is captured for making off with a slave, Korga loses his glove and all his newfound consciousness. Returned to slavery, he is less content, and even begins instructing other slaves to point their hands to the stars.

Reading this reminded me of the passage from Frederick Douglass's autobiography where he talks about how his master didn't believe slaves should learn how to read because it would only make them unhappy. Douglass didn't regret literacy, but came to realize that his master was right: An intelligent slave is a more unhappy slave. Delany's SF variation on Ellison, Morrison, Reed, and the slave narrative confronts American racial history more directly than any of his other work, even *Dhalgren*. If you've read that 879-page opus, this statement may strike you as rather skewed: *Dhalgren,* after all, is set in an American city after an apocalyptic black uprising has driven its white citizens away and left the run of the town to black gangs and the various countercultural types who wander in to slum around. Delany savvily realized that a science-fiction novel about blacks doesn't have to be set in another galaxy far far away—here and now is weird enough. But the blacks in the book are peripheral to the walking dream state of his amnesiac antihero Kidd, who experiences them more as products of his interior landscape than as characters with lives outside of his head. Rat Korga's prologue is different because it dramatically parodies the victimization of blacks by American racism.

In his criticism, Delany often mentions that he wants to imagine futures where the race question has been resolved. As an adolescent, he had an epiphanic moment reading Heinlein's *Starship Troopers*; it came when the hero of the book, whom Delany had assumed was white, is described in passing as a person of color. I told Delany I received a similar jolt reading *Starboard Wine* when I came across a speech he gave at the Studio Museum of Harlem. "We need images of tomorrow," he said, "and our people need them more than most." The "our people" business surprised me because it was the first time I'd come across anything in his work that indicated he openly identified with, well, the rest of us colored peoples.

I've always found Delany's racially defused futures problematic because they seem to deny the possibility that the affirmative aspects of black American culture and experience could survive assimilation. By which I mean not just the obvious things like the genius present in black music, speech, and style but the humanity and range of personas born of black people's sense of communion. Until I read that passage, I figured Delany for if not an Oreo then somebody who wasn't interested in being labeled black. And while his fiction is full of black and other protagonists of color (Rydra Wong, Oriental poet, linguist, and starship commander of *Babel II*; Lorq Von Ray, the interstellar mulatto of *Nova*; Kidd, the native American antihero of *Dhalgren*; Lo Lobey, black mutant Orpheus of *The Einstein Intersection*) the race of these characters is not at the core of their cultural identity. Which used to bug me out like a mug because what I expected from our one black science-fiction writer was SF which envisioned the future of black culture as I'd define it, from a more or less nationalist stance. (That Delany was for so long the only black science-fiction writer reminds me of Eugene Genovese's observation that black Americans have tended toward pragmatic rather than prophetic leadership.) The trick thang about Delany is that while his black characters don't wear their negritude on their sleeves, they're not exactly upstanding members of tomorrow's black bourgeoisie either. Consider how many of them have been poets, musicians, and/or outlaws whose art and intelligence have gained them social mobility within the dominant culture and the option of rejecting its values whenever it suited them.

One thing I've learned from Delany is that black writers need to address not only the complexity of the black community but the complexity of the world. By sidestepping the race question, he's been able to criticize sexual, racial, and economic oppression in America and depict a wider range of human, alien, and mutant characters than you'll find in books by other black writers—not to mention books by other American writers, except for Pynchon and DeLillo. And as in *Gravity's Rainbow* and *Ratner's Star*, some of the most lyrical and stirring passages in Delany's work fuse the juncture between art, technology, and social science. Here's one from the chapter in *SIMPLGOS*, where Dyeth describes Korga's rescue by the Web:

> *The synapse-jamming technique first surfaced on a moon of Rhyonon's cousin world, Jesper, here in the Tyon-Omega system, as a medical method for dealing with certain social intractables. It was squelched by the Web as inhuman and was finally superseded, on that moon, by a program of drug therapy . . . it resurfaced as part of the practice of an extremely violent art form: For some twenty-five years during Rhyonon's second century many of the artists in various geosectors of Rhyonon's southern hemisphere, when the emotional stringencies of their craft became too great, would voluntarily subject themselves to this form of mental suicide—during which time the practice gained great social prestige. . . . At some time in the past Korga had apparently been offered, by a benevolent society, a chance at what had been up till recently, on his world, the* ave atque vale *of artists and priests: the chance to have the paths in the brain through which worry forces us to grow closed over forever and detours about those troublesome crossroads left permanently open. . . . It's precisely those 'anxiety' channels which Radical Anxiety Termination blocks. . . . Rat Korga will never get all those little neurological transmitters wired in the crevices in the top five vertebrae that will hook into whatever local GI system happens to be around.*

This means that Korga's mind can't be controlled by the Web, a typical Delany bit of irony: The same operation which made Korga a slave gives him freedom in an overdetermined universe. Korga gets access to GI's computers without allowing them access to his brain through a batch of hand rings made for Vondramach Okk, legendary dictator, poet, world-conqueror, and bohemian sybarite. Her connection with Korga sets up messianic possibilities Delany will undoubtedly deliver on when the second volume of his SF diptych appears late next year and, needless to say, I can't wait.

February 1985

UNDER NIGHTWOOD

By Edmund White

DJUNA: THE LIFE AND WORK OF DJUNA BARNES
By Phillip Herring

NIGHTWOOD: THE ORIGINAL VERSION AND RELATED
DRAFTS
By Djuna Barnes
Edited and with an introduction by Cheryl J. Plumb

For American writers growing up in the 1950s and '60s (as I did), there
were few examples of the other tradition in our literature, that is, of
native fiction other than the action and dialogue adventure realism
epitomized by Hemingway. Djuna Barnes, the author of *Nightwood*—a
slim novel about American expatriates in Paris, about lesbians and a
male transvestite and a dubious, dolorous Austrian aristocrat—was perhaps the most prominent signpost pointing in another, more mysterious
direction.

Barnes had concocted her novel out of Elizabethan poetry and
Gothic props, out of a rush of imagery inspired by Synge's play *Riders to
the Sea*, a vivid sense of melodrama linked to Emily Brontë, and an
unlikely blend of satire with tragedy. She had few antecedents in America—Hawthorne's and Melville's haunted fiction, suggestive of doom
and hinting at allegory, Henry James's "supersubtle fry" maneuvering
dangerously in Italian or English salons—and in the 20th century she
could look toward only Gertrude Stein, who'd broken with realism in a
far more radical way, and the poets Pound and Eliot, who like Barnes
had left America for Europe, not as skirt chasers fleeing Prohibition,
but as genuine students of world culture.

In our day, American fiction has become monosyllabic, regional,
and catatonic (the final decadent version of the bluff realistic tradition
and a style in synch with contemporary American isolationism and self-
absorption), but Djuna Barnes remains a reminder of the Road Not Yet
Taken—international, devious, perverse, verbally abundant, psychologically subtle.

For two centuries Americans have been undecided whether their destiny is to inherit the European (or African or Asian) past or to invent a uniquely American future. Pound decided to take the past and "Make It New" according to the abrupt, gnomic strategies of streamlined American modernism. Djuna Barnes, like Melville, had no sense of historic or cultural restrictions, and just as in *Moby Dick* Shakespearean language is joined to a Yankee plot and Christian symbols are invoked but not embraced, in the same way in *Nightwood* an artificial, elevated language is put in the mouths of contemporary American women who are pursuing a tragic destiny. In her own way, Barnes is as syncretic as Pound.

Perhaps Barnes's work gave permission to Jane Bowles to write *Two Serious Ladies*, which may be high-flown, but which is every bit as original and spooky as *Nightwood*; Barnes's writing also cleared a space for Edward Dahlberg's beautiful, touching, and utterly improbable memoir, *Because I Was Flesh*, a recasting of his family story (his mother was a barber in St. Louis) in the terms of Greek mythology. Today the poetic and visionary novelist Carole Maso reads as though she'd been enabled by Barnes's example. In fact, one could make a case that American lesbians have written some of the most exalted books of the 20th century—Nathalie Barney (who wrote in French), Gertrude Stein, Willa Cather, Djuna Barnes, Jane Bowles, and Carole Maso.

Barnes, of course, was not only a superlative (and unprecedented) writer, but also a legend. According to the myth, she was supported for years by Peggy Guggenheim (to whom *Nightwood* is dedicated), edited by T. S. Eliot, befriended by James Joyce (who told her to write about the ordinary in fiction and the extraordinary in journalism). She lived on the Left Bank in Paris in the '20s and '30s before returning to Greenwich Village, where she settled in at Patchin Place (one of her neighbors was e. e. cummings). She lived on and on but after *Nightwood* wrote just one important work, *The Antiphon*, a verse play that Dag Hammarskjold translated and managed to have staged in 1961 at Stockholm's Royal Dramatic Theater. She became an old curmudgeon whom Darryl Pinckney worked for and describes in *High Cotton*. She created endless problems for Peter Klappert, who wrote a magnificent poetic monologue for her character Dr. O'Connor in his book-length poem, *The Idiot Princess of the Last Dynasty*. The late Howard Moss, former poetry editor of *The New Yorker*, once told me that he published two of her poems and then was summoned to her apartment. She complained about her poverty, resisted all his advice, and when he told her how much he admired her, grumbled that all her problems were due to that damn Tom Eliot who'd said that she had no talent (in fact T. S. Eliot had written a blurb for *The Antiphon*: "It might be said of Miss Barnes, who is incontestably one of the most original writers of our time, that never has so much genius been combined with so little talent").

Barnes, alas, has not been fortunate in her biographers. Andrew Field, the same man who turned in a strangely misleading biography of Nabokov, took on Barnes in 1983 in a superficial study called *Djuna: The Life and Times of Djuna Barnes.* Now Phillip Herring has joined his excellent research to an almost total inability to organize his material. He repeats the same anecdote several times, jumps back and forth in time, and seems overwhelmed by what was essentially an uneventful life. Nor is his heavy-handed style one that would have pleased his subject. What would Barnes have thought of this sentence, for instance: "She was born in 1892, just north of West Point, on the Hudson River, to an English mother, who wished to be a celebrated poet, an American father, an itinerant musician, painter and writer who was content to be supported by his own mother's journalism while he fiddled and sowed his seed wherever a field was in want of a plowshare"? This quotation is a good representation of the Herring style—impacted information poked into one long grammatically complex sentence complete with a final stab at pedantic humor. Nor are we reassured when Herring tells us: "The writing of this biography thus springs from my own ignorance and confusion, and from my certain knowledge that this important writer has eluded us modernists so completely that her textual strategies continued to perform tricks while she hid behind a curtain of obscurity, smiling at our gropings." That "us modernists" and "gropings" are worthy of one of Nabokov's buffoons. Elsewhere Herring, usually suitably self-effacing, hazards a bit of questionable philosophizing: "Given that life is suffering, the greatest crime would be procreation, which seems to give homosexuality the edge as a preferred lifestyle, since it promotes the extinction of the human species."

But Herring does at least tell his tale and in his version the Barnes legend takes on substance. She was born into a weird bohemian menage. Her father was a ne'er-do-well who kept changing his name and whose talents included house building, opera composing, wood carving, painting, and inventing (he published a pamphlet about a bicycle-driven airship). "Djuna" was another of his inventions, a corruption of a name in Eugene Sue's *The Wandering Jew*; when Shirley Walton, a friend of mine, opened a feminist bookshop near Patchin Place named Djuna Books, Barnes phoned her up hopping mad, denounced Shirley, feminism, and the "theft" of her name. She even said that her father had given her such an original name because he didn't want her to be saddled with a name shared and thereby sullied by other people. Three of his sons he named Thurn, Saxon, and Shangar.

Her father's fecklessness, his espousal of free love, the many children he spawned, and his energetic promiscuity (he was a sort of erotic circuit-rider and Djuna later claimed he kept a sponge tied to his saddle to mop his genitals as he rode about the country between assignations)— all these traits made the girl come to depise procreation. She later wrote a friend that "father and his bastard children and mistresses had thrown me off marriage and babies."

The evidence is shadowy but her father, apparently, either seduced Djuna himself when she was an adolescent or arranged for one of his cronies to do the job. In any event, to her it seemed like rape and an experience so ghastly that she was still brooding about it half a century later when she wrote *The Antiphon* (published in 1958). She told the poet George Barker that "she believed her Lesbianism to have been the consequence of her father raping her when she was a very young girl" (although the theory about lesbianism sounds uncharacteristic and Barker may just have been working up an after-dinner story).

The decisive influence in Djuna's childhood was her paternal grandmother, Zadel Barnes, a woman who began to publish when she was 13 and who supported with her pen her shiftless son and his brood (his household at one point counted 13 members).

Zadel was a spiritualist who conducted seances in which she impersonated the dead. She was also a poet of the John Greenleaf Whittier school (typically, she writes: "Speed hither, winds, and blend in noble mirth/The many chorded harmonies of earth . . .). In 1880 *McCall's* magazine sent her as a correspondent to London, where she became friendly with Speranza Wilde (Oscar's mother) and Karl Marx's daughter Eleanor. (Zadel introduced them to each other—there's a meeting that would make a good subject for our poet Richard Howard!)

In *The Antiphon* Djuna describes the Zadel figure as an "abolitionist, free thinker, *raconteur*, abstainer, known for her turbans: seizures; wit." She was ill with cancer, exhausted from a life of overwork, reduced to writing begging letters to the rich and famous people she'd known in her palmier days.

Barnes's biographer toys with the Oprah-idea that Djuna may have also been seduced by her grandmother. Djuna slept beside Zadel during her first 15 years and named her grandmother's breasts "Redlero" and "Kedler." Zadel drew funny pictures for Djuna in letters in which one nude woman is shown lying on top of another. Zadel called breasts "Pink Tops" or "P.T.s." Not much of a dossier for an incest inquest, especially considering how passionately Djuna loved her grandmother; in 1935 she wrote a friend, "I always thought I was my grandmother, and now I am almost right." Nor do participants in incest speak so openly and cheerfully of their partners. Professor Herring has apparently never read the Mozart family correspondence, full of scatology, nor other intimate letters written before the universal id was repressed by Freud.

Certainly Djuna grew up in a strange household in which her mother (who'd been raised in a family of English gentry) had to work like a servant and failed to disguise her resentment of her husband's mistress (later his second wife). In this household Zadel read out loud from all the standard authors while her beloved son was scoring an opera, writing a verse drama, or seducing a neighbor—and the children ran wild. Barnes received only the most rudimentary education, and after her mother separated from her father and moved to the Bronx (in 1912 when Barnes was 20), the gifted young woman became the main support of her mother and brothers by working as a journalist for the *Brooklyn Daily Eagle*.

By 1915, Djuna had left her mother's house and moved to Greenwich Village (first to 42 Washington Square South, then to 220 West 14th Street, finally 86 Greenwich Avenue). She had a number of adventures with men, one common-law marriage, and a two-year live-in love affair with Courtenay Lemon, alcoholic drama critic and reader of manuscripts for the Theatre Guild. In 1917 she wondered out loud in print why "there existed no man, young or old, who could draw the slightest, faintest word of interest from me apart from my drawing or some abstract thing connected with themselves." She attended art school, met the most visible Village bohemians, made her living by interviewing theater celebrities and even the evangelist Billy Sunday. She managed to publish *The Book of Repulsive Women*, which she later renounced. And she bore the crushing burden of supporting her mother and siblings.

In 1921 she was sent as a correspondent to Paris and soon met the love of her life, Thelma Wood, another American. The affair in its strongest form lasted some seven years but afterward Barnes was never able to escape from the obsessive thought (which she expressed in a letter): "I have *had* my great love, there will never be another." Barnes frequently told the overinquisitive, "I was never a lesbian—I only loved Thelma Wood." Thelma was as heavy a drinker as Barnes; when she became really drunk Thelma would comb the Paris cafes looking for partners of either sex. Barnes demanded that Thelma report on all her infidelities, but Wood often couldn't comply, so total were her blackouts. Thelma was nearly six feet tall, wore boots, and the two women must have made quite an impression as they strode the boulevards in black capes and men's hats; Djuna said she loved Thelma because she resembled Zadel, Djuna's grandmother. Djuna persuaded Thelma to take up silverpoint, a medium in which she drew plants and animals with a modicum of success.

Eventually, Thelma left Djuna for a rich woman, Henriette Metcalf, with whom she stayed for about 16 years. The failure of Barnes's affair with Thelma was the direct inspiration for *Nightwood*, which she wrote largely at Hayford Hall, an English house Peggy Guggenheim rented in the summers of 1932 and 1933. There Barnes was encouraged by Peggy, a vague dilettante who seldom finished a sentence but who had a genuine passion for the arts, and her lover John Ferrar Holms, a brilliant alcoholic who knew everything and did nothing. More important, the household included Emily Coleman, an American novelist (her book *The Shutter of Snow* was about her stay in an insane asylum) who turned herself inside out over several years helping Djuna organize, complete, and finally place her masterpiece.

The Dalkey Archive Press has just published a new, definitive edition of *Nightwood*, which gives the related drafts and restores many of the cuts censored from the original manuscript because they were considered too risque at the time, either by Emily Coleman or by the editor she found, T. S. Eliot at Faber & Faber. Everything about this strange novel was problematical, starting with the title. Earlier titles included "Bow Down" (now the title of section one), "Anatomy of the Night," and so on. Although Andrew Field credits Eliot with coming up with *Nightwood*, in fact it was Barnes herself, who wrote Coleman on June 23, 1935: " 'Nightwood,' like that, one word, it makes it sound like night-shade, poison and night and forest, and tough, in the meaty sense, and simple yet singular. . . ." Later Barnes discovered that the name could be a reference to Thelma—"Nigh T. Wood—low, thought of it the other day. Very odd."

According to the introduction to the Dalkey version by Cheryl J. Plumb, the novel may have been first conceived as early as 1927, the year of the first breakup with Thelma. The book was rejected by many publishers and went through three full drafts, but at no point did Barnes want to resort to what she called the "safety" of realism. What she did accept were Coleman's suggestions to simplify and unify the action. For instance, Matthew O'Connor's long disquisition about love, "Watchman, What of the Night?," the bravura center of the book, at one point was addressed not to Nora (the Barnes stand-in), who is hopelessly in love with Robin (the Thelma character), but to another woman altogether, Catherine. Coleman was responsible for the condensation of the text. It was she who convinced Eliot (whom she originally approached through the poet Edwin Muir) to give it a careful reading.

On April 27, 1936, Eliot wrote Coleman that he thought *Nightwood* could be published if changes could be made to avoid the suppression of publication by the censor. Previous commentators have assumed that Eliot made extensive editorial changes in the manuscript, but Plumb has shown that most of the changes were suggested by Coleman: "All in all, the editorial hand was light; certainly because he anticipated potential difficulty with censors, Eliot blurred sexual, particularly homosexual, references and a few points that put religion in an unsavory light. However, meaning was not changed substantially, though the character of the work was adjusted, the language softened." For instance, in the original text Dr. O'Connor asks, "Or is confessing bottom up (though keeping the thread in the tatting), to a priest who has the face of a butcher, and the finger of our own right hand placed where it best pleases?" Eliot suppressed this passage because of its sexual and anticlerical ring, but in the Dalkey edition it is restored—as are countless other details. Or when O'Connor says that he haunts the *pissoir* "in search of my man," just as "I've seen the same thing work in a girl looking for her woman," Eliot suppressed the two homosexual references.

Despite these changes, *Nightwood* remained even in its original version an overwhelming, anarchic cry of passion (Nora's love for Robin) and an ingenious threnody about the disreputable nature of desire (take the scene where O'Connor tries to masturbate at St. Merri's church but remains impotent). The passage is worth quoting in full because it demonstrates better than any paraphrase the linguistic drama that animates every page of the edgy cri de coeur: "I was crying and striking my left hand against the *prie-Dieu*, and all the while Tiny O'Toole was lying in a swoon. I said, 'I have tried to seek, and I only find.' I said, 'It is I, my Lord, who know there's beauty in any permanent mistake like me. Haven't I said it so? But,' I says, 'I'm not able to stay permanent unless you help me, oh Book of Concealment! *C'est le plaisir qui me bouleverse!* The roaring lion goes forth, seeking his own fury! So tell me, what is permanent of me, me or him?' And there I was in the empty, almost empty church, all the people's troubles flickering in the little lights all over the place. And I said, 'This would be a fine world, Lord, if you could get everybody out of it.' And there I was holding Tiny, bending over and crying, asking the question until I forgot, and went on crying, and I put Tiny away then, like a ruined bird, and went out of the place and walked looking at the stars that were twinkling and I said, 'Have I been simple like an animal, God, or have I been thinking?'"

Nightwood is in fact haunted by animals, which provide most of the defining metaphors or similes for the human characters. Jenny Petherbridge, for instance, races like a squirrel in her cage, whereas when Robin Vote is first introduced it's at a circus and a lioness crouches in its cage before her and appears to weep. In the last scene, Robin even couples with a dog. But this fierce animality is matched by a loneliness, a yearning, that seems tragically human. One could say that the characters in *Nightwood* are like those Egyptian beings that combine human and animal characteristics to produce deities.

November 1995

TRANNY SUBSTANTIATION

William Goyen's Arcadio

By Darcey Steinke

I am going to tell you about Arcadio the hermaphrodite transvestite, and how she escaped the China Boy brothel located over the Chinese restaurant alongside the dead river in Memphis, Tennessee, but first I have a story of my own to tell. Now this happened at a party in the late '80s in the days before Miss Hogg went to work for Courtney Love. I was still waitressing at the Mafia restaurant in Brooklyn where the basement was full of black-market stereos and the bar was littered with small-time dons in toupees and Elvis sunglasses. Miss Hogg was my boyfriend's roommate and every Saturday night as we woke from our disco nap he would come traipsing through the doorway wearing his blond wig, a full face of makeup, a pig's snout, his nurse's uniform, and white Hush Puppies and parade around our bed. At first this shocked me—that a chubby, balding guy could transform himself so thoroughly into a creature of bovine dimensions—though eventually I got used to Miss Hogg biting the heads off Barbie dolls and intentionally catching her hair on fire while eating Hostess fruit pies.

But my story isn't about Miss Hogg's excesses. This story centers on the night I danced with Connie Girl, the tall black luminous drag queen. As a minister's daughter, I had been raised on images of the smooth-bodied, flowing-haired Jesus as well as told, before I could even speak, that a guardian angel hovered sparkly and dreamy-eyed against the ceiling of my bedroom. So I was particularly susceptible to Connie Girl's thin shoulders and glittering makeup. *What else is an angel but a beautiful man in all-out divine drag?* I had watched her over many Saturday nights, in her touching, waiflike disco outfits—sequined tube tops and latex stretch pants—dancing with her Puerto Rican boyfriend. It wasn't only her glamour that affected me, but also her singular sadness; she seemed homesick for her own planet. And while I always wanted to ask her to dance (me of the messy ponytail and moth-eaten, leaf-raking sweater), I was way too intimidated. But one night, emboldened by a particularly good hit of Ecstasy and charmed by her '70s ensemble—

platform sandals, teardrop-pocket jeans, and a ribbed purple skinny—I worked up the courage.

To my complete surprise she acquiesced immediately, and as we took the dance floor, the mirror ball sent out little leaflets of light and I felt like the prince in the Disney movie, dancing for the first time with my slender, glass-slippered Cinderella. Connie Girl didn't move much, but the strands of her hair swayed around her face like a seductive veil and I felt mesmerized by her transitory image as it shifted from girl to boy. My mind couldn't place her within its pre-established IN or OUT boxes, so Connie Girl hovered in that limbo, neither man nor woman but a shimmering changeling with high teacup breasts and shapely teenage-boy biceps.

For the few moments that dance lasted, Connie Girl was my own private Arcadio. Though Arcadio, as created by William Goyen, the master Texan storyteller, is an actual hermaphrodite and a creature containing nuances of both divinity and vulgarity, a creature tormented by the sad story of Jesucristo and the particularities of both male and female lust. Goyen's Arcadio is so vividly rendered that, like Hamlet before her, she has escaped the pages of her book and I often think I see her late at night, bathing her dual genitalia in the stone fountains around New York.

Goyen, born in 1915, died just before *Arcadio* was published in 1983. He was a friend of Katherine Anne Porter, a supporter of his first novel, *The House of Breath*. As well as his numerous novels, Goyen wrote erotically charged and gothic short stories. In my favorite, "In the Icebound Hothouse," an insane poet tells the tale of a nude coed who jumps from a brick academic building, shattering the roof of the orchid-filled, icebound hothouse. Goyen's work in general, and *Arcadio* in particular, isn't for those who favor the demure cancer-in-Connecticut novels or the ones that raise 12-Step lingo and psychobabble into an idiotic poetry. The language of *Arcadio* is operatic: a mixture of the King James Bible, African-American and Mexican dialects, as well as channeled communiques from the world of the dead. Every page is permeated with a de Sadean eroticism that threatens to upset the social order and implode the universe: "My breasts was frosted with semen my eyes glued with that glue my stomach was spread with it like a mayonnaise, my hair set in a marcel of come and my face a running icing that strung down to my neck . . . and the pieces of men and women like soggy peaches broken open sopping against me."

Arcadio's struggle to unite with God through the conduit of sex is central to the novel's theme of sin and redemption. After leaving the China Boy brothel, Arcadio goes to work at a freak show. There, he sits on a golden throne inside a jeweled wagon and reveals himself to paying customers. One day a little white Bible is passed over the red velvet curtain that encircles his chair and with the help of Eddy Gonzales, an atheist dwarf, he reads about the struggle of Jesucristo and is able to free himself from carnality and begin his journey into the id. First he searches for his whore mother, whom he remembers in her winking green dress and bruised green shoes, then for his flesh-fiend father who lets his member lead him through life day after day, like a dog on a rope.

Arcadio's trip eventually blossoms out to include a vivid cast of eccentric characters—among them Hondo Holloway, who is looking for Ethelreda, the gigantic sister of his tiny former girlfriend; and Tomasso, Arcadio's half brother, who was born in a jailhouse and now sings with the Deliverance Church gospel choir.

Though all those quested for are eventually found, the finding is not entirely satisfactory and Arcadio realizes that he has actually been searching all the while for God. This realization helps him to forgive his family and accept his sexual duality and enter the spiritual realm. "I have come up living from those nails, the woman part has closed up like a flower closes and the man has given up its bitter sting on me. They are *espléndido*, at splendid rest." Arcadio's quieted genitalia are a metaphor for the unification of the tormented and divided soul. It's also why androgyny is so powerful—why drag queens like Connie Girl are so sublime; they embody a blendedness many of us long for. Even Jesus, in the gnostic gospel of Thomas, teaches that combining the sexes can bring on salvation. "When you make the two one, and when you make the inside like the outside, and the outside like the inside, and the upper like the lower and when you make male and female into a single one, then you will enter the kingdom."

All Goyen's work, while drenched in sex, is ultimately about the soul's progress toward redemption, and like a lot of novels that have been out of favor in the last 20 years, it's not particularly politically correct; aging women are referred to as "old trout," and there's a whole lot of fucking. Not the soft-focus heterosexual variety but all-out animalistic copulation. Worst of all in terms of the contemporary literary scene, *Arcadio* is filled with God-hunger. Angels hover overhead—not the sweet sexless Hallmark-card variety, but huge sexual beings with "hair of light streaming" and eyes glowing as lanterns. Arcadio longs to unite, through them, with the Godhead. This is where the power of *Arcadio* lies: By the end of the novel, as he kneels down to unbuckle the white-haired angel's silver shoes, we glimpse, not some freaky hermaphrodite, but our own flawed and yearning selves.

April 1999

THE SOLOIST

Albert Murray's Blues People

By Joe Wood

THE SEVEN LEAGUE BOOTS
THE BLUE DEVILS OF NADA: A CONTEMPORARY
AMERICAN APPROACH TO AESTHETIC STATEMENT

Lesson 1: Albert Murray is not famous.

Murray has long argued his opinions with the ferocity of a dragon fighter, ever since the publication of his first book, *The Omni-Americans,* in 1970. Back then he was trying to outpoint the youthful black Barakas of the day, trying to peel away the long shadow of his friend Ralph Ellison, trying to find his own voice for fiction at age 54. Twenty-five years later there is a shelf of accolades: a National Book Award nomination, a membership in the Century Club, publication of one of his titles in the Modern Library series. And yet, Murray remains something of an unknown. He is an unattended teacher, the last of an endangered breed of literary-political thinkers.

The hope for a change in the weather is minimal. Except: National fascination with well-read black people (see "black public intellectuals") is at a postmodern high, perhaps commensurate with the equally popular notion of black intellectual inferiority (see Charles Murray). Except: Interest in black conservatism, that species of political behavior often lauded as *honest* for its unflattering descriptions of black folk, is also selling like hotcakes. Except: If Stanley Crouch is the mind of Wynton Marsalis, as one writer recently put it, Murray is the mind of the mind of Wynton. When Lincoln Center recently decided to give the jazz program Crouch and Marsalis run equal standing with its European classical side, the Center bowed to one of Murray's lifelong projects. "The objective was to be a part of that . . . ," he has said. "Once I'm at Lincoln Center, (the place) is different. (The objective) is not to be *like* them. It's to make Lincoln Center like *I* think it should be."

Lesson 2: The Omni-Americans *is his motherlode.*

One of my favorite professors used to say that most intellectuals have one idea, which they struggle with all their lives. If they succeed in expressing it well once, they are very lucky. What this luck usually amounts to, the teacher said, is one good film, one good book of essays, one good novel. In Murray's case, that book would be *The Omni-Americans*, in which he argues that blues, like all fine aesthetic idioms, tells universal tales.

Omni is a book about American literature. It borrows heavily from the work of other thinkers. From historian Constance Rourke's *American Humor,* in which the author argues that *"homo Americanus"* is made of one part entrepreneurial Yankee, one part frontiersman/Indian, and one part Negro, comes to the title conception: Murray's "omni-American" is the product of a rich "mulatto culture" which has given a much to black people as blacks have given to it. "It is all too true that Negroes unlike the Yankee and the backwoodsman were slaves whose legal status was that of property," he writes in *Omni*. "But it is also true—and as things have turned out, even more significant—that they were slaves who were living in the presence of more human freedom and individual opportunity than they or anybody else had ever been before. That the conception of being a free man in America was infinitely richer than any notion of individuality in the Africa of that period goes without saying."

Murray also relies on Kenneth Burke's distinction between frames of rejection and acceptance. "Out of the frame of rejection, you get the plaint, the elegy, the complaint, you get moral outcry, you get protest, you get the idea of victim," he told me when I saw him recently. "That's because you're rejecting the human condition. The other frame that we've talked about is a frame of acceptance. Not the acceptance of injustice, inequality, or any of those things like that. But acceptance of the fact that life is a struggle." Murray singles out Frederick Douglass and Harriet Tubman as particularly obvious paradigms of this type of acceptance, and says they represent true American heroism.

The writer's interest in heroism bears the stamp of his favorite literary figures, all stalwart Modernists: W. H. Auden, James Joyce, T. S. Eliot, Ernest Hemingway, Andre Malraux, Thomas Mann. What he likes is their focus on the predicament of the individual human being, the struggle to face the worries of existence, and to negotiate a place among other people. "So that's where the blues comes in," he explained to me. "Where we get my thing in is to say the blues is an aesthetic device for confrontation and improvisation."

Of course, he had put it plainly enough before:

(In the blues) there is, for instance, the seemingly inherent emphasis on rugged individual endurance. There is also the candid acknowledgement and sober acceptance of adversity as an inescapable condition of human existence—and perhaps in consequence an affirmative disposition toward all obstacles, whether urban or rural, whether political or metaphysical . . . but perhaps above all else the blues-oriented hero image represents the American embodiment of the man whose concept of being able to live happily ever afterwards is most consistent with the moral of all dragon-encounters: Improvisation is the ultimate human (i.e., heroic) endowment.

This improvisation in the face of what Murray calls "antagonistic cooperation" from the challenges of human existence is dialectical, but not in a Marxist sense. Good writers present heroes who struggle with dragons and blue devils honorably using all the swords and other weapons at hand. In the process, such writers create two kinds of examples. Their "representative anecdoctes" show the best ways to struggle with life's chaos, and the writer's own improvisations demonstrate the fact, and beauty, of human possibility.

Lesson 3: Albert Murray likes to teach.

I began our conversation by complaining that his man Marsalis sounds more like a curator than a musician. I wondered when Wynton will take the musics he grew up with and transform them in the way that people used to transform Cole Porter songs.

"I see what you mean," he said. His face tightened like a young surgeon's. "But it's a bigger problem for Wynton to do it, simply because he knows more (than funk musicians). If you operate on the level of convention, James Brown and those guys are not responding to as much music. What complicates the quest is what Harold Rosenberg called 'the tradition of the new.' I think a number of the commentators have backed into the tradition of the new. . . . Anybody who thinks that innovation is the prime imperative for the creative person does not know anything about art or the history of art. Because that is pursuit of novelty. Nothing could be more superficial or ephemeral," he said, laughing from his chest.

Lesson 4: Albert Murray thinks jazz can save American lives.

M urray says the blues idiom's encouragement of confrontation and improvisation helps the nation survive. According to him, jazz artists have "synthesize(d) all the (American) forces as nobody else has done," largely because black people's cultural slate was wiped clean when they arrived on these shores. He might even call the jazz idiom—a child of African America—the savior of the nation. "Today, America's only possible hope is that the Negroes might save us, which is all we're trying to do," Murray recently told *The New Yorker.* "We've got Louis, Duke, Count, and Ralph (Ellison), and now we're trying to do it with Wynton and Stanley. That's all we are—just a bunch of Negroes *trying* to save America."

Lesson 5: Albert Murray takes his individualism seriously.

H ow different from the solitude of writing literature jazz seems, now that the music has come to signify the respectful conversation of a team, each player gracefully enabling the improvisations of another. But the striking thing about Murray's passion for good literature and music is how similarly he sees these art forms. To him, both are heroic idioms. And when he does discuss artistic collaboration, he mostly means engaging the masterworks. "Creative effort means entering a dialogue with the form," he told me. "Each new effective aesthetic statement alters the existing emotional scale. So it's not simply a dialogue, it's a colloquy."

To Murray, a good artist fashions gold out of the ore of folk art—songs, pop writing, television, movies—and ordinary experience. His fine art must finally respond, however, to the best of what has happened or is happening in its tradition. This is a tenet of modernism—in literature as in music, the artist should engage in colloquy with the work of dead masters, and with the few who are alive today.

But and but: What comes through after a session of close listening to the man's work—even on jazz—is not an interest in collaboration as an end, but as a means for the individual player. Heroic self-expression is what counts. Louis Armstrong, Murray suggests in the latest book of essays, "was not unaware of the fact that he was in effect a culture hero (not unlike, say, Prometheus), the bringer of indispensable existential equipment for the survival of humanity." Count Basie, an accompanist par excellence, worked other musicians like a quiet god:

Sometimes the accompanist, for all his unobtrusiveness, actually leads and prompts the soloist. Sometimes he only follows, perhaps most often as if he were whispering yes, yes, yes; and then, and then, and then; go on, go on, go on; amen, so be it. Even when he engages in call and response exchanges, it is always as if the soloist is carrying on a dialogue with someone who is either absent or totally imaginary. But always the accompanist is there to keep the melodic line and its frame of reference intact and the soloist in key, in tune, and in time.

There was also Duke, whose place in the national pantheon was "not a matter of election campaigns. You must earn your own way in as gods and heroes have always had to do, through the intrinsic merit of what you do and how you do it, and as a result of the undeniability, the depth and scope, and the durability of its impact. And, of course, that is exactly what Duke Ellington had done."

Their godliness, Murray says, makes these musicians very similar to their literary cousins. While he admires the scholarship—the ability to converse with tradition—men like Thomas Mann and Ernest Hemingway bring to their work, he finally loves them for being able to improvise a singular synthesis of all they know, with courage. In doing so, and in producing art which reflects these values, such artists demonstrate humanity's best attributes. He elaborates in the middle of an essay on Ellington in his latest book of nonfiction, *The Blue Devils of Nada:*

No one can seriously accuse the Hemingway hero of not using his head. With the exception of Harry Morgan, the typical Hemingway hero is almost always not only a thinking man but also a reading man and frequently a writing man. He does not indulge in academic abstractions and intellectualized cliches and slogans but neither does he rely on tribal instinct, superstition, magic, or hand me down rules of thumb. He proceeds on concrete information, his discipline being that of an empiricist who responds in terms of what he personally knows and feels rather than what somebody else has decided he would know and feel. . . . Robert Penn Warren once wrote that the Hemingway hero was becoming aware of nada. Perhaps one might add that he is someone who has the blues (is bedeviled by blue devils) because, like Ecclesiastes, he has confronted the absurdity of human existence and knows that each moment and each experience count.

This passage can only be read as Murray's conception of the ideal temperament of the literary artist. Murray's "auteur" conception sticks to the mainstream modernist concern about the individuality of any artist, whether musical or literary.

But and but and but: Murray neglects the artist's need to collaborate with her audience. One suspects the process is more obvious in the case of jazz performers than writers. No matter how much chaos they face down, musicians have never been inattentive to their audiences—or they couldn't play in public for very long. Murray himself points out that Ellington worked many crowds—he wrote music for films, dance halls, opera houses—with integrity but with flexibility. But he doesn't see that this makes Duke an artist collaborating with other artists collaborating with listeners. Not only does Murray's emphasis on individual heroism distort the first kind of collaboration, it neglects the second.

Lesson 6: Albert Murray doesn't believe in a "black audience."

he extent of the collaboration between writers of fiction and their readers is a matter best taken up by academicians. But at the end of the day the fact of that collaboration is undeniable, if only because writers must use a shared tongue. Sometimes sharing causes fights. For the black writer especially the audience can be a difficult partner. Two of her audiences—the blacks and the whites—share a tongue but are at odds. Nobody has written about the difficulty this creates for the black writer as well as James Weldon Johnson did in his 1928 essay, "The Dilemma of the Negro Author."

> *The moment a Negro writer takes up his pen or sits down to his typewriter he is immediately called upon to solve, consciously or unconsciously, the problem of the double audience. To whom shall he address himself, to his own black group or to white America? Many a Negro writer has fallen down, as it were, between these two stools.*

Today's landscape is more complicated than the one Johnson describes. Numbers of Latino and Asian readers have increased since the time when Johnson wrote, and racial attitudes among all readers have changed considerably. Also, many black writers write in part to traditions and audiences that are not European or American: There is Gabriel García Márquez in Toni Morrison's writing and Chinua Achebe, too. Still, Johnson's dilemma is still as real as the chasmic split over the O. J. verdict.

Johnson goes on to explain the conflicting expectations of the two audiences, which amount to a white demand for stencils of docile or savage Negroes, and a black demand for respectable and "nice" Negroes. The way out is not easy:

> *I judge there is not a single Negro writer who is not, at least secondarily, impelled by the desire to make his work have some effect on the white world for the good of his race. It may be thought that the work of the Negro writer, on account of this last named condition, gains in pointedness what it loses in breadth. Be that as it may, the situation is for the time one in which he*

is inextricably placed. Of course, the Negro author can try the experiment of putting black America in the orchestra chairs, so to speak, and keeping white America in the gallery, but he is likely at any moment to find his audience shifting places on him, and sometimes without notice.

Murray's answer is to insist on the essential sameness of all Americans. Since Negroes are part of America, Negro expression can't help but keep in mind (and heart and body) Americanness; Du Bois's veil of "double consciousness" doesn't exist. For Murray, Louis Armstrong's music "is if anything even more representative of American affirmation and promise in the face of adversity than the festive reiterations of the most elaborate display of any Fourth of July fireworks. . . . Indeed, during the year following World War II the sound of Ambassador Satchmo came to have more worldwide appeal than the image of Yankee Doodle Dandy ever did, not to mention the poster image of Uncle Sam. . . ." And whites are no less culturally mulatto than the Ambassador. In one essay Murray quotes a friend's approving remarks about Hemingway's attention to the truth. "For Ellison, everything Hemingway wrote 'was imbued with a spirit beyond the tragic with which I could feel at home, for it was close to the feeling of the blues, which are, perhaps, as close as Americans can come to expressing the spirit of tragedy."

Implicit is this idea: When you're addressing the American audience, a mulatto audience, you're talking to everybody without regard to race. This saves America—it tells the entire nation of the facts about itself, and reminds it of its ideas in a nonpartisan fashion.

Except there's a hidden set of concerns. When Johnson concludes—

The making of a common audience out of white and black America presents the Negro author with enough difficulties to constitute a third horn of his dilemma. It is a task that is a very high test for all his skill and abilities, but it can be and has been accomplished. The equipped Negro author working at his best in his best known material can achieve this end; but standing on his racial foundation, he must fashion something that rises above race, and reaches out to the universal in truth and beauty. And so, when a Negro author does write so as to fuse white and black America into one interested and approving audience he has performed no slight feat, and has most likely done a sound piece of literary work.

—he sounds like Murray, or vice versa, but the difference between the two men is substantial. While Johnson acknowledges the dilemma in the first place, Murray is evasive. He contends the color line doesn't matter, yet he always keeps it in mind. "I have more white guys and gals reading my books than colored guys simply because they read more books," he told me. "You're not hoping to reach but so many Afro-Americans or whatever it is they call themselves today. You're not going to reach them because they don't read books. They certainly don't read books that have the ambition to be on the same level as Kenneth Burke or Malraux." Like his books, for example.

Murray was talking out of both sides of his mouth. First, he said black artists need to keep in mind their mulatto Americanness. Then he said there are almost no blacks in the audience. Surely a mulatto culture implies a heterogeneous audience—even if it's at war with itself.

Lesson 7: Albert Murray likes his "representative anecdotes" to reflect "ancestral imperatives."

    sipped on the cup of tea Mr. Murray's wife had set down beside us. Murray explained his representative anecdote idea. "Even if it's a 900-page novel, it's an anecdote. All of Proust is an anecdote of turn-of-the-century France. . . . The Hemingway section (of *The Blue Devils of Nada*) keeps it as simple as I think I can make it, which is, you write about what you know about. Try to get how you really feel about it. If your sensibility is comprehensive enough and your craft is good enough, then what you come out with is probably a representative anecdote." He used Richard Wright's *Native Son* as an example of a book that is not a representative anecdote. "What is mising in (Bigger) Thomas was that he was not a representative character. And yet people interpreted the book (this way): 'This tells me what it's like to be a Negro in America.'"

I wondered whether he could see what I meant *this* time. Mostly I listened like a good young man. I should have said: Surely black people knew that Bigger isn't representative of all black people, even if the characterization was off. To whom, in Murray's eyes, was Wright *misrepresenting* black people? Those misled "people" simply have to be *white*, which concedes Johnson's point without conceding it: Murray knows the two American audiences bring very different sensibilities to their reading chairs.

I asked Murray whether he thought Jake Barnes, the protagonist in Hemingway's *The Sun Also Rises*, is representative of any community. The "white" community for example.

"(Hemingway) was writing about the predicament of man. So that's the challenge. Do these guys identify with Scooter (the protaganist in Murray's novels) or do they receive it as news as to what it's like to be a black boy in America? And yet I wanted authentically—you get all the local color, all of the specifics are there. (The protaganist) doesn't have to be a character with no specific cultural affiliation. The problem of the artist is to take these idiomatic particulars and process them in a way that gives them universal impact."

He went on, "I can think of very few of my friends or very few people that I know—and we're not from professional families or anything like that—[who resemble Bigger]."

But that's a big burden, I said. I should have said: Why does a writer have any responsibility to authentically "represent" people who don't read her?

He explained that the representative anecdote should reflect the "ancestral imperatives"—God, I would have thought he was making this up as he went along, except I'd seen the idea in his books. The ancestral imperatives are various, but the best ones enable a people to survive; blues confrontation and improvisation fit the bill. Only people like Richard Wright didn't get it. "This guy can't swing. You wouldn't have thought he was within 10,000 miles of Earl Hines, and the Grand Terrace."

So now I wanted to know whether the blues-oriented Hemingway shared ancestral imperatives with black people. Were their imperatives the same?

"I don't know whether I'm interested in that or not," he said. He couldn't see himself having the same ancestral imperatives as the son of a doctor from the Midwest, but he did share a dialogue with the very literary masters Hemingway engaged. And these writers are white. "You can't have a dialogue with a form that does not exist. If you're going to be a writer, and you want to be a good writer, and you're writing novels, you're either going to be an American novelist, a French novelist, or a German novelist. You're not going to be an African novelist, because they don't write. . . . Shit, you can't do that."

"But," I said, "you can have a dialogue with your audiences." Any good writer—Africans included—wants to and does speak to living souls, not just Flaubert and Hemingway. Or even Soyinka. He might want to speak to certain Africans.

Murray's voice rose. "But that's not what your audience is. Can't you understand? I'm talking about being a writer. Just like a guy talking about being a movie actor. That's not the same as dancing in front of a chief. You say, 'Well that's performing, too.' But that's crap. Anybody who can't see the difference between a movie star and a slave dancing in a mudhole. . . ."

I listened obediently to the man who suddenly seemed elderly, his age. He couldn't hear all that well, his back kept him hobbled. He was at the mercy of young doctors and he was running out of time. I remembered the last sentence of a recent newspaper interview he'd done: "the most radical thing that you can do," he'd told the Boston journalist, "is to be a nice-looking, brown-skinned American guy, well-dressed, well-educated; that's the most dangerous sonofabitch in the country!" I got the point: He really is interested in having some effect on the white reader for the good of the race.

He wants us to be respectable.

Lesson 8: Albert Murray slams the lid on black protest literature.

▊ remind you that his big idea is that blues voices laugh in the face of the oppressive or just plain entropic forces, and that writers should write characters who live despite the chaos, and without complaining too much. He told me:

> *You confront the fact that life is a low down dirty shame. Anybody who can see the natural history of Negroes in the United States can see that. You wake up in the morning and you're a slave, you're not going to kid yourself. It's unjust. Some guy will just complain about it and moan about it. Another guy will listen around and whatnot and find out about the Underground Railroad. So he accepts the fact that he's a slave as a necessity for struggle. That qualifies him as being a part of the heroic or epical mode. You see, because he can extend from one to many, that is, he's an example. That's why he's a hero. He inspires other people to accept that.*

Murray never goes so far as to suggest that anybody ignore the dragons of racism, but he is very impatient with art that spends a lot of time talking about them. "American protest fiction . . . concerns itself not with the ambiguities of self-improvement and self-extension, not with the evaluation of the individual as protagonist, but rather with representing a world of collective victims whose survival and betterment depend not upon self-determination but upon a change of heart in their antagonists, who thereupon will cease being villains and become patrons of social welfare!" Murray is careful not to condemn propagandistic art in general; elements of propaganda, he concedes, appear in all literature. "Nevertheless, there are many reasons why it is all but impossible for a serious writer of fiction to engage his craft as such in a political cause, no matter how worthy, without violating his very special integrity as an artist in some serious way. . . ."

A few pages later he goes even further:

> *Writers have always thrived on oppression, poverty, alienation and the like. Feodor Dostoevski, for example, was very poor, much oppressed. . . . He was imprisoned; and one time he came within minutes of being officially lynched. But he wrote good books. Because he liked good books. . . .*

> *But the sad fact is that there is very little to show that very many U.S.*
> *Negro writers have ever actually tried to write major novels.*

Major novelists, then, do not complain about racism. White folks—the only audience Murray imagines—don't need to hear those complaints because all they do is tell the dragon he has power over black life. Would-be major novelists, he contends, ought to enter the complex lives of their characters, which in the case of Negroes are always circumscribed but rarely defined by racism.

The last point is brilliant. There is a certain formula to black lamentation and a good writer can master it in a very short time. Until the recent change in climate, such lamentation seemed to be the kind of black writing preferred by liberal whites. Now the rage is for stories by and about well-adjusted and responsible black people. As with the older predigested formulation, good writers can run the current line with their eyes closed—but good writing forces an encounter with the demands of those often conflicting white and black audiences. If the writer displeases too many blacks, she loses fellow strugglers on her side of the great divide. If she displeases too many whites, she may find herself unable to publish at all.

The serious writer simply can't help conversing with the world around her. In this way her fiction is collaborative. If she is hip to the spirit of the age, if she is writing in America, if her characters are black, if their lives are affected by the forces that help shape the lives of most black Americans, if she is aware of the complex moral and existential issues facing them, she will write damning words about white supremacy. Murray's well-dressed black man knows that, but he may not realize this: If the novelist chooses not to make any of her characters heroic, even tragically heroic, she can be sure that some critics will dismiss the book as lacking in sublety. They will say she is too *angry*. That she protests too much. Others will suggest that she is insufficiently angry or that she does not love her people enough. And she might answer with that old perfect riddle: *I listened to what the characters had to say.* Only her serious readers (women, men, black, white, brown, yellow, American, global) will get the joke.

Lesson 9: Albert Murray dons his uniform.

Murray's distaste for black "protest fiction" has roots outside of literary modernism. While his embrace of edifying heroism also resembles W. E. B. Du Bois's Talented Tenth formulation, it more directly stems from the mind of Booker T. Washington. In *Up From Slavery*, the founder of Tuskegee shows the philosophy he peddled to students like Murray and to turn-of-the-century whites:

[I told them] that the whole future of the Negro rested largely upon the questions as to whether or not he should make himself, through his skill, intelligence, and character, of such undeniable value to the community in which he lived that the community could not dispense with his presence. I said that any individual who learned to do something better than anybody else—learned to do a common thing in an uncommon manner— had solved his problem, regardless of the color of his skin.

Now hear Murray, graduate of Tuskegee, in *The Hero and the Blues.* "Heroism, which is, among other things, another word for self-reliance, is not only the indispensible prerequisite for productive citizenship in an open society; it is also that without which no individual or community can remain free."

Both Washington and Du Bois were privately skeptical about the intentions of white people, and both valued heroic leaders. In public they parted company on the efficacy of collective protest. Du Bois's heroes are loudly and collectively resistant; they do not "accept" the fact that they are oppressed. Washington's spend time making sure they improve themselves economically, and in this way help "the black community" by individual achievement. Ultimately Washington is more optimistic about American possibility; he also seems like a more convinced individualist.

Murray sides with Washington. "I'm not a politician," he says, but like any good citizen, he does have an opinion. He admires the nonviolent strategies associated in this country with Dr. Martin Luther King Jr. "They had a device which would turn the guy's strength against him. . . . I thought that was sophisticated stuff." But he thinks the anticapitalists ruined things. "The rhetoric of Marxism came in. The strategy for recruiting Negroes was a strategy of alienation. Protest and alienation took the way over drive and initiative and go-getum. See, they wiped out Horatio Alger and the dymanic of the self-made man. Because it was, 'Are you a comrade?'"

Murray told me he would put *Up From Slavery* in the American literary canon because he considers it a representative anecdote. "It's simply Horatio Alger in brown skin! It is the cliche of the times. . . . In other words, I can make it—give me my chance and I will. That's not just the Negro, that's the United States. . . ." He pointed to a special brandy he wanted me to try. He knows and loves fine spirits almost as much as books.

Murray's other selections included *The Narrative of the Life of Frederick Douglass* and some of the poetry of Dunbar, though he thinks it's "lightweight." Murray once had an affection for James Weldon Johnson, but now he considers much of his work "light." Certainly, "Ellison would be the most illustrious [Negro] representative." The point is to put forward black individuals who are ready to compete. "We're taking them to Yankee Stadium, man. And you're gonna put Langston Hughes in there with T. S. Eliot? Or Ezra Pound? Or Yeats?"

Murray would select social realist Richard Wright—if Dreiser, Steinbeck, Upton Sinclair had to go in. But "political pamphlets like *The Fire Next Time*," he said, "don't belong in the pantheon." Why *Up from Slavery* and not *The Fire Next Time*? Well . . . never mind the brilliance of Baldwin's technique or the fact that *Up From Slavery* was ghostwritten. "What do you see as representative about *The Fire Next Time*?" he asked.

"I'm not sure that I would use that criterion for putting it into the literary canon." I lifted my glass.

"The biggest impact," he said, "that *The Fire Next Time* had was that it served, alas, to legitimize—to a certain extent for some people— Malcolm X."

I said *Fire* thoroughly criticizes Elijah Muhammed and the Nation. But he didn't hear the objection.

"They don't represent the ancestral imperatives," he says. "The ancestral imperatives are to become American. That's what Frederick Douglass and these guys, to me, represented. One way or the other. One guy takes this route, the other guy takes the other route to do it. One guy says, 'Well, you've got to start down here right with the soil. Then you've got to work your way up and you get your money. If you got enough money, and you got enough power, and you've got enough skill, nobody's going to bother you.' The other guy says, 'No, we've got to have our rights first. We want our dignity and so forth.' The (first) guy says, 'Dignity don't mean shit if you're hungry. . . . You don't have to go around asking him for anything if you've got something he wants.' That's the American way! These guys weren't out there protesting. They were out there going West, getting the Indians out of the way. 'The Indians are in the way, Jack. We *need* this. . . .' I'm not for Sitting Bull winning. I'm for whatever Custer represented. They took it from somebody, somebody took it from them."

Lesson 10: Albert Murray steps to the plate.

(H) e wanted to put one in the stands. "Wright was from Mississippi, but he wasn't near Faulkner. Faulkner got some of the most admirable Negroes there ever was. Hardly any Negroes admirable in Richard Wright, you see, and I couldn't find that with Duke, Louis, Count, Jack Johnson, Joe Louis. . . . I got to account for them. Because I was going to be the Joe Louis of literature. Me and Ralph."

Nowhere are Murray's ideas about literature and life more immanent than in his fiction. In *Train Whistle Guitar*, *The Spyglass Tree*, and *The Seven League Boots* the author offers representative anecdotes which describe the heroic journey of his alter ego, Scooter. Like Murray, Scooter is a native of a small town in Alabama, was a star pupil at Mobile County Training School, attended a college very much like Tuskegee Institute. Scooter is the pride of his hometown and he understands his role at a very early age. He does not betray the trust—Scooter digs the girls, but he also studies hard and succeeds. By the time of the third book in the series, *The Seven League Boots,* Scooter has taken up bass, become an apprentice to a bandleader who is very much like Duke Ellington, then struck out on his own. The books, then, can be seen as part autobiography and part wish fulfillment, and as a flesh-and-blood outline for saving America.

One would hope, however, that Murray's fiction would be more than a mere servant of his theories. Even though his essays never resolve the contradiction between his desire for universality and his stated interest in "saving America," Murray's novels could, like the blues, look beyond either concern to the complexity of actual life. His friend and fellow Tuskegee grad Ralph Ellison's willingness to grow, bend, explore in this way is precisely what made the man such a brilliance. There is a range of opinions in Ellison's work—in *Shadow and Act,* for instance, the writer celebrates the confrontational quality of *Native Son* in "Richard Wright's Blues," and later delivers a careful attack on the shortcomings of the novel, as well as a delineation of his differences from Wright. Ellison, for one, was no polemicist.

Lesson 11: Albert Murray swings and misses.

F or the most part, his fiction doesn't work. Murray makes Scooter's environment totally subservient to Scooter, to the point of unintentional absurdity—there is no pessimism, no ambiguity, no ambivalence about America the beautiful. Instead, the novelist hands out paean after paean to his own ingenious insights about the ways of Man and the ways black people should act. Here is some wisdom from Scooter in *The Seven League Boots:*

> *Most people I know don't know anything at all about the point Booker T. Washington was trying to make when he said what he said in that famous speech. They just take what he said at that point as a very wise old saying about not overlooking something valuable right under your nose so to speak. To them it goes right along with what old Booker T. also had to say about our people prospering in proportion as we learn to dignify and glorify labor and put brains and skill into the common occupations of life.*
> *That's what it all adds up to for me too, I said, and I also knew a*

few other things about that historic speech in Atlanta. And I've read the inscription directly from the monument at Tuskegee. But what Booker T.'s bucket always brings to my mind is a church song that goes as far back in my memory as the Sunday school shout that goes "Jesus wants me for a sunbeam."

More trying are Murray's attempts to stitch together the styles of his favorite writers. Faulkner's italicized streams of consciousness, Hemingway's spare attention to detail, Mann's speculative meanderings, Joyce's play with the music of language—it's all in there, absolutely undigested. What's missing most is novelty. Murray's desire to talk to the old masters comes at the expense of his characters; Scooter never gets a chance to breath our air. Instead, he coughs out passages from the books on Murray's reading list, including the author's own. Which is perfectly reminiscent of the curatorial compositions of too many well-dressed Wyntonites.

Lesson 12: Albert Murray has the last word.

There is an irony in the old man's failure to synthesize and improvise and face the truth—the very imprecisions he has railed against in much of his writing. "Craftsmanship does not necessarily add up to artistry," he said during our last talk. "And that's where a lot of people (go wrong). They look at the notes, they look at the paper, and nobody feels anything for their playing songs, I was playing so and so flat, I did this and the tempo was this. And you say, 'Yeah, OK.' So he's going to try to win a goddamn argument with some intellectual stuff and he's not communicating. Then they want to browbeat you intellectually into it. 'Well, I'm smarter than they are. You can't tell me that because (you don't) know enough about it.'" Whether or not Murray ever notices this failing in himself, his observation makes me a student as much as a critic, and it makes Murray the teacher, perfectly.

When we finished, I gulped down the last of my brandy, the end. Mr. Murray showed some of his old photgraphs. "That's Jimmy Baldwin." "That's Ralph." "That's Kenneth Burke." I smiled and packed up my recorder. He signed my books and I shouted good-bye to his wife in the bedroom.

He was in the mood for a final lesson. Gesturing toward my hands, the old man said, "These books are serious books. And they keep coming out. None of them is a bestseller (so that) everybody running around (is) talking about Albert Murray. But the sommabitch ain't stopped. He's pretty close to 80. I think that's what you should do. I'm not broke, you know. I'm sharp," he grinned. "I got a pretty wife. Got a million dollars in paintings (by friend Romare Bearden) in sight. All out of serious stuff and no bullshit anywhere."

Downstairs, I opened the pages of the books Stanley Crouch had given me, long ago, when I first started writing for publications. "You should read these," Stanley said back then, handing me his copies of *The Omni-Americans* and *The Hero and the Blues*. I scanned the signatures Albert Murray had left. I particularly liked the one he wrote on the title page of *The Blue Devils of Nada*, gentle reader. "For Joe Wood. Who plays his own riffs on this stuff."

February 1996

A SAINT AND A STRANGER

By Rick Moody

BURNING YOUR BOATS: THE COLLECTED SHORT STORIES
By Angela Carter

Reviews of unrestrained praise don't have much to recommend them. Therefore, I have to warn you about the case at hand—*Burning Your Boats: The Collected Short Stories* by Angela Carter. There's nothing to complain about. On the contrary. All I'm going to do here is pile up a bunch of superlatives, one after another, with increasing vehemence, relying heavily on my Microsoft Word thesaurus to avoid "brilliant," "pellucid," "limpid," "trenchant," and other degraded modifiers as I get intoxicated by my responsibilities. Continue at your own risk.

Of course Angela Carter, who died in 1992, was a novelist of considerable accomplishment and reputation (*The Passion of New Eve, Nights at the Circus*), and a wicked social critic (*The Sadeian Woman*), but she also worked frequently with shorter forms. Several compendia of her stories appeared on this side of the Atlantic—*The Bloody Chamber, Fireworks*, and *Saints and Strangers*. This new volume assembles all of this work as well as an entire collection unpublished in the U.S. (*American Ghosts and Old World Wonders*), three early stories, and a troika of uncollected later efforts. *Burning Your Boats*, then (hey, wait, maybe I have one criticism after all: mediocre title), makes a case for Carter as a writer of range, fills out her profile so that we remember of her that she was as comfortable in the short as the long, as inventive with the fictional as the nonfictional.

As with *The Bloody Chamber*, which Salman Rushdie, in an occasionally condescending introduction, rightly terms the "masterwork: the book in which her high perfervid mode is perfectly married to her stories' needs," most of *Burning Your Boats* derives from the storytelling impulses and forms of folk tales. Carter addresses this point herself in an afterword appended here (dating from 1973): "The limited trajectory of the short narrative concentrates its meaning. Sign and sense can fuse to an extent impossible to achieve among the multiplying ambiguities of all extended narrative. I found that, though the play of surfaces never ceased to fascinate me, I was not so much exploring them as making abstractions from them, I was writing, therefore, tales." In the three early stories, "The Man Who Loved a Double Bass," "A Very, Very Great Lady and Her Son at Home," and "A Victorian Fable (With Glossary)," from the early '60s, it's fascinating to see the author, confined during her apprenticeship to a more literal realism, nonetheless begin to edge toward the fabulism and grandly anachronistic folklore (especially in "A Victorian Fable") that would come to serve her so well in *The Bloody Chamber*.

Similarly, from the early collection entitled *Fireworks* we have the somewhat realistic narratives dating from Carter's travels in the early '70s to Japan ("A Souvenir of Japan," "The Smile of Winter")—with their affectionate Asian exoticism, their preoccupation with cross-cultural love relationships—doing a sort of deranged English jig with the fairy tale structures of "The Executioner's Beautiful Daughter," in which, for example, a mythic executioner pursues an incestuous relationship with his daughter, or "The Loves of Lady Purple," about a puppeteer and his voracious puppet.

Fireworks in this (chronological) assemblage of the Carter oeuvre then gives way to her magnum opus, *The Bloody Chamber*, and its preternaturally canny pursuit of English literature's roots among the disenfranchised—peasants, vagrants, agrarians. The origins of this antibourgeois dramatis personae are apparent earlier in "The Executioner's Beautiful Daughter": "This nominal ruler is in reality the poorest beggar in all his ragged kingdom. Heir of the barbarous, he is stripped of everything but the idea of omnipotence." But in *The Bloody Chamber*, the political and narrative coloration of the folk tale are even more in the forefront, though here embued with the fierce language and the elegance of Carter's more realistic aspect: "It is northern country; they have cold weather, they have cold hearts. . . . When they discover a witch—some old woman whose cheeses ripen when her neighbor's do not, another old woman whose black cat, oh, sinister! *follows her about all the time*, they strip the crone, search her for marks, for the supernumerary nipple her familiar sucks" (from "The Werewolf"). Or this: "The grave-eyed children of the sparse villages always carry knives with them when they go to tend the little flocks of goats that provide the homesteads with acrid milk and rank, maggoty cheese. Their knives are half as big as they are, the blades are sharpened daily" (from "The Company of Wolves"). There are, in *The Bloody Chamber*, politically acute versions of stories about Little Red Riding Hood, Beauty and the Beast (no relation to the Disney confection), Puss-in-Boots, and Bluebeard. In fact there are *two* Little Red Riding Hood stories (three if you count the lycanthropes of "Wolf-Alice") and two different Beauties with their Beasts, as if there's a polysemy to the contemporary folk tale. In Carter's formulation, you have the basics of a plot, you have the sub-conscious ("The Gothic tradition . . . ignores the value systems of our institutions: it deals entirely with the profane"—from the afterword), and you have a rich literary palette—but the meaning of the work is completely flexible, contingent, multifarious.

Without doubt, *The Bloody Chamber* is so playful ("So may all your wives, if you need them, be rich and pretty; and all your husbands, if you want them, be young and virile; and all your cats as wily, perspicacious and resourceful as: PUSS-IN-BOOTS"), so infectious, and so original that it must have been difficult to improve upon. What seems to happen in *Black Venus*, therefore, Carter's next collection, is that the author allows the pendulum to swing back slightly toward her much reviled "bourgeois realism," with its "technical and emotional complexity," with its characters who "learn to think." The stories begin to be peopled with historical or actual personages (as Rushdie likewise notes in his introduction). "Black Venus," then, a harrowing, sad, and it seems to me, perfect story heroizes Baudelaire's black mistress Jeanne Duval, while it also splendidly delineates the conflicts between high European style and *the literature of the people* that is so important to Carter's work. "He said she danced like a snake and she said, snakes can't dance: they've got no legs, and he said, but kindly, you're an idiot Jeanne; but she knew he'd never so much as *seen* a snake . . . if he'd seen a snake move, he'd never have said a thing like that." "The Cabinet of Edgar Allan Poe," which follows in *Black Venus*, is a reverent embroidery upon the beleaguered childhood of our American Gothic architect, and "The Fall River Axe Murders" is the first of two elucidations in *Burning Your Boats* of the psychology of New England's celebrated murderer Lizzie Borden.

There are a couple of fairy tales in the *Black Venus* collection, too—last alternate takes from a particularly satisfying recording session: "Peter and the Wolf" and "The Kiss." The latter imagines a folk narrative for communist Uzbekistan ("This is a story in simple, geometric shapes and the bold colours of a child's box of crayons"). Fine, beguiling stories, sure, like the best of *The Bloody Chamber*, but by the time *Burning Your Boats* turns its attentions to Carter's last collection, *American Ghosts and Old Wonders*, the archaisms and quaint imagery of the folk tale have mostly given way to an interest in the more contemporary mythmaking apparatus of Hollywood cinema. Three of these stories, "John Ford's *'Tis a Pity She's a Whore*," "Gun for the Devil," and "The Merchant of Shadows," rely to varying degrees on American cinema—mainly upon the symbology of the western. "John Ford," e.g., is an often hilarious commingling of the work of John Ford, director of *Stage-coach*, with John Ford, Jacobean tragedian. In this coproduction, an incestuous brother and sister of the American prairie pronounce their doomed love sometimes in couplets ("What, chang'd so soon! hath your new sprightly lord/Found a trick in night-games more than we could know in our simplicity?"), sometimes in the Hollywood pseudo-frontier vulgate ("Reckon I never properly knowed no young man before").

Fiction in an era of cinema, however (I'm paraphrasing John Barth), is like rail travel in the jet age. With these later stories, in spite of their virtuosic language, their wisdom about cinematic aesthetics, their comic warmth, I couldn't help feeling that Carter was distracting herself, writing *divertissements*, in contrast to her "emotionally and technically complex" earlier work. But, on the verge of criticizing these last hundred pages of *Burning Your Boats*, a justification for this late style seems unavoidable to me. Angela Carter was dying. In 1990, three years prior to the publication of *American Ghosts*, Carter fell ill with lung cancer. As you approach the last published works of this volume, then, you approach the work—I'm theorizing—of someone mired in a dread ordeal. Thus a willingness to be distracted by the silver screen, to be a little distracted in general. And thus the last two (chronologically speaking) stories here, "Alice in Prague," an elegy for the work of Czech filmmaker Jan Svankmayer, and "Impressions: The Wrightsman Magdalene," each filled with manifestos for Carter's work and style ("'Reason becomes the enemy which withholds from us so many possibilities of pleasure,' said Freud"), and the latter with its illuminating autobiographical confessions: "When I was in labour, I thought of a candle flame. I was in labour for nineteen hours. At first the pains came slowly and relatively light; it was easy to ride them. But when they came more closely together, and grew more and more intense, then I began to concentrate my mind upon an imaginary candle flame."

As a reader, I was grateful for the three uncollected stories (from the '70s and early '80s) that close out *Burning Your Boat*, especially grateful for the generous first person of the final story, "The Quilt Maker." Here, a younger Angela Carter finds the high European art of painting much indebted to the arts and crafts of the housewife. "It took a hundred years for fine artists to catch up with the kind of brilliant abstraction that any ordinary housewife used to be able to put together in only a year . . . without making a song and dance about it." These stories leavened an ache in the *American Ghosts* volume, for me, restored it to a context, and reminded me of the singular accomplishments of *Fireworks*, *The Bloody Chamber*, and *Black Venus*.

I should add, by way of disclosure, that I knew Angela Carter, that I was her student for a year when she lived in Rhode Island, that I corresponded with her during the last years of her life. She was a fabulous, sympathetic, selfless, and sometimes ornery teacher who corrected my efforts well into my professional career. To read *Burning Your Boats* for me, therefore, was to lose Angela over again, to lose someone I loved. She once said to me of Polish writer Bruno Schulz (killed by a Nazi on the street, days before Armistice) that it was hard not to read the biographical drama of his life backward onto his stories. I noticed the same tendency here, though I wished I hadn't, because of the chronological ordering of this collection. On the other hand, Angela has been gone five years now, and it's hard not to encounter her subversive, joyful, incendiary imagination, especially in such a generous, important, comprehensive volume, hard not to encounter her preoccupations with lions, cats, wolves, mirrors, sex, lice, comedy, storytelling, the history of art, unusual words; it's hard not to encounter Angela Carter's spectacular fictional legerdemain without the certainty that it will last, that it will be read, that it will be admired. *Ars longa, vita brevis:* "We know when we are born but—the times of our reprieves are equally random."

May 1996

❶ ❷ ❸ ❹ ❺

Signs of the Times:

Capturing a Cultural Moment

*T*he 1980s was the era of the culture wars: ferocious debates over identity politics and the canon, cultural studies, and the alleged closing of the American mind. At heart, this was a struggle over what "culture" actually meant. Was it civilization—values set in stone, art raised to a lofty zone towering over the commonplace, a fortress to be defended against insurgent forces of barbarism? Or was it something much closer to everyday life—owned by the people, by definition turbulent and fluid, and sufficiently vital not to need anybody's protection?

Tending toward the latter definition, *VLS* writers sifted through the signs of the time. Ellen Willis's 1982 review of books by bell hooks and Angela Davis moved boldly through the dual minefield of race and gender allegiances, confronting dangerous questions about the racism of white feminists and the sexism of black men. In 1986 Richard Goldstein's desire to shatter the silence surrounding AIDS drove him to search for meaning and tradition in the literature of plagues past in Daniel Defoe, E. A. Poe, Mary McCarthy, Albert Camus.

Academia in the '80s and '90s was the front line of the culture war, and our critics made theory look as cool as sex, drugs, and rock 'n' roll. Using the machete of supreme lucidity, Michael Bérubé blazed a path through the jargon jungles of postmodernism and deconstruction, while Michael Warner did a similarly sterling job mapping queer theory. Anticipating the now trendy discipline of "whiteness studies," Scott Malcomson wrote about anthropology as a honky's history of the world. In the age of multiculturalism, he found the field riddled with self-loathing, often backward attempts to get down with the "Other."

Tremors in literary terrain often presage seismic shifts in the wider culture, and *VLS* writers kept a close watch on the Zeitgeist's Richter scale. Walter Kendrick, locked in his own love-hate relationship with Freud, documented escalating attacks against the father of psychonalysis, while Thulani Davis identified Terry McMillan as the harbinger of a new genre of assimilationist Buppie fiction. Playing off the Clinton-Lewinsky melodrama, Lynne Tillman revealed the dangerous liaisons between politics and fiction, and defended the novelist's knack for true lies.

NOT JUST ANOTHER OEDIPAL DRAMA

The Unsinkable Sigmund Freud

By Walter Kendrick

> THE ASSAULT ON TRUTH:
> FREUD'S SUPPRESSION OF THE SEDUCTION THEORY
> *By Jeffrey Moussaieff Masson*
>
> IN THE FREUD ARCHIVES
> *By Janet Malcolm*
>
> THE FREUDIAN FALLACY:
> AN ALTERNATIVE VIEW OF FREUDIAN THEORY
> *By E. M. Thornton*
>
> THE REPRESSION OF PSYCHOANALYSIS:
> OTTO FENICHEL AND THE POLITICAL FREUDIANS
> *By Russell Jacoby*

All last autumn and winter, it was impossible to attend a cocktail party, even one billed as only mildly intellectual, without braving a buzz of gossip about Freud. Hearing that I'd written on that inexhaustible subject, people would come up to me with doleful questions: Was Freud really a sniveling coward? How could he and Wilhelm Fliess have done those gruesome things to Emma Eckstein? Wasn't it a surprise that psychoanalysis had been dead wrong from the very beginning? Behind the earnest eyes and clucking tongues, I detected joy; the Germans call it *Schadenfreude*, delight in someone else's misfortune. So, fearing reprisals, I agreed with everything. Yes, yes, yes, I said; Freud was a worm, and the discipline he founded—which has made us what we are, for good or ill—was a silly mistake.

Arguing about Freud has been one of the world's favorite pastimes since the 20th century began, but it's entered a new stage that might be terminal. Freud's old opponents used to lambaste him for cynicism, obscurity, and simple dirty-mindedness; they were horrified by what he told them and resisted it with all their strength. They lost. For at least two generations now, we've more or less accepted Freud's view of human nature; art and literature have embraced it—not to mention the thousand brands of therapy that all owe their origin to psychoanalysis—and it's been so thoroughly absorbed by popular thinking that you don't need to have read a word Freud wrote in order to understand "Freudianism." Freud can't shock us anymore; we hate him now for a new set of reasons. He betrayed us: The truth he told us hasn't made us free.

If Freud had been content to write philosophy—or anthropology, sociology, any other abstract study—he'd never have riled us up with such violence. He gets his nagging endurance from the fiendish coupling of metaphysical speculation with a practical technique; "psychoanalysis" means both, to everybody's detriment. The technique doesn't work and never did, yet no illusion in the history of the human race, except religion, flourishes so mightily in the absence of all successful results. Freud himself likened religion to obsessional neurosis and ascribed its power to the Oedipus complex; in 1927, he feistily forecast that "a turning away from religion is bound to occur with the fatal inevitability of a process of growth, and that we find ourselves at this very juncture in the middle of that phase of development." Sixty years later, psychoanalysis stands where religion used to be, and Freud probably lacks God's staying power.

Last fall's flare-up of the Freud furor was Janet Malcolm's fault, thanks to her two brilliant *New Yorker* articles detailing the intricate insanity of Jeffrey Masson's speedy rise and fall within the psychoanalytic establishment. We've now got a slightly revised version, *In the Freud Archives*, another one of those precious little Knopf volumes that everyone has read before they come out. It forms a companion piece to Malcolm's *Psychoanalysis: The Impossible Profession* (1981), also *New Yorker*-born and recycled through Knopf. Malcolm has proven herself our best behind-the-lines reporter in the bizarre, murky realm of entrenched psychoanalysis; she knows it all thoroughly, both as a theory and as a way of life, and she possesses the rare talent of immersing herself in lunacy without losing her head. As she tells the tale, it seems almost reasonable that grown-up men and women, driven to distraction by the talking cure, should rage and shriek like a mob of deranged children.

The contents of *In the Freud Archives* are tangled enough in their own right, but external circumstances have made the mess even weirder. "I'm writing a book," says Masson, quoted by Malcolm. "And when my book comes out there is not a patient in analysis who will not go to his analyst with the book in hand and say, 'Why didn't you tell me this? What the hell is going on?'" When Malcolm's *New Yorker* articles appeared, we could gleefully look forward to breadlines full of shrinks; for a couple of months, though, we've had the book Masson was cackling about, *The Assault on Truth*, and the promised exodus seems not to have happened. When we read Malcolm again, renewing the forecast, we'll hardly know which end of the carriage the horse goes on. Ideally, the two books should be read simultaneously; but, if you have only one pair of eyes, choose Malcolm. She tells you everything Masson does, and more.

In the Freud Archives stands quite well on its own as a peculiar episode in late 20th-century social history. Ten years from now, though, if anyone still wants to read *The Assault on Truth*, Malcolm's book will serve as a user's manual, to explain why Masson gets so breathless. Masson's personal story is much more entertaining than his book, especially when Malcolm tells it, though if it came from any other milieu it wouldn't have made such a splash. A woman pushing 90 was prone to vagueness and protective of the past, an aging nabob at the pinnacle of his profession grew infatuated with a charismatic young colleague, an egomaniacal hotshot won the chance of a lifetime and blew it—these are perennial stereotypes of the muddled human condition. But when the parts were played by Anna Freud, Kurt Eissler, and Jeffrey Masson (the first two world-famous and the third hell-bent on becoming so), and when the stage was the citadel of psychoanalysis (where the muddle is supposed to get unraveled), *that* was news.

In the introduction to *The Assault on Truth*, Masson runs through his story again, leaving out the compromising details of passions and personalities that Malcolm supplies. In 1980, after years of negotiation, he was given carte blanche to assemble a full, annotated edition of Freud's letters to Fliess, written between 1887 and 1902, the most important evidence we possess of how psychoanalysis was born. Number 20 Maresfield Gardens, Freud's London home where his daughter still lived, was thrown open to Masson; he was allowed to examine Freud's library, rummage through his desk, and even delve into an intriguing "large black cupboard outside Anna Freud's bedroom." In addition, he became one of the directors of Sigmund Freud Copyrights and was named Eissler's heir apparent as head of the Freud Archives.

It remains unclear why the old guard should have decided, after so long, to let some light into the crypt. An abridged edition of the letters to Fleiss, reduced by about half, had been published 30 years earlier as *The Origins of Psychoanalysis*, with no indication of where the cuts were made. But the silent censorship of Freud's letters has always been standard practice; so far as I know, the only untrimmed volume is the *Freud/Jung Letters* (1974), which also gives both sides of the correspondence. The excuses for this policy, though they raise suspicions, are at least halfway plausible: Most letters, even those of a genius, are dull ("Yes, I'll be there for tea on Tuesday"); in Freud's case, embarrassing facts about living people were frequent. By now, however, anyone Freud stripped naked for Fleiss is bound to be dead, and perhaps we're willing to endure repetition and triviality, as long as Freud's name is attached. These might have been the reasons for agreeing to publish the Freud-Fleiss letters in full, or maybe the custodians of the archive only got weary at last of accusations that such elaborate secrecy must mean there's something sinister to hide.

Masson gives no real explanation, but Malcolm makes it a matter of animal magnetism exerted upon two susceptible old people. In any case, the elders couldn't have made a worse mistake: They fell in love with Nancy Drew, detective. The tasks they handed Masson, though they did him honor, were huge and should have taken years to complete. The Freud-Fleiss letters were only the beginning; he was also supposed to catalogue all the Freud materials in the Library of Congress, some 150,000 documents. Within a few months of getting the go-ahead, however, Masson had short-circuited everything: He concocted a theory which, according to him, turns psychoanalysis on its head and drastically alters the world's view of Freud. He read preliminary accounts of his "findings" at closed professional meetings in London and New Haven, then blurted the whole thing to *The New York Times*; before long, he was out on his ear, and the portcullis clanged down behind him.

Masson contends that Eissler & Co. are hateful for dumping him (I think they're pathetic for embracing him in the first place), but it's understandable that they've recoiled from his brazen campaign to barge into the limelight. As a rule, translators and archivists lead placid lives; their names seldom appear in headlines. Having boldly gone where no man went before, Masson wasn't about to sink into obscurity for a few decades. He wanted fame, and he won it—briefly. All we got from the brouhaha was a couple of cheap thrills, when we might have had something priceless: unrestricted access not only to the Freud-Fleiss letters, but also to those reams of other papers, some of which are locked up till the 22nd century. Once led astray, the psychoanalytic watchdogs are unlikely to turn so docile again; whoever ends up succeeding Eissler will no doubt be a company man, colorless and safe.

This is a shame, much more lamentable than the fate of Jeffrey Masson, who's sure to rise from his ashes. Of course, Masson would counter my uncharitable interpretation of his actions with the claim that the discoveries he made in Freud's letters were so shocking that he *had* to speak out, damn the torpedoes. Well, *The Assault on Truth* contains the whole scandal, and I, for one, remain skeptical. The questions it raises are disturbing enough, but I wish Masson had waited till he calmed down (if he ever does) and could assess them soberly. His book is strident and hasty, driven by a Carry Nationish fervor that gets wearisome by about page two. It seems not to conceal any facts, but it's occasioly sloppy about them. (Joan Riviere's death date, for example, is omusly given as "?" as if she'd wandered off into the Yucatan with Ambse Bierce. Actually, Mrs. Riviere—Freud's foremost English trans-latoext to James Strachey—died under thoroughly respectable cir-cumances in 1962; Strachey wrote her obituary for the *International Jouıl of Psycho-Analysis.*)

asson's case against Freud might be damning, if it weren't so nar-rowıd lurid. He focuses in on the moment which all commentators havehosen as the origin of psychoanalysis—September 21, 1897, when Freuwrote to Fleiss, "I no longer believe in my *neurotica*." Until then, he h taken his neurotic patients at their word when they traced their aduldisorders to sexual molestation in childhood, usually by the fatheFor some time, Freud had been finding it "hardly credible that pervıed acts against children were so general"; he was also coming to see tlt "there is no 'indication of reality' in the unconscious, so that it is imıssible to distinguish between truth and emotionally-charged fic-tion.'The convergence of these two ideas produced the portentous hypoıesis that, from the point of view of adult illness, it didn't matter whetir the hysteric had really been raped by Papa or had dreamt the deed p; the resulting neurosis would be the same.

Tis letter to Fleiss wasn't published till 1950, but Freud's change of heartad long been apparent from his essays. In the 1896 "Aetiology of Hystıa" (reprinted by Masson as an appendix), Freud stated unequiv-ocallyhat "at the bottom of every case of hysteria there are one or more occurınces of premature sexual experience." By 1905, this necessary pre-condiın had become an "accidental influence"; and in 1914, the myth of thebirth of psychoanalysis was made complete with the declaration that sxual experience (as distinct from fantasy) had been "a mistaken idea."'Initial error led to a profound discovery," bubbled Ernest Jones in 1924. Few episodes in the history of scientific research provide a more dramaic test of true genius than the occasion on which Professor Freud made he devastating discovery that many of these traumas to which he had ben obliged to attach aetiological significance had never occurred outsidı the imagination of the patients. The realization that an imag-ined event could in certain psychological circumstances produce an effect exactlyequivalent to that of an actual event was one that only an inves-tigator gifted with a supreme feeling for psychology could have achieved."

Jones was a fathead, but a powerful one. Through sheer doggedness and slavish devotion, he made up for manifest shortage of intellect to become the most influential psychoanalyst after Freud himself. Weary of defectors, Freud welcomed such unqualified loyalty, though he was never wholly blind to his henchman's flaws: "Jones is hardly a happy prospect for the future," he wrote to Max Eitingon in 1932, on Jones's

election to the presidency of the International Psychoanalytic Assoc-
tion. It was Jones who canonized the myth that psychoanalysis entd
the world when Freud stopped believing his patients; Freud was rer
so unambiguous. Masson's target in *The Assault on Truth* is at st
double, though he doesn't seem to know it. He fulminates against Fid
the man as if all the subsequent failings of psychoanalysis were due a
single dereliction by its founder; but the real culprit, it seems to n is
neither Freud nor even Jones, no individual at all. The hardest trut to
accept are the kind that obviate both villains and heroes, that trac vil
results to the best of motives. Everything we know of human hiry
tells us that no effect is produced by a single cause; more insisttly
than any other modern philosophy, psychoanalysis tells us that.

Behind evil Freud, in the fable Masson spins, stood a sillier moter,
Fliess. Among other crackpot notions, Fliess had conceived the tory
that there was a direct connection between the nose and the gital
organs, especially in women. So enamored was Freud of his only intimate friend that he swallowed this malarkey, even letting Fleiss oprate
on his own nose and referring patients to him. Among the patien was
Emma Eckstein, whom Freud was treating for various hysterical smp-
toms, including irregular and painful menstruation. Emma may ave
been sexually abused as a child; Masson insists that she had bee and
quotes some remarks of Freud's that seem to imply it. Nothing her
childhood, however, could have matched the violence she suffered s an
adult at the hands of her two trusted doctors.

Since Emma's problems centered in her genitals, Fleiss's daffy logic
declared that her nose should be cut open. After some hesitatin—it
would be Fleiss's first major surgery of this kind—Freud sent Emma
under the knife. It's not recorded what Fleiss carved out (possibly the
turbinal bone), but within a month there was trouble: infection, leed-
ing, and terrible pain. So Emma was opened up again, this tine by
Robert Gersuny, a competent doctor. He cleansed and closed her; couple of days later the bleeding resumed; a drainage tube was inerted;
more days, more bleeding, then finally, during Emma's fourth or fifth
operation, yet another surgeon, I. Rosanes, grabbed hold of the truth.
As Freud wrote to Fleiss on March 8, 1895, "suddenly he pulled at
something like a thread, kept on pulling and before either one of us had
time to think, at least half a meter of gauze had been removed from the
cavity. The next moment came a flood of blood."

The event was nauseating enough (Emma's pulse briefly stopped,
and even Dr. Freud felt sick), but the sequel, says Masson, was worse.
Though the apparent cause of her distress was gone, Emma didn't get
better; menstrual problems continued, now accompanied by nosebleeds.
Fleiss's operation had been a failure in more senses than one, leaving the

old "hysterical" symptoms untouched and adding a new source of pain. Freud was in an extremely awkward position: His dear Wilhelm was obviously a quack, if not also a madman, but he was Freud's only close friend, and the two men shared what even stodgy Ernest Jones had to call a "passionate" attachment. Then there was poor Emma, still suffering, still bleeding. Freud's ungraceful escape from this impasse was to announce that Emma's nosebleeds, too, were hysterical, that she bled "out of *longing*" and not because a clumsy man had done horrible damage to her nose. That, according to Masson, was the real birth of psychoanalysis—not a bold thrust of genius, but a coward's recoil from the truth. On this false cornerstone, a false edifice has rested ever since.

Most of the information Masson supplies on the Emma Eckstein affair isn't new; though all references to Emma were expurged from *The Origins of Psychoanalysis,* Max Schur translated and published the bulk of the relevant letters in 1966. Schur expressed amazement and outrage in private notes, but his public pronouncements were mild: The episode served to elucidate the Freud-Fleiss relationship and to clarify the famous "Dream of Irma's Injection" in *The Interpretation of Dreams* (1899). Scholarship alone won't do for Masson; he wishes to explain literally everything, Freud's entire career and the subsequent history of psychoanalysis throughout the world, as the consequence of this single snafu. If Freud had stuck with his first idea, Masson maintains, and had gone on regarding childhood molestation as the sole cause of neurosis, psychoanalysis would do some actual good. Instead, Freud fled into fantasy, running away from the horror that lustful adults wreak on innocent children.

Emma Eckstein's story is the centerpiece of *The Assault on Truth,* flanked on one side by an account of Freud's extensive reading in the literature of child abuse and on the other by a chapter on Sándor Ferenczi, who tried to revive the seduction theory in the early 1930s. From Masson's point of view, the assault on Freud wins or loses via Eckstein, but in his hubris he overlooks a few details. For instance, nowhere in Freud's letters to Fleiss does he say that Emma's first hemorrhages were not brought on by the gauze in her nose; only the repetitions were hysterical, the product of "longing." "When she saw how affected I was by her first hemorrhage," Freud wrote on May 4, 1895, "she experienced this as the realization of an old wish to be loved in her illness, and in spite of the danger during the succeeding hours she felt happy as never before." Emma might have gone on bleeding as the aftereffect of Fleiss's hatchet job—Masson makes this the only possible explanation, though he can provide no proof—but she might just as well have healed completely once the gauze was ripped out, bleeding again for the reason Freud gave.

I can come up with a much better scenario for Freud's abandonment of the seduction theory, one hardly more flattering to Freud and calling on no suppressed documents. If neurosis were caused exclusively by violation of children, psychoanalysis would have become merely a specialized form of therapy. Freud was too ambitious for that; he wanted to account for the whole of human culture, all the way back to the caves, and he never could have done that with a technique tailored to a minority. Ambition, then, rather than cowardice, was his motive—nothing to be proud of either, if it really led him to launch an attack on "truth," as Masson contends.

I'm never comfortable with books that bandy "truth" about, especially when the author claims to have sacrificed everything in truth's name. The contrast between Masson and Freud (both à la Masson) is suspiciously neat: bravery vs. cowardice, clear sight vs. illusion, truth vs. lies. All they seem to have in common is monumental ego, along with a fierce determination to wipe out their precursors. Do you suppose Masson's feelings toward Freud might be (ahem) Oedipal? The concept of the Oedipus complex grew directly out of the junking of the seduction theory; if one falls, so must the other. By reinstating the reality of seduction, Masson would discredit the theory that best explains his own behavior, thereby exonerating himself for the umpteenth time. Maybe he's not so different from his version of Freud after all.

The Assault on Truth stacks every card: If you want to refute it, you apparently have to come out in favor of child abuse. Masson can rely on the fact that none of his readers will be able to consider this issue dispassionately; he cleverly blurs the distinction between the "truth" of battered children and the "truth" of his own crusade, making it seem that he's the first psychoanalyst who ever recognized that children do get raped and beaten. We all know that the incidence of child molestation is greater than was ever supposed, but it can hardly be universal; Masson cites no figures. Nor does he distinguish between the effects of a single act of brutality and of "a childhood filled with sexual violence." If you're going to make yourself the champion of "reality," you ought to pay attention to gradations like these; otherwise, you run the risk of joining your opponents, the hidebound shrinks, who claim that reality doesn't matter.

But Masson isn't interested in nuances. As *In the Freud Archives* and *The Assault on Truth* both demonstrate, he's after shock and scandal, seasoned with self-justification. Actually, though Malcolm's book is far superior to Masson's, the public response to the case was more interesting than either. Masson isn't alone, evidently, in his Oedipal relation to Freud; to judge from cocktail-party conversations, newspaper articles, and a new surge of debunking books, the whole world shares it. Small wonder: If contemporary civilization has a father, Freud's only close rival is Christ, and Freud seems to be winning. Nowadays, psychoanalysis is our closest equivalent to what the Catholic Church must have been for Voltaire—manifestly rotten but apparently indestructible, it enables us to think and at the same time stifles us.

Kill the Father!—whether or not you can derive all motives from this ancient imperative, as Freud thought you could, it certainly accounts for the latest wave of assaults on psychoanalysis. The thinking of most new anti-Freudians is almost pathetically naive: discredit Freud the man, and, like a rank of dominoes, the technique, the philosophy, and the century that swallowed both will tumble after him. As the high priest of modernism, Freud deserves to be defrocked; the impotent voodoo that calls itself psychoanalysis has earned all the abuse it gets; "Freudian" art and criticism are too insipid for words. The wish to be rid of these millstones is wholesome, yet to think the job can be done by kicking down a single idol plays foolishly into the idol's tarnished hands. How can you simply kill the Father who taught you that his death must be your desire?

Rebellion is simmering everywhere, though in this instance as in most others, it's taking a feeble form. With no more subtlety than the scriptors of *Dallas*, anti-Freudian polemicists like Masson continue to whittle down a century of intellectual and cultural history into a tacky fable. When Freud wanted a universal myth, at least he went to a tragedy that had proved its fascination for over 2000 years. The best that can be done by Freud's *Nachkömmlinge*—another tasty German word; it means "little things that come after"—are creaky horror tales that Stephen King would sneer at. There are exceptions; now and then a critic of psychoanalysis has the sensitivity to restrain his rage, and the dedication to work hard puzzling out a sad tale that grants no easy answers. Drowned in sensationalism, however, such quiet, thoughtful books seldom receive a proper hearing. Russell Jacoby's *The Repression of Psychoanalysis* is one of these, worth a cartload of Massons. Before I get to it, I want to dispose of a couple more screamers.

Alice Miller's *Du sollst nicht merken* appeared in 1981, in the midst of the Masson hoopla; the English version, *Thou Shalt Not Be Aware: Psychoanalysis and Society's Betrayal of Children*, translated by Hildegarde and Hunter Hannum, is published by Farrar, Straus & Giroux. Miller has a couple of pixilated walk-ons in *In the Freud Archives*, complaining of defective swimming goggles and screwing up a dinner party. At the time, she was, as Masson told Malcolm, his "only remaining supporter," though he had to admit that her earlier book, *Prisoners of Childhood*, wasn't "scholarly—but it's on the right track, and I owe her a great deal." The track of *Thou Shalt* runs straight backward, asserting the "innocence" of children, their freedom from all sexual desire prior to puberty. The Freudian scheme, postulating sexuality that goes underground about age five and sprouts again when pubic hairs do, is dubious enough—but this reversion to a pre-Freudian idea, an idea that's literally pre-everything, appalls me.

It's ridiculous to suppose that human beings, uniquely among living creatures, give birth to things that hang around for 15 years or so before they get a glimmer of the business that brought them on earth in the first place—that is to say, sex. Miller acknowledges that no one in history has ever believed this; nevertheless, she asserts it. If you can overlook its wacky premise, though, her case against psychoanalysis is more telling than Masson's. While he wallows in infantile rape scenes, she suggests—not systematically; coherence isn't her forte—that the very state of being a child, a small, helpless entity hemmed in by big, strong adults, is an arena of violence. Daddy doesn't have to stick his penis inside you for you to feel raped; all he has to do (Mommy goes along) is to run the world without your consent. They were mewlers and pukers once, and abused this way, so they just continue it. The cycle revolves; simply being alive damns us all.

Miller works up a fine head of steam over our plight, but it seems rather futile, since by her own account the problem has been with us forever (even *before* the expulsion from Paradise), and she offers no solution to it. I don't see how there very well could be one, unless we let actual babies run for president. *Thou Shalt Not Be Aware* doesn't propose this, though it comes close; it's a silly book, yet at times it almost made me weep. I can't resist Miller's idea that for 2000 years we've been misjudging Jesus, attributing all his accomplishments to that heavenly Father of his and neglecting the earthly one, Joseph. Sure, it helped to have God in the family; but, according to Miller, God was "demanding, distant, invisible, and infallible"—no fun at all. Little Jesus was much better off with Joseph, "who never called attention to himself, who protected and loved Mary and the child, encouraged the child, assigned him central importance, and *served* him." God gave Jesus his vocation, but Joseph made him nice.

This is delicious. Miller stands up for every underdog in sight, and you can't help liking her. Amid all the goofiness, however, a good idea flashes out now and then—undeveloped, dizzily presented, yet superior to Masson's tawdry tale of a psychoanalysis raped at birth. Miller seems to have had no access to Masson's shocking revelations (she never mentions him), but she comes to the same conclusion: that psychoanalysis betrayed us all when Freud rejected the seduction theory. The difference is that, in her version, Freud isn't personally guilty. Raised under the system of "poisonous pedagogy" that has prevailed since the dawn of time and still rules us, he merely capitulated to the myth of noble parenthood, as all his successors have done. Unable to face the fact of innocent childhood, he devised a theory of "drives" and "infantile sexuality" that blames the world's woes on children, salvaging the honor of adults. But Western culture had always done that, in one way or another, so Freud was nothing worse than a deluded child of his time.

Fair enough—impossible to refute, at any rate. If only Miller weren't so scatterbrained, if she'd focused in on this idea and worked it out more carefully, *Thou Shalt Not Be Aware* might have laid down a coherent argument, rather than a heap of half-baked assertions. It might have approached, that is, the cool, highly scientific structure of our next blow against the empire, E. M. Thornton's *The Freudian Fallacy*. At the heart of Thornton's book lurks a madness far more profound than Miller's giddiness or even Masson's megalomania; yet you can't fault its documentation, its bland, sane style, or the logical progress of its indictment. It was published last year in England as *Freud and Cocaine*, but the American publishers must think this gives too much away. Right: It gives *everything* away.

We've known for a long time that Freud was deeply into coke in the mid-1880s; Ernest Jones spilled those beans in a chapter of his biography called "The Cocaine Episode." Elated by this new wonder drug, Freud used it freely, recommended it to everybody, and made it out to be the universal remedy. Evidence of overdose and addiction began to pile up, however, and when the discovery of cocaine's only legitimate medical function—local anesthetic in eye surgery, still the only one— was made in 1887 by Carl Koller, Freud supposedly dropped the stuff for good. This is the orthodox version, though there have been some people (Peter Swales for one, me for another) who looked at Freud's formidable literary output, his lifelong regimen of patients all day and scribbling half the night, and wondered whether coke had really been just an "episode."

According to Thornton, Freud not only used cocaine till at least 1912, he was firmly addicted to it and made up all his nasty theories under its influence. Fleiss was an addict, too—hence his obsession with noses—and the letters between the two men were nothing more than an exchange of increasingly wacked-out delusions by a pair of druggies. There's no such thing as the unconscious (just drug-dreams), no infantile sexuality (drugs make you horny), and no point in struggling through the denser passages of Freud's writing (bad effects of same on expository style). All of Freud's early patients were epileptics, not neurotics; they took coke, prescribed to them by the Doctor, so everything they said can be traced to the same source. Once again, at the touch of a single idea, psychoanalysis and its history vanish as if they'd never been.

From Thornton's point of view, we have no spiritual life, only a bank of little switches flicking on and off. This is the standard ultramedical position; until the end, in fact, Freud clung to the hope that what he described as "mental" would turn out to have a physical basis. Physiologists of various brands have often attacked psychoanalysis on this ground, though I've never seen anything to equal the sweeping absoluteness of *The Freudian Fallacy*. That, of course, is a fallacy in itself. I feel as though I'm constantly harping on the same string, but in the face of this new deluge of cures for Freud, it seems the point can't be made too often: Nothing so intricate, complex, and subtle as psychoanalysis, so deeply ingrained in our culture and so powerfully influential on the very people who put it down, is going to disappear at the wave of a wand.

I mistrust the nostalgia for prelapsarian innocence that pervades these simpleminded campaigns. I'm also wary of their ignorance of history. Masson, Miller, and Thornton come at psychoanalysis from different angles and do their demolition work in different ways, but along with a frenzied desire to pulverize Freud, they share the naive belief that they can wipe out the 20th century in the process. None of them so much as attempts to explain why an egregious card-house like psychoanalysis, ready to crumble at the impact of any feather, was bought wholesale by an entire culture that still dwells in it. All of them seem to think that today's psychoanalysis remains more or less as Freud left it, that by deep-sixing him they can abolish the institution he founded. The optimism is touching but wrongheaded; the shrinks hardly need to lift a finger in self-defense—as Masson found out when his celebrated megatonnage did the damage of a cherry bomb. Asked whether Masson's exposé would mean the end of their profession, various eminent shrinks smiled condescendingly. Of course not, they replied; we don't pay much attention to Freud nowadays. We're "eclectic"—a little from here, a little from there, each of us forging his own distinctive technique. So even if Freud was a coward, a child molester, *and* a coke addict, nothing will change.

True, and no reason to rejoice. The oddest thing about the professional response to Masson (which would greet Miller and Thornton, too) is that the attackers and the pooh-poohers range themselves backward, taking what seem to be the wrong sides of the fence. Ordinarily, the members of an establishment are willing to acknowledge at least some kinship with its founder, but when the shrinks are accused of fidelity, they retort with proud assertions of faithlessness. None of our current anti-Freudians allows for that line of defense; they simply assume that today's psychoanalysts are Freud's direct descendants and go at them accordingly. Indeed, though it saves the shrinks for this round, it might end up a risky line to take, because it raises the natural question of where, if not from Freud, these highly paid technicians do come from. They really shouldn't let us ask that.

They're secure for the time being, however, since it's evident that few critics of psychoanalysis are willing or able to undertake the labor of finding an answer. Their hearts are in the right place, but their weapons are pitiful—garish little melodramas of dubious truth and proven ineffectiveness. Alone among the newest crusaders, Russell Jacoby has made the better effort: his *Repression of Psychoanalysis* isn't content with simple stories and easy outrage. He sees psychoanalysis not as the dastardly deed of a wicked individual, but as a discipline of thought developing through history, acted upon by many forces both good and evil. The pernicious sterility of contemporary psychoanalysis is due, for Jacoby, to a plot unfolding across three generations and employing scores of actors. The plot had no spinner, but it's no less tragic for that.

Jacoby focuses on the career of Otto Fenichel (1897–1946), whom specialists today know principally as the author of *The Psychoanalytic Theory of Neurosis* (1945), a standard textbook that Jacoby calls "conservative to a fault." But Fenichel hadn't always been so cautious: In the 1920s, he was a leading light among the new generation of analysts who gathered in Berlin, then the world center of psychoanalytic thought and practice, outstripping even Vienna. In November 1924, Fenichel organized a group of younger analysts for a series of informal meetings that soon became known as the *Kinderseminar* ("Children's Seminar"); they met unofficially, at one another's homes, to discuss matters too minor or too risky for public airing. Among the riskier subjects (though not yet fully taboo) was politics, the engagement of psychoanalysis in social action.

Gazing upon our present psychoanalytic establishment, no one would believe that this reactionary clique is the direct heir of a radical, even subversive tradition. That's Jacoby's point: psychoanalysis has "repressed" its past, obliterating where it came from in the interest of getting fat. Fenichel's career makes a sad paradigm. For almost nine years, the Children's Seminar convened regularly (168 meetings), taking no specific political stand but freely debating questions of socialism, communism, sex education, and the role of psychoanalysis in all these controversial movements. After the Nazi takeover in 1933, the group dispersed, expecting an early reunion but never to have one. Starting the following year and continuing till just before his death, Fenichel endeavored to keep the *Kinder* together by a barrage of *Rundbriefe* ("round" or "circulating letters," from a single sheet to more than 20 pages, in at least six carbons); Fenichel typed all 119 of them. He acted as clearinghouse for the other members, who sent questions and comments to him for distribution. The outside world had no inkling that such a fifth column existed, that well-known figures like Fenichel, Edith Jacobson, and Annie Reich were carrying on an underground correspondence. Psychoanalysis would later repress their memory, but they began by repressing themselves.

In his last chapter, Jacoby briefly considers the "Americanization of Psychoanalysis," an important factor in the repression and often discussed by other critics. He sums it up succinctly: "professionalization and medicalization; the insecurity of refugee analysts; the gap between American and European culture." The spectacle of Fenichel's last days is a poignant illustration. Since his Austrian medical degree wasn't valid in the United States, Fenichel decided—in his late forties, overweight, with an imperfect command of English—to enter on a course of internship. So this polished European gentleman, squeezed into an ill-fitting white uniform, went dashing down the corridors of Cedars of Lebanon Hospital, trying to keep up with a herd of callow Americans 20 years younger than he. The strain probably brought on the cerebral hemorrhage that killed him.

There are parallel cases, and they're heartbreaking. For Jacoby, however, the most drastic effect of exile to America was the havoc it wrought in the "delicate arena where psychoanalytic culture is passed from generation to generation." Any hint of socialist or communist affiliation would have discredited emigré analysts in the brave new American world, so they kept silent, letting their radical philosophy petrify into a prop of the status quo. But the process had set in earlier: The Nazi advance across Europe had driven psychoanalysts from one city to another before they fled the continent; it had cut their lines of communication and shattered their continuity; worst of all, it had induced within psychoanalysis itself a reflex of fear and self-censorship that prepared the way for cooptation across the Atlantic.

Last year, in *Fury on Earth*, Myron Sharaf told the disquieting story of Wilhelm Reich's expulsion from the International Psychoanalytic Association in 1934, at the hands of Ernest Jones and with the certain collusion of Freud. Reich's sins were numerous, but the most grievous of them seem to have been his membership in the Communist Party and his campaign to distribute contraceptives among the proletariat. Fenichel was never so controversial—though he and Reich were close for several years, they eventually split up—but he felt the necessity, if psychoanalysis was to maintain any sort of political involvement in those frightening days, to keep such activities secret both from the civil authorities and from the leaders of his own profession. At about the same time, Sándor Ferenczi was also on the way out—as Masson would have it, because he wanted to revive the seduction theory, but probably for a more significant reason.

The final chapter of *The Assault on Truth* is devoted to Ferenczi, in an effort to show that Freud's Eckstein phobia lasted till the end of his life. At the 12th International Psychoanalytic Congress in Weisbaden (1932), Ferenczi read a paper, "Confusion of Tongues" (another appendix in Masson), which proposed, along with a reconsideration of the reality of childhood trauma, a general relaxation of the relationship between analyst and analysand. For some time, Ferenczi had been working on his "active" technique, which involved the touching, even the kissing of patients; Reich, too, had been experimenting with physical contact. Ferenczi was moving in the direction of "mutual analysis," as his diaries reveal: If any of his own hang-ups happened to coincide with those of his patient, he would confess them, breaching the wall of silence that was (and is) supposed to separate the two.

Ferenczi's paper was duly published in German; English translation, however, which would bring it before a much wider audience, was delayed by Jones till 1949—too late for any gain to Ferenczi, who died in 1933. Once he was gone, a myth grew up (Jones codified it in his Freud biography) that Ferenczi had been going to pieces for years, that the honchos had stuck by him till the end, even when his derangement was undeniable, that his later work should be dismissed because it came from a madman. None of this holds water, as Masson shows. Again, as in the case of Reich and the Fenichel circle, established psychoanalysis withdrew from any member who threatened to make himself controversial in a hostile political environment. There's plenty of cowardice here, though not of Masson's soap-opera kind; it's the cowardice of small-minded, self-serving people, blinkered by the present and blind to the future.

The Repression of Psychoanalysis is the only one of these new critiques that disdains shortcuts and cocktail-party psychologizing. It isn't the kind of story your grandmother used to tell you, so it's unlikely to have the impact of the other muckrakers. Who wants painful nuances when you can get fairy tales? If Masson is any example, the others won't last long; the glare of hype that surrounded him has already died, making Malcolm's *In the Freud Archives* ancient history even before it was published. Nevertheless, it can't be an accident that so many anti-shrink books, solid or trivial, should come on us all at once. For a long time, we've been thinking of ourselves as postmodern, poststructuralist, post-post-post—but we're not yet post-Freud. If nothing else, these books are signals of readiness: Maybe eventually, instead of trying to kill this crafty last Father, we'll learn how to do an end-run around him—and out of the century he made his own.

June 1984

SISTERS UNDER THE SKIN?

Confronting Race and Sex

By Ellen Willis

> WOMEN, RACE AND CLASS
> *By Angela Davis*
>
> COMMON DIFFERENCES: CONFLICTS IN BLACK AND
> WHITE FEMINIST PERSPECTIVES
> *By Gloria I. Joseph & Jill Lewis*
>
> AIN'T I A WOMAN: BLACK WOMEN AND FEMINISM
> *By bell hooks*

Recently, at a feminist meeting, a black woman argued that in American society race is a more absolute division than sex, a more basic determinant of social identity. This started an intense discussion: If someone shook us out of a deep sleep and demanded that we define ourselves, what would we blurt out first? The black woman said "black woman." Most of the white women said "woman"; some said "lesbian." No one said "white person" or "white woman."

I'm not sure it makes sense to say that one social division is more absolute than another. I wonder if it isn't more a matter of different kinds of division. Most blacks and whites live in separate communities, in different social, cultural, and economic worlds, while most women and men share each other's daily, intimate lives and cooperate, even if unequally, in such elemental activities as fucking, procreating, and keeping a household going. On the other hand, a man and a woman can spend their lives together and have such disparate versions of their "common" experience that they might as well live on different planets. Do I feel more distant from black women than from white men? Everything else (class) being equal? (Except that it usually isn't.) In some ways yes, in some ways no. But whatever the objective truth, my sex feels more basic to my identity than my race. This is not surprising: In a sexist society it's impossible to take one's femaleness for granted; in a racist society whiteness is simply generic humanness, entirely unremarkable. Suppose, though, that a black revolution were to seriously challenge my racial privileges? Suppose I had to confront every day, every hour, the question of which side I'm on?

Such questions excite and disturb me. Like talk about sexuality, discussions of the racial-sexual nexus radiate danger and taboo—a sign that the participants are on to something. Lately such discussions, mostly initiated by black women, are happening more often. They raise the heartening possibility of connecting, and in the process revitalizing the unhappily divergent discourses of feminism and black liberation. This could be the first step toward creating a new feminist radicalism, whose interracial, interclass bonds go deeper than lowest-common-denominator coalition politics.

One of the women at the meeting suggested that I read *Sally Hemings*, Barbara Chase-Riboud's controversial historical novel about Thomas Jefferson's black mistress. I found it a devastating study of the psychology of masters and slaves, the politics of romantic love, the relations between black and white women, and the institution of the family. Much of its power lies in the way the author merges the race and sex of each character into a seamless whole, bringing home the point that to abstract these categories is already to falsify experience. So long as whiteness and maleness remain the norm, white women can think of themselves as "women," black men as "blacks"; but black women, doubly the Other, must be constantly aware of their dual identity at the same time that they suffer from both racial and sexual invisibility. In forcing the rest of us to see them, they also present us with new and far less tidy pictures of ourselves.

This suggests that confronting the oppression of black women means more than taking in new information or taking up new issues. It also means questioning the intellectual frameworks that the (male-dominated) black and (white-dominated) feminist movements have set up. If race and sex are experientially inseparable, can we (should we) still analyze them separately? If all women are subject to male supremacy—yet black and white women play out their relations with men (both inside and outside their own communities) in different ways—do they still have a common core of female experience, a common political oppression *as women?* Theoretically, the different situations of black women and black men should raise the same sort of question. But in practice black women single out their relation to white women and feminism as the more painful, problematic issue. This subject is now bursting through a decade's sediment of sloganeering, ritualistic condemnations, and liberal apologies to inform some provocative new writing.

But first, I feel I have to say something about Angela Davis. *Women, Race and Class* may have been inspired by all this ferment, but the kindest judgment I can make is that it misses the point. From Davis's orthodox Marxist perspective (still CP after all these years!), in which economic relations determine all, while sexual relations have no material status and sexism is merely a set of bad attitudes, the question of how racial and sexual politics interact loses its meaning. Davis strips racism of its psychocultural dimension and treats it strictly as a form of economic exploitation; she tends to ignore sexism altogether, except when invoking it as an excuse for white bourgeois feminists to undermine the struggles of black and working people. (For instance, she rightly condemns the racism of white suffragists outraged at the prospect that black men would get the vote before white women—but rationalizes the sexism that prompted black men to sell out women of both races by agreeing that the black male vote should have priority. Black men's "sexist attitudes," Davis argues, were "hardly a sound reason for arresting the progress of the overall struggle for Black liberation"—and never mind the effect on that struggle of denying the vote to half the black population.) Still, it would be a mistake to simply dismiss Davis's book as an anachronism. In more subtle and ambiguous forms, its brand of left antifeminism continues to influence women's thinking. Besides, Angela Davis is a public figure, and *Women, Race and Class* will undoubtedly outsell both the books I'm about to discuss.

Gloria I. Joseph is black; Jill Lewis is white. In *Common Differences: Conflicts in Black and White Feminist Perspectives*, they attempt to explore their separate histories, confront misunderstandings, and move toward "collaborative struggle." The book has the flavor of an open-ended political conversation; for the most part the authors write separate chapters, each commenting from her own perspective on various aspects of sexual politics. The result is uneven, full of intellectual loose ends and contradictions, and both writers have an unfortunate penchant for clotted, obfuscatory prose. But *Common Differences* does help to clarify touchy areas of black-white conflict. Joseph's chapters—which taught me a lot, especially about black mothers and daughters—are a valuable counterweight (and an implicit rebuke) to the tendency of white feminist theorists to base their generalizations about the female condition on white women's experience. In discussing black women's lives, Joseph uses a time-honored feminist method: She records group discussions and individual comments, picks out common themes and contradictions, and tries to draw conclusions. The immediacy of this material exposes white feminist parochialism more effectively than any abstract argument.

Without denying the movement's shortcomings, Lewis sets out to debunk the stereotype of the spoiled, elitist "women's libber." The feminist movement, she maintains, deserves recognition as the only social movement to challenge the status of women as women. She argues that white feminists have been struggling toward a deeper understanding of race and class, and that even those sectors of the movement most narrowly oriented to white middle-class concerns "have engaged in and won concrete struggles that potentially open up new terrain for *all* women."

In their introduction, Joseph and Lewis agree that "as a political movement, women's liberation did and does touch on questions which in different ways affect *all* women's lives." But *Common Differences* is much more about difference than about commonality. In *Ain't I a Woman: Black Women and Feminism* bell hooks strides boldly beyond pluralism to the rockier ground of synthesis. While hooks also stresses the uniqueness of black women's experience and the ways it has been discounted, her aim is to enlarge the theoretical framework of feminism. To this end she analyzes black women's condition in a historical context, tracing the basic patterns of black female oppression to slavery and developing three intertwined themes: black men's sexism, white women's racism, and the effect of white men's racial-sexual politics on the relations between black and white women. Hooks is a contentious writer, and I don't always agree with her contentions, but *Ain't I a Woman* has an intellectual vitality and daring that should set new standards for the discussion of race and sex.

The central political question these books raise is why the contemporary feminist movement has been so white. Most critics of the movement have offered a simple answer: White feminists' racism has driven black women away. This indictment is true as far as it goes, but it already takes for granted facts that need explaining. Why, in the first place, was it primarily white women, rather than black women or both groups simultaneously, who felt impelled to mobilize against sexism? And why did so many politically conscious black women reject the movement (in some cases the very idea of feminism) out of hand, rather than insisting that it purge its theory and practice of racism, or organizing groups committed to a nonracist feminist politics? Antifeminist leftists have typically argued that sexual politics are inherently a white middle-class crotchet, irrelevant to women who are "really"—i.e., economically and racially—oppressed. Or else (this is Angela Davis's main strategy) they redefine feminism to mean women fighting together against racism and capitalism, and conclude that black and white working-class women have been the leaders of the *real* feminist struggle. Either way they imply that sexism is not a problem for black women, if indeed it is a problem at all.

Hooks, Joseph, and Lewis reject this idea. They assume that black women have a stake in women's liberation, and see white feminists' racism as part of a complex social history that has shaped black women's politics. Bell hooks argues that estrangement between black and white women goes all the way back to slavery. The terms of the conflict, as she sees it, were defined by white men who applied racism to a Victorian sexual (and class) ideology that divided women into two categories: good (chaste, delicate, to be protected and idealized) and bad (licentious, unrefined, to be exploited and punished). While the white upper-class southern woman represented the feminine ideal, black female slaves were stigmatized, in schizoid fashion, both as bad women—therefore deserving to be raped and beaten—and as nonwomen: In doing the same work as men, black women threatened the ideology of female inferiority, a contradiction resolved by defining them as neuter beasts of burden.

At the same time, the white woman's power to collaborate in oppressing blacks softened and obscured the reality of her own inferior position. She exercised this power most directly over female slaves, whom she often treated with the special viciousness of the insecure boss. No doubt the degraded status of black women also reminded her, subconsciously at least, of what can happen to any female who provokes men into dropping the mask of patriarchal benevolence. As hooks observes, the manifest cruelty of white women's own husbands, fathers, and brothers "served as a warning of what might be their fate should they not maintain a passive stance. Surely, it must have occurred to white women that were enslaved black women not available to bear the brunt of such intense antiwoman aggression, they themselves might have been the victims." As a result, the very identification that might have led white women to black women's defense probably had the opposite effect. White men's sexual pursuit of black women also exposed white women's humiliating position: They could neither prevent their husbands' behavior nor claim a comparable freedom for themselves. Instead they expressed their anger, salvaged their pride, and defended their own good-woman status by vilifying black women as seducers and sluts.

Hooks shows that what she calls the "devaluation of black womanhood" did not end with slavery but remains a potent source of black women's rage. Her account of how black women are systematically disparaged as whores, castrating matriarchs, and sexless mammies explains a crucial ingredient of black female hostility to the women's movement. Clearly, when white feminists ignored black female experience and in effect equated "women" with "white woman," the insult had a double meaning for black women: It suggested that we were not only reinforcing white supremacy but trying to have it both ways by preserving our monopoly on femininity and its rewards (respect, status, financial support) while demanding the option of rejecting it. This perception of bad faith fueled the angry denunciations of feminism as "white women's business."

But envying white women's "femininity" is a trap for black women, as hooks is well aware. Idealization of the white woman's status has tended to divert black women from demanding sexual justice to attacking black men for their inability to support stay-at-home wives. Many black women have endorsed black male demands for female subservience in the hope that at last they would get a crack at the pedestal. At the same time, their envy of white women has been mixed with contempt, an emotion that led some black women to insist they didn't need a movement because they were already liberated. Another illusion in hooks's relentless catalogue: Strength in adversity and the need to make a living are not the same thing as freedom.

Gloria Joseph emphasizes the painful collisions of black and female identity. As she says, "an individual cannot be two separate entities." Yet black women suffer from two modes of oppression and so are implicated, like it or not, in two social movements at once. At best this involves a double burden, at worst a continuing conflict of loyalties and priorities. Joseph shows that deep ambivalences permeate black women's thinking—on black men (distrust and antagonism mixed with solidarity, affection, and protectiveness), on sex ("a 'desirable no-no,' an 'attractive nuisance'"), on feminism itself (most of Joseph's respondents reject the movement but endorse its goals). Her argument suggests that black women have been slow to commit themselves to feminism—especially the more radical aspects of sexual politics—for fear of weakening their ties with the black community and the black struggle. Jill Lewis points out that white middle-class women could focus singlemindedly on feminism because "they did not have the stakes of *racial* unity or solidarity with White men that the Black women had with Black men" and because their privileges left them "free of the survival struggles that are priorities for minority and working-class women." If anything, class and racial privileges (particularly education) spurred their consciousness of sexual injustice by raising expectations that were thwarted purely because they were women.

Ironically, Joseph exemplifies the dilemma she describes: Like many other black women who define themselves as feminists, she draws the line at calling black men oppressors. While Joseph and Lewis agree that black and white women are oppressed as women, they uncritically assume that male supremacy is a product of white culture, and that the concept does not really apply to male-female relations among blacks, except insofar as all white institutions and values shape black life. Lewis asserts that institutionalized sexism in America was imported by European immigrants, as if Native American, African, and other nonwhite cultures were free of male dominance. In fact, no anthropologist, feminist or otherwise, has ever come up with convincing evidence of a culture in which some form of male dominance does not exist.

Lewis and Joseph argue that because black men do not have the same worldly power as white men, "Male dominance as a salient problematic factor in male-female sexual relationships cannot be considered as a universal trait applicable to all men." But Joseph's own descriptions of black women's attitudes toward sex, men, and marriage—not to mention their struggles to bring up children alone—belie this view. Rather, her evidence confirms that despite black men's economic and social subordination to whites they share with all men certain male supremacist prerogatives, including physical and sexual aggression, the assumption of male superiority, and refusal to share responsibility for child rearing and housework. Joseph and Lewis also make the puzzling claim that sexist repression is more severe for white women because "Black women can be kept in their places via racism alone." Does racism alone account for black women's oppression as mothers, workers (including domestic workers), welfare recipients, prostitutes, victims of rape and sexual exploitation?

All this adds up to a bad case of conceptual confusion. You can't simultaneously agree that black women need feminism and deny the basic premise of feminism—that men have power over women. Women who engage in this form of doublethink still have a toe or two in the camp of left antifeminism; while rejecting crude economism of the Angela Davis variety, they assume that sexism is perpetuated not by men in general but by a white capitalist ruling class.

Hooks insists on the reality of black male sexism. Discussing the experience of female slaves, she angrily refutes the cliché that "the most cruel and dehumanizing impact of slavery . . . was that black men were stripped of their masculinity." This idea, she argues, merely reflects the sexist assumption that men's experience is more important than women's and that "the worst that can happen to a man is that he be made to assume the social status of woman." In fact, though all slaves suffered brutal oppression, "black men were allowed to maintain some semblance of their societally defined masculine role." Noting that American blacks came from African patriarchal cultures, hooks rejects the idea that black men learned sexism from whites and the myth (repeated once again by Angela Davis) that within the slave community men and women were equal. On the contrary, the slaves accepted the concept of male superiority, and black families maintained a sexual division of labor, with women doing the cooking, cleaning, and child care. Nor did slaveholders assign black men "women's work." Black women, however, were forced by their white masters to perform both "masculine" and "feminine" functions, working alongside black men at backbreaking labor in the fields, while also serving as houseworkers, breeders, and sexual objects.

Hooks implicitly links what she sees as black women's false consciousness about sexism with their political isolation: While the sexism of black male activists has forced black women to choose between asserting themselves as women and maintaining racial solidarity, the racism of white feminists has reinforced and justified that split. *Ain't I a Woman* describes how this combination of pressures undermined black women's efforts to participate in both 19th- and 20th-century feminist movements. In dissecting the rhetoric of the contemporary black and women's movements, hooks shows how sexism has been promoted as a cure for racism, sisterhood as a rationale for ignoring it. Black power advocates, confusing liberation with the assertion of their "manhood," embraced a white man's contention that a black matriarchy was the cause of their problems, and called on black women to advance the black cause by being submissive; some even suggested that sexual equality was a white racist idea, indicative of the white man's effeteness and decadence. Black Muslims tried to reverse the racist Victorian paradigm, defining black women as the feminine ideal and white women as devils (and establishing rigid patriarchal families).

Meanwhile the early radical feminists were claiming that the division between men and women was the most basic social hierarchy, and that since men had ruled every known political system, racism was basically a male problem ("men dominate women, a few men dominate the rest"—Redstockings Manifesto). This analysis, which I and most of my political cohorts then subscribed to, has had a good deal of influence on the movement as a whole. It has two erroneous implications: that it's impossible for white women to oppress black men, and that racial conflict between black women and white women has no objective basis, but is (on both sides) an inauthentic antagonism that only serves the interests of men. Radical feminists understood, theoretically, that to build female unity white women had to oppose racism and change their own racist attitudes and behavior. We were sharply critical of liberal feminists who defined women's freedom in terms of professional careers and formal equality within a racist, class-stratified social system. Yet emotionally our belief that sex was a more basic division than race allowed us to evade responsibility for racism. It was tempting to imagine that simply by doing what we wanted most passionately to do—build a radical feminist movement—we would also be fighting racism; tempting, too, to play down how much we benefited from being white. For a while feminism seemed a way out of the classic bind of white middle-class radicals: We no longer had to see ourselves as privileged people wondering where we fit into the revolutionary struggle; we too were part of an oppressed class with a historic destiny.

Hooks's anger at this refusal to be accountable is well-deserved. But when she gets down to specifics, she tends to oversimplify and at times rewrite history. In her indictment of "white upper- and middle-class feminists" (Abby Rockefeller aside, who are these upper-class feminists I keep hearing about?), the movement becomes a monolith. The political differences between liberals and radicals, the social conditions that allowed the former to co-opt and isolate the latter, the fierce intramovement debates about race and class are ignored or dismissed. White feminists' main aim, hooks charges, has been to join the male power structure; the movement has posed no threat to the system.

This is silly. The women's movement has been no more or less opportunistic than the black movement, the labor movement, or any other mass movement successful enough to attract power mongers. Feminists have not succeeded in making a revolution (neither, I believe, has the rest of the left), but—as Jill Lewis ably argues—we did create a new political arena and set a revolutionary process in motion. (Among other things, we established the political context in which a book like *Ain't I a Woman* can be written and read.) The best measure of our threat to the system is the virulence of the reaction against us.

Hooks also indulges in overkill when she tries to explain white feminists' appropriation of female experience in terms of two different, even contradictory forms of racism. My own view is that the right explanation is the obvious one: We were acting on the unconscious racist assumption that our experience was representative, along with the impulse to gloss over racial specificities so as to keep the "complication" of racism from marring our vision of female unity. Hooks makes these points, but she also argues that white feminists have shared the racist/sexist perception of black women as nonwomen. In the process she accuses white feminists of claiming that black women are oppressed only by racism, not sexism, and denying that black men can be oppressive. These charges are, to put it mildly, befuddling. If there was any point radical feminists insisted on it was that all women were oppressed because of their sex, and that all men had the power to oppress women. In response, antifeminist black women (along with black and white male leftists) made the arguments hooks now puts in our mouths, and denounced us as racists for attributing a "white problem" to black people. Inevitably, many white women have echoed these arguments, but it's perverse to blame feminists for them.

In fact, white feminists have generally been quite conscious of black women *as women;* it's their blackness we've had trouble with. Straightforward reactionary racism exaggerates differences and denies commonalities; liberal racism, more typical of white feminists, does the opposite. Since the denial of black women's "femininity" is such a central issue for hooks, she mistakenly assumes that protecting an exclusive claim to femininity is equally an issue for all white women. On the contrary, white feminists felt free to challenge received definitions of femininity because we took for granted our right to be considered women. And it was precisely because our claim to womanhood was not an issue for us that we were insensitive to black women's pain at being denied it by racial fiat. Many white feminists recognized that the division between white women and black women had something to do with good girls and bad girls. (Shulamith Firestone, in *The Dialectic of Sex,* discusses this idea at length.) What we didn't see was the asymmetry: We could decide to be bad, or play at being bad; black women had no choice.

Hooks's misperception of white feminists' psychology also leads her to argue that their analogies between women and blacks were designed "to evoke in the minds of racist white men an image of white womanhood being degraded" by association with black people, especially black men. Again, the "image of white womanhood" had much less resonance than hooks imagines, either for white feminists or for the white liberal and leftist men who were our immediate targets. The main reason that '60s feminists relied so heavily on comparisons between sexism and racism is that white male politicos recognized the race issue as morally legitimate, while dismissing feminism as "a bunch of chicks with personal problems." If anything, we were trying to evoke in these men the same guilt about sexism that they already felt about racism; since we hadn't yet experienced the drawbacks of liberal guilt, we craved its validation. We also hoped, naively enough, to convince black men to renounce their sexism and identify with the feminist cause.

Hooks takes a hard line on analogies between women and blacks. She argues that they always imply a comparison between white women and black men, that they make black women invisible, obscure the issue of white women's racial privilege, and divert attention from racism to white women's problems. Certainly racial-sexual analogies have been misused in all the ways hooks cites, but I don't see these misuses as either invariable or necessary. Many feminists have made analogies between women and blacks in full awareness that they are talking about two overlapping groups; what they mean to compare is two sets of oppressive relations, male-female and white-black. And though the dynamics and effects of racism and sexism differ in important ways, the parallels—legal, social, ideological—do exist. Which is why antiracist movements have been so instrumental in stimulating feminist consciousness and revolt.

Hooks refuses to recognize this. Scoffing at the idea that abolitionism inspired the first feminist wave, she says, "No 19th-century white woman could grow to maturity without an awareness of institutionalized sexism." But of course 19th-century white women—and for that matter my generation of white women—did exactly that. It is the essence of institutionalized sexism to pose as the natural order; to experience male dominance is one thing, to understand that it is political, therefore changeable, is quite another. For me and most feminists I know, that politicizing process was very much influenced by the civil rights and black power movements. Conversely, though feminism was not a miraculous antidote to our racist impulses and illusions, it did increase our understanding of racism.

Surely, the answer to exploitative comparisons between women and blacks is not to deny the organic link between antisexist and antiracist politics. Here hooks, too, gets trapped in contradictory thinking. She argues that the issues of racism and sexism cannot really be separated, yet she repeatedly singles out racism as an issue that is not only separate from sexism but prior to it. According to hooks, "American society is one in which racial imperialism supersedes sexual imperialism," and all black people, black men included, are absolutely lower on the social scale than any white woman. In other words, it is illegitimate for feminists to regard sexism as a category that can, at least theoretically, be abstracted from (and compared to) racism; but no comparable stricture applies to black liberationists.

Gloria Joseph agrees that "in the end, it is a question of priorities, and given the nature of racism in this country, it should be obvious that the Black liberation struggle claims first priority." Most black feminists whose views I know about take a similar position. It is easy to see why: Because racism is intertwined with, and in part defined by class oppression, black people as a group suffer an excruciating combination of economic hardship and social indignity that white middle-class women and even most white working-class women escape. (Of course this does not necessarily hold true for individuals—it can be argued that a middle-class educated black man is a lot better off than a white welfare mother from an Appalachian rural slum.) Besides, as hooks points out, women without the insulation of racial or class privilege are also the most vulnerable to sexist oppression: A white professional woman can buy liberation from housework by hiring a black maid; she can also (for the time being) buy the legal abortion Medicaid patients are denied.

Left antifeminists have often used this line of reasoning to suggest that sexual issues should wait until racism and poverty are abolished. Black feminists, by definition, have rejected that idea. But what then does it mean, in practical political terms, to say that despite the irreducibly dual character of black women's oppression, their sex is less immediate an issue than their race? Specifically, what does this imply for the prospect of an antiracist feminist movement, or, more modestly, "collaborative struggle" between black and white women?

While hooks never really focuses on strategic questions, Joseph and

Lewis often write as if black and white women are on fundamentally separate tracks. They refer, for instance, to "White feminism," a concept as self-contradictory as, say, "male socialism"; while one can speak of a feminism limited and flawed by white racist bias, it is *feminism* only to the extent that it challenges the subjection of women as a group. (The mechanical pluralism underlying the notion of separate-but-equal "White" and "Black" feminisms also impels the authors to capitalize "White." Though capitalizing "Black" may make sense as a polemical device for asserting black pride, racial self-assertion by white people is something else again.) But in discussing abortion, Jill Lewis endorses a specific approach to integrating feminism with race and class struggle. The strategy she describes has developed as a response to the abortion backlash, but the basic idea could be applied to almost any feminist issue. Since I think it's both appealing and fallacious, I want to discuss it in some detail.

Lewis argues that to "isolate" abortion as an issue and defend it in terms of freedom for women betrays a white middle-class bias: Since black women suffer not only from being denied safe abortions but from sterilization abuse, inadequate health care, and poverty—all of which impinge on their reproductive choices—a radical approach to "reproductive rights" must address all these concerns. The trouble with this logic is that abortion is not just one of many medical or social services being rolled back by Reaganism; nor does the present opposition to abortion stem from the same sources or political motives as pressure toward sterilization. Abortion is first of all the key issue of the new right's antifeminist campaign, the ground on which a larger battle over the very idea of women's liberation is being fought. In essence, the antiabortionists are arguing that women who assert their free agency and refuse to be defined by their childbearing capacity are immoral. (In contrast, no one defends poverty or forced sterilization on principle.) So long as this moral attack on women is gaining ground, presenting abortion primarily as a health or social welfare measure is ineffective because it evades the underlying issue. Our choice right now is to defend abortion as a pivotal issue of women's freedom, or lose the battle by default. This is not to belittle the urgency of opposing sterilization abuse (which is, among other things, another expression of contempt for black femaleness) or demanding better health care. Nor is it to deny that all these issues are linked in important ways. My point is only that the reproductive rights strategy does not resolve the touchy question of priorities. Rather, while purporting to cover all bases, it submerges sexual politics in an economic and social welfare program.

Is this good for black women? Gloria Joseph points out that on the issue of abortion rights, "Black women have even more at stake, since it is they who suffer more from illegal and abusive abortions." They also suffer more from having unwanted children under horrendous conditions. If a sexual-political strategy offers the only real chance to preserve legal abortion and restore public funding, it is clearly in black women's interest. Since black women are faced with so many urgent problems, they may well have other priorities, but it doesn't follow that white women who concentrate on abortion are indulging a racist bias. On the contrary, they're doing a crucial job that will benefit all women in the end.

All this suggests that the question of whether racism is worse (or more basic, or more pressing) than sexism matters less than the fact that both are intolerable. Not that I agree with the white feminists bell hooks castigates for dismissing racial differences on the grounds that "oppression cannot be measured." It's clear to me that in demonstrable ways, some oppressed people are worse off than others. But I do question whose interests are really served by the measuring. Once it's established that black women are the most victimized group, and that most black men are more victimized than most white women—then what?

In my experience, this kind of ranking does not lead to a politics of genuine liberation, based on mutual respect and cooperation among oppressed groups, but instead provokes a politics of *ressentiment*, competition, and guilt. Black men tend to react not by recognizing the sexual oppression of black women but by rationalizing their antifeminism as a legitimate response to white women's privilege. White women who are sensitive to the imputation of racism tend to become hesitant and apologetic about asserting feminist grievances. As for white women who can't see beyond their own immediate interests, attempts to demote them in the ranks of the oppressed do nothing but make them feel unjustly attacked and confirmed in their belief that sexual and racial equality are separate, competing causes. The ultimate results are to reinforce left antifeminism, weaken feminist militance, widen the split between the black and feminist movements, and play into the divide and conquer tactics of white men ("We can do something for blacks or for women, but not both, so you folks fight it out"). Black women, caught in the racial-sexual crossfire, stand to lose the most.

Insistence on a hierarchy of oppression never radicalizes people, because the impulse behind it is moralistic. Its object is to get the "lesser victims" to stop being selfish, to agree that their own pain (however deeply they may feel it) is less serious and less deserving of attention (including their own) than someone else's. Its appeal is that it allows people at the bottom of social hierarchies to turn the tables and rule over a moral hierarchy of suffering and powerlessness. But whatever the emotional comfort of righteousness, it's a poor substitute for real change. And we ought to know by now that effective radical movements are not based on self-abnegation; rather, they emerge from the understanding that unless we heal the divisions among us, none of us can win.

The logic of competing oppressions does not heal divisions but intensifies them, since it invites endless and absurd extension—for every person who has no shoes, there is always someone who has no feet. (One might ask, by this logic, what bell hooks has to complain about next to a woman from a dirt-poor third world country who was sold to her husband and had her clitoris cut off at age four.) White women will not become committed allies of black women because they're told that their own suffering is unimportant. What white women must be convinced of is that it's impossible to have it both ways—that the privileges we cling to are an insuperable obstacle to the freedom and equality we long for. We need to learn this lesson again and again. Good books help.

June 1982

VISITATION RITES

The Elusive Tradition of Plague Lit

By Richard Goldstein

A JOURNAL OF THE PLAGUE YEAR
By Daniel Defoe

THE WHITE PLAGUE
By René and Jean Dubos

THE PLAGUE
By Albert Camus. Translated by Stuart Gilbert

MEMORIES OF A CATHOLIC GIRLHOOD
By Mary McCarthy

BRING OUT YOUR DEAD: THE GREAT PLAGUE OF
YELLOW FEVER IN PHILADELPHIA IN 1793
By J. H. Powell

EPITAPHS FOR THE PLAGUE DEAD
By Robert Boucheron

AND THE BAND PLAYED ON: POLITICS, PEOPLE AND
THE AIDS EPIDEMIC
By Randy Shilts

SIGNIFICANT OTHERS
By Armistead Maupin

A RECENT MARTYR
By Valerie Martin

"Epidemics have often been more influential than statesmen and soldiers in shaping the course of political history, and diseases may also color the moods of civilizations. . . . [Yet] their role is rarely emphasized by historians." So wrote René and Jean Dubos in their landmark study of tuberculosis, *The White Plague* (1952). They might as well have included novelists among the oblivious. With the notable exception of TB, whose association with creativity inspired reams of inspirational verse and fiction, some of our favorite operas, and one certified literary masterpiece (*The Magic Mountain*), the literature of epidemics is as scant—or at least scantly remembered—as those tomes on phrenology that once graced transcendentalist coffee tables.

Do we need a Visitation Lit? In the current crisis, it hardly seems like a priority: Give us a vaccine, a cure; give us condoms that work and laws that protect. But our failure to devise an effective response to AIDS is partly a product of the silence of our culture. We are raised to regard epidemics as relics of distant lands and ancient eras; when an outbreak does occur, it seems unprecedented, unnatural. We cast about for a strategy, ceding the task to medicine and politics (though we don't really trust either profession), because we have no alternative. There is no cultural tradition that gives meaning and order to the chaos of an epidemic. There is only religion, with its mechanisms of suppression and control. Art has abdicated its authority to counsel us in time of plague. And this absence of an aesthetic is part of our helplessness.

Why are there so many novels about World War I and so few about the influenza epidemic that followed it, killing many more people? Why doesn't plague inspire literature the way war does? Perhaps because, at least until the spectre of nuclear annihilation, combat never threatened our hegemony over the environment. War is something men declare, but epidemics are a force of nature, and until we unravel their codes and learn how to repel them, they subject us to assault on their own, inhuman, terms. War is politics by other means, but epidemics have no purpose or intention; they happen, often as an unintended consequence of social mobility, sometimes by chance. War is, in some sense, as deliberate as fiction. But plague is accidental history.

The Grim Reaper notwithstanding, epidemics are hard to personify. An invisible enemy versus a small band of crusaders, reeking more of disinfectant than manly sweat, is hardly the stuff of heroic fantasy. War is butch; it is the strange fruit of masculinity. To die in combat is a confirmation of gender, but epidemics are androgynous, and the loss of control they induce is usually represented as emasculating. Men who fall victim to disease are champions brought low, given to heroic speechifying; women just lie there in paler and paler makeup. They are the ones who whisper about love and memory; men weep over their loss of mastery. (Think of Sly Stallone as the leukemia victim in *Love Story*). And real men die of some inner defect, not an infectious disease. Long before AIDS, we believed that epidemics strike—indeed, signify—the effete. Thomas Mann's social critique proceeds from this assumption, and his apprehension about sexuality finds a ready emblem in diseases like cholera and tuberculosis. Aschenbach and even Hans Castorp enter into the state of illness almost by consent, as a logical expression of character. Susceptibility is fate.

Mann's message takes a Nietszchean twist in America, where health is your own business and you'd better take care of yourself. The self-help cults that have arisen in response to AIDS reflect our assumption that illness is a character flaw made manifest, and usually preventable by good behavior. The process of "freeing ourselves from the bonds of karma, disease, problem relationships" (as an ad for those New Age nabobs, the Ascended Masters, puts it) suggests that not just desire, but nature itself, can be consciously controlled. The Eastern jargon is purely decorative; this view of the environment as a "peaceable kingdom" is central to American culture, and it persists—partly because literature has failed to deconstruct it—in direct denial of our actual history.

P estilence may have an old-world ring, but epidemics were, until quite recently, a recurring feature of urban life in America, as well as a force in such emblematic events as the Civil War and the great westward trek. Congress could not be convened in 1793 until George Washington rode through the streets of Philadelphia to assure himself that an outbreak of yellow fever, which had decimated the city, was under control. As J. H. Powell's riveting account of that outbreak, *Bring Out Your Dead*, reveals, the barbaric responses we associate with AIDS were commonplace in 1793: Refugees were stoned, shot, or left to starve as they wandered the countryside; newspapers from the capital were boiled in vinegar before anyone would read them; and the task of caring for the afflicted and burying the dead fell largely to impoverished blacks. This is an America you will not read about in fiction. There are no epics about the epidemics that struck New Orleans with such regularity that the death rate in that city remained higher than the birth rate for the entire 19th century; no chronicles of the devastation that disease wrought upon the '49ers as they headed west. You can read all about cannibalism on the Donner Pass, but not about diarrhea.

When we aren't discreet about the subject, we leave it to the likes of Bette Davis to set the tone of American rhetoric about epidemics—turgid and romantic. In *Jezebel*, she plays the ultimate coquette, all taffeta and eyelashes, who's brought to her senses by a bout of "yellowjack" that strikes her jilted beau. The film ends with the essential American image of vanity chastened by pestilence: Davis on a crowded wagon, rolling through the shuttered streets of Charleston, nursing her love in quarantine. There's a similar epiphany in *Arrowsmith*, when the young doctor's wife dies during a Caribbean outbreak of the same disease, and he breaks the rules of his profession by providing experimental serum to the natives without a control group. Though Sinclair Lewis meant his novel to be both a critique of scientism and a testament to its rigors, in the movie, such ambiguities are lost to the epidemic as otherworldly spectacle, complete with darkies chanting among the fronds.

The fabricator of pestilitential rhetoric in America is Poe, whose interest in the subject confirms its disreputability. "The Masque of the Red Death" is a paradigm of the dread epidemics arouse in us: Their terrible swift sword seems aimed directly at our hubris and hedonism—two sins Americans simultaneously celebrate and excoriate each other for. If the Red Death resembles any known disease, it is influenza of the sort that killed 20 million people in 1918. But in Poe, it comes on preternaturally, with profuse bleeding from every pore that kills in half an hour. What better setting for this Visitation than a primordial kingdom with a party-hearty sensibility too splendid to survive? When plague strikes, the royals retreat in a vain attempt to banish death. He enters anyway, dressed like the rogue in *The Desert Song*. "And one by one dropped the revelers in the blood-bedewed halls of their revel." In other words, the party's over.

Poe's maunderings could only have meaning in a culture so phobic about disease that the subject must be addressed in terms of retribution. We get the fate we deserve for living like Vincent Price. At the core of Poe's masque are guilt and denial, the very evasiveness our literature stands accused of displaying toward love and death. An epidemic calls up the same response, since it forces us to confront both the intensity of human need and the fragility of all relationships. As a culture whose optimism is its most enduring trait, we cannot bear to look directly at this experience, except through the lurid refracting lens of moral causality.

Compare Poe's Red Death with the description of influenza that opens Mary McCarthy's *Memories of a Catholic Girlhood*. It occupies less than a page, yet this account, as seen through a child's eyes, says more about the grotesque incongruity of an epidemic than any allegory. Traveling from Seattle to Minneapolis in a closed compartment, the entire family was stricken as the train proceeded east.

> *We children did not understand whether the chattering of our teeth and Mama's lying torpid in the berth were not somehow a part of the trip . . . and we began to be sure that it was all an adventure when we saw our father draw a revolver on the conductor who was trying to put us off the train at a small wooden station in the middle of the North Dakota prairie. On the platform at Minneapolis, there were stretchers, a wheel chair, red-caps, distraught officials, and, beyond them, in the crowd, my grandfather's rosy face, cigar, and cane, my grandmother's feathered hat, imparting*

*an air of festivity to this strange and confused picture, making us chil-
dren certain that our illness was the beginning of a delightful holiday.*

McCarthy's perspective belongs to another, far more naturalistic,
tradition of Visitation Lit. It is not to be found in fiction, but in the less
hallowed venues of journalism and memoir. From Pepys, we get the
sense of pestilence as an ordinary experience—one of life's elemental
indignities. From Defoe, we get the larger picture of a social organism
convulsing under bacterial siege. *A Journal of the Plague Year* (1722) is
the first example of that paradoxical form we now call the nonfiction
novel: It is "reported" as fact, but constructed as fiction, and all the
more potent for its formal confusion. Defoe invented the "plot" we still
impose on epidemics, and he intended it not just to convey but also to
shape reality as a tangible expression of his ideology.

As a Dissenter, Defoe was subject to professional and personal harassment by the Anglican authorities. The stance of a rebellious rationalist
informs his tone, perhaps even his choice of subject matter. The extremis
of plague gave Defoe a chance to rail at irrational "tradition"—in everything from quack cures to the futile quarantining of whole families when
one member took sick. And nothing revealed the sanctimoniousness of
his peers like the high, theocentric prose in which epidemics were cus-
tomarily described: "Now Death rides triumphantly on his pale horse
through our streets," read one typical account of the bubonic plague
that ravaged London in 1665. "Now people fall as thick as the leaves in
autumn, when they are shaken by a mighty wind." Defoe, in contrast, is
blunt, sensory, reportorial: "It came at last to such violence that people
sat still looking at one another, and seemed quite abandoned to despair;
whole streets seemed to be desolated . . . windows stood shattering with
the wind in empty houses for want of people to shut them."

What comes handed down to us as "objectivity" was actually a rhetoric of rebellion against the political and religious institutions that put
Defoe at personal risk. His response must have seemed like the proverbial
shoe-that-fits to Albert Camus, the Communist/resister who set out in
1947 to construct a metaphor for the German occupation and all it evoked
in the French. Camus intended plague to universalize the circumstances
of his own oppression, but so did Defoe. From the old Dissenter, Camus
borrowed not just the specter of a city stricken by bubonic disease but
the perspective of a rationalist in extremis, the antiliterary style, and
the very form of *The Plague*. The subject attracts the alienated, perhaps
because they sense the power of an epidemic to shatter social orthodoxy.

Both Defoe and Camus set out to instruct us about life beyond the
boundaries of personal control. Both call up the impotence and isolation—
even in fellowship—of those who must inhabit "a victim world secluded

and apart," as Camus describes Oran under quarantine. Camus could not have constructed his deliberately modern paradigm of "death in a happy city" without Defoe's radical vision of plague as a landscape where virtue and survival do not follow as the night the day. And though their subject is bubonic plague, with its ancient rhythm of explosive death, the dry rage and mordant irony Camus and Defoe share, their abiding sense of life's precariousness, are the personality traits of an AIDS survivor.

There was no plague in Oran during the years Camus wrote, and as far as is known, he never actually experienced an epidemic. Rather, he assembled his description from secondary sources—as did Defoe, a child of five when the outbreak he describes took place. So the "plot" these journalists impose on epidemics is a fictional contrivance. More to the point, it is a contrivance that we inherit as reality. We still trot out Defoe and Camus to class up think pieces about AIDS because we trust their reporting, even though its authenticity is an illusion. The model they created gives meaning to the meaningless; it shapes an event that is terrifying precisely because it seems chaotic. Can anyone who has never experienced an epidemic imagine, in purely naturalistic terms, the terror of an invisible entity, not to mention the ghastly, often abrupt, changes an afflicted body undergoes? In a literary work, no matter how grim, there is order, progression, response; when you add journalism's claim to objectivity, and its obsession with good and bad behavior, an epidemic can be fitted with a tangible structure of cause and effect. This—and not just verisimilitude—is the power of reportage.

As for the plot: It is a tale without a protagonist. The "hero" is a collective—the suffering multitudes, called up in a thousand images of mortification of the flesh. At first, they refuse to acknowledge anything out of the ordinary, and the narrative feeds on this denial (*we* know why the rats are dying). But there comes a moment when, as Defoe describes it, "the aspect of the city itself was frightful." Denial gives way to terror, and the suspense is not just who will live and die, but whether society will endure. Pestilence brings the collective into high relief. It must protect the uninfected, care for the stricken, and dispose of the dead. That it does function is—for both Camus and Defoe—a source of chastened optimism. Plague, the despoiler of civilization, has become an agent of social cohesion.

T his existential saga is the shape we still give to epidemics. And in America, where the subject is seldom approached straight-on, it is also the point of countless horror movies, in which the monster is like a scourge raining death out of Camus's indifferent blue sky. The first victim is always an emblem of normality—a carefree bather yanked under the waves, or a baby-sitter ambushed by something in the closet. Then comes the warning—

"They're here!"—but to no avail. It's too weird to be credible, and anyway, no one wants to frighten the citizenry. Finally, the system is brought to its senses—in the nick of time.

The horror movies of my youth in the '50s were a plug for scientific progressivism, and a none-too-subtle plea for civic vigilance. But in recent years, the fatalism that underlies those tales of transformation we inherited from Europe has crept back into horror-consciousness. In *The Fly* and *Invasion of the Body Snatchers*, to mention two postmodern remakes, the alien intrudes almost like a bacterium out of Mann, with the victim's tacit consent; and the afflicted pass through all of Kübler-Ross's stages, from denial to rage to resignation. In *The Andromeda Strain*, the denial stage becomes a premise: Can the doctors stop an alien organism before it kills so many people that the government will have to acknowledge its existence? In *Jaws*, an implacable force of nature has "vetoed pleasure" in Amity, just as it did in Camus's Oran. Except for the rugged individualist (a/k/a crusty old shark hunter) who holds the key to survival, it is easy to imagine the author of *The Plague* set loose on this terrain.

Randy Shilts's history of the AIDS epidemic, *And the Band Played On*, draws its power from precisely this tradition: It is a journalistic work with a fictional form. Its plot, as constructed by Defoe, renovated by Camus, and apotheosized by journalistic thrill mongers like Robin Cook and Stephen King, is the unexpected appearance of a deadly microbe; its stealthy progression, fostered by obliviousness and indifference; and the gradual emergence of a collective response. Shilts writes of death and denial with all the lurid energy of the Old Dissenter. His alienation from (gay and straight) orthodoxy is entirely true to form, and so is his judgment on all the players—from government to media, from the afflicted to the immune. The journalist shapes the event—has done so ever since Defoe.

Of course, the model of Visitation Lit doesn't entirely fit the reality of AIDS. Shilts's fiercest rage is directed at the breakdown of community when pestilence strikes. In Camus and Defoe, everyone is equally at risk, and therefore everyone must overcome indifference. But in Shilts, the collective that emerges consists of isolated groups—the infected and their doctors. The larger society is insulated by contempt for the afflicted and an illusion of immunity. The pariah experience that AIDS creates cannot be found in Visitation Lit (except perhaps in a didactic potboiler like *The Nun's Story*, with its doting on leprosy as a test of godliness). There are ample accounts of shunning those who show the "tokens" of bubonic plague or yellow fever, but AIDS is a lifelong condition that leaves no visible mark until it becomes activated; shunning is decreed by the technology of diagnosis and, often, by the presumption of belonging to a group at risk. We can monitor the development of AIDS in both the afflicted and the infected, but we cannot improve their prognosis. The psychic and social bind generated by our helpless efficiency is also an unprecedented product of this disease.

The precedent for AIDS in our culture is the "slow plague" of tuberculosis, which has shifted in its iconography from a disease of the artistic to a scourge of the impoverished. In the late 19th century, as word of its contagiousness spread (and before there was conclusive evidence that exposure does not usually result in infection), the image of the afflicted changed as well. Once they had been held in such esteem that the problem for epidemiologists was convincing the families of consumptives to *stay away.* But by the turn of the century, TB patients were thought to be dissolute, if not degenerate; later still, Mann's elegant mountaintop retreat became a state-run sanitorium to which they could be committed against their will. The parallels with AIDS are striking but not exact. Sexually transmitted diseases carry a distinct stigma, and so do homosexuals and intravenous drug users, the main groups at risk for AIDS. In the culture at large, there is no gay or junkie equivalent of the virtuous poor.

The AIDS epidemic, which is a highly literary event (the death of people in their prime always is), cannot be written about in traditional literary terms; because it shatters the social contract, it forces us to break with form. Those who live through this Visitation will have to invent not only their own *communitas* but a new system of representation to make that process meaningful. So far, only the rudiments of such a system are in place. The AIDS plays that drew so much attention to the epidemic are all traditional in form: Larry Kramer's *The Normal Heart* leans heavily on Ibsen's ideology of the heroic outsider ("The strongest man . . . is he who stands most alone"); William Hoffman's *As Is* makes a comforting mélange of Maxwell Anderson and William Inge; even *Jerker,* the controversial (because it is homoerotic) series of blackouts by Robert Chesley, veers toward the familiar modernism of Ionesco via Menotti. Only *Beirut* attempts to project AIDS into the dreamlife of our culture, but unfortunately it achieves its nightmare edge by misrepresenting the transmissibility of the disease.

In fiction, it was mostly the gay presses that produced the first responses to AIDS. But these novels, like the plays, have been either didactic tracts or domestic dramas. Both are important themes—the danger of social violence is real enough, and the bond of love between men is rare enough, in or outside the context of sexuality, to be worth expressing. But, so far, these good intentions don't achieve the power and range of literature, in part because the subject (homosexuality) is still so culturally arcane, and in part because it takes more than a season—or five—for the best authors to transform trauma into art.

Epitaphs for the Plague Dead, a small volume of formal, traditional verse, is a semi-breakthrough. Robert Boucheron has turned to Tennyson for a formal framework that is both strikingly antique and oddly abstract—giving his subject matter, the histories of gay men dead of AIDS, a timeless entombed air. The content is often trite, sometimes clumsy; but these epitaphs, in a colloquial discourse rendered stately by iambics and rhyme, have the effect of ennobling not just the ordinary but the shunned. This is form in the service of a new idea, something the literature of any epidemic must achieve if it is to matter in the long run.

It may be too much to hope for parody as a weapon in the fight against AIDS, although the satiric edge in Boucheron's poetry, Shilts's journalism, and Kramer's play is what most sets these gay writers apart from other chroniclers of plague. It is almost as if the rich vein of camp has been tempered into a mordant comedy of manners. What this promises for the future of both gay culture and Visitation Lit is anyone's guess, but the spirit of Thackeray (not to mention Mann) must hover at the shoulder of any reasonably acute homosexual who thinks about AIDS. It certainly informs the picaresque fiction of Armistead Maupin, whose work is a model of what the epidemic has done to gay sensibility. By the latest installment, *Significant Others,* AIDS has become a recurring motif that grounds the narrative. The characters we've been following through volume after volume haven't so much changed their ways as their perspective—on each other, on mortality. And Maupin's tone has grown softer and fuller, as if to acknowledge the "feminine" emotions that gay rage suppresses right now.

M elancholy is the literary legacy of AIDS, for all of us. It informs the texture of more and more popular fiction, if only in its fascination with pathology. A glance through *Publishers Weekly* reveals these plot premises, all from books due out this fall: A woman engaged to be married discovers that she is a carrier of Tay-Sachs disease, raising painful questions about her true paternity and changing her life. . . . A crotchety old truck driver, watching his wife die of cancer, reverts to wetting his bed. His anguish is heightened when she reveals the details of an extramarital affair that spawned their late son, a teenage victim of meningitis. . . . A young cancer patient, withdrawn from chemotherapy by his mother, is placed in a halfway house for "roomers with tumors." But when the boy's estranged father tries to put him back in chemo, mom, son, and a handsome hospice worker run away to a hideaway in the redwoods, where. . . .

Then there is Leslie Horvitz's *The Dying,* a just-published novel of "biological horror" (actually another of those pesky Poe-like flus that kill in the flip of a page) complete with a dust jacket admonition that

THE PLAGUE YEARS ARE HERE. And Sharon Mayes's *Immune,* whose protagonist, "at once a highly professional doctor and researcher, and a wild, erotic woman, addicted to cocaine," must confront the threat of AIDS. That it "leads her to a re-discovery of responsibility and a nostalgia for a more stable and structured past" makes *Immune* "a tragedy of our time." Or so the blurb insists.

As a culture, we are losing our sense of immunity to disease and our confidence in sexuality as a route to self-discovery. These may have been constructions in the first place, but they were crucial to my generation, and now they have been shattered. The assumption that AIDS will compel us to remake the libido in more "mature" terms is as cockeyed as any belief in human perfectibility, as utopian as the sexual revolution we are now exhorted to forsake. Only in a TV movie will this epidemic teach heterosexuals to value commitment and homosexuals to find their identity in rodeos and Proust. More likely, we will pull the wool over each other's eyes in erotic masques of safety and salubrity. The gap between public morality and private behavior will promote the very passions it suppresses. Those who can't or won't be locked in place will exude a faint aroma of mortality whenever they have sex. And if the epidemic is not contained, we will come to inhabit a landscape where death and desire go hand in hand.

This is a very ancient landscape, but also the thoroughly modern setting of Valerie Martin's novel *A Recent Martyr,* which takes place in a contemporary New Orleans mired in corruption, civil chaos, and a burgeoning epidemic of bubonic disease. Sainthood and sexual obsession vie for women's souls, while men hover, in their passion, between brutality and helplessness. It has nothing to do with the current health crisis, but a great deal to do with the emotional climate AIDS is generating. Martin's model suggests that any epidemic—whether or not the disease is sexually transmitted—affects the libido, if only because it places ecstasy and imminent death on the same chaotic primal plain.

"The plague continues, neither in nor out of control," Martin writes at the conclusion of her reverie, "but we have been promised a vaccine that will solve all our problems. We go on without it, and life is not intolerable. Our city is an island, physically and psychologically; we are tied to the rest of the country only by our own endeavor. . . . The future holds a simple promise. We are well below sea level, and inundation is inevitable. We are content, for now, to have our heads above water."

This is the looking glass fiction can fabricate. Gazing into it, we confront what journalism cannot imagine: the possibilities.

October 1987

DON'T WORRY, BE BUPPIE

Black Novelists Head for the Mainstream

By Thulani Davis

> LONG DISTANCE LIFE
> *By Marita Golden*
>
> TROUBLE THE WATER
> *By Melvin Dixon*
>
> BABY OF THE FAMILY
> *By Tina McElroy Ansa*
>
> DISAPPEARING ACTS
> *By Terry McMillan*

Now that the '90s are at hand, it's inevitable that someone will announce a new generation of writers, folks who'll be the bridge to the next century. (WOW!) The "new generation" of African-American writers, novelist Terry McMillan said not too long ago, are "different from a generation before" because "they are not as race oriented, and they are not as protest oriented." I wondered at first who she was talking about. The novelists being published right now are, for the most part, around 40. Most of them began getting published 20 years ago, but those who were the talk of the '70s seem wildly different—and I mean wildly—from the crew McMillan is describing. The young writers back then were full of the anger, rhythms, sexuality, and wicked humor of jazz, r&b, and the '60s. I doubt if anyone would have guessed that the next generation was going to be less "race oriented."

In the poets' cafes Ntozake Shange, Wesley Brown, Charlotte Carter, Pedro Pietri, Gylan Kain, Pat Parker, Victor Hernández-Cruz, David Henderson, and Lorenzo Thomas were ripping the lid off our neat and tidy preconceptions. Floating from hand to hand were out-of-print copies of J. J. Phillips's *Mojo Hand* and Carlene Hatcher Polite's *Sister X and the Victims of Foul Play*. Ishmael Reed's early books introduced us to the trickster, and Gayl Jones's novels spared us nothing. The energy was outside the mainstream, as it usually is for young writers, and that energy became a credo: Let it be raw and raggedy, intense, black, and yes, self-righteous. It was fun.

All of us who're now somewhere around 40—whether we were in the marches, or in the Panthers, or the lonely Negroes at Hendrix concerts, or none of the above—were in the first generation to go en masse into white institutions when the Civil Rights Act and affirmative action took force. Before that time, we knew white America, north or south, largely by way of television (which we watched with some restriction because it was new, and our parents were understandably frightened of it). Like our parents and grandparents, we were, and are still, different. We started out life in a truly separate culture inside America, and therefore first learned to think, like it or not, with Race Mind, the black half of what W.E.B. Du Bois called double-consciousness. African-American literature of the '60s and '70s made the self-conscious choice to give voice to that black language *without* the explanatory context of earlier work. In today's self-censoring atmosphere, Race Mind is carefully muted. The white half of that double-consciousness is more often used for public presentations: Jesse Jackson uses it in speeches, and yet his Race Mind is coded within what he says.

If four novels published in the past few months, including one by McMillan, are any indication, there *is* a crop of African-American fiction coming in the '90s, written by 40ish folk, that's less interested in race and protest. It speaks in the practiced tongue of white mainstream literature. Melvin Dixon, Marita Golden, Tina McElroy Ansa, and McMillan show in their work a silent—in some cases maybe unconscious—struggle with assimilation. Each of their books describes some part of the lonely, self-involved journey of the middle-class African American who has access to some little piece of the Dream and is as deeply ensconced in American mass culture as in our boisterous yet closely held black world.

More Bup Art than Black Art, these African-American writers' current work shares bourgeois mores and values with lots of other work by the 40-something generation. Buppism moves literature toward the middle of the road: conservative stylistic choices in form and language taken from mainstream American models; a personal focus, as opposed to the ever-enlarging worldview that shifted from Mississippi to internationalism in the late '60s, '70s, and early '80s (and, in the case of Alice Walker, included several millennia); the death of the heroic figure, so prominent in black literature as recent as *Beloved* (Morrison raised questions about the nature of heroism in the African-American context); and an absence of protest, which has been replaced by homilies to survival.

Following Baldwin's edict to "take the language apart," African-

American writers have been for some time revising or destroying forms to make them more expressionistic. The '90s writers return to story-telling as a private act, the exorcism of existential demons that could be viewed as nonracial. The old Race Mind, once a necessity for survival, is being lost to a naïve pragmatism: We can imitate and join. Despite many efforts to salvage them, the old sayings of the village have one by one been consigned to the place where America put the dog-tags, ankle-cuffs, and bills of sale for the village folk.

Twenty years after the introduction of Africana studies in American universities, African-American scholars have institutionalized the study of black life; they now argue that their black students need the courses to know who they are. As the culture continues to evolve, the language of black experience is disseminated and assimilated by the mass white audience almost as soon as it appears. Race Mind is marketed as late-night style with Arsenio Hall. The larger, more profound wisdom and practice is being lost to a culture that erases everything but success, and does not replenish the spirit.

As we turn the corner of the century, the shared yearnings based on race, gender, generation, or family so common to black fiction could become inscrutable relics of the past, like the Motown records a Bup executive retrieves from the garbage in George Wolfe's play *The Colored Museum*, or those mama-on-the-couch shows he parodies, which actually did once say something about how we folks felt behind the veil in America.

arita Golden's *Long Distance Life* tracks a black family from the '20s to the present as they wend their way in America's Great Procession—a material climb predictably marked by a spiritual decline. Although Golden's theme is migration, the idea has little connection to the book, which rarely opens up beyond the tidy rooms of a middle-class Washington D.C. home, and which shuts the reader out of the characters' inner journeys. (Golden's memoir, *Migrations of the Heart*, has a similar plot.) In earlier American novels of the Great Procession of immigrants, and earlier African-American novels, the mother country/culture proves hard to repress within the people who migrate towards the American mainstream.

Doris Jean Austin covered some of the same turf in her 1987 first novel, *After the Garden*, another story of a northern migration, which is interesting because the white world gets filtered through the tough, sur-viving country culture of the family matriarch. Everything from World War II to the urban lives of her children and neighbors gets a dose of withering Alabama wisdom. Even though the signposts and labels are there, the black homeground in *Long Distance Life* is a much less compelling, or even defining, culture; there is no strong sense of place or language or system of beliefs from which to migrate.

The first half of the novel (which has more typos than any book I've ever seen) is the story of Naomi Johnson, the family matriarch who leaves her North Carolina home in the 1920s for Washington. Naomi is a driven woman who gets into real estate and becomes part of the new D.C. bourgeoisie as the Depression wanes. Rayford, the man she marries, is more lore than flesh—a black intellectual composite figure who reads his daughter Chesnutt, Hughes, and Dunbar at bedtime. (Most of Golden's other characters haven't heard of Rayford's black heroes; Jackie Robinson and Clark Gable loom larger.) The city itself, which seems intended to be a secondary character, gets the same kind of composite treatment—pages of historical background here and there: "Emancipation Day, April 16, was in those days celebrated with a parade of floats from Anacostia to the White House and down Pennsylvania Avenue, to the Capitol and then to Lincoln Park, where Frederick Douglass might deliver a speech to mark the historic proclamation. And every year, in honor of John Brown, there was an excursion to Harpers Ferry."

The second half of *Long Distance Life* is about Naomi's daughter Esther, who lacks her mother's drive; she leaves college and jettisons the dreams of the previous generation. An obsessive relationship with a married man brings her first a child, then a nervous breakdown. When she comes out of the hospital, she decides, perversely I think, that what ails her will be cured by running off to the Civil Rights movement. On her return, she picks up her life—as if the migration south had no effect—giving birth to a second son, Nathaniel, whose murder at the beginning of the book forces the family into uncomfortable introspection.

Nathaniel's death—destined, like his drift away from his folks, to remain mysterious—is proof of the family's dysfunction. No one knew the listless, alienated ball player who apparently turned to drug dealing for the excitement and sense of power. (He didn't get high and didn't need the money.) Why didn't Nathaniel connect? Unfortunately the most intriguing question of the book is never answered. Grandmother Naomi's last word on the boy is: "Nathaniel got caught up in all that ugliness, not because he didn't know better but because he didn't know. He didn't know how to be afraid. How to fear God. That's what's killing everybody now. . . . We did all we could, but we couldn't do no more than our hearts would let us. And in every family there's pitiful few pure hearts."

All the characters, like actors with a skimpy script, try to take on the seemingly sensible personal problems given them, but the guts are missing. They get along, without shouting matches or tears, without the church, the bar, or the bogeyman of their thwarted dreams. They survive with a practiced sameness, and it's hard to see what's making them tick. Emotional issues are tough for Golden; she avoids them—her characters say they cannot speak of feelings. *Long Distance Life* is hemmed in for want of one strong idea to drive the narrative forward. Golden doesn't take the naturalistic line that the family is being unraveled by a destructive society; nor does she make her characters responsible. Each of these passive souls has been emotionally abandoned somewhere down the line; still, they hardly seem meant to be emblematic of anything uniquely African American. They have the problems people bring every day to Oprah Winfrey for a big hug.

T hings are also falling apart in *Trouble the Water*, but Melvin Dixon manages to pull them together. Dixon sticks close to tradition in his poetry, illuminates and extends it. In his first novel, he has the same respect for convention, hewing closely to principles of well-made structure and character development, and he has produced a smartly crafted novel which seems anything but risky until you get into the heart of the story. Still, *Trouble the Water* is essentially a private story, the tale of a pivotal event in a young man's past.

Jordan Henry, a successful African-American professor in a northern college, returns home to Pee Dee, North Carolina, to bury his grandmother and relive the horror that drove him running from the ancestral home 20 years before. Dixon's most luminous writing recalls the death of Jordan's childhood friend and his youthful realization that he loved the boy, body and soul. His fierce and unforgiving grandmother, Harriet Henry, served him with a blunt and stunning rejection of his confession about the boy, and tried to force him into an act of vengeance.

The countryside of that childhood, the secret paths through the woods, the forays to the edge of the Pee Dee River are at the emotional center of the book. The river, scene of Jordan's early happiness and isolation, is haunting: "Drunk with thaw from the Carr Mountains, the Pee Dee River raised its muddy arms and hugged the shore. Months into spring the river was still drinking. Ripples on its surface arched into blue-black lips that puckered and belched with every swallow. . . . But when it rose, the river became as sloppy and inebriated as molasses." The tenderness and vulnerability of the two boys, echoed through children Jordan encounters on his return home, make for the book's best writing.

Jordan Henry remains something of an enigma because so much of his own transformation is not visible; but his rural family, whose life in a craggy, hard-farming river valley has barely changed since he left, is marvelously drawn. (I *was* curious about whether they ever watched television, where they shopped, stuff like that.) The language Dixon gives them is satisfying, blunt, untroubled. At Jordan's long-awaited arrival in Pee Dee, he is announced with a simple, "He's here. . . . He's got a girl with him. His wife." Change, or perhaps the falling away of the past, is measured by a different yardstick: "It were a freight train what pass there and sometime a train with passengers stop there. Now it's only one freight train every two days when it used to be three, four times a day you'd hear that whistle coming through." And one delightful character, straight from the African-American tradition, leavens the basically heavy goings-on: a New Orleans conjure woman who keeps slipping up on the spells and misplacing her false teeth.

On the other hand, scenes of the northern college town where Jordan and his wife, Phyllis, live threaten to derail the book with blandness. Phyllis remains fairly elusive, recognizable as she is (you know the type—smart, hip, educated, a poet, smart-ass, and emotionally needy). She perks up after she gets used to the bugs and burrs down south, and the book's conclusion suggests that all their marriage really needed was an honest-to-god crisis.

What's wrong with this picture? Well, I wonder what happened to Jordan over the 20 years that made up the bulk of his life. The only member of his family to have gone off to college, or to live somewhere else, is obviously no longer like the homefolks, and constantly reminded of it by them. Having left that "different" world of hard-farming and wacky conjuring, he walks, talks, acts, and dreams differently than the Henrys of generations past. What did he carry up the dark road that night besides the memory of his friend's blood on the asphalt? What did he shed? Everything but the survival tools? Dixon leaves the matter more or less where Jesus flung it.

Novels of everyday African-American life—unadorned realism largely free of the broad social strokes that Wright or Petry applied, or the deeply spiritual base of the tradition Baldwin gave us—have been around since the 19th century. They contained, however, certain assumptions about the possibilities of black life. If the novels served no greater purpose, they acquainted readers—especially modern ones—with the strictures of that time. In *Trouble the Water* and *Long Distance Life*, it isn't clear what the characters feel are the parameters of their world, and yet they live and die, suffer and prosper, by how they adjust to that world. For this reason big changes like integration have almost no impact in these books: There is no apparent shock in the passage from the Pee Dee to New England, or from mama's comfy kitchen to a Mississippi tent city.

Tina McElroy Ansa hails from the Georgia Sea Islands, and so her first novel, *Baby of the Family*, promised at least a peek at the lore of that region. The story is as precious as its title—Buppiedom at its worst. *Baby* is built of slight pieces, fragments of true-to-life-sounding anecdotes that lack metaphorical power or universal currency. Lena, *Baby's* baby, is born with a caul over her face, which supposedly confers powers, and might have been the premise for a magic tale drawn from genuine African-American riches. Not this baby. The novel reads more like the story of a kid with two left feet. Lena's very modern mother, in an ironically symbolic act, throws away the caul tea made by the midwife, and thus ends the most interesting section of the book: the midwife's close attention to an ancient rite.

Lena does have powers and visions, is sometimes visited by ghosts, and because of her mother's mistake, she sees the nasty kind. These events turn out to be remarkably uninteresting, and Lena's otherwise uneventful, well-to-do life of pretty dresses, pretty cars, and would-be colorful local folk is bland stuff. One chapter opens with: "Car trips were something at which Lena's family excelled." *Baby* is hardly a picture of black life. If anything, it's a warning that African Americans can be boring. And I don't mean the kind of boring the neo-cons talk about ("those people blame everything on racism")—Ansa's folk haven't bumped into racism yet. As in all of these books, there are no white characters and the white world never comes crashing in. Some of the older family members feel a little anxious when Lena's father gets lost on a car adventure, but you'd have to know something about the south to understand why anyone was worried.

Throughout the book Lena takes in next to nothing of the world beyond the lawn sprinkler, her parents' fights, and the poor girl who lives next door and is lost to her forever when the neighbors move across town. The flat, uninventive prose chokes off what might have been made of any of this "[Lena] felt more and more alone. The girls at school didn't even slip up and speak to her by mistake anymore. And the boys only wanted to see how close they could get to putting their eager hands on her breasts as if it were a game. Even if her brothers didn't understand her any more than anyone else did, they loved her just the same." Yeah, and they move away. Since Lena views her specialness as the worst curse a girl could have—depriving her of friends and dates—she never gets beyond her own shining. Baby of the family indeed.

Bup art is distinguished from Black art of the past by its self-involvement, a narrow focus on the struggling individual, and in some cases a narcissism downright unusual for African-American literature. Early in the '70s, the psychological mirror fascinated a number of writers, particularly poets, and the black me-generation spawned a school of imitators who explored life through the first-person narrative voice. The struggling individual's self-involvement took some original, even bizarre, forms: Look at the early short fiction of Alice Walker or Ntozake Shange. In these four new books the characters are cut off from their folks, in a sad limbo where there's nobody listening. They're ordinary people, inured to the dullness of work, the banality of day-to-day racism, the random dissatisfactions of relationships.

D*isappearing Acts*, like Terry McMillan's first novel, *Mama*, is an energetic and earthy book that takes place wholly within the confines of an intense relationship. While the narrator of *Mama* sounded like a character in the story, in this book McMillan uses two alternating voices that speak directly to the reader. The whole world is filtered through the self-naming, self-mythologizing first-person monologue—from racism to masturbation, parental conflicts to staying on a diet. And because there's no one obvious for Zora Banks or Franklin Swift to tell it to—they are loners in every way—the question is whether these folks are for real. In many ways they are quite ordinary, in other ways they are hardly tangible.

Zora is a young black woman on the lookout for the right man while she pursues singing ambitions; Franklin is a construction worker frustrated by his inability to get steady work in a closed industry. Zora sounds a lot like the narrator of *Mama*, in spite of her *Essence*-style self-improvement rap: "When I started visualizing myself less abundant, and desirable again, that's how I think I was able to get here—to 139 pounds." She likes to tell you straight up how it is: "I've got two major weaknesses: tall black men and food." Though reviewers have said that Franklin dominates the book, he has the same brassy, up-front, I'm gon'-tell-you-exactly style as Zora. "Don't ask me why I did some stupid shit like that. Ringing that woman's doorbell at that time of morning. And with a lame-ass line like, 'You drink coffee?' . . . She was still pretty, though, even with no makeup. Her skin looked like Lipton tea. I saw them thick nipples sticking out through that pink bathrobe, and I felt Tarzan rising." Yes, a tall black man whose swinging thing was made in Hollywood.

Even though Zora and Franklin are last-week contemporary, they are also like classic folklore characters come to life in Brooklyn. She's the wily black woman of yore, smart-talking Eve who's always got a little something on the rail for the lizard, as we used to say. She's also a sophisticated shopper who likes fancy cheeses and bottled water, and she says shit all the time. Zora has all the pulls and tugs of feminism versus the feminine that a modern black woman who's read Walker and Shange is supposed to have. She's not unlike Zora Neale Hurston's sassy folk women—characters *Cosmo* would never dare to pop-psychoanalyze.

Complicated as Franklin is supposed to be, he is a savvy urban John

Henry—he don't take no tea fo' the fever. An intellectual Tina Turner meets a hardhat Ike. They are both bricks and though they may chip each other, they ain't never gonna blend. They live and work in New York City, but are in a very insulated world; their problems are completely personal. Their relationship is doomed by mutual expectations and ended by an outburst of gratuitous male violence. Let's just say it wasn't needed for the love affair to fall apart.

These two are as they are; like other folk heroes, they don't change much, or drag skeletons out of the closet, and they learn their lessons the hard way. They've been created by years of past mythologizing, drawn their images from popular culture, black and white. They are black, sho 'nuff—the last thing I would say about McMillan's people is that they ain't black—but they're black in big, bold strokes. And that means her work will continue to raise questions among African Americans about the fuzzy line between realism and popular misconception. And at the same time, McMillan is, as she said, less race-conscious. She confines herself to the day-to-day life struggle, as told from behind the mask Claude McKay so poignantly described. McMillan uses, almost exclusively, the performance side of black character, emphasizing the most public, most familiar aspects of us. If you smell a little song and dance in the self-sufficient ribaldry, it's there.

Still, hard as it may be to imagine, for me at least, I suppose the time had to come when race would cease to be the obsession of African-American writers, and in its place would be some form of ordinary life—stripped in varying degrees of "context," depoliticized. If I can feel it in the street—the dislocation that can no longer be healed by inspiring leaders—I shouldn't be surprised to find it in our literature. I hope for some understanding from novels about African-American life, but perhaps it isn't there to be had. Welcome to the '90s.

The work of Marita Golden, Melvin Dixon, Tina McElroy Ansa, and Terry McMillan seems ambivalent and narrowly focused after nearly two decades of uninterrupted literary conjuring from those fabulous wild women of the '70s and '80s black-lit boom. Morrison, Walker, and company continue to write books that are ambitious, intensely lyrical, and profoundly disturbing; yet clearly their work is only one end of the spectrum. These new novels show that African-American fiction is miscegenating. Though the white world does not intrude in the form of characters, it is very much alive—recognized or not—in the minds of the blacks. The African Americans in these four works have become garden-variety Americans. They seem confined by the African-American culture that has defined and nurtured writers before them.

In the '70s, cultural nationalists ranted about black women writers, vilifying them/us as purveyors of "mulatto consciousness." I was amused by the clumsiness of the term, and, as intended, insulted. Was black culture so circumscribed that we could not merengue, or talk about men, or whatever it was that upset this crew of fuddy-duddies? Or were they just talking about the lightness of certain writers' skin? That happened too. A few weeks ago I heard Trey Ellis, self-appointed propagandist for the New Black Aesthetic invented by my colleague Greg Tate, proudly defining HIS (30ish) generation as "cultural mulattoes." While I think Tate observed that cultural appropriation is a common denominator among a certain cadre of artists, Ellis seems to be defining his generation by the conditions of their upbringing: We are therefore we are, something like that. It sure ain't like announcing you're the New Negro.

The writers of the '90s are sitting in the middle of a big mess—among critics and other artists screaming "Who are we?" while the newspapers holler that black music and white performers equal popular magic. American culture has not been a blending pot so much as a river Lethe for all its peoples, their languages and arts. Have we baptized our children there only to wonder later to whom they pray? I think George Wolfe is right—this cultural nervous breakdown is likely to land us in the Colored Museum. Collard greens and bean pie will be served at the snack bar.

May 1990

JUST THE FAX, MA'AM

Or, Postmodernism's Journey to Decenter

By Michael Bérubé

In the waning moments of the 1970s, *Eraserhead* was playing at the Waverly in the West Village, and David Lynch, its director, was not exactly a household word, though he did find some kindred spirits who'd always known there were puffy-cheeked women singing under the radiator. When he was given a TV series in the spring of 1990, eyebrows went up nationwide, and everyone waited to see whether the Apocalypse would follow from the historic encounter between David Lynch and prime-time network TV. But Lynch's relentlessly strange and provocative *Twin Peaks* became so widely acknowledged a critical success that it wound up being explained to—and defended from—the uncomprehending masses by none other than the house organ of the uncomprehending masses, *USA Today*, whose "Life" section loudly protested the show's hiatuses and eventual cancellation by ABC. *Soap Opera Weekly* checked in from time to time with astute, sympathetic, and theoretically sophisticated assessments of the show's development, and large segments of middle America were served up Lynch's hallucinogenic Northwest, along with a side of pie, for over a year.

Meanwhile, back in the late '70s, a few miles north of the Waverly, Kool DJ Herc and Grandmaster Flash were busy recycling vital cultural products in some strange new ways. A mere decade later, "rap," a/k/a hiphop, has become the single largest music on the block—*any* block. On the technical tip, hiphop's dazzling blends of traditional and electronic musical forms, together with its dexterous pillaging of various recent cultural archives, have launched (among other things) a thorough, multimedia examination of blackness and the technological means of cultural reproduction. And in the space of a few years, hiphop has made its way from turntables to TV ads for cola, throat lozenges, and kids' breakfast cereals, all the way from the Bronx to Bel Air—surviving its many cooptations and crossovers at every little step. Not even MC Hammer and Vanilla Fro-Yo have frozen out Ice-T and Ice Cube; and while black radio in Philly and elsewhere keeps trumpeting its new "no-rap" programming, grain-fed American youth can still hear the latest singles from L.L. Cool J and Monie Love on central Illinois's best mix of yesterday and today. Hiphop has become a national music whether it likes it or not, our most politically important music *despite* (or alongside of) its gradual citation-and-absorption by fast-food chains and *People*.

Hiphop and David Lynch have little else in common, but between them they do go to show that postmodernism isn't merely a "style" located somewhere in cultural products; at a much greater reach, it involves new configurations of cultural transmission, the means by which artifacts (and "copies" thereof) circulate in the general culture. It isn't that pomo gives you 30 per cent more modernism for your money (more uncertainty, more fragmentation, more playful self-consciousness), and it's not that postmodernism is modernism's evil dwarf twin, hell-bent on knocking down everything modernism took such a long time to build. Instead, what's going on involves a more subtle and elusive cultural shift, in which it's getting harder (and more challenging) to determine what it means that ostensibly "avant-garde" cultural works are available in so many media so instantaneously.

And these disseminations, these "new configurations," are by no means limited to the work of our contemporary "avant-gardes"; on the contrary, they include the retransmission of what was once the modernist avant-garde—which has, in the past 50 years, gotten itself distributed in such a way that it is now more likely to show up on the walls of corporate offices than in cafés or garrets. Yet when we try to gauge the relation between mo and pomo, it doesn't help to ask yet again what modernism was, because (as we'll see later on) even that's a distinctively modernist question. Rather, what pomo wants to ask is this: How do we understand modernism's circuitous route into our general culture, whereby *The Waste Land* wound up in every classroom and *faux* Piet Mondrian wound up in the packaging design of L'Oreal mousse and hair spray? And does the transmission of Eliot and Mondrian involve the same processes by which Lynch and hiphop likewise became part of our cultural lingua franca?

Of course, it's easy to claim that postmodernism simply entails the corporate cooptation of everything in sight, since postmodernism seems to follow from (and accelerate) modernism's own absorption into the general culture. As *New German Critique* editor Andreas Huyssen puts it, the irony here is that "the first time the U.S. had something resembling an 'institution art' in the emphatic European sense, it was modernism itself, the kind of art whose purpose had always been to resist institutionalization." Why then should we be mourning the passing of the modernist avant-garde in the first place? In 1991, when you can't tell anymore where the garde is, it's a fair bet that you don't know whether you're avant of it or not. And as a result, "avant-gardism," even in these troubled times, has come to seem gestural if not downright reactionary.

This is what Huyssen means when he calls ours a "post-avant-garde" society. For Huyssen, as for a legion of younger cultural critics, it no longer makes any sense for artists or critics to claim positions on the "margin" or in the "center" of the culture, because the contemporary cultural landscape resists precisely such static confrontations. And if there are no margins and centers, there's no vanguard; and if there's no vanguard, there's no site of authentic, unsullied, "pure" cultural production, immune to the technologies of economic and cultural *re*production.

Them's fighting words, you know, to people who continue to see themselves as "avant-garde." Yet even if there were a bona fide, certified-authentic vanguard out there, who's to say that its cultural work would be more important than—or even distinguishable from—the kinds of stuff we find in what we still call "mainstream" media? It may yet come to pass that 30 years from now, when we look back at how the '80s replayed the '50s with a knowing but deceptive wink, we will care less about the "media image" photographs of Cindy Sherman than about Nick at Nite's relentlessly campy promotions for its reruns of *The Donna Reed Show,* which fill your late-night TV screen with a graphic style composed of equal parts early *Jetsons* and late John Waters. Besides, who needs artists and writers to "lay bare the device" of contemporary culture, when laying bare the device has become standard business practice anyway? As Kirk Varnedoe and Adam Gopnik, the directors of *High & Low: Modern Art and Popular Culture,* have written, "in the age of Joe Isuzu, a hardened knowingness about the value-emptied amorality of media culture, was, far from being the preserve of a small cadre of vanguard thinkers, the sour, commonplace cynicism of the whole commercial culture." The *High & Low* show itself was brought to you by the folks at AT&T, who urge you to reach out and touch someone by giving the gift of modern art, the gift that keeps on giving.

How did we get to this strange party? Who's responsible for these lousy hors d'oeuvres? Uh—can we come in again?

Sure, we can *always* come in again; postmodernism means never having to say you've been here before. In fact, the word "postmodern" has been bruited about for over four decades now, by art critics as by *Spy* magazine and real estate agents, and in the process of going through a few demi-generational changes, it's become a kind of "essentially contested" term that many people are just tired of contesting. Even Ihab Hassan, who had been using the word since way back in the '60s, when John Barth was Prince of Pomo and everybody was talking about the "literature of exhaustion"—even Hassan recently dropped his pen in fatigue, writing, "I have already written enough of these matters, and I would let postmodernism rest." (Thud. Snore.)

Well, who wouldn't be tired, confronted with all these postmodernisms, this L=A=N=G=U=A=G=E writing, MTV, ACT UP, e-mail, junk bonds, Madonna, smart bombs, poststructuralism, Reaganism, terrorism, colorization, Houstonization, and, if you order right away, much, much more? And as if this profusion weren't enough, we now have a number of constituencies for whom the adjective "postmodern" signifies little more than a new brand name, as in the case of "Postmodern MTV," a seemingly redundant phrase which, as one of my students suggested last spring, merely denoted "things that sound like Morrissey."

However, we do have some idea of why a unified field theory of "postmodernism" is neither possible nor desirable, and before I get to my own concerns about postmodernism and history, I want to suggest two reasons why postmodernism remains a cultural field distinguished by internal dissensus.

For one thing, one man's postmodernism is another woman's poison. In some ways, all of post-1960s feminism is postmodern, because it has destabilized "universal" languages, questioned gender and subjectivity, and rewritten our dominant historical narratives. But then again, not every feminism *wants* to be postmodern, since the suspicion remains that pomo will dissolve all possibility for political resistance in a bubbling vat of textuality and ironic self-parody. In 1983, in an essay entitled "The Discourse of Others: Feminists and Postmodernism," the late Craig Owens convincingly charged his fellow theorists with sustaining a systematic neglect of feminism's role in pomo, practice and theory; but six years later, in *The Politics of Postmodernism*, Linda Hutcheon claimed that postmodernism lacks any theory of agency, without which feminism is impossible. So either the question is whether pomo should acknowledge the feminists in its midst, or whether feminism should acknowledge the postmodernism sitting next to it on the bus and mumbling to itself about Max Headroom and identity politics. Does one of these isms bracket the other? You tell me.

Thing number two has to do with "facts." To wit, it's hard to determine the relevant facts and features of pomo when so much of pomo has questioned how "facticity" is constructed. David Byrne opened the '80s by intoning, in "Crosseyed and Painless," that "Facts don't do what I want them to/Facts just twist the truth around." Ronald Reagan, having been reportedly "brutalized" by facts before a 1984 debate with Walter Mondale, closed the decade by stammering, "Facts are stupid things." In the meantime, we switched over painlessly to a government by the photo op, of the photo op, and for the photo op, and the neofascist Institute for Historical Review offered $50,000 to anyone who could disprove its claim that the Holocaust never happened. In what may have been facticity's last stand, in 1985 the IHR was defeated in court by a Holocaust survivor, Mel Mermelstein; nonetheless, the IHR's director, Tom Marcellus (a man apparently immune to fact), replied that the defeat was "the best outcome we could have had," since "we did not have to compromise any of our positions."

On another front altogether, 50 years of "theory" from people as diverse as Ludwig Wittgenstein, Thomas Kuhn, and Michel Foucault have led the cultural left to argue that objects of knowledge are locally and historically specific, and that they become available for human understanding only within certain "language-games," "paradigms," or "discursive formations"—not that these are three names for the same thing, either.

So we have multiple histories of postmodernism, which are themselves licensed by postmodernism's multiplicity. And they're also a result of pomo's propensity for searching out and destroying unitary, linear historical narratives—the kind that serve up clear origins and straightforward plot development (whether of rise or decline). This "antifoundationalist" aspect of postmodernism has sometimes been taken to be a potentially liberating tool, since it suggests that our beliefs and practices are culturally "contingent," subject to ongoing revision, bound to no historical determinism. And by the same token, we've found that "proof" is a more slippery thing than we'd thought—something that depends more on rhetoric, power, consensus, and history than on "incontrovertible fact."

It's not that there are no "facts" in pomo, or that anything goes so long as everybody's happy; rather, it's that pomo has paid acute attention to how various human communities go about deciding what will count as "facts." As Kuhn argued in *The Structure of Scientific Revolutions* (1962), revolutionary "paradigm-shifts" occur when one dominant theory supersedes another, but the new paradigm doesn't simply "falsify" or "disprove" the older model. Instead, writes Kuhn, paradigm-shifts are matters in which "neither proof nor error is at issue," because past scientific communities were simply seeing different "facts" even when they were looking at what we now think are the same phenomena: "theories, of course, do 'fit the facts,' but only by transforming previously accessible information into facts that, for the preceding paradigm, had not existed at all."

But even while pomo's encounters with antifoundationalism and feminism have rendered us unable to conceive of a single, monolithic thing called "History," postmodernism has been acquiring a history of its own. And this alone should provoke us into some historical reflection, because as far as I can see, the recent history of pomo's shifting definitions can be charted largely in terms of how people have determined pomo's relation to history. Perhaps nothing has been so widely misunderstood about pomo as this; indeed, in some cases, the postmodernism we thought to be lamely ahistorical has now been judged by some recent histories of pomo to be nothing less than the very spur to revisionary historicism. To put matters another way; although postmodern historicism flaunts its inability to capture the past "the way it really was," it has also quite effectively exploded the claims of other historicisms (such as marxisms) to be able to do so either.

OK, I know this one takes some explaining, so let me back up a second and fill in the details.

For much of the first half of the 1980s, critics from Left and Right spent a good deal of their time forming two neat, separate lines to take turns bashing postmodernism. On the Left, Charles Newman found pomo to be facetious, pointlessly playful, and possessed by an attitude toward history not unlike that of *Bill and Ted's Excellent Adventure*; on the Right, Hilton Kramer found pomo to be facetious, pointlessly playful, and possessed by an attitude toward history not unlike that of *Total Recall*. Ageless modernist torchbearer Denis Donoghue complained that "postmodernism is content to let a thousand discrepancies bloom," because in pomo, "no artist's desire reaches out for spontaneity or an original relation to the world"; and the earl of Duke, Marxist critic Frederic Jameson, proposed that postmodernism and late capitalism had bequeathed us "a world in which stylistic innovation is no longer possible, all that is left is to imitate dead styles." Donoghue and Jameson? Kramer and Newman? Golly, it finally looked as if *something* had gotten these boys to stop fighting and play nicely—and that something was pomo. It was a happy time, and soon "rock" musicians stopped suggesting that they wanted to die before they became old enough to do 25th Anniversary Reunion Tours, and started singing instead that they were working out 'most every day, and watching what they eat.

Just as it was getting hip to be square, squares were getting hip to whimsical Left-Banker Jean Baudrillard's notion (first advanced in 1983) that our era is distinguished by what he called "the precession of simulacra." In the era of the simulacrum, Baudrillard declared, when "the map engenders the territory" and everything is a 20th-generation copy of everything else, we find a suspiciously compensatory cultural reflex—"a proliferation of myths of origin and signs of reality . . . a panic-stricken production of the real and referential." This Baudrillard calls the "hyper-real," and no doubt it's here to stay, since we hear so frequently that real people purchase real food for real people and drink beer that's as real as it gets, 'cause you can't beat the real thing. Except maybe if you have 200 Elvis impersonators ringed around a replica of the Statue of Liberty.

Baudrillard's essay has now become something of a postmodern classic, so much so that it's been invoked to explain everything from the art of Jeff Koons to the Iran-Contra hearings: simulacra of roadside kitsch, simulacra of parliamentary "justice." And in an appropriately Baudrillardian way, "The Precession of Simulacra" has itself had a significant impact on postmodern writers and artists whose work Baudrillard's theories are then called upon to explain, in rather circular fashion.

Yet I think Baudrillard's essay—and its influence—may be remembered less as a definitive description of postmodernism than as an index of what the pomo debate looked like in the mid-1980s. For it wasn't hard to see, even five or six long years ago, that what people feared or celebrated about postmodernism had to do with issues of tangibility and thinginess. Hence all the apocalyptic rhetoric about the disappearance of the referent, the death of Man, the end of philosophy, the death of the author, the dissolution of the subject, and the impossibility of apocalyptic rhetoric. In a 1986 lecture, Jameson opined, almost off the cuff, that word processors were to postmodernism what the typewriter was to modernism: That is, in the breaking point between mechanical reproduction (keys, ink, hammers, machinery, industrial economies, sweaty Socialist Realist men in overalls) and electronic transmission (laser printing, modems, microchips, information economies, Steve Jobs on the cover of *USA Today*) lay the distinction between mo and pomo. Sort of like the difference between pinball and video, and who *wouldn't* be nostalgic for the days when pinball games had no microchips, no sound effects, and a top score of 99,999?

The only problem was that while the Right hated pomo for fairly obvious reasons (having never even learned to play pinball, the Right naturally figured that Space Invaders was the death knell of reflective thought), the Left—including Baudrillard—seemed paralyzed by dreams of days when things were better, days when things were *thingy*. You know, when the proletariat and the haute-bourgeoisie wore recognizable uniforms, and sat down facing each other at heavy, wooden tables, and argued about *real* wages—silver dollars, doubloons, and florins. None of this "simulacra" nonsense, none of these credit rollovers and reinvested pension funds, and most of all, none of these dang teleconferences.

Of course, not all of the Left felt this way. But perhaps it was only the repeated interventions of women, ethnic minorities, and variously queer theorists that finally shattered the pernicious sense of nostalgia to which so many men on the antipostmodernist Left fell victim. Or perhaps it wasn't until pomo began to come to grips with the various social liberation movements of the past generation that it began to take stock of what it might mean to retheorize recent history from the vantage point of *plural*, discontinuous, multiply constituted "public spheres." Surely, it is hard to imagine any group other than white male intellectuals who would be in the position to tell stories about exhausted literature, or about our decline and fall from the Golden Age of the public intellectual; and in this sense, "history" simply wasn't available for postmodern scrutiny until the disenfranchised showed up and put it on the table. As Barbara Ehrenreich has recently said, one reason we shouldn't make the mistake of confusing "multiculturalism" with the Left is that "the left is not sufficiently multicultural to deserve being confused with multiculturalism, at least not yet."

Either way, in the past few years, it seems that only a few pointed words from people like Nancy Fraser, Gayatri Spivak, Douglas Crimp, and Cornel West have gotten most of what remains of the Left to check its books and think again about the project of going back to the future. As for the rest of the erstwhile antipomo "Left," the mugged-liberal crowd who thought social justice was a good thing so long as they didn't have to get their own coffee, live in bad neighborhoods, or put up with men kissing each other in public . . . well, the less said about that bunch the better.

Besides, I don't mean to revive the false dichotomy between postmodernism and the Left; my point is simply that the Left has had a number of misgivings about pomo's alleged erasure of materiality, and about its relation to history. If, for instance, postmodernism has troubled the distinction between consumption and production (as it certainly has), then the Left has some reason to say that pomo is no different in this respect from consumer capitalism, in which consumption has itself become a kind of "production" (and notoriously so in the merger-mad '80s). Obviously, the same can be said for much of recent literary and cultural theory, especially "reception theory," which, in its more interesting formulations, maintains that cultural artifacts are "produced" only by means of their continued consumption.

But pomo isn't just consumerism with a veneer of theory—not in hip-hop (which "consumed" disco only to spit it back out in scratching and sampling), and not in the work of artists like Hans Haacke. When Haacke foregrounds the means of cultural transmission, he doesn't do so in order to glorify consumption; on the contrary, Haacke's work rigorously interrogates the socioeconomic conditions of art's "ownership," and contests the corporate reprivatization of the arts. From the perspective of Haacke's Left-postmodernism, you could say that what makes Philip Johnson's famous AT&T building postmodern is not its funny Chippendale top, but its tax-abatement "plaza," which, as Herbert Schiller noted in *Culture, Inc.* (1989), is marked by a revealing sign of the times:

PUBLIC SPACE
Owned and Maintained
By AT&T
550 Madison Avenue, N.Y.C.

In AT&T's "public space," as in the critical reception of Haacke and hiphop, we find that postmodernism isn't without enemies in its reconfiguration of the means of cultural transmission; even as pomo culture spans the globe and appears in your living room, the global culture of "free-market" capitalism is doing its best, often (and paradoxically), to *restrict* circulation, to *reprivatize* culture, to *recapture* public spheres, museums, airwaves, and Xerox machines, and to *reinforce* the laws of copyright, ownership, and Authorship. In pomo's future tenses, Right and Left will very likely duke it out over the availability of "public" information; and postmodernism's politics will involve a struggle for control—not over the means of production, but over the means of *replication*. Who cares about the funny Chippendale top? Not me.

What's crucial here is that whenever we speak of "the means of cultural transmission," we're also speaking of the processes of *historical* transmission. And no one theorist illustrates the recent history of postmodernism's history so well as Frederic Jameson, who's spent most of the last decade calling pomo the "cultural dominant" of our era. Jameson's latest brief, a gorgeously produced 400-page document (*Postmodernism, or the Cultural Logic of Late Capitalism*, 1991), begins by suggesting that "it is safest to grasp the concept of the postmodern as an attempt to think of the present historically in an age that has forgotten how to think historically in the first place." That sounds like a prescription for heroic failure to me, however beset by cultural amnesia we may be. But in the opening pages of his hundred-page "Conclusion," Jameson takes issue with the mistaken notion that he is either a "vulgar Marxist hatchet man" or a "post-Marxist" who's stopped worrying and learned to love the boom. "I write," he now writes,

> as a relatively enthusiastic consumer of postmodernism, at least of some parts of it: I like the architecture and a lot of the newer visual work, in particular the newer photography. The music is not bad to listen to, or the poetry to read; the novel is the weakest of the newer cultural areas and is considerably excelled by its narrative counterparts in film and video.

All well and good. Still, the first versions of Jameson's argument do sound pretty dour in retrospect. In "Postmodernism and Consumer Society" (1983), he'd held that postmodernism could only attempt pastiche, rather than parody, because "there remains somewhere behind all parody the feeling that there is a linguistic norm in contrast to which the styles of the great modernists can be mocked." Whereas today, thanks to our cultural fragmentation and hypertrophy of cultural styles, we have no linguistic norm, and "that is the moment at which pastiche appears and parody has become impossible." Pastiche, then, is like everything you've had before, all mixed up—but "without parody's ulterior motive, without the satirical impulse, without laughter."

To Jameson, pomo pastiche was most painfully evident in "nostalgia" films like *Star Wars*, which evoked without irony the era of Saturday afternoon serials. But in his suggestion that the movie *Body Heat* is a "distant remake" of *Double Indemnity*, Jameson sounded an ominous note:

> *It seems to me exceedingly symptomatic to find the very style of nostalgia films invading and colonizing even those movies today which have contemporary settings: as though, for some reason, we were unable today to focus our own present, as though we have become incapable of achieving aesthetic representations of our own current experience. But if that is so, then it is a terrible indictment of consumer capitalism itself—or at the very least, an alarming and pathological symptom of a society that has become incapable of dealing with time and history.*

In Don DeLillo's *White Noise* (1985), a massive chemical spill (the novel calls it an "airborne toxic event") gives people a false sense of déjà vu—that is, it makes them think they have déjà vu even though they don't. Such is the world Frederic Jameson once described; DeLillo's point, and Jameson's, was that we had plenty of evidence that consumer capitalism's frenetic production of new, improved I-forget-whats does in fact work to erase our sense of, um, did I mention *Total Recall* yet?

But in another sense, the moment for this kind of historical despondency is itself a part of pomo's past; one might even venture to say, these days, that there's reason to be cheerful. Long ago, in a galaxy far, far away, we thought postmodernism was a world of sheer depthlessness and virtual reality, where presidents confuse World War II with World War II movies, and the torched tenements lining the Cross Bronx Expressway get plastered with Slum-Kote, a space-age facading polymer designed to make unsightly urban blight vanish in seconds. But lo, postmodernism has turned out to have developed a critical edge after all—and you know, it even takes a serious attitude toward history (now understood to be the sum of the processes of historical transmission). It hasn't fixed the Bronx, but it has brought some of the Bronx to my own MTV, and what's more, it's forced us to rethink just what it is we're post- in the first place.

According to Andreas Huyssen's surefooted negotiations of mo and pomo, "postmodernism is far from making modernism obsolete. On the contrary, it casts a new light on it and appropriates many of its aesthetic strategies and techniques, inserting them and making them work in new constellations." And one of the things we may now understand about our modernist legacy is that our century's art need not necessarily proceed, as do missile delivery systems, capitalisms, or the works of James Joyce, developmentally into systems of ever-increasing complexity. For if we read "postmodernism" with less emphasis on the dismissive prefix and more on the presence of the name-within-the-name, we can position pomo against modernism without having to claim that postmodernism is either new or improved. What looks to one person like a rehashed pastiche of hi-modernist panache, therefore, may appear to another (me, say) as a trenchant reworking of traditional modernist tropes and aesthetic strategies.

As I mentioned earlier, item one on this agenda is the question of whether modernism was truly, always and everywhere, an avant-garde movement after all. Since we can't very well rope together T. S. Eliot, Dada Berlin, Djuna Barnes, André Derain, Isadora Duncan, and Igor Stravinsky, maybe we should go back up to the attic, sort through this pile of boxes our great-grandparents left us, and try to determine whether all this stuff is as oppositional and corrosive as its labels claim. And here, we have to ask not only about the Modernists themselves, but also, and more crucially, about modernism's publicists and promoters.

Modernist promoter Philip Rahv once claimed that even Eliot's *Four Quartets* should by rights be ascribed to the "venturesome spirit" of "the avant-garde which must be given credit for the production of most of the literary masterpieces of the past hundred years." But by the time Rahv wrote that sentence, Eliot was a conservative Anglican royalist on his way home from picking up the Nobel Prize. And ever since then, many American critics have been embroiled in the non-dispute over who "owns" modernist poetry—T. S. Eliot, Ezra Pound, or Wallace Stevens. The correct answer is none of the above, but just the same, even if literary modernism *were* reducible to the venturesome work of one ultraconservative white man, what does it mean for us in 1991 that modernism has so long been *classic?* Again, this is not the same question as the question of what modernism "was"; nor can it properly be asked from "within" modernism, for when modernist theorists ask how modernism became so routine in our daily lives, they just can't see around their own edifice.

In a 1983 article entitled "The Making of the Modernist Canon," for instance, Hugh Kenner concluded that the modernist canon, far from being the construction of critics like Kenner, was organically grown "chiefly . . . by the canonized themselves." Kenner was seconded a few years later by fellow modernist fan Helen Vendler, who averred in the face of all evidence to the contrary that "canons are not made by governments, anthologists, publishers, editors, or professors, but by writers." So you can try to ask modernist critics and apologists about who *transmitted* modernism—but they'll only shake their heads, look at you quizzically, and reply with knotted brow that modernism simply transmitted itself.

And—now here's the catch—modernists will claim also that when modernism transmitted itself into the cultural center, it *died*. For those of you who were wondering why the avant-garde is dead, you may take comfort in knowing that the question is older than many of the people asking it, and that it just doesn't have an intelligible answer outside of modernist assumptions about centers and margins. Probably the best case in point is Anglo-American modernist literature, which, having established itself in the academies and anthologies in the 1940s and 1950s, was at once retrospectively theorized as an avant-garde whose force lay in its resistance to institutionalization, and whose success was therefore its failure.

In a famous 1957 *Partisan Review* essay, entitled "The Fate of the Avant-Garde," Richard Chase wrote that "the insurgent movement in this country which defended 'modernism'—that is, the aesthetic experimentalism and social protest of the period between 1912 and 1950—has expired of its own success." Chase concluded by charging that modernism "has been institutionalized by the universities and the publishers, which by definition means that in its modern phase it has to come to an end." Modernism, in other words, has no shelf life: Its expiration date is by definition the date when it first shows up in a central store.

Fair enough; by the '50s Anglo-American modernism had indeed been "institutionalized" in those tiny little padded cells known as "classrooms," and by 1965 Lionel Trilling could write that the teaching of modern lit effectively kills its subject, by making The Abyss into something every well-rounded person should encounter in college. But isn't there something wrong with this picture? Look again: In the passage above, Richard Chase's canonical "modernism" allows him to conflate aesthetic experimentalism and social protest under one sign, that of an "insurgent movement" which "defended 'modernism.'" Chase's account leaves no room for avant-garde social/aesthetic protest that attacked (or was at best ambivalent about) modernism, no room for *New Masses*, the early-'30s Edmund Wilson of *Axel's Castle*, the militant Suffragette campaigns in prewar Britain, or any of the writers of the Harlem Renaissance. (Surely, no one in the Harlem Renaissance wound up expiring of success.) The lessons here, then, are that not all of modernism was "insurgent," that not all insurgents liked modernism, and—most of all—that most of our *truly* insurgent modernisms were, as Cary Nelson's *Repression and Recovery* (1989) has shown, utterly obliterated from the cultural record when, in the postwar years, "modernism" was incorporated under the sign of Eliot/Pound Enterprises.

But then the inevitable question follows: Who impoverished and monologized "modernism" and why?

The pomo jury is still out on this one, but Andrew Ross has offered one explanation I find persuasive. In *No Respect: Intellectuals and Popular Culture* (1989), Ross tackles the various intellectual formations that sought to "contain" mass culture after the collapse of the Old Left in the late 1930s. For what really "consolidated" modernism, in the 1940s and 1950s, was a conglomeration of strange modernist bedfellows, as critics of the anti-Stalinist Left lined up with critics of the Right in a bi- or multi-partisan agreement that nothing could resist the twin evils of fascism and mass culture—nothing except the transcendent masterpieces of the modernist "avant-garde." Over the soul-saving virtues of modernism, even the liberal/socialist lambs and the agrarian-conservative lions were agreed: Clement Greenberg and T. S. Eliot, F. O. Matthiessen and Cleanth Brooks, Lionel Trilling and Allen Tate. As Ross puts it, "the mass society critique was first advanced on the left as an explanation for the failure of socialist movements, and the growing successes of fascism. . . . As a result, the picture of mass culture as a profitable opiate, synthetically prepared for consumption for a society of automatons, won favor among the anti-Stalinist, and mostly Trotskyist, intellectuals grouped around the little magazines like *Partisan Review, Politics,* and *Dissent*."

Therefore, there could have been no passing of the modernist cultural moment, in these terms, until we saw the realignment of "high art" and "mass culture," a realignment provoked by Pop Art, television, feminism, roadside architecture, camp, the Black Arts movement, deconstruction, and a contradictory host of critical forces dedicated to the common cause of asking whether modernism and mass culture actually were polar, binary opposites in the first place. In other words, modernism didn't die when it was absorbed into the university and the supermarket; it was cryogenically preserved amid the mass culture it affected to despise, living on into an era which no longer needs (or finds it possible) to maintain a binary opposition between the High and the Mass. From the twin peaks of pomo, indeed, it's come to look as if modernism and masscult were the yin and yang of the early 20th century—or, in Huyssen's words, as if "their much heralded mutual exclusiveness is really a sign of their secret interdependence." For Huyssen, postmodernism works to destabilize the high/mass opposition from within; and for Andrew Ross and critics working out of the British Cultural Studies tradition, what's most important to postmodernism is the passing of the "coercion" theory of masscult, the dogged notion that masscult's consumers (of, for example, TV, pornography, and romance novels) are purely passive potatoes.

The current upshot of reassessments of the "culture" in mass culture, concludes Ross, is that today, an "intellectual activism" disconnected from "the vernacular of information technology and the discourses and images of popular, commercial culture will have as much leverage over the new nomination of modern social movements as the spells of medieval witches or consultation of the *I Ching*." If this means that academics and policy consultants have to stop quoting Eliot and start watching *The Simpsons,* so be it: Either our self-appointed intellectual and artistic vanguards learn what Ross calls "lessons about the business of contesting popular meanings without speaking from above," or—read my lips—they can eat my shorts.

The landscape looks exciting, and the field of critical inquiry (like the field of cultural and artistic production) has expanded considerably if not downright vertiginously: The passing of "avant-gardism" has left us a world in which cultural subversion and political quietism may turn up anywhere on the dial, even hand in hand—and a world in which yesterday's subversions can very easily become tomorrow's quietisms. Such a state of affairs should keep us up at night pretty regularly, but let me tell you, it beats watching *The Donna Reed Show.*

In fact, for my money, the only unambiguously regrettable development in all this is the sad fate of poor old modernism. Where once the stuff had the power to disturb, shock, transform, and energize its audiences, it's now fallen into the hands of the sorriest bunch of cultural reactionaries you'll ever want to see, people like Hilton Kramer at *The New Criterion*—the kind of critics who appear without fail, every generation, staff in hand, to grouse volubly about how culture took a fatal turn for the worse precisely 10 years before they were born, and how the art of "our" past can sustain us in these trivial times if only we venerate it sufficiently. What do you think happens to people like Kramer when pomo points out that their "classic" modernism and mass culture have something to do with each other? Well, it isn't pretty. All Kramer has to do is walk into the *High & Low* exhibit, and the popping of his blood vessels becomes downright audible: "We know straightaway," if we're a we, "that in 'High & Low' we are in the presence of one of the most unconscionable intellectual swindles we have ever seen in a serious museum."

But surely this too is to be expected: As "classicity" touches everything from Braque to Coke, there will be a growing number of reactionaries who'll resist any historical inspection of the Real Thing. Soon, no doubt, the same curmudgeonly people who complained about pomo's playfulness will be screeching that pomo is Politically Correct. And by then, we can expect two things. Thing one will be that postmodernism's complex and indeterminate projects of cultural critique, wherever on the dial we find them, will have drawn some blood from the vastly complacent culture they inhabit. Thing two is that postmodernism will shortly thereafter be defended by *next* century's reactionaries as the scale of classicity in which future generations will once again be weighed and found wanting.

And by *then*, if memory serves, pomo's institutionalization will look to us like it's déjà vu all over again.

October 1991

FROM QUEER TO ETERNITY

An Army of Theorists Cannot Fail

By Michael Warner

The appeal of "queer theory," like the appeal of "cultural studies," has outstripped anyone's sense of what exactly it means. I discovered this abruptly not long ago when I used the phrase, in passing, to a lesbian theorist of sexuality whose work I respect. With an air of embarrassment that may or may not have been Socratic, she said, "Wait—what is queer theory?" I thought of this as her attempt to educate me into being clear; she must know, I thought, since her book is one that I am citing as an example of queer theory. On the other hand, she may have been simply (and rightly) puzzled. Like many other theorists, she doesn't use the word *queer*, because she wrote most of her book before the word had currency. Academics now are talking about queer theory as a Movement. As recently as two years ago the phrase would not have rung a bell.

Queer theory is nothing if not hot. Routledge makes a regular trade of it. Book series in queer theory have been started by Columbia and Duke (Duke's is called "Series Q"). In the Rutgers English Department, where graduate students take exams in a theory or method of their choice, more students are choosing queer theory this year than Marxism and deconstruction combined.

Yet when these students make their reading lists, they come up with things that have been around for years: Foucault, lesbian feminism, Lacan, postmodernism, cultural studies. Part of the attraction is that queer theory isn't a well-defined field; being interested in queer theory is a way to mess up the desexualized spaces of the academy, exude some rut, reimagine the publics from and for which academic intellectuals write, dress, and perform. Nervous over the prospect of a well-sanctioned and compartmentalized academic version of "lesbian and gay studies," people want to make theory queer, not just to have a theory about queers. For academics as well as activists, queer gets a critical edge by defining itself against the normal rather than the heterosexual, and normal includes normal business in the academy.

"Queer" is also a way of cutting against mandatory gender divisions, though gender continues to be a dividing line. Men in queer theory, as well as women who write about gay men or AIDS, tend to be strongly influenced by Foucault and constructionist theory in general. They infuse queerness into their work through a mixture of tempered rage and carnivalesque display. Women who write about women, by contrast, typically refer to French feminisms (Monique Wittig, Luce Irigaray, Julia Kristeva) and Anglo-American psychoanalytic feminism, especially in film theory (Teresa de Lauretis, Judith Mayne, Sue-Ellen Case, Judith Roof, but also Judith Butler and Diana Fuss). As Fuss points out in her influential book *Essentially Speaking*, this tradition of lesbian feminism has made lesbian theorists more preoccupied with the theme of identity—the attempt to define (or, more recently, ironize) the common core of lesbian or female subjects. "A certain pressure is applied to the lesbian subject," Fuss points out, "to either 'claim' or to 'discover' her true identity before she can elaborate a 'personal politics.'" For lesbian theorists, queer theory offers a way of basing politics in the personal without acceding to this pressure to clean up personal identity.

The idea of queer theory may involve some generational mythmaking as well. At the otherwise partylike Lesbian and Gay Studies Conference last year, a young critic named Arlene Stein gave a talk called "Sisters and Queers: The Decentering of Lesbian Feminism." Stein argued that lesbian feminism traditionally has relied on a myth of identity through sisterhood, a notion that all women or at least all lesbians are in some ways alike enough to have common interests and shared understanding; *queer* is a better term, she said, because it emphasizes what can't be assimilated, and therefore allows people to acknowledge more diversity. Many heads were nodding at this; Stein was expressing what has come to be a common sentiment. But others, particularly older lesbians in the room, were not convinced. Sisterhood, they said, was not in all places and times reductive or unreflective.

The objection was more than theoretical. Many of the women in the room had been working without recognition or reward for years—some as independent scholars, others as academics who often suffered in their careers for doing lesbian work—only to see a younger generation cashing in professionally for having the same interests. To them, there was some irony in the anti-assimilationist rhetoric of the first lesbian and gay generation to enjoy academic celebrity.

The republication of *Out of the Closets* partly bears out the views of these lesbian elders. *Out of the Closets* was state-of-the-art lesbian and gay liberation theory in 1972. Three years after the Stonewall riots, it offered ambitious left-wing theories about what a lesbian and gay liberation movement might do, not just about homophobia, but about oppression of all kinds. It made available Radicalesbians' "The Woman-Identified Woman," as well as Carl Wittman's "A Gay Manifesto"—both classics from which much can still be learned.

Lesbian and gay liberation thinking of this sort tends not to be what people have in mind when they talk about queer theory, and I suspect that few in the queer generation will have read it until now. *Out of the Closets* is dated in many ways (not all of which are corrected by the new introduction; the editors, who don't seem to get out much these days, remark that AIDS "has made sexual conservatism necessary," a piece of phony wisdom that Douglas Crimp's *AIDS: Cultural Analysis/Cultural Activism* should have buried forever). Nevertheless, its republication shows that many insights and aspirations now associated with queer theory have long histories—including self-conscious dialogue among lesbians, as well as between lesbians and gay men, about their multiple differences.

If you compare it to the recent special issue of *differences*, "Queer Theory: Lesbian and Gay Sexualities," you find a remarkable continuity of interest. This issue has had much to do with popularizing the term "queer theory" among academics; it came out at the same time that many political activists were shifting from "lesbian and gay" to "queer" (not so long ago—Queer Nation only started in 1990), and its attempt to address seriously racial and ethnic differences among queers struck a chord with those attuned to problems of coalition activism. But most of the *differences* issue has a long history in the movement: its interest in racial difference, for example; or in the way power relationships shape sexuality; in the way feminist resistance to male domination and lesbian/gay resistance to compulsory heterosexuality require each other; in a sense of alienation from most available ways of affirming identity.

But in other ways queer theory marks a departure. Queer theorists are much more at ease with the idea that queerness is necessarily an effect of representation. They have less interest in what it means to be lesbian or gay than in the kinds of fantasy, performance, display, and talk that make sexuality as queer as it is. In part, this is because queer theory is a way of teaching culture; very few of the contributors to *Out of the Closets* were academics, but queer theory almost always comes from universities, particularly from literature or film departments. Almost everything that would be called queer theory is about ways in which texts—either literature or mass culture or language—shape sexuality. Usually, the notion is that fantasy and other kinds of representation are inherently uncontrollable, queer by nature. This focus on messy representation allows queer theory, like nonacademic queer activism, to be both anti-assimilationist and antiseparatist: You can't eliminate queerness, says queer theory, or screen it out. It's everywhere. There's no place to hide, hetero scum!

Lesbians in queer theory have been particularly drawn to such arguments given the problem of lesbian invisibility. Madonna comes in for analysis, of course. But consider the range of texts discussed in Judith Roof's *A Lure of Knowledge: Lesbian Sexuality and Theory:* Anaïs Nin, Freud, Kristeva, Rita Mae Brown, Emily Dickinson criticism, journalism about professional tennis, *Lianna,* straight porn, *I've Heard the Mermaids Singing.* What do these things have in common? They are occasions for Roof to describe the problem of bringing lesbian sexuality into view without pathologizing or mythologizing it, as well as dominant culture's inability to keep it entirely hidden. For Roof there is no simple solution, such as coming out, to these problems. Nor are they in all ways lamentable. She does not try to attribute certainty, identity, or mastery to lesbians; she wants instead for lesbian sexuality to be a movable threat, a variable pleasure.

In her widely cited essay "Toward a Butch-Femme Aesthetic," Sue-Ellen Case took a similar approach to the dynamics "within" lesbian sexuality, emphasizing performance and fantasy identifications as a way of showing that lesbianism is not an easily isolated, stable, or homogenous thing. Case's work opened the way for theorists to find lesbian sexuality in places that had always been thought of as male and heterosexist, even in voyeurism and fetishism. In most queer theory these two emphases—on the public forms that display sexuality and the fantasy scenarios that make up sexuality—go together. Teresa de Lauretis offers a synthesis of such arguments in "Film and the Visible," her contribution to *How Do I Look?: Queer Film and Video.* Probably the most influential example of this trend, however, is Judith Butler's *Gender Trouble.*

Butler goes farther in this direction than any other major queer theorist, replacing the emphasis on identity with an emphasis on performance. It has made her the object of controversy. AIDS activist Simon Watney, in a recent issue of *NYQ* (now *QW*), complained about the "virtual deification" of Judith Butler in queer theory. Noting that Butler was cited approvingly in almost every panel session of the recent Lesbian and Gay Studies Conference at Rutgers, Watney accused Butler of arguing that coming out can only be a way of embracing a fixed identity defined by the heterosexual system, and therefore just as oppressive as the closet. In his view, this is theory only for academics. If the rejection of identity politics is what "queer theory" means, Watney says, then who needs it?

Watney's criticism relies on a superficial reading of Butler's work, though one that she at times seems to invite: "If I claim to be a lesbian," she writes in her contribution to *Inside/Out: Lesbian Theories, Gay Theories*, "I 'come out' only to produce a new and different 'closet'." The "only" in this sentence is the sort of thing that gets Watney's back up, because it implies that there is no politically relevant difference between being closeted and being out. Butler goes on to say, however, "I am not legislating against the use of the term. My question is simply: Which use will be legislated, and what play will there be between legislation and use such that the instrumental uses of 'identity' do not become regulatory imperatives?" She wants to emphasize the queerness of queers. She wants an anti-assimilationist way of being a "lesbian" or a "gay man" so that these queer identities will not be mere alternatives to "straight," parallel to it in every way. She wants queerness to challenge the very nature of heterosexual self-understanding, and it can't do that by simply being another kind of identity in the world.

This part of her argument has been embraced by the queer generation because it solicits a praxis of fun making, and because it makes the in-your-face attitude of queer politics unfold from the intrinsic nature of sexuality. In this respect it has an authorizing power. Have fun and make trouble, it tells us. Or better yet: Sexuality already, of its own logic, makes trouble. This is why many of the same people who admire Simon Watney's aggressive criticism of homophobia in the media also admire Butler's philosophical-psychoanalytic account of gender and sexuality. It's an argument that seems to fit with urban lesbian culture's shift toward public visibility, queer fashion, butch/femme resurgence, girl bars with back rooms, blurry lines between lesbian and bisexual practice, and other kinds of mayhem. And by giving a central role to cross-identifications of various kinds, it recognizes the appeal that a work of lesbian-feminism might have for gay men and others.

Butler's work further appeals to the queer generation for the ways it seems to break with previous generations of lesbian and gay activists in the U.S. For instance, it practically reverses the position of "Woman-Identified Woman." Where Radicalesbians saw lesbian-feminism as sharpening the contrast between male and female—lesbian sexuality being the purest form of gender solidarity—Butler sees lesbian-feminism as erasing, or at least "troubling," the distinction between male and female, as well as between hetero and homo. "The anachronistic notion of 'male identification,'" she writes, "ought to be discarded from a feminist vocabulary"; women, in her view, should be expected to have male identifications, and should be encouraged to act them out parodically, just as lesbians can be expected to act out (again parodically) het roles.

Radicalesbians began their manifesto, "What is a lesbian? A lesbian is the rage of all women condensed to the point of explosion." If Butler could be persuaded to regard the question "What is a lesbian?" as one worth answering, she might respond that a lesbian is the incoherence of gender binarism and heterosexuality condensed to the point of parody. Radicalesbians spoke of making individual integration more available to women. They spoke of self-love, sense of self, autonomy, and dignity; and they spoke of the common identity and interest of "all women." Butler speaks of "resistance to classification and to identity as such." (When Simon Watney attacks Butler for this sort of position, I think he forgets that it is addressed largely to a lesbian-feminist audience, for whom the problem of the supposed unity of women has been abiding and difficult. As gay men, Watney and I don't have the same history of worrying about the unity of all men; we will therefore tend to have a different stake in the argument.)

In another way, however, Butler fundamentally agrees with a key premise of liberationist theory: the notion that nonstandard sexuality is the political medium for opposing gender domination. Like the Radicalesbians, Butler sees lesbian sexuality as a subversion of patriarchy, here understood as phallogocentrism. Her book is subtitled "Feminism and the Subversion of Identity"; because Butler regards compulsory heterosexuality as the means for consolidating the oppressive illusions of gender identity, subversion of identity is an attack simultaneously on masculinism, gender, compulsory heterosexuality, and the metaphysics of presence.

These large claims do not entirely originate with Butler; her strongest arguments are influenced by the early work of Gayle Rubin and by Monique Wittig. Wittig's *The Straight Mind*, which now makes accessible her brilliant, provocative essays from the last 12 years, might finally give her the recognition she deserves in queer circles. (Rubin continues to be known mainly to academics, mainly through two diamondlike essays of 1975 and 1984, but her work is of no less importance; I can only hope that someone will republish her essays and interviews soon.) Both Rubin—at least in her early essay "The Traffic in Women"—and Wittig establish a strong link between male domination and normative heterosexuality. And both advocate radical measures in response, Wittig in particular often embracing a language of revolution.

Like many of the current queer theorists, however, Butler has shed the specifically political part of her forebears' radicalism. Heterosexuality in her account turns out to be subverting itself already.

Heterosexuality offers normative sexual positions that are intrinsically impossible to embody, and the persistent failure to identify fully and without incoherence with these positions reveals heterosexuality itself not

> *only as a compulsory law, but as an inevitable comedy. Indeed, I would offer this insight into heterosexuality as both a compulsory system and an intrinsic comedy, a constant parody of itself, as an alternative gay/lesbian perspective.*

Without entirely disagreeing, I find it hard to be content with this. When Butler calls heterosexuality an inevitable comedy, one might well ask: inevitable for whom? In everyday life the comedy seems more than evitable; and if heterosexuality, as Butler says again and again, is bound to "fail," it's been failing for centuries, with great success (much the way "late" capitalism seems to be on the rise). Post-identity theory such as Butler's may help legitimate sexual dissidence within expert culture, but it has almost ceased to distinguish between descriptive normative projects. What politics follows if heterosexuality already inevitably seems to do what we want it to do—that is, fail? The answer mainly seems to be that queers should dramatize its failure, but we are already supposed to be doing that merely by being queer.

Does queer practice consist entirely or even mostly in identification and desire? Is the parodic subversion of queer performance immediately visible in all publics, all media, all institutional contexts? Butler speaks of the social force of language as a way of arguing for the power of subversive identifications, but language in her account typically means the lexicon of identities (do I call myself "gay" or "queer"?); the pragmatic interactions, genres, and media of language are not distinguished (why do I say gay in one context and queer in another, where in other contexts there would be no question of what I might say?). Such a one-dimensional analysis can hardly clarify the main ambitions of queer theory, which include bringing sexuality, academic expertise, state politics, and public media into a more mutually critical relation—something that can't be done if these levels are not distinguished in the first place.

At any rate, the political remains undertheorized in Butler's work, which seldom discusses class, race, or nationality, let alone the state and other institutions. In *Inside/Out*, she herself asks, "Is it not a sign of despair over public politics when identity becomes its own policy?" but surely when ironized identity becomes its own policy, public politics remains equally empty. Fuss writes that "simply *being* gay or lesbian is not sufficient to constitute political activism," and neither is being queer. I think Butler and Fuss would agree on this point, but the focus on identity has led to a kind of negative identity politics in queer theory.

One of the lessons the republished *Out of the Closets* might bring at this point is that lesbians and gays have been struggling for decades with many of the same public institutions. The editors write that in

1972 four stood out particularly: government, health care, organized religion, and the mass media. We're still there.

The most important theoretical work on this front in recent years is Cindy Patton's *Inventing AIDS*, though given its focus it has more to say about gay men than lesbians (some of Patton's uncollected essays, however, shift the focus to women). Patton reflects on the organizational contexts that bring gay men, lesbians, heterosexual women, African Americans, IVDUs, and sex workers together. Conceptually risky and densely detailed, *Inventing AIDS* describes the relation of these different organizing contexts to each other, and just as importantly, to the national state. Politics, in her analysis, consists of competing discourse frames and institutional layers, and she shows that you can't determine the politics of anything in the abstract without considering its conflicting concrete manifestations. Where middle-class white activists rapidly adopted the knack of organizing around AIDS as a single-issue cause, for example, activists of color and IVDUs were more inclined to pursue the "full-plate" approach to a wide range of government services, meaning that they were often left behind in the scramble for AIDS resources.

Patton's work is the clearest example of how queer theory can take some of its cues from the implicit theoretical intuitions of queer activism. Academic theory need not be simply a handmaiden, but it can learn from activism. *How Do I Look?* shows how this might be done, as does a new essay by Lauren Berlant and Elizabeth Freeman, "Queer Nationality" (in the current *boundary 2*), or all of *Nationalisms and Sexualities*. These writers have realized that queer activism consists of a largely intuitive and half-articulate theory about precisely these questions: How do you avoid being brokered into assimilation by the national political system? How do you deploy one medium or context against another—street theater, for example, against national television? How do you define a public space that isn't nationalist, that isn't ungendered or desexualized or racially homogenous? How can you short-circuit the machine of het self-congratulation? How can you cut down the toxic waste from the culture industry? The field of queer theory is at a boom point, and it is only going to get queerer still.

June 1992

HOW THE WEST WAS LOST

Writing at the End of the World

By Scott L. Malcomson

THE HOLD LIFE HAS: COCA AND CULTURAL IDENTITY
IN AN ANDEAN COMMUNITY
By Catherine J. Allen

THE WRITING OF HISTORY
By Michel de Certeau

WORKS AND LIVES: THE ANTHROPOLOGIST AS AUTHOR
By Clifford Geertz

PEREGRINATIONS: LAW, FORM, EVENT
By Jean-François Lyotard

LES PRIMITIFS, NOS CONTEMPORAINS
By Frédéric Rognon

Where are the primitives of yesteryear? Once the planet was covered with them, and to the savannahs, pampas, atolls, and yam gardens came pale emissaries in unusually large wooden boats. In the early days, explorers, missionaries, and economic mercenaries could claim ownership of entire continents after discovering the teeniest beach. And they could draw portraits of new lands and peoples virtually as they pleased. Terra incognita could be a Woman waiting for European seed, fertile territory ripe for exploitation, a tropical inferno peopled by hostile lunatics, the European subconscious come terribly or wondrously to life; it could harbor cannibalistic primitives, or childlike innocents, or noble savages. The primitives of yesteryear could be almost anything that was not Europe, which was their allure and their crime.

Pioneering white travel writers and conquerors came from a Europe that was still very diverse, you might even say primitive: a Europe of Black Forest trolls, weird sisters cackling over cauldrons, Auvergne sorcerers, and Kerry leprechauns. The ethnic other might be just a few valleys away; the socioeconomic other could be alternatively in the castle or toiling on the plain; the deep otherness of time and death could be found in God, magic, political fate, and transparent repetitions of myth. Which is not to say that premodern white people were without history. They just hadn't yet partaken of the modern idea of history, or of ethnicity.

As Renaissance slipped into Enlightenment, white folk got a grip on themselves. You could call it white nationalism, or you could call it civilization. All sorts of bizarre ideological tricks were tested out in the effort to construct whiteness—like classicism, that deft sleight-of-hand whereby two millennia of white history were made to disappear merely by concentrating on Greece and Rome. (Who'd have imagined! Italians and Greeks as the Ur-white people!) Aided by technology and the written word, the metropoles slowly consolidated Gauls and Bretons, Angles and Scots under the slightly less restless, if no more obviously credible, banners of the nation-state. This "civilizing" process has always been tenuous and contradictory—nation-states still have to define themselves against each other, white or not—but it was solid enough that some obscure burdens of the Dark Ages could be shifted onto the Dark Continent. The nonwhite primitive was put in the thankless position of acting as civilization's repressed subconscious, its former self, an unwilling and uninformed analysand in geopolitical therapy.

If the transition from feudalism was in part a struggle between the secular state and tribal religion, Europe's postfeudal relationship with the rest of the world took an even stranger form: a struggle between the white superstate of civilization and a planet's worth of enemies who were ultimately distinguishable only by, of all things, their skin color. Throughout this process, of course, economic and political undercurrents churned along. But at the ideological level it was largely a question of religion and, later, civilization. By the 19th century there was even a science of white-nonwhite relations: anthropology. The primitive could at last be subjected to rational classification. Lists could be made. With classic encyclopedist assurance, one might actually believe that, with enough time, money, and manpower, all of humanity would be recorded in one very big book, with chapter headings like "Myths and Legends," "Kinship Structures," and "The Sexual Division of Labor."

It would be a stretch to say anthropology ever had a unified theory, but it did, for a time, have the next best thing: disciplinary self-confidence. During anthropology's heyday, say from 1890 to sometime between the wars, practitioners at least knew the difference between Us and Them and could believe, vaguely or fiercely, that We were better. After the tribal slaughters of World War I, a subtle yet corrosive relativism began chipping away at Enlightenment confidence. Despite the Eisenhower hiatus of American supremacy, it chipped and chipped until, in the '60s, the terms of Us and Them were briefly and unevenly inverted. It was possible to be white and anticolonial at the same time.

Anthropology reaped short-term gains as it provided access to nonwhite cultures, now problematically collectivized into the Third World. But the '60s didn't last, and neither did the insecure admiration of many white students for the nonwhite world.

And, in the aftermath, the science of white-nonwhite relations had to scramble. Was it pro-Enlightenment, anti-Enlightenment, or what? Neocolonial, anticolonial, postcolonial? What were young anthropologists to think of themselves after landing at the Port Moresby airport, wading through the discarded beer cans that clog the city streets, catching a bus to the Guinean Highlands and searching, with a weird desperation, for one last premodern kinship structure? Were they the inquisitive shock troops of white cultural hegemony, or anti-Western empiricist guerrillas, preserving other cultures in a kind of antidiluvian Save the Whales maneuver? How could they be either and still keep a clean conscience and a straight face?

Where are the primitives of yesteryear? Building nation-states, forgetting pasts, remembering them and making them up, fighting wars of liberation and immiseration, constructing identities amid the chaos of postmodern life. Making history. That was supposed to be a white prerogative but something seems to have gone awry. Many white people are worried by this since it means the end of civilization as we know it. (We?) They hold séances for the Enlightenment and Western Civ. They wonder, Did civilization fall on its sword or was it pushed? They huddle about the wheezing body and fight to hear its last words. Maybe "The feminists got me," or "It was the poststructuralists," or "The Negroes put the knife in . . ."

Personally, I think the cause of death will be slow asphyxiation. Modern white civilization—which is but a burp, really, in the meal of history—is losing its Others, and they are the air it has needed to breathe. The primitives are gone, and with them, one hopes, the white people of yesteryear will depart as well.

One irony of contemporary English-language anthropology is that Clifford Geertz is its best-known practitioner. This is not only ironic but indicative because Geertz, apart from some early work in Indonesia, doesn't "practice anthropology" so much as write about practicing anthropology. His 1973 *The Interpretation of Cultures* was decisive in turning anthropology inward to ask the hard questions. Until roughly the time of its publication, Claude Lévi-Strauss had somehow managed to take anthropology on one last joyride. Lévi-Strauss wasn't much of a field-worker either—a 1938–39 trip to central Brazil was as close as he ever came to serious labor *sur le terrain*. But he produced a lifetime of tomes on the darker peoples, using received data to spin out structuralist dichotomies like a librarian on amphetamines. Subsequent criticism has pretty much buried structuralist theory, which now looks like the last desperate gasp of Durkheimian dualism.

Geertz's *Works and Lives*, a beautifully written state-of-the-discipline update, has a chapter on Lévi-Strauss that gives him his due and probably a little more. "I regard [Lévi-Strauss's] construction of an entire discourse realm from a standing start as a stunning achievement, altogether worthy of the attention it has received. Lévi-Strauss is clearly one of the true 'authors' in anthropology—if originality be all, perhaps the truest." Not that Geertz likes structuralism; he cheerfully admits "skepticism" about it as research technique and "outright hostility" to its philosophy. But he does appear to like Lévi-Strauss, not least because he, however briefly, made anthropology seem like king of the academic hill.

Works and Lives is subtitled "The Anthropologist as Author," and it is as an author, in the grand sense, that Lévi-Strauss earns Geertz's admiration. The book contains three other profiles, of E. E. Evans-Pritchard, Ruth Benedict, and Bronislaw Malinowski. Geertz sets out to defend these big four. He doesn't defend them as bearers of anthropological truth—each had a very different method in any case—but as anthropological authors, people who had the confidence, talent, and epistemological wiring to create discourses. That is, anthropologists who weren't afflicted with what Geertz sees as the signal contemporary ailment: "grave inner uncertainties, amounting almost to a sort of epistemological hypochondria, concerning how one can know that anything one says about other forms of life is in fact so." Later, he elaborates: "What is at hand is a pervasive nervousness about the whole business of claiming to explain enigmatical others on the grounds that you have gone about with them in their native habitat or combed the writings of those who have."

Geertz wants to perk up his colleagues, many of whom (particularly the youngsters) he apparently sees as dangerously spineless whiners, so crippled by self-doubt that they can barely leave their offices or write memos, let alone mount the physical and textual expeditions of times past. Geertz's colleagues are, emphatically, not the white people of yesteryear (nor is Geertz, though his *Lives* do have the feel of cautious rehabilitations). If anthropology was once part of a grand therapy session in which white civilization acted as analyst for the uncivilized other—pretending to treat the dark patient while actually treating itself—anthropologists are now mired in a miserable auto-therapy, at once self-mutilating and precious.

"Whether the period immediately ahead leads to a renewal of the discursive energies of anthropology or to their dissipation, a recovery of authorial nerve or its loss, depends on whether the field (or, more exactly, its would-be practitioners) can adjust itself to a situation in which its goals, its relevance, its motives, and its procedures all are questioned." Geertz figures that "whatever use ethnographic texts will have in the future, if in fact they actually have any, it will involve enabling conversation across societal lines—of ethnicity, religion, class, gender, language, race—that have grown progressively more nuanced, more immediate, and more irregular." As a call to arms this is pretty timid, but it is also honest.

One young anthropologist who has answered Geertz's call, if not explicitly, is Catherine J. Allen in *The Hold Life Has: Coca and Cultural Identity in an Andean Community*. Allen is neither founding a discourse nor even reviving "authorial nerve," but she is certainly engaging in conversation. In fact, her methodology is that of a friendly chat: "I have learned the most (and I think this is true of most fieldworkers) from a few individuals whom I can genuinely call friends and teachers, and who see themselves in this light. I did not actually choose these people as informants; we became friends because we enjoyed each other's company. With Luis, Erasmo, and Basilia, 'hanging out' coincided with my most profitable fieldwork, not to mention my happiest moments in Sonqo [the Andean village in which her book is set]." Throughout *The Hold Life Has* Allen is disarmingly modest. She recognizes in passing the epistemological predicament of ethnography, but doesn't let it get her down. "Ethnographers, of course, arrive on the scene with their own habitus, and try to learn the new one from scratch— a slow process that meets with partial success at best. . . . Here the anthropologist has much in common with an actor preparing a role." No epistemological nervousness here.

One wonders who would read a book like Allen's. I read it largely because I was once in the Andes myself. I have friends ("informants") there too, people I hung out with and from whom I learned various things, as well as occasionally having a good time. As it happened I was there to a great extent because there's a war in the Andes; preoccupied with that, I missed out on the habitus Allen is investigating. So *The Hold Life Has* was an opportunity to fill in some blanks.

I mention my motives because the kind of anthropology Geertz is proposing—the "conversation" kind—is likely to find nonprofessional readers only through some personal quirk. Without the legitimizing edifice of Science behind them, any future installments in ethnography will have to compete on the same terms as any other novel or travel book.

Unless, that is, they find some new and impressive "discursive energy." Yet, for better or worse, the authorial nerve Geertz believes is now missing was inextricably bound to its authors' pretensions, whether Evans-Pritchard's Oxbridge self-confidence or Lévi-Strauss's structuralist monomania. And the viability of those pretensions in turn depended on the pretensions of readers. In anthropology nowadays the nervousness Geertz dislikes is precisely the greatest source of authorial verve. I liked *The Hold Life Has*, but for rhetorical energy it can't compare with Frédéric Rognon's blistering *Les Primitifs, nos Contemporains*. Rognon's book is, needless to say, tortured and negative, a critique. He is pissed off at anthropology, with its "ethnocentrism," heedless utopianism, imperialist tendencies, and general manipulativeness. Primitives were "chimeras prepared for consumption" by, as he says elsewhere, "the only civilizations that have generated racist theories, not to mention scientific pretension and colonial expansion, the methodical exploitation of a foreign land and the systemic enslavement of its population ... [that is] the Occident and to a certain extent the Arab world." This is the authorial energy of outrage, and its echoes can be found elsewhere in current anthropological literature; the excellent 1986 anthology *Writing Culture: The Poetics and Politics of Ethnography* (University of California Press) is particularly well stocked.

What makes Rognon intriguing, at least symptomatically, is that his outrage takes him well beyond the "Whither anthropology?" sighing that Geertz attacks but has trouble escaping. Instead of projecting a calm future of respectful conversations in the Allen mode, Rognon goes right over the top and dumps on the ex-primitives themselves, or rather their indigenous, post-anthropological representatives, the "evolved," educated natives who now speak on behalf of their dark brothers and sisters. "Anthropology is menaced simultaneously by the loss of its object and by those objects having taken up, by themselves, their own monologues. The Savage speaks ... and what does he say? He recites books of ethnography. Oof! The anthropologists let out their breath! The Savage has learned his lesson well."

Rognon is something of a maniac, and his recitation of anthropology's ills is rapidly becoming old news. But his point about the primitive learning to speak in his master's voice captures, however hysterically, the bitter dilemma that Geertz evades: When the newly emerging primitive wishes to speak, he or she may find the discursive possibilities very limited indeed, just as nervous white practitioners have.

For example, in Tahiti these days there is a nationalist spirit, particularly among the young. Tahiti, or rather French Polynesia, of which it is a part, is a French colony, retained because of its convenience as a nuclear test site and its vague utility in the mythopoetics of French nationalist self-esteem. The most visible manifestation of Polynesian nationalism is tattooing. Traditional tattoos have been revived and are worn proudly by the young. But from where did the tattoo designs come? Not from elderly Polynesian guardians of culture, as there are none left: The designs are lifted from books by the turn-of-the-century German anthropologist Karl von den Steinen.

A trivial example, maybe, but there are others. The thankless ideology of the nation-state has been adopted wholesale by the Third World, with the same sanguine results that its adoption produced in Europe and the U.S. Ditto for economic development, progress, ideals of beauty . . . there are a billion small exceptions to this but not, I believe, any big ones. So Rognon can be forgiven for concluding that "the primitives, our contemporaries" is not necessarily a comforting sign of global unity—it could just mean They are as fucked up as We are.

D oubtless it's wrong to separate theory and practice, but I think the way out of Rognon's dilemma requires that some difference be recognized between what is written and what is done. I imagine discourse and reality walking together in a klutzy embrace, like lovers trying to cross the street while making out (or having a fight). Rognon's nightmare is a vision of discourse run amok; Geertz's nightmare is of discourse tired and spent, a self-recriminating drunk crying over spilt beer. An anthropologist might note (under "Myths and Legends"?): Toward the end, white civilization began to have serious problems with discourse.

The late French historiographer Michel de Certeau was in many ways just such an anthropologist. His early work was mostly in the history of Western religion; erudite in the extreme, de Certeau proceeded to wander through psychoanalysis, literary theory, anthropology, and, it seems, just about every other discipline relevant to the relationship between discursivity and the human sciences. *The Writing of History*, his first major work to be translated into English, muses on that relationship. De Certeau is an exceedingly difficult writer—it took me months to make it through this book, small dose by small dose. He's also brilliant and rewarding.

L'écriture means "writing" but it also means "scripture," and de Certeau treats written discourse in the human sciences as an evolution of religious discourse: They are both Scripture. As he sees it, religion in 17th-century France, faced with competing doctrines, was obliged to isolate mystical thought outside of religious discourse—it was construed as the other of a scriptural rationality. Religion became a dialogue between doctrine and mysticism, subject and object, consciousness and its repressed. The scriptural ground was thus laid for the state and civil society, whose various discourses would be devoted to controlling their respective others: state policy and popular desire, anthropology and non-Western culture, written history and the passage of time, or death.

De Certeau conceives Western discourse as an effort to enlist time itself in the service of Civilization: to make it inevitable, to make "our" history identical with history itself. "Modern Western history essentially begins with differentiation between the *present* and the *past*. In this way it is unlike tradition (religious tradition). . . . This rupture also organizes the content of history within the relations between *labor* and *nature*; and finally, as its third form, it ubiquitously takes for granted a rift between *discourse* and the *body* (the social body). It forces the silent body to speak. It assumes a gap to exist between the silent opacity of the 'reality' that it seeks to express and the place where it produces its own speech, protected by the distance established between itself and its object." Like an exorcist treating someone possessed, the historian listens to the words of the past then translates them, "forces the silent body to speak," gives them meanings in the language of the present. The historian gives to the dead a voice that isn't their own—it's the voice of the present. Historical discourse isn't so much a science as a Western ancestor cult; "it aims at calming the dead who still haunt the present, and at offering them scriptural tombs."

As is usually the case with tombs, the writing of history both honors the dead and guarantees their silence. De Certeau believes the same is true of anthropological writing: It listens to the cultural other as a method of exorcism and control. In a chapter on demonic possession, he writes, "Similar problems appear in the relation maintained by the ethnographical tale with the 'other society' that it recounts and claims to make heard. With respect to the possessed woman, the primitive, and the patient, demonological discourse, theological discourse, and medical discourse effectively assume identical positions: 'I know what you are saying better than you.' . . . In ethnographical texts and travel literature, the savages—like the possessed woman—are *cited*, in both juridical and literary fashion, through the discourse which positions itself in their place, saying about these unknowing people what they do not even know about themselves."

Ever abstract, de Certeau is shaky on the question of motives, but he apparently believes the main reason for discourse having taken this form is Reason itself, God's replacement in a Western civilization that had lost its faith in "a providential time, that is . . . a history decided by an inaccessible Subject who can be deciphered only in the signs that he gives of his wishes." And with Reason came Progress, the articulation of Reason over time. Religion became, at best, useful, one aspect in the greater elite plan of social utility and the (material, at least) betterment of humanity.

As civilization needed progress to replace its lost god, it needed the primitives to replace its lost mystics. In effect, the primitives were not outside civilization at all (they should be so lucky); rather "the relation between the civilized and the savage [became] a relation inherent within modern societies—according to which some of the forces or values circulating in a society receive the privilege of representing the 'predominant factor,' the 'progress,' or the 'essential' and are used in categorizing all of the others. The central place awarded to one category of signs establishes the possibility of classifying others as 'delays' or 'resistances,' and furnishes the base—or the partial base—for a 'coherence,' for a 'mentality,' or for a system to which everything is referred." De Certeau is discussing anthropology, but he could as easily be talking about the United Nations or the International Monetary Fund, which divide the world's countries into "underdeveloped," "developing," and "developed." Needless to say, it is the system of the developed countries "to which everything is referred," the rest of the world being a collection of delays and resistances.

W hat is the anthropologist to make of Michel de Certeau's "Myths and Legends" treatment of Western civilization? De Certeau is heavily influenced by psychoanalysis, particularly the work of Jacques Lacan; his final chapter, on *Moses and Monotheism,* portrays Freud as mourning two originary losses—of place (Israel) and of the "father" (in various guises). Death, absence, and loss appear throughout de Certeau's book, but the volume is decisively turned up in his last chapter. He concludes that the writing of history—and, perhaps, "discourse" generally—"assimilates traditions in order to speak in their place, in the name of a site (of *progress*) authorizing it to know better than do these traditions exactly what they are saying."

So what, enquiring minds want to know, about the writing of *The Writing of History?* It is, after all, a discourse itself; given that the dead can't attend their own funerals, what loss is de Certeau mourning? It seems to me that he's mourning the loss of Western, civilized, white discourse itself. For that discourse is precisely the "tradition" in whose place he is speaking, knowing "better than do these traditions exactly what they are saying." De Certeau's point of view is postmodern; postmodernism speaks to writing, discourse, and history as they—a "they" created, of course, by postmoderns themselves—once spoke to primitives and the possessed. What de Certeau says of Western discourse might as well be said of his own: "it creates these narratives of the past which are the equivalent of cemeteries within cities; it exorcises and confesses a presence of death amidst the living." The corpse, in this case, is Western civilization. No wonder the favorite postmod color is black.

Jean-François Lyotard is nothing if not postmodern, so it's particularly striking that his most recent book to be translated into English, *Peregrinations: Law, Form, Event,* concludes with a eulogy. "A Memorial for Marxism" is partly Lyotard's memoir of his great friend and former ideological comrade, the French Marxist Pierre Souyri. After spending much of the postwar years together in the left-intellectual group Socialisme ou Barbarie, Lyotard and Souyri broke in the '60s when Lyotard rejected the discourse of Marxism. Lyotard writes of Souyri:

> *The dialectic was his way of thinking, a component part of the dialectic he tried to uncover in things. Theoretical experience proceeded for him like a practice of contradiction, just as contradiction formed for him the nervure of historical reality. But on my side, this perseverance in thinking and acting according to the dialectic, as if for forty years the revolutionary movement had not suffered one failure after another—which Souyri moreover had no trouble admitting because that was the very thing he wanted to understand—seemed to me more and more alien to the exigencies of thought. Was one able to think, after these failures, without recognizing in them, first of all, the failure of a way of thinking?*

Lyotard is building for his friend a scriptural tomb; he is building a cemetery for Marxism in his postmodern city. Two things are remarkable about Lyotard's memorial: his frankly emotional tone, and his implicit recognition that postmodern discourse has evolved in quite specific historical circumstances. Most postmodern writing tries hard to avoid both. At its worst it attempts timelessness, being nothing in itself, but secure in the knowledge that it is *after* everything else. Postmodern, post-industrial, post-Marxist, postfeminist, postwar, post-Enlightenment . . . Lyotard is daring to weep openly at the funeral of white Western civilization, revealing the enormous emotional investment postmodernist discourse has in those other discourses that it seeks to bury. Perhaps he felt that he owed at least that much to his departed friend.

Lyotard, de Certeau, Geertz, and Rognon are all attending the same funeral. The discourses they mourn—Marxism, historiography, anthropology—come from the same social body, namely that of "our" civilization. One could extend the metaphor to much current literary theory, which often feels like an endless wake for the omniscient first-person plural; "we" must henceforth always put "we" in quotes.

There is a distinct ethnic cast to this wailing and keening. The "we" in all four books is white (and, to a great extent, male, heterosexual, and bourgeois, but those are other stories). I've often wondered why ethnicity is almost always absent from postmodern writing. After all, race is one of the most glaringly obvious aspects of contemporary life, whether one is in the Third World or in Paris (or Chicago). But the only place where it appears in postmod literature is in anthropology—and there, perhaps, lies the explanation for its absence everywhere else. Anthropology was the "human science" charged with taking care of race, with discursively knowing the racial other better than it knew itself, as de Certeau might say. It was supposed to take care of racial business so that the other human sciences—particularly history and philosophy—could carry on as if the civilization from which they sprang had nothing to do with race, its exclusive whiteness being simply a coincidence.

It doesn't seem to have worked, does it! Of all the civilized discourses postmodernism is now mourning, white ethnicity is for me the least important. Who wants to get up every morning and dress for a funeral just because white doesn't make right anymore? But this is probably a minority opinion. Civilization was the mythic anchor of modern whiteness; postmodern whiteness has no such anchor. The resurgence of white ethnic quarrels in Europe, among other things, suggests that civilization met a fundamental "racial" need. It's possible that the collapse of transhistorical whiteness will return us white folk to Serbs and Balts, Gauls and Scots.

Apart from lost ethnicity, narrowly defined, the decline of civilized discourse has decidedly undermined political/economic ideology. Without Progress and Reason, what happens to the ideological base of political activity? Ideology at least broached the questions of material exploitation in a practical way, something postmodernism has yet to do; it also undercut the centrality of the nation-state, a centrality that has since returned with a vengeance. Well Lyotard might mourn the death of Marxism, and of ideological discourse in general—they provided, however ambiguously, a grip on historical "truth." Lyotard ends up pushing the metaphor of clouds—"clouds of thought," "clouds of community"—as a model for postmodern thought, which may be appropriate, but isn't exactly mobilizing.

In any event, the sooner postmodernism realizes that it is partly a discourse of race, and not of life in general, the better. For Western intellectuals might then find themselves in a world freed from the terror of a Master Discourse (or its loss), and open themselves to the multiple discourses and realities of a vast and fascinating globe. They might cease at last polishing the tombs of 1890s Vienna and entre-deux-guerres. The "postmodern predicament" needn't be a synonym for angst; it can be a chance for liberation.

Discourse and reality are indeed lovers, and while some discourses are more equal than others (capitalism and the nation-state come immediately to mind), it is arrogant to assume, as Rognon does, that a Discourse exists with the power to bury history altogether. That Discourse, the essential postmodern product that permeates all these books and countless others, is a specific historical phenomenon; it is the textual trace of a white civilization that is losing its tribal grip on itself and on the world. The primitives of yesteryear are all around us, putting us in quotation marks; they have undermined "the unspeaking opacity of a 'real,' lived as a continuity of blood," as de Certeau writes of Freud and the Jewish origin. Certainly white people have a right to mourn the end of this continuity of blood that has sustained them for centuries. The white people of yesteryear deserve a nice scriptural cemetery in the postmodern, multiracial city.

April 1989

THE TRUTH ABOUT FICTION

By Lynne Tillman

What place does fiction have here, where we live? Once upon a time, reading fiction was necessary to understand the world. Novels were argued about the way movies are now. Into the 1960s, intellectuals saw fiction as part of their work and related it to an ongoing dialogue about social, aesthetic, and philosophical issues and the content of American life. In the U.S., an especially intense discussion existed in the '30s and '40s, then diminished and in a way disappeared by the late 1960s. Cold War McCarthyism must have played its palling, nefarious role, shutting down a freer, bigger flow of ideas. By the 1970s, greater specialization, more disciplines, the decline of humanism and with it questions about the canon—what does one *need* to read or know?—further unsettled fiction's hash. Written by generalists, fiction was often ticketed for lacking "information." Relegated to the purview of literary critics and book reviewers, fiction began to drop out as a major player in the cultural big leagues. It moved into the outfield.

After Vietnam and Watergate, a traumatically scrambled America didn't believe in anything or anyone. Punk rock and the blank generation responded with anarchic, apposite anthems. Fiction turned inward with metafictions that revealed their own ploys and provided their own rigorous critiques. Antinarrativists decried narrative's seductions—closure, illusion, linearity—as if they were lies. Though life and art without illusion is an illusion, the disavowal of narrative that emerged after World War II and the Holocaust found new recruits.

The trenchant distrust of everything metamorphosed into a more general fear of fantasy, imagined worlds, invention—fiction's possibilities that live in what may not be seen, heard, or instantly accessible. Reagan's America was soon inundated with memoirs, "real-life" stories and "accounts based on real life." In the parlous environment of the '80s and '90s, their appearance mounted a case with startling evidence of America's desperate need for absolute meaning. "True" was relentlessly linked to "real" events, meaning and meaningfulness conflated with "actual." Any event was supposedly self-explanatory.

When literalism rules, fiction suffers. It often uses actual events, always has; biographical and autobiographical elements, crimes and political events are boxed in writers' storage rooms—memory, childhood, news, everything human and inhuman is material. But fiction's territory represents what can never be recovered. Its field is as much inexperience and lack of experience as experience, absence as much as presence. What one wants to happen is as valid as what does. Fiction's domain, in part, is fantasy's psychic reality, whose underground operations secretly make the world turn. There are things we don't know or will never fully understand. Fiction leaps in to imagine the unimaginable and the underimagined.

"Life is stranger than fiction," and "no one could have made this up" are boringly repeated. Reality wins, apparently, though unless it's represented, whatever it is, it's gone. But reality, as Timothy Leary quipped, is an opinion. Life's meanings aren't obvious. They beg explanation and interpretation, and are rewarded with speculations and ideas, with fictions in diverse formal displays.

Fiction thrives in testing truths and rejecting absolutes. The insoluble, irrational, and unknowable, the normal and the perverse, march through its wide, wild door. Every genre—literary fiction, mystery, science fiction, thrillers—appeals to our need for pleasure and knowledge, to our interest in ourselves, a permanent narcissism. Fiction's métier is consciousness, novels containers for it. As old as modernity and the Gutenberg press, novels reflect, effect, distort, and concoct consciousness. Fictions allow for the reversals, surprises, disruptions—deaths—that humans cannot stomach in so-called real life.

But nothing's dead or stays dead, since matter returns in different guises, undressed, dressed up—as parody, imitation, homage. There's a huge rear window of opportunity to stare out; every genre has its mise-en-scènes, and everything's there, ready to be used. Look at the good hand fiction was inadvertently dealt in the late '90s. Force-fed on the minutiae of the Clinton-Lewinsky matter, we Americans were confronted with a story whose every event—the stain on the blue dress—was subject to speculation. DNA proved the stain was the president's semen, yet what it meant about Clinton was endlessly argued. Was Clinton ever a reliable narrator of the events of his life?

Usually under assault for its virtues, fiction's methods were trotted out to explicate a so-called true story. Character, motive, interests, time, all played their parts. If invented, a tale about the Office of the President taking orders from the Office of Impulse and Desire would have as little or as much profundity, depending upon how well it was written, as the spectacle we watched. It wasn't stranger than fiction, it was like fiction. Thorny, contradictory truth required fiction's crafty devices to rescue it from the stranglehold of American fundamentalism—stupefying literalism.

The Bible's a magnificent literary work of history, faith, theory, psychology. Job fights furious fate, like a character from Beckett. Imagining a Job—or a Clinton—is what fiction does. In the face of detractors who just want the facts, with sagacious pleasure, contemporary fiction invents true stories of doubt and complexity. It bravely risks its own irrelevance, especially when not spouting the prevailing pieties. Whatever reality is, it is not reliable and can't simply be recorded. But fiction goes on the record and doesn't promise what it can't deliver. Just suspend disbelief and read.

February 2000

❹ F O U R

Pulp Friction: Obsessing over Pop Culture

A t the start of the 21st century, it's hard to recall a time when popular culture wasn't taken seriously. But when *VLS* began, the borders between high and low were still fiercely patrolled. *VLS* represented a new generation of critics for whom it was second nature to see connections between avant-garde and mass-market entertainment. It wasn't a daring, Sontag-like gesture or a case of highbrows slumming, but simply the only sensible way to approach culture: no preconceptions.

The apotheosis of this all-gates-open sensibility was *VLS*'s annual Summer Trash issue. Fearlessly forwarding the proposition that smart people can appreciate pablum, Summer Trash spawned several pieces in this chapter: Paul Berman's playful but provocative take on the Pentagon catalog, Hilton Als's corrosive review of Sammy Davis, Jr.'s showbiz memoir, and Vince Aletti's fond remembrance of the pre–Gay Pride beefcake parade offered by men's physique magazines. In a similar vein, Lisa Jones delights in taking seriously the doubly despised subgenre of black romance novels, while Dorothy Allison's interview with Goth goddess Anne Rice revels in the dark voluptuary of her vampire fiction.

Elsewhere, Geoffrey O'Brien pays tribute to a forgotten genre, "classic comics" (the Western canon rendered as pulp graphics), while Guy Trebay leafs through Andy Warhol's diaries and hoists the Pop Art milieu by its own gossipy petard. Jonathan Lethem's mordant elegy for the lost promise of science fiction mourns the banishment of its experimental vanguard. Greil Marcus's impassioned treatise on Situationism's revolutionary struggle against boredom became the seed for his classic punk rock book *Lipstick Traces*. Reckoning with the fin de millennium extremism documented in Adam Parfrey's cult anthology *Apocalypse Culture*, Mark Dery wonders how much mileage is left in the notion of aesthetic terrorism.

SEX, SIN, AND THE PURSUIT OF LITERARY EXCELLENCE
Anne Rice's Triple Threat

By Dorothy Allison

Late in 1969, 27-year-old Anne Rice, living amid the crazy ferment of Haight-Ashbury, had the notion to write a short story about interviewing a vampire, to give that caped romantic figure a chance to explain himself. "The idea was Oscar Wilde in vampire drag," she says, "an aristocrat looking at modern life with great wry humor."

It was a good idea, and it could have made a bitterly funny story, but when Rice sat down to revise it she found herself beginning, not with Wildean witticism, but with grief, the grief of Louis, the vampire, at the death of his much-loved younger brother. Over the course of a frenzied six weeks, the short story became a novel dominated by that somber vision. Rice acknowledges that *Interview with the Vampire* is full of her grief at losing her young daughter to leukemia and sad memories of her childhood in New Orleans—that lush, old-guard Roman Catholic society in which everything seemed fixed and timeless. But despite its melancholy tone, the novel throbs with intense and extravagant eroticism.

The erotic charge that permeates Rice's imagination becomes more and more obvious with each of her novels. Her voluptuous prose draws readers into an erotic landscape where the sensual delights are dark-edged, terrifying, and utterly compelling. In the novels published under her married name, Anne (O'Brien) Rice, that emotionally intense voice has presented characters of enormous sensual hunger in situations where their survival, sanity, and honor are tested. Using the pseudonyms A. N. Roquelaure and Anne Rampling, she has tuned her voice to a different pitch and explored less complex but equally compelling characters and situations.

Over the past ten years, Rice has published nine novels, four under her own name, three as Roquelaure, and two, including her most recent, as Rampling. With the exception of *Feast of All Saints*, they have proved popular, but the Roquelaures and Ramplings have been dis-

missed by *Publishers Weekly* as "pornography pure and simple," while
those that appeared under her own name have won praise for "literary
merit." This would seem to be more a question of genre than of writing
skill, since most reviewers have also noted the craft and style Rice
brings to her erotic prose. Curiously, her recent revelation that she is
also these two other writers has not yet received much attention. The
literary establishment hesitates to treat the author of graphic sexual
fantasies with the same respect it gives a "serious" writer.

In her sexually explicit novels, Rice poses a direct challenge to our
myths and prejudices about erotic writing. Traditionally, such fiction
has been banished to the territory of triviality and contempt. Pornography, blasphemy, trash—why do they write that stuff anyway? Certainly
no "good," no "reputable," no "serious" writers publish pornography—
not under their own names anyway. Sexually explicit writing is the
country of the pseudonym, the alias, the cloaked and secreted identity—Samuel Steward publishing as "Phil Andros," "Pauline Réage"
writing *Story of O*, Anaïs Nin withholding her privately distributed erotica until after her death. Pornography (like gothics and science fiction)
is sometimes seen as a gateway undertaking, work done in preparation
for a "real" career or as a way to finance one's young and hungry years.
There is no recognition that such writing touches on vitally important
ideas and themes, that it draws on a writer's most deeply held beliefs
and insights, that, in fact, emotionally powerful erotica is one of the
greatest tests of a writer's craft and range. The cloaking of sexual fantasy makes our sexual realities more dangerous and despised.

To the writer, the need for disguise—pseudonyms, delayed publication, and secrecy—may be crippling, or may allow greater experimentation. While Rice says, "Pornography has no value if you're going to be
guarded and worried about what people think," she also believes that
the Roquelaure pseudonym let her go to extremes she might not have
tried otherwise. Regardless, she is convinced that the time for change
has arrived, and she has chosen to do it by putting her skills to the service of an acknowledged erotic literature.

Rice spent her childhood in a Catholic girl's school, writing novels
that she passed around to friends and hid from the nuns. Like many
other women, she developed early a sense of herself as an outsider. "I
think," she told me recently, on the phone from San Francisco, "if you
grow up a passionate child, particularly a passionate woman child, you
grow up being told that you're not in some way feminine. You grow up
an outsider, isolated from the idea of your own kind and it takes time to
begin to believe in yourself and your desires."

That vision has so far produced the 70-year-old vampire child, Claudia, in *Interview*, with her six-year-old body and raging woman's mind;

Marcel in *The Feast of All Saints*, who passes from innocence to mystery at 14; Guido, the castrato composer in *Cry to Heaven*, who first experiences a "wicked little pleasure" at six, just before he is castrated; Lisa, the dominatrix of *Exit to Eden*, who describes orgasms at age eight and "ugly memories of feeling freakish, like I carried a secret within me that made me feel like an outsider"; and Belinda, the heroine of Rice's latest book, who has a lesbian affair at 12 and by 16 is in love with the 44-year-old Jeremy Walker.

What is most fascinating in *Belinda* is Jeremy's argument with himself and his friend Alex on the merits of confronting the world with the "truth." Jeremy the painter could be the voice of Rice the writer. Both produce forbidden work—suspect, erotically specific images. Both face the risk of losing all their hard-won status by acknowledging their pornographic work and its source, forbidden passion. By tracing Jeremy's slow working-out of his own fear of exposure, Rice presents all the arguments for and against acknowledging her Roquelaure and Rampling novels; she comes down finally, as she has in life, on the side of confronting the public with the truth. Jeremy reasons that "truth makes art and people know it," and "it doesn't make a damn bit of difference whether truth sells." But he also believes, with Rice, that the public longs for truth.

Interview with the Vampire was a total revision not only of the idea of the vampire, that damned spawn of the devil, but of the Catholic certainties Rice had learned as a child. Awakening in his eternal night, the vampire finds no god, no supernatural power, no grand scheme of good and evil. There is only a self-determining thirst for blood, a constant confrontation with the fact that his very existence depends on the death of innocents. Louis, the vampire who records the night-long *Interview*, is damned in his own mind; but Lestat, the vampire who made him, is beyond such paltry notions. He is, paradoxical as it sounds, *innocent*— like a wild animal feeding on its prey. It is this inspired sense of innocence, this noble vision of the vampire, that surprised Rice's early readers. With that simple stroke, Rice created an antihero for the '80s— an essentially immoral figure who transcended old superstitious notions of good and evil.

Superstition is a word Rice uses freely. After leaving New Orleans, she went to college in Texas, and she speaks pensively of the first time she walked into the campus bookstore. "I stood in front of all those shelves of books, the whole literature of the Western world, and shelves and shelves of them were books that as a Catholic I was not supposed to touch." She faced the age-old choice between reason and faith, the intellect and the religious life, the 20th-century world of the mind and the medieval conviction of damnation without God's grace. For Rice there was no choice—superstition could not hold her—but there was still sorrow at the loss of conviction described so wonderfully in the vampire books. The loss of her religious faith did not mean a loss of moral convictions; her books have a consistent moral emphasis, asking provocative questions about the meaning of good and evil, and she sees her writing, particularly the pseudonymous erotic novels, as a real moral cause. She sees how sexuality and sexually specific writing are treated as a product of ancient superstitions, which she hopes to counter with vigorous and passionate prose. Without engaging in the controversies over women's pornography, she has set out to make a pornography for men and women that provides new information about women's desire, simply because it presents her vision of what that desire can be.

"There's this idea that it's wrong to sexually excite the reader," Rice says. "But exciting the reader, provoking and stimulating the reader—that's really about changing the reader, which is what all writers want to do. Obscenity definitions notwithstanding, sexual provocation is as good a reason to write as any, and I see nothing wrong with writing sexually titillating scenes that have no redeeming social value. I totally believe in it."

Rice is outspoken in her rejection of censorship. "I enjoy reading pornography and I don't make these distinctions people talk about between erotica and pornography." "The movement toward personal freedom and sexual integrity is ongoing," she insists, noting that in all her travels around the country, she has experienced little difficulty as a "pornographer." "The first novel I wrote was inspired by reading the *Story of O*; I called it the *Suffering of Charlotte*. Unfortunately, the only existing copy of it was stolen, but it was important for me to write it. And after having been raised on Catholic censorship, I can't give in to another wave of it with regard to the written word."

The only limit Rice places on her own imagination is refusing to write stories in which anyone is killed or commits suicide because of an attempt to gain sexual gratification. "I don't want to tell the same old myth," she says. All her erotic novels have happy endings, because she believes this is what we need now, novels in which women have intensely satisfying sexual and emotional relationships. "Women have only been out of the closet for about 50 years," she says. "We don't need anything put in our way."

Listening to Rice talk about sex, I recalled Lisa, in *Exit to Eden*, telling her friend, Martin, "Nobody has ever been able to convince me that anything sexual between consenting individuals is wrong. I mean it's like part of my brain is missing. Nothing disgusts me, it all seems innocent." Martin replies: "I remember I asked you if you could love the people who came to my house. You told me that in a real way you loved all of the sexual adventurers who didn't hurt others, that it was impossible for you to feel any other way towards them. . . . You said that you were they and they were you." That love, and that wholly human passion for passion itself, is the current that flows through all Rice's books, both literary and erotic; tracing it is itself a labor of love.

The Anne Rice novels have been novels of history; each has explored the period in which it is set, from *Interview* and *Lestat* (the mores and morals of the 18th-century materialist mind), through *Feast of All Saints* (the hidden violence in the lives of the free people of color of New Orleans), to *Cry to Heaven* (the ethical and sexual conflicts of a society in which only first-born sons may marry or inherit). For Rice, the mind of the age is a real being, one she loves to embody in her characters. Louis, for example, is a perfect 18th-century man. When he protests that no, he is not the spirit of his age, that he has always been at odds with everything, he only confirms his role. "Everyone feels as you feel," he is told. "Your fall from grace and faith has been the fall of a century. . . . You reflect your age. . . . You reflect its broken heart."

Interview with the Vampire contains all the elements that mark the later work of Anne Rice: the agnostic materialism that nonetheless treasures individual human life; the lush sexual power of the language; the sexuality that plays itself out more in metaphor than orgasm (her vampires are as sterile as the castrati of *Cry to Heaven*), without reference to limitations of gender or generation; the complicated link between fear and sexual excitement; the concentration on outsiders—vampires, homosexuals, rebellious women, carnal children—and the nominal perversions—pedophilia, s/m, and necrophilia.

The Roquelaure novels rewrite the story of Sleeping Beauty, so that Beauty is carried off not into marriage, but to a fantasy castle where the most exquisite erotic punishments are performed in an atmosphere that makes such behavior seem completely natural. Described as novels of "tenderness and cruelty for the enjoyment of men and women" and written in an elegant prose with few of the gothic overtones of Rice's more "respectable" fiction, the Beauty novels are straightforward in their exploration of sexual desire as a path to enlightenment. They are also remarkable studies of the psychology of sexual submission, vulnerability, and selfish desire. The princes and princesses taken away to serve in the Queen's castle are told that through their servitude they will learn "humility, grace, all the virtues." They do—but, once perfected, they return to their kingdoms to pine for the splendid education they leave behind. Beauty's accomplishment is that she takes that education to the limit and manages to bring the prince and the adventure home with her.

What in most fairy tales is rendered obliquely turns physical and immediate in these novels. Lust is not only natural, it bears witness to a philosophical imperative, the desire to know oneself completely, to explore one's most hidden nature. Beauty's progress from the castle to the village is a search for reality rather than facade. And like all of Rice's novels, these are full of love for all things human, both flesh and spirit, fear as well as desire. The fairy tale approach is a wonderful way of enlivening the traditional utopian landscapes of sexual fantasy. Rice-Rampling uses much the same method in creating the private island in *Exit to Eden* and Jeremy's Victorian house in *Belinda*. It's as if these scenes were posted—"Warning, here sex happens in all its raw and beautiful complexity."

Rice has labeled the Rampling voice "contemporary American" in contrast to the "European" voice of *Interview with the Vampire*. This difference has less to do with style than characterization. The Rampling characters, particularly those in *Belinda*, are much less fully developed, and the fiction suffers for it. The contemporary settings, beautifully detailed as they are, have less romantic resonance than the historical settings of the Rice novels. The whole leads to the impression that Rice's "American" voice is a thinner one than the "European" voice of *Interview of the Vampire* or *Cry to Heaven*. It is as if she were writing at only 60 per cent of her full power; perhaps the past more thoroughly engages her imagination. The Roquelaure novels, after all, are much more powerful than the Rampling books, and the Castle is long ago and very far away.

All of Rice's women, however, are contemporary. Full-blooded creatures, characters of rage and desire, all are motivated by intellectual and sexual longing. From Claudia, Mademoiselle Freniere, and Eleni in *Interview*, to Lisa in *Exit to Eden* and Gabrielle and Akasha in *Lestat*, I have been enthralled by them. Where else do you find women like these?—"ah, the women were glorious, naked in the spring warmth as they'd been under the Egyptian pharaohs, in skimpy short skirts and tuniclike dresses, or wearing men's pants and shirts skintight over their curvaceous bodies if they pleased. They painted, decked themselves out in gold and silver, even to walk to the grocery store. Or they went fresh scrubbed and without ornament—it didn't matter. . . . For the first time in history, they were as strong and interesting as men."

Gabrielle, in *The Vampire Lestat*, may be the most fascinating of Rice's women, partly because of her integrity. While Rice consistently portrays women in rebellion against the imposed definitions of female fragility, shallowness, and submission (including the not at all submissive Beauty, who hungrily demands the utmost in her own exploration of masochism), Gabrielle is the most opaque. She seems the incarnation of that 18th-century ideal of La Belle Dame Sans Merci, saying exactly what is on her mind and no more. She seeks to please no one but herself, holding true to her own ideal of love and courage, submitting to no man's definition of what her life should be. Lestat hides in cellars and coffins, but she digs into the living earth. While he clings to civilization and its issues, she strikes out into the wilderness, the wide empty world where man is incidental or, better yet, absent. Rice has been accused of writing with a male sensibility; she herself believes that her spirit is one "not generally recognized as feminine." But to me, the mind that made Gabrielle feels completely lesbian; the mind that made Lestat, male and gay; while the mind that gave us Elliot Slater in *Exit to Eden* could be nothing but heterosexually female. Anne Rice may in fact be the first trans-gender writer, too multifaceted for shorthand categories of sex and sexual preference.

She told me of her need to write ahead, to keep in mind the readers of 50 or 100 years from now. When I reminded her that all her erotic works had been completed before the full impact of the AIDS crisis, she replied that, even so, she wouldn't change them. "I grew up an outsider, alienated from my belief in my own femininity because I was told that my desires were inappropriate. It's so important to me to say that desire is appropriate, that sex is good. Catastrophes like the AIDS crisis can make us pull back from our ideals, our commitment to sexual freedom, and I believe that it's important to fight that impulse, particularly for writers. I keep my audience in mind—all those people who will need my books someday, and take from them the message that sex is good and the sexual revolution is continuing."

What all writers hope for is readers who understand, who love the same ideas, the same ideals as the writer, who engage fully with the writer's imagined world. This dream audience is like the crowd at a rock 'n' roll concert, standing and beating time to the music and words, cadence to the energy and power of the artist's vision—Bruce Springsteen at the Meadowlands, in front of an audience that calls out the lyrics before he can sing them. Anne Rice possesses the power to take literature into the realm where one can scream of good and evil, proclaim characters angels or devils, and provoke mortals to stand up and cheer.

December 1986

LOVE AFRICAN-AMERICAN STYLE

Happily Ever After with Black Romances

By Lisa Jones

DARK EMBRACE
By Crystal Wilson-Harris

INDISCRETIONS
By Donna Hill

ISLAND MAGIC
By Loraine Barnett

LOVE SIGNALS
By Margie Walker

MIDNIGHT WALTZ
By Barbara Stephens

ROOMS OF THE HEART
By Donna Hill

YAMILLA (PROUD TRUTH)
By Mildred E. Riley

There's a scene in Barbara Stephens's *Midnight Waltz* that made me howl: Copper-colored heroine Sylvia Random dreams she's being chased by a man with a diamond engagement ring the size of an egg. Had to call my friend Deandra to ask if she ever had a nightmare like that. Hell no, said Deandra, these days you can't even get a man to admit he's seeing you, let alone *think* about buying you a rock. (If you thought the girlfriend gripe session in *Jungle Fever* was heavy-duty, come over to Deandra's one Saturday night and watch the divas use testicles for target practice.) Deandra was surprised to learn that *Midnight Waltz* is part of a romance line that features African-American belles and beaux and is published by a black company out of Maryland. Black romance, said the jaded Deandra, isn't that an oxymoron?

Publisher Leticia Peoples set up Odyssey Books last year, armed with the data that romantic fiction accounts for 32 to 40 per cent of all paperback sales. Peoples estimates that at least one quarter of romance readers are women of color. But of the 120 romance novels published each month, you'd be hard-pressed to find any with characters or milieux that reflect an African-American, Hispanic, or Asian cultural experience. Dell put out an "ethnic romance" line for four years starting in 1979, but canceled it because of low sales (which makes one wonder about marketing support). Harlequin Books, whose titles account for half of the romance pool, has never published an ethnic series. Of the company's 800 romance writers, only two are African-American, and they don't write about black characters.

Odyssey has five books out (including a historical romance, *Yamilla*, about an enslaved African princess and her female descendants) and one more scheduled for this month. Hot on the heels of Odyssey is Marron Publishers and their series, Romance in Black, also launched last year. Publishers Marquita Guerra and Sharon Ortiz, West Indian–born New Yorkers, want their line to take on a range of diaspora cultures. Their second novel, *Island Magic*, written by Guerra under the pen name Loraine Barnett, involves a steamy affair between a Barbadian and a Trinidadian, both editors at *West Indian World* magazine, and is set in Barbados and Brooklyn. Along with publishing two more RIB titles this winter, Marron has another line in the works, Romance En Rojo (Romance in Red), which will feature Hispanic characters and appear in Spanish and English versions.

Book-cover design sums up the difference between the two companies. Odyssey holds on to classic romance-novel illustrations, while Marron opts for racy black-and-white photographs of bare-chested men and nearly bare-chested women. (The Marron partners do everything—from editing to photographing the covers—out of Guerra's Queens home.) The contrast carries over to content: While Odyssey novels have more substance than your average romance (*Indiscretions* has criminal lawyer Khendra Phillips butting heads with Atlanta's white legal establishment), they're still firmly rooted in fantasy. Marron, on the other hand, solicits in its manuscript requirements a "thoughtful, but not morbid" discussion of "real-life" topics like adultery, unemployment, drug abuse. Its two titles so far do tread new territory for romance. *Island Magic*'s heroine Rhonda Baptiste comes to terms with being a love child; radio executive Patrice Mason wrestles with single parenthood in *Love Signals*.

Both imprints aspire to provide tidy, positive images of black men and women. Maybe it's the genre, but what might be heavy-handed elsewhere comes off as charming here. Cultural references are always tied to prestige or sex appeal: *Midnight Waltz*'s Sylvia Random, a buyer for the chichi Nook of International Treasures in Houston who's described as being as much at home at a Brahms recital as a gospel revival, gets dressed in a strapless gown for an Anita Baker concert. *Rooms of the Heart*'s Tempest Dailey, an interior designer, tries to patch up her marriage to her husband the arrogant politician over dinner at Jezebels, New York's spot for gourmet soul food. (Food appears often—heroes can cook, calaloo or gumbo, usually better than heroines can.) This priceless moment comes from *Midnight Waltz*: The mysterious artist with whom Sylvia Random is obsessed reads poetry to her from an anthology of Negro verse and compares himself to a Nigerian mask in her art collection—"Her breath caught in her throat and she could feel herself submitting to his will. 'This is from Africa. . . . ,' she said. Her speech was labored. 'This is too,' Justin countered, moving his face closer to hers. 'Via the U.S. of A.'"

The first ladies of black romance—all successful career women—deal with male problems by throwing themselves into their work. They even have an intellectual life: Editor Rhonda Baptiste, who writes poetry, leaves the States to start her own magazine and grapple with being abandoned by her father. Radio general manager Patrice Mason is politicized by her opposition to apartheid. True to the romance formula, though, the strengths of these women exist only to be sapped by a powerful, difficult man. He insults them, they admire him—they surrender and learn through love that their professional ambitions were just narrow self-absorption.

The war between the sexes that's raging in black America provides a spicy subtext here. Lots of single black women complain bitterly about the scarcity of "good brothers"—eligible men who are willing to commit (you know the figures, more black men in prison than in college). Men who do fall into that category are such a rare breed—they can have their pick when it comes to women and they ain't in a rush to sign on the dotted line. There are so many references to "possession" in the novels, it's spooky. These heroines don't rely on men for money, status, or companionship (they all have warm, supportive relationships with their mothers and women friends.) Yet having been two-timed by other men in the past, they have a need to be "claimed" by a man, acknowledged as his one and only. When the radio exec's lover-man, who's provost at Banneker University, tells her he's taking her "off the market," she gets to breathing heavy.

The sex runs from demurely suggestive to borderline soft-porn, which matches the range available in mainstream romance. Is it a coincidence that all but one of these novels contains a cunnilingus scene? And not just any old cunnilingus scene, but scenes that show the men absolutely reveling in it. ("He drank of her like a vintage wine," says *Rooms of the Heart*—are these books written by women, or what?!) For inspirational sex and healthy female imagery, the prize goes hands down to *Island Magic*. Aggressive in the sack, protagonist Rhonda Baptiste distinguishes between sexual and emotional needs and chooses her men accordingly. She has ample hips, hamhock thighs, a big dancing butt, short natural hair, full lips, *and* is spoken of, in flowery romance lingo, as irresistibly attractive and feminine. Lest you thought *Island Magic* was totally right-on, like the other novels, it holds on to predictable skin codes. Rhonda is a light-skinned woman whose love interest is a dark-skinned man with "good hair" and "light eyes."

More sizzling than the sex are the class dynamics. Not only are these heroines independently wealthy, but they have the opportunity to turn down even larger sums of money offered by men. A few have house-keepers. (Tempest Dailey's housekeeper Clara has been with her since she was a girl and is described in such familiar terms—"beefy hands on her broad hips"—she might as well be a mammy.) And you've never read more hilariously conspicuous descriptions of material wealth. (Patrice Mason's flat "smells of just-off-the-showroom-furniture inter-mingled with the slight hickory fragrance from the burning pignut wood.")

There is a clear-cut difference between these class fantasies and those popular in mainstream romance. The heroines here aren't heiresses fixated on the dangerous brute from the other side of the moors or poor damsels yearning for the Lord of Bentlecock; they are working women who've labored hard to get to the top. The Prince Charmings of the black romance circuit weren't born with silver spoons in their mouths either. This is definitely buppie love, grounded in a shared work ethic. (Patrice Mason and her beau the provost bond by sharing stories of how they pulled themselves up by the bootstraps.) You can almost see the benevolent god of Booker T. Washington superimposed over the scene, like one of Van DerZee's ghosts, smiling down on these ambitious ones as they share their first hot kiss over the office water cooler.

October 1991

STRIP SHOW
Classics *Comics Get Back to Basics*

By Geoffrey O'Brien

There is no canon like your first canon.

Before I ever heard about the Great Books of the Western World with their various Greco-Roman and Judeo-Christian glories, I already knew there were such things as classics. I had found a box of them in an attic, scattered among back issues of *Little Lulu* and *Casper the Friendly Ghost*. They were comic books, but of a hitherto unknown kind, their panels crowded with disturbing and inexplicable images: a ragged child threatened by a madman with a knife (*The Prince and the Pauper*), a cowled monk murdered by a dwarf (*The Talisman*), a mother poisoning herself and her young son (*The Count of Monte Cristo*), a one-eyed old woman chaining a young girl to a cellar wall (*The Mysteries of Paris*). In the dark world these comics depicted, a ray of hope was provided by the assurance that each was "a complete, faithful adaptation of a great classic." I had discovered *Classics Illustrated*, and would immerse myself in them for many years to come. Such cultural literacy as I possessed by the age of 10 owed incalculably to their tutoring.

They were an extraordinary publishing enterprise, deeply expressive of what culture was ordinarily supposed to be in the '40s and '50s, naïve and cunning, often crassly commercial yet at times so faithful to their sources that by today's standards they might seem almost esoteric. (A reader lacking the basics of 17th-century French history might find the 1948 *Man in the Iron Mask* utterly mystifying.) Initiated in 1941 by Gilberton Company of New York, *Classics Illustrated* for some 20 years worked industriously at repackaging the plots of a stable of "immortal authors." The front runners were Shakespeare, Dickens, Dumas, Scott, and Mark Twain, but what gave the list its flavor were the secondary figures, names now rich with the aroma of literary oblivion: Frederick Marryat, Jane Porter, Edmond About, R. D. Blackmore, Henryk Sienkiewicz, G. A. Henty. It was a flexible canon, ranging from *The Iliad* to *Bring 'Em Back Alive*; there was no real danger of ever running out of classics to adapt, although toward the end, with titles like *Castle Dangerous* and

The Conspirators and *Tigers and Traitors*, the selection committee was evidently put on its mettle.

Classics Illustrated thrived on contradictions, teetering eternally between the exploitive and the educational. Ultimately the educational won, so that by the time the series petered out in the early '60s, the comics had succumbed to officially sanctioned blandness. But their roots were pure pulp, and in the early days, despite their claim to be "the world's finest juvenile publication," they were often as lurid as any of their competitors in the mystery and horror line. In *Three Famous Mysteries*, for instance, Guy de Maupassant's "The Flayed Hand" provides the excuse for a string of horrifying (and horrifyingly ill-drawn) vignettes. A jaundiced, fang-toothed madman stares out at the reader and declares: "All men are my enemies! I will rob, burn and murder until the world is destroyed!" Moments later he dispatches his wife with an ax whose blade, dripping with blood, is hoisted into center frame. The same number features a version of "The Murders in the Rue Morgue" which manages to amplify the violence of the original and culminates with Auguste Dupin engaging in a most uncharacteristic bit of gunplay.

The writing and artwork in these early *Classics* tended toward the primitive. (In the '50s, as the company went about changing its image, many of the old versions were withdrawn to make way for more faithful, and more anemic, adaptations.) A ramshackle *Moby-Dick* features a stick-figure Captain Ahab whose dying speech consists of: "Toward you I roll, unconquerable whale. To the last I grapple with you. . . . With all my hate, I GIVE YOU MY SPEAR! YAAA-A-GGGGG!" But gradually the publishers, evidently hoping to win acceptance from schools, began to take their literary responsibilities a little more seriously. By the late '40s the scripts were hewing more closely to the originals, and in the hands of artists like Henry C. Kiefer and Alex Blum, the art attained a modicum of precision and expressiveness. Not that *Classics Illustrated* ever stirred up the kind of excitement comics freaks looked for in *Plastic Man* or *The Vault of Horror*; the *Classics* were more like comic book equivalents of salon paintings or M-G-M literary adaptations. But however word-dominated and earnestly rectilinear their visuals, they did reveal new possibilities in the comics medium simply because of the variety and complexity of their source material. To compact the multiple disguises, conspiracies, and hideous family secrets of *The Count of Monte Cristo* into a 62-page comic book created, almost automatically, a powerful aesthetic effect. The narrative was so complicated that the frames were reduced in size to get more on a page; yet even so, virtually every frame was burdened with a major plot development.

By reducing a long and elaborate novel to a frantically speeded-up sequence of tableaux vivants, *Classics Illustrated* produced something more than illustration. They diagrammed a culture. A 20th-century medium served to lay bare the ghosts of the previous century. In fact, the compartmentalized structures of Dickens, Hugo, Wilkie Collins, and Eugène Sue lent themselves naturally to this form. It was simply a further extension of earlier theatrical and cinematic versions, another road-show engagement of the 19th century's greatest hits. The *Classics* edition of *Uncle Tom's Cabin*—still in circulation in the late '50s, although by now it must be among the rarest of all—enacted one last time the traditional spectacle of Eliza fleeing across the ice and Little Eva ascending to paradise. Poetic classics like *Lady of the Lake* and *The Song of Hiawatha*, on the verge of forced retirement from the center stage of literary history, were permitted this final bow—and benefited enormously. Their verse, broken up, rearranged, wedged into speech balloons, gained new strength from being thus rudely decontextualized. The way the words worked with the pictures suggested—and still suggests—possibilities for a new kind of poetic text.

This suggestion, like many of the *Classics'* most interesting effects, was largely inadvertent. Yoking together all these immortal stories and reducing them to a common grid-pattern activated unsuspected correspondences. The texts cohabited with one another, all the more so because the artists tended to use the same faces over and over, with the result that Prince Rudolf of Gerolstein, Rudolf V of Ruritania, Roderick Dhu, and Ulrich von Rudenz appeared to be aliases for the same eternal mustachioed leading man. Plot mechanisms seemed to spill over from book to book. The stories were part of a vast serial, the product of an impersonal narrative machine. One might move the frames around like postage stamps, to generate endless variants. In the end the "immortal authors" were robbed of their authorship. The stories existed in their own world, a shared world whose tunnels and trapdoors connected up somewhere just beyond the page.

A rough geography and chronology began to emerge. The further back in time you went the more open the structures became. The narrative grew more fluid in exact proportion to the quantity of robes and togas sported by the characters; *The Odyssey* and *A Midsummer Night's Dream* suggested lightness, freedom, ultimate harmlessness. Distance produced the same effect. *The Jungle Book* and *The Adventures of Marco Polo* could be endlessly reread because their episodic narratives promised relief from the claustrophobic contingencies of plot. The exotic vistas of jungle and ocean offered a breathing space.

But these were the exceptions. Mostly one was in Europe, in the 19th century, in the labyrinths of Zenda and Ballantrae. If the *Classics* held a secret, it was the sickness that lay at the end of plot, a weariness with the inevitable disasters that tightened around Jane Eyre or Oliver

Twist. A story was a trap, an evil destiny. Would you really walk into that with your eyes open, accept lodging from the smiling man who would try to kill you, ignore the locket with its crucial evidence, come back too late to save your family from the king's hired murderers? The comics medium did away with whatever illusion of free action might have inhered in the original novel's descriptions and characterizations. Everything was stripped down to its basic motives. The ritual nature of the stories became glaringly evident. Personal motivation didn't enter into it; things happened because otherwise the necessary catastrophes would not take place.

The inadequacies of the *Classics'* scripts and drawing brought about an involuntary alienation. The "London" and "Paris" of the stories often seemed another planet, populated by strange stiff creatures decked in beards and brooches. This unreality added to the fascination. Most comics, like most movies, were based on a principle of identification. The *Classics*, by contrast, exuded at their best an air of reptilian detachment. They had their heroes and heroines, but what lingered most powerfully was a hint of cruelty built into the tales themselves, the cruelty of old places and old cultures. From these raw materials it was possible to construct a mythology of a world quite different from the outward face of '50s America.

The series was founded on the illusion that the other world, the old world, was beloved, and would always be beloved. The titles adapted were books in the library of someone's parents, a fixed body of tradition to be handed on. But the ground was already shifting. Many of the ostensibly deathless works were in fact dying. How many would ever again seek out *Lorna Doone* or *Under Two Flags* or *The Scottish Chiefs*? Rather than celebrating the renewal of tradition from generation to generation, the *Classics* became testimony to a tradition's gradual erasure, a four-color funeral rite.

Even *Hamlet* and *David Copperfield*, although they were not about to go away, would never again be read so guilelessly. From here on in they would have to be taken apart, broken down just as the comics had broken them down into frames. For years *Classics Illustrated* had hawked, in its back pages, "handsome, durable, permanent" simulated leather bindings in which readers were meant to preserve their comics. I never heard of anyone actually buying these, but they reinforced the notion that great works of literature had the same durability and permanence. Today the comics that promulgated that notion are scattered bits of rapidly decaying paper: proof, if any were needed, that stories also die.

January 1989

BLACK NARCISSUS

By Hilton Als

WHY ME?: THE SAMMY DAVIS, JR., STORY
By Sammy Davis, Jr., and Jane and Burt Boyar

Dear Sammy: At first I wasn't going to write this as a personal letter because personal letters are just that—personal. But then I thought, This has to be as much about me as it is about you because that's how you want your readers to react. Because what this book is about, man, is love. Totally. I know what you're getting at here because I'm all about that myself—love. So that made me think, Why not, *why not* write this as a personal open letter in response to your openness as revealed in your second autobiography in however many years it is since *Yes I Can*, your first, was published. *Yes I Can* was a pretty long book, remember, and how much can one man *alone*, albeit a superstar, have to say? I could never have that much to say even though I, too, have been a man alone, have been there, suffered and come back. And although I am not a superstar yet, I am in a similarly exciting, dangerous, compelling, grateful, amazed, personal, humble, exciting, personal, and incredibly humble field—the writing thing. Writing is something that *really* brings you to your knees and makes you want to sing *The Impossible Dream*, isn't it? It's a field that always requires my personal best as well as yours, Sammy, and you give your all to it in *Why Me?* because that's just the way you are, that's what you do. And you know what makes you incredible just as you'll know what makes me incredible after you read this because, dig, I had the *guts* to lay this all on the line in a personal way; I had the *guts* to write yet another boring piece that contributes to the general confusion of Negroes representing their own Negroness and being personally critiqued by other Negroes in front of a largely white audience. I mean, who needs it. Not you. Because what you have written here is Everynegro's Autobiography. It is all of our stories rolled into one even though many of us have not had the millions that you've had so we could leave the country whenever things became personally unbearable, or picked up a Swedish first wife, or made any of those personally complicated gestures such as adopting Judaism as our personal faith. I've often wondered if you did that so that you would have some place, *somewhere* to dump the anxiety that many of us feel by identifying with the oppressed but not necessarily your own oppressed. And did you think your Judaism would then lead to some kind of—like crazy man!—assimilation? Sammy, you bring new meaning to the idea of the signifying monkey. But dig, such personal heaviness is eclipsed for me, Sammy, by the beautiful and heavy, personal but open way certain other gestures in your personal and public lives have put you right up there as yet another empty symbol of achievement. Remember that deep hug on Nixon, Sam old boy? I mean *man* . . . And even though, as you explain so movingly in *Why Me?*, the mouth *bleeds*, superstardom as a goal can become a curse. And even though you have to know what it is you don't want once you have it and you don't want to be any more famous than you already are, which is kind of the book's *moral*—or one of them—then why write a book in the first place, the superstar auto(didact)biography being just a little more grist for the personal publicity mill? I'm telling you, Sam, all of this heaviness cooks on a low flame for a long time in the back of my mind (what's left of it) because it's all so funny I can't cry for laughing. (That last bit was a little Negroism, which your book is peppered with. Usually you put it into the mouth of your father, a song and dance man himself, kinda like a hipster Uncle Remus.)

But the fame thing was such a kick in the head, Sammy, because it acted as a beautiful chick does, in terms of the effect you wanted it to have on your personal life—to maybe make you believe that after all the tuxedoes and pinky rings and relaxed hair, somebody could really, really, personally *like* a boy who was more or less self-educated, had a glass eye and a flat nose and a weird way of twisting his mouth to the side when he sang. But isn't that the beauty of showbiz, Sammy? The illusion thing? I know just what you mean. Regardless of that weird dichotomy, Sammy, when it's beautiful it's *beautiful*.

August 1989

THE LONG WALK OF THE
SITUATIONIST INTERNATIONAL

By Greil Marcus

SITUATIONIST INTERNATIONAL ANTHOLOGY
Edited and translated by Ken Knabb

In the U.S.A. the Situationist International is mostly known, if it is
known at all, as a small group of dadaist provocateurs that had something to do with the May 1968 uprising in France. The name has been
batted around in reference to punk, because Sex Pistol Svengali Malcolm McLaren was supposedly connected with the situationists—or
was it that, like a lot of 1960s U.K. art students, he favored situationist
rhetoric about revolution arising out of the boredom of everyday life?
The situationists were, ah, sort of like the Yippies, one hears. Or New
York's Motherfuckers, who once tore into Berkeley, firebombed a cop,
and left a black bystander holding the bag. Or the Frankfurt School—
not known for their firebombings, but the ideas were similar, right?

Situationist International Anthology—the result of years of work by
Ken Knabb, an American acolyte of the group—makes it clear that the
Situationist International was something considerably more interesting: perhaps the most lucid and adventurous band of extremists of the
last quarter century.

1

first became intrigued with the Situationist
International in 1979, when I struggled through
"Le Bruit et la Fureur," one of the anonymous lead articles in the first
issue of the journal *Internationale situationniste*. The writer reviewed
the exploits of artistic rebels in the postwar West as if such matters had
real political consequences, and then said this: "The rotten egg smell
exuded by the idea of God envelops the mystical cretins of the American 'Beat Generation,' and is not even entirely absent from the declarations of the Angry Young Men . . . They have simply come to change

their opinions about a few social conventions without even noticing the whole *change of terrain* of all cultural activity so evident in every avant-garde tendency of this century. The Angry Young Men are in fact particularly reactionary in their attribution of a privileged, redemptive value to the practice of literature: they are defending a mystification that was denounced in Europe around 1920 and whose survival today is of greater counterrevolutionary significance than that of the British Crown."

Mystical cretins ... finally, I thought (forgetting the date of the publication before me), someone has cut through the suburban cul-de-sac that passed for cultural rebellion in the 1950s. But this wasn't "finally"—it was 1958, in a sober, carefully printed magazine (oddly illustrated with captionless photos of women in bathing suits), in an article that concluded: "If we are not surrealists it is *because we don't want to be bored* ... Decrepit surrealism, raging and ill-informed youth, well-off adolescent rebels lacking perspective but far from lacking a cause—boredom is what they all have in common. The situationists will execute the judgement contemporary leisure is pronouncing against itself."

Strange stuff—almost mystifying for an American—but there was a power in the prose that was even more seductive than the hard-nosed dismissal of the Beat Generation. This was the situationist style—what one commentator called "a rather irritating form of hermetic terrorism," a judgement situationist Raoul Vaneigem would quote with approval. Over the next decade the style never really changed, but only became more seductive and more hard-nosed, because it discovered more seductive and hard-nosed opponents. Beginning with the notion that modern life was boring and therefore *wrong*, the situationists sought out every manifestation of alienation and domination and every manifestation of the opposition produced by alienation and domination. They turned out original analyses of the former (whether it was the Kennedy-era fallout shelter program in "The Geopolitics of Hibernation"—what a title!—or the Chinese cultural revolution in "The Explosion Point of Ideology in China") and mercilessly criticized the timidity and limits of the latter. In every case they tried to link specifics to a totality—why was the world struggling to turn itself inside out, and how could it be made to do so? What were the real sources of revolution in postwar society, and how were they different from any that had come before?

The Situationist International Anthology contains pre-S.I. documents, 250 pages of material from the situationist journal, May 1968 documents, two filmscripts, and far more, stretching from 1953, four years before the Situationist International was founded, to 1971, a year before its formal dissolution. It is exhilarating to read this book—to confront a group that was determined to make enemies, burn bridges, deny itself the rewards of celebrity, to find and maintain its own voice in a world where, it seemed, all other voices of cultural or political resistance were either cravenly compromised or so lacking in consciousness they did not even recognize their compromises.

2

The attack on the Beat Generation and the Angry Young Men—in 1958, it is worth remembering, considered in the English-speaking world the very *summa* of anti-Establishment negation—was an opening round in a struggle the situationists thought was already going on, and a move toward a situation they meant to construct. "Our ideas are in everyone's mind," they would say more than once over the next ten years. They meant that their ideas for a different world were in everyone's mind as desires, but not yet as ideas. Their project was to expose the emptiness of everyday life in the modern world and to make the link between desire and idea real. They meant to make that link so real it would be acted upon by almost everyone, since in the modern world, in the affluent capitalist West and the bureaucratic state-capitalist East, the split between desire and idea was part of almost everyone's life.

Throughout the next decade, the situationists argued that the alienation which in the 19th century was rooted in production had, in the 20th century, become rooted in consumption. Consumption had come to define happiness and to suppress all other possibilities of freedom and selfhood. Lenin had written that under communism everyone would become an employee of the state; that was no less capitalism than the Western version, in which everyone was first and foremost a member of an economy based in commodities. The cutting edge of the present-day contradiction—that place where the way of life almost everyone took for granted grated most harshly against what life promised and what it delivered—was as much leisure as work. This meant the concepts behind culture were as much at stake as the ideas behind industry.

Culture, the situationists thought, was "the Northwest Passage" to a superseding of the dominant society. This was where they started; this was the significance of their attack on the Beat Generation. It was a means to a far more powerful attack on the nature of modern society itself: on the division of labor, the fragmentation of work and thought, the manner in which the material success of modern life had leaped over all questions of the quality of life, in which "the struggle against poverty . . . has overshot its ultimate goal, the liberation of man from material cares," and produced a world in which, "faced with the alternative of love or a garbage disposal unit, young people of all countries have chosen the garbage disposal unit."

I have presented a bare outline of the situationist perspective, but perhaps more important for a contemporary reader is the use the situationists made of that perspective. Unlike many with whom they shared certain notions—Norman Mailer, the Marxist sociologist Henri Lefebvre, the *gauchiste* review *Socialisme ou Barbarie*—the situationists were bent on discovering the absolute ability to criticize anyone, anywhere, without restraint, without the pull of alliances, and without self-satisfaction. And they were bent on turning that criticism into events.

3

The situationists thought of themselves as avant-garde revolutionaries, linked as clearly to dada as to Marx. One could trace them back to Saint-Just—the 22-year-old who arrived in Paris in 1789 with a blasphemous epic poem, *Organt* (an account of nun-rape and endless sexual adventures), and became the coldest, most romantic, most brilliant, most tragic administrator of the Terror. Prosecutor of Louis XVI in 1793, he gave his head to the king's guillotine a year later.

More directly, situationist thinking began in Paris in the early 1950s, when Guy Debord and a few other members of the Lettrist International—a group, known mostly to itself, which had split off from the Lettrists, a tiny, postwar neo-dada movement of anti-art intellectuals and students—devoted themselves to *dérives*: to drifting through the city for days, weeks, even months at a time, looking for what they called the city's psychogeography. They meant to find signs of what lettrist Ivan Chtcheglov, writing under the pseudonym Gilles Ivain, called "forgotten desires"—images of play, eccentricity, secret rebellion, creativity, and negation. That led them into the Paris catacombs, where they sometimes spent the night. They looked for images of refusal, or for images society had itself refused, hidden, suppressed, or "recuperated"—images of refusal, nihilism, or freedom that society had taken back into itself, co-opted or rehabilitated, isolated or discredited. Rooted in similar but intellectually (and physically) far more limited surrealist expeditions of the 1920s, the *dérives* were a search, Guy Debord would write many years later, for the "supersession of art." They were an attempt to fashion a new version of daily life—a new version of how people organized their wishes, pains, fears, hopes, ambitions, limits, social relationships, and identities, a process that ordinarily took place without consciousness.

The few members of the grandiosely named Lettrist International wanted to reshape daily life according to the desires discovered and affirmed by modern art. Dada, at the Cabaret Voltaire in 1916, "a laboratory for the rehabilitation of everyday life" in which art as art was denounced and scattered, "wanted *to suppress art without realizing it,*" Debord wrote in 1967, in his book *The Society of the Spectacle.* "Surrealism wanted *to realize art without suppressing it.*" In other words, dada wanted to kill off the claim that art was superior to life and leave art for dead. Surrealism wanted to turn the impulses that led one to create art into a re-creation of life, but it also wanted to maintain the production of art works. Thus surrealism ended up as just another debilitated, gallery-bound art movement, a fate dada avoided at the price of being almost completely ignored. The Lettrist International thought art had to be both suppressed as separate, special activity, *and* turned into life. That was the meaning of supersession, and that was the meaning of a group giving itself up to the pull of the city. It was also the meaning of the L.I.'s attack on art as art. Debord produced a film without images; with the Danish painter Asger Jorn he created a book "'composed entirely of prefabricated elements,' in which the writing on each page runs in all directions and the reciprocal relations of the phrases are invariably uncompleted." Not only was the book supposedly impossible to "read," it featured a sandpaper jacket, so that when placed in a bookshelf it would eat other books.

In 1952, at the Ritz, the L.I. broke up a Charlie Chaplin press conference, part of the huge publicity campaign for *Limelight.* "We believe that the most urgent expression of freedom is the destruction of idols, especially when they present themselves in the name of freedom," they explained. "The provocative tone of our leaflet was an attack against a unanimous, servile enthusiasm." (Provocative was perhaps not the word. "No More Flat Feet," the leaflet Debord and others scattered at the Ritz, read: "Because you [Chaplin] identified yourself with the weak and the oppressed, to attack you was to strike the weak and oppressed, but in the shadow of your rattan cane some could already discern the policeman's nightstick . . .") The lettrist radicals practiced graffiti on the walls of Paris (one of their favorite mottoes, "Never work," would show up fifteen years later during May 1968, and thirteen years after that in Bow Wow Wow's "W.O.R.K.," written by Malcolm McLaren). They painted slogans on their ties, shoes, and pants, hoping to walk the streets as living examples of *détournement*—the diversion of an element of culture or everyday life (in this case, simply clothes) to a new and displacing purpose. The band "lived on the margins of the economy. It tended toward a role of pure consumption"—not of commodities, but "of time."

From *On the Passage of a Few Persons Through a Rather Brief Period of Time*, Debord's 1959 film on the group:

VOICE 1: That which was directly lived reappears frozen in the distance, fit into the tastes and illusions of an era carried away with it.

VOICE 2: The appearance of events we have not made, that others have made against us, obliges us from now on to be aware of the passage of time, its results, the transformation of our own desires into events. What differentiates the past from the present is precisely its out-of-reach objectivity; there is no more should-be; being is so consumed that it has ceased to exist. The details are already lost in the dust of time. Who was afraid of life, afraid of the night, afraid of being taken, afraid of being kept?

VOICE 3: That which should be abolished continues, and we continue to wear away with it. Once again the fatigue of so many nights passed in the same way. It is a walk that has lasted a long time.

VOICE 1: Really hard to drink more.

This was the search for the Northwest Passage, that unmarked alleyway from the world as it appeared to the world as it had never been, but which the art of the 20th century had promised it could be: a promise shaped in countless images of freedom to experiment with life and of freedom from the banality and tyranny of bourgeois order and bureaucratic rule. Debord and the others tried to practice, he said, "a systematic questioning of all the diversions and works of a society, a total critique of its idea of happiness." "Our movement was not a literary school, a revitalization of expression, a modernism," a Lettrist International publication stated in 1955, after some years of the pure consumption of time, various manifestos, numerous jail sentences for drug possession and drunk driving, suicide attempts, and all-night arguments. "We have the advantage of no longer expecting anything from known activities, known individuals, and known institutions."

They tried to practice a radical deconditioning: to demystify their environment and the expectations they had brought to it, to escape the possibility that they would themselves recuperate their own gestures of refusal. The formation of the Situationist International—at first, in 1957, including fifteen or twenty painters, writers, and architects from England, France, Algeria, Denmark, Holland, Italy, and Germany— was based on the recognition that such a project, no matter how poorly defined or mysterious, was either a revolutionary project or it was nothing. It was a recognition that the experiments of the dérive, the attempts to discover lost intimations of real life behind the perfectly composed face of modern society, had to be transformed into a general contestation of that society, or else dissolve in bohemian solipsism.

4

Ⓐorn in Paris in 1931, Guy Debord was from beginning to end at the center of the Situationist International, and the editor of its journal. *The Society of the Spectacle*, the concise and remarkably cant-free (or cant-destroying, for that seems to be its effect) book of theory he published after ten years of situationist activity, begins with these lines: "In societies where modern conditions of production prevail, all of life presents itself as an immense accumulation of *spectacles*. Everything that was lived has moved away into a representation." Determined to destroy the claims of 20th-century social organization, Debord was echoing the first sentence of *Capital*: "The wealth of societies in which the capitalist mode of production prevails appears as an 'immense collection of commodities.'" To complain, as French Marxist critics did, that Debord missed Marx's qualification, "appears as," is to miss Debord's own apparent qualification, "presents itself as"—and to miss the point of situationist writing altogether. Debord's qualification turned out not to be a qualification at all, but rather the basis of a theory in which a society organized as appearance can be disrupted on the field of appearance.

Debord argued that the commodity—now transmuted into "spectacle," or seemingly natural, autonomous images communicated as the facts of life—had taken over the social function once fulfilled by religion and myth, and that appearances were now inseparable from the essential processes of alienation and domination in modern society. In 1651, the cover of Thomas Hobbes's *Leviathan* presented the manifestation of a nascent bourgeois hegemony: a picture of a gigantic sovereign being, whose body—the body politic—was made up of countless faceless citizens. This was presented as an entirely positive image, as a utopia. In 1967, *Internationale situationniste #11* printed an almost identical image, captioned "Portrait of Alienation": in a huge stadium, countless Chinese performing a card trick which produced the gigantic face of Mao Zedong.

If society is organized around consumption, one participates in social life as a consumer; the spectacle produces spectators, and thus protects itself from questioning. It induces passivity rather than action, contemplation rather than thinking, and a degradation of life into materialism. It is no matter that in advanced societies, material survival is not at issue (except for those who are kept poor in order to represent poverty and reassure the rest of the population that they should be satisfied). The "standard of survival," like its twin, the "standard of boredom," is raised but the nature of the standard does not change. Desires are degraded or displaced into needs and maintained as such. A project precisely the opposite of that of modern art, from Lautréamont and Rimbaud to dada and surrealism, is fulfilled.

The spectacle is not merely advertising, or propaganda, or television. It is a world. The spectacle as we experience it, but fail to perceive it, "is not a collection of images, but a social relationship between people, mediated by images." In 1928, in *One-Way Street*, writing about German inflation, Walter Benjamin anticipated the argument: "The freedom of conversation is being lost. If it was earlier a matter of course to take interest in one's partner, this is now replaced by inquiry into the price of his shoes or his umbrella. Irresistibly intruding upon any convivial exchange is the theme of the conditions of life, of money. What this theme involves is not so much the concerns and sorrows of individuals, in which they might be able to help one another, as the overall picture. It is as if one were trapped in a theater and had to follow the events on the stage whether one wanted to or not, had to make them again and again, willingly or unwillingly, the subject of one's thought and speech." Raoul Vaneigem defined the terrain of values such a situation produced: "Rozanov's definition of nihilism is the best: 'The show is over. The audience get up to leave their seats. Time to collect their coats and go home. They turn around . . . No more coats and no more home.'" "The spectator feels at home nowhere," Debord wrote, "because the spectacle is everywhere."

The spectacle is "the diplomatic representation of hierarchic society to itself, where all other expression is banned"—which is to say where all other expression makes no sense, appears as babble (this may be the ironic, protesting meaning of dada phonetic poems, in which words were reduced to sounds, and of lettrist poetry, in which sounds were reduced to letters). The spectacle says "nothing more than 'that which appears is good, that which is good appears.'" (In a crisis, or when the "standard of survival" falls, as in our own day, hierarchic society retreats, but maintains its monopoly over discourse, the closing of questions. The spectacle "no longer promises anything," Debord wrote in 1979, in a new preface to the fourth Italian edition of *The Society of the Spectacle*. "It simply says, 'It is so.'") The spectacle organizes ordinary life (consider the following in terms of making love): "The alienation of the spectator to the profit of the contemplated object is expressed in the following way: the more he contemplates the less he lives; the more he accepts recognizing himself in the dominant images of need, the less he understands his own existence and his own desires. The externality of the spectacle in relation to the active man appears in the fact that his own gestures are no longer his but those of another who represents them to him."

Debord summed it up this way: "The first phase of the domination of the economy over social life brought into the definition of all human realization the obvious degradation of *being* into *having*. The present phase of total occupation of social life by the accumulated results of the economy"—by spectacle—"leads to a generalized sliding of *having* into *appearing*." We are twice removed from where we want to be, the situationists argued—yet each day still seems like a natural fact.

5

his was the situationists' account of what they, and everyone else, were up against. It was an argument from Marx's *1844 Economic and Philosophical Manuscripts*, an argument that the "spectacle-commodity society," within which one could make only meaningless choices and against which one could seemingly not intervene, had succeeded in producing fundamental contradictions between what people accepted and what, in ways they could not understand, they wanted.

This was the precise opposite of social science, developed at precisely the time when the ideology of the end of ideology was conquering the universities of the West. It was an argument about consciousness and false consciousness, not as the primary cause of domination but as its primary battleground.

If capitalism had shifted the terms of its organization from production to consumption, and its means of control from economic misery to false consciousness, then the task of would-be revolutionaries was to bring about a recognition of the life already lived by almost everyone. Foreclosing the construction of one's own life, advanced capitalism had made almost everyone a member of a new proletariat, and thus a potential revolutionary. Here again, the discovery of the source of revolution in what "modern art has sought and *promised*" served as the axis of the argument. Modern art, one could read in *Internationale situationniste # 8*, in January of 1963, had "made a clean sweep of all the values and rules of everyday behavior," of unquestioned order and the "unanimous, servile enthusiasm" Debord and his friends had thrown up at Chaplin; but that clean sweep had been isolated in museums. Modern revolutionary impulses had been separated from the world, but "just as in the nineteenth century revolutionary theory arose out of philosophy"—out of Marx's dictum that philosophy, having interpreted the world, must set about changing it—now one had to look to the demands of art.

At the time of the Paris Commune in 1871, workers discussed matters that had previously been the exclusive province of philosophers—suggesting the possibility that philosophy could be realized in daily life. In the 20th century, with "survival" conquered as fact but maintained as ideology, the same logic meant that just as artists constructed a version of life in words, paint, or stone, men and women could themselves begin to construct their own lives out of desire. This desire to begin such a construction, in scattered and barely noticed ways, was shaping the 20th century, or the superseding of it ("Ours is the best effort so far toward getting out of the twentieth century," an anonymous situationist wrote in 1964, in one of the most striking lines in the 12 issues of *Internationale situationniste*). It was the desire more hidden, more overwhelmed and confused by spectacle, than any other. It had shaped the lettrist adventures. It was the Northwest Passage. If the spectacle was "both the result and the project of the existing mode of production," then the construction of life as artists constructed art—in terms of what one made of friendship, love, sex, work, play, and suffering—was understood by the situationists as both the result and the project of revolution.

6

To pursue this revolution, it was necessary to take all the partial and isolated incidents of resistance and refusal of things as they were, and then link them. It was necessary to discover and speak the language of these incidents, to do for signs of life what the Lettrist International had tried to do for the city's signs of "forgotten desires." This demanded a theory of exemplary acts. Society was organized as appearance, and could be contested on the field of appearance; what mattered was the puncturing of appearance—speech and action against the spectacle that was, suddenly, not babble, but understood. The situationist project, in this sense, was a quest for a new language of action. That quest resulted in the urgent, daring tone of even the lengthiest, most solemn essays in *Internationale situationniste*—the sense of minds engaged, quickened beyond rhetoric, by emerging social contradictions—and it resulted in such outrages as a six-word analysis of a leading French sociologist ("M. GEORGES LAPASSADE," announced almost a full page of *I.S. # 9*, "EST UN CON"). It led as well to a style of absurdity and play, and to an affirmation that contestation was fun: a good way to live. The situationists delighted in the discovery that dialectics caused society to produce not just contradictions but also endless self-parodies. Their journal was filled with them—my favorite is a reproduction of an ad for the Peace o' Mind Fallout Shelter Company. And the comics that illustrated *I.S.* led to the *détournement* of the putative heroes of everyday life. Characters out of *Steve Canyon* and *True Romance* were given new balloons, and made to speak passionately of revolution, alienation, and the lie of culture—as if even the most unlikely people actually cared about such things. In the pages of *I.S.*, a kiss suggested not marriage but fantasies of liberation: a sigh for the Paris Commune.

The theory of exemplary acts and the quest for a new language of action also brought the situationists' pursuit of extremism into play. *I.S. #10*, March 1966, on the Watts riots: "All those who went so far as to recognize the 'apparent justifications' of the rage of the Los Angeles blacks . . . all those 'theorists' and 'spokesmen' of international Left, or rather of its nothingness, deplored the irresponsibility, the disorder, the looting (especially the fact that *arms and alcohol* were the first targets for plunder) . . . But who has defended the rioters of Los Angeles in the terms they deserve? We will." The article continued: "The looting of the Watts district was the most direct realization of the distorted principle, 'To each according to his false needs' . . . [but] real desires begin to be expressed in festival, in the *potlatch* of destruction . . . For the first time it is not poverty but material abundance which must be dominated [and of course it was the relative affluence of the Watts rioters, at least as compared to black Americans in Harlem, that in the 1960s so mystified observers of the decade's first outbreak of violent black rage] . . . Comfort will never be comfortable enough for those who seek what is not on the market."

"The task of being more extremist than the S.I. falls to the S.I. itself," the situationists said; that was the basis of the group's continuation. The situationists looked for exemplary acts which might reveal to spectators that that was all they were. They cited, celebrated, and analyzed incidents which dramatized the contradictions of modern society, and contained suggestions of what forms a real contestation of that society might take. Such acts included the Watts riots; the resistance of students and workers to the Chinese cultural revolution (a struggle, the situationists wrote, of "the *official owners of the ideology* against the majority of the *owners of the apparatus of the economy* and the state"); the burning of the Koran in the streets of Baghdad in 1959; the exposure of a site meant to house part of the British government in the event of nuclear war; the "kidnapping" of art works by Caracas students, who used them to demand the release of political prisoners; the Free Speech Movement in Berkeley in 1964; the situationist-inspired disruption of classes taught by French cyberneticians in 1966 at Strasbourg, and by sociologists at Nanterre in 1967 and 1968; and the work of Berlin actor Wolfgang Neuss, who in 1963 "perpetrated a most suggestive act of sabotage . . . by placing a notice in the paper *Der Abend* giving away the identity of the killer in a television serial that had been keeping the masses in suspense for weeks."

Some of these actions led nowhere; some, like the assaults on the cyberneticians and sociologists, led to May 1968, where the idea of general contestation on the plane of appearances was realized.

The situationist idea was to prevent the recuperation of such incidents by making theory out of them. Once the speech of the spectacle no longer held a monopoly, *it* would be heard as babble—as mystification exposed. Those who took part in wildcat strikes or practiced cultural sabotage, the situationists argued, acted out of boredom, rage, disgust—out of an inchoate but inescapable perception that they were not free and, worse, could not form a real image of freedom. Yet there were tentative images of freedom being shaped which, if made into theory, could allow people to understand and maintain their own actions. Out of this, a real image of freedom would appear, and it would dominate: The state and society would begin to dissolve. Resistance to that dissolution would be stillborn, because workers, soldiers, and bureaucrats would act on new possibilities of freedom no less than anyone else—they would join in a general wildcat strike that would end only when society was reconstructed on new terms. When the theory matched the pieces of practice from which the theory was derived, the world would change.

7

The situationist program—as opposed to the situationist project, the situationist practice—came down to Lautréamont and workers' councils. On one side, the avantgarde saint of negation, who had written that poetry "must be made by all"; on the other, the self-starting, self-managing organs of direct democracy that had appeared in almost every revolutionary moment of the 20th century, bypassing the state and allowing for complete participation (the Soviets of Petrograd in 1905 and 1917, the German Räte of 1919, the anarchist collectives of Barcelona in 1936, the Hungarian councils of 1956). Between those poles, the situationists thought, one would find the liberation of everyday life, the part of experience that was omitted from the history books.

These were the situationist touchstones—and, oddly, they were left unexamined. The situationists' use of workers' councils reminds me of those moments in D. W. Griffith's *Abraham Lincoln* when, stumped by how to get out of a scene, he simply had Walter Huston gaze heaven-ward and utter the magic words, "The Union!" It is true that the direct democracy of workers' councils—where anyone was allowed to speak, where representation was kept to a minimum and delegates were re-callable at any moment—was anathema both to the Bolsheviks and to the Right. It may also have been only the crisis of a revolutionary situa-tion that produced the energy necessary to sustain council politics. The situationists wrote that no one had tried to find out how people had actually lived during those brief moments when revolutionary contes-tation had found its form—a form that would shape the new society—but they did not try either. They spoke endlessly about "everyday life," but ignored work that examined it both politically and in its small-est details (James Agee's *Let Us Now Praise Famous Men*, Foucault's *Madness and Civilization*, the books of the Annales school, Walter Ben-jamin's *One-Way Street* and *A Berlin Chronicle*, the writing of Larissa Reissner, a Pravda correspondent who covered Weimar Germany), and produced nothing to match it.

But if Lautréamont, workers' councils, and everyday life were more signposts than true elements of a theory, they worked as signposts. The very distance of such images from the world as it was conventionally understood helped expose what that world concealed. What appeared between the signposts of Lautréamont and workers' councils was the possibility of critique.

Pursued without apparent compromise or self-censorship, that cri-tique liberated the situationists from the reassurances of ideology as surely as the experiments of the Lettrist International had liberated its members from the seductions of the bourgeois art world. It opened up a space of freedom and was a necessary preface to the new language of action the situationists were after. A single example will do: the situa-tionist analysis of Vietnam, published in *I.S. # 11* in March 1967—almost frightening in its prescience, and perhaps even more frightening in its clarity.

"It is obviously impossible to seek, at the moment, a *revolutionary* solution to the Vietnam war," said the anonymous writer. "It is first of all necessary to put an end to the American aggression in order to allow the real social struggle in Vietnam to develop in a *natural* way; that is to say, to allow the Vietnamese workers and peasants to rediscover their enemies at home; the bureaucracy of the North and all the propertied and ruling strata of the South. The withdrawal of the Americans will mean that the Stalinist bureaucracy will immediately seize control of the whole country: this is the unavoidable conclusion. Because the invaders cannot indefinitely sustain their aggression; ever since Talley-rand it has been a commonplace that one can do anything with a bayo-net except sit on it. The point, therefore, is not to give unconditional (or even conditional) support to the Vietcong, but to struggle consistently and without any concessions against American imperialism . . . The Vietnam war is rooted in America and it is from there that it must be rooted out." This was a long way from the situationists' rejection of the Beat Generation, but the road had been a straight one.

If the situationists were fooled, it was only by themselves; they were not fooled by the world. They understood, as no one else of their time did, why major events—May 1968, the Free Speech Movement, or, for that matter, Malcolm McLaren's experiment with what Simon Frith has called the politicization of consumption—arise out of what are, seemingly, the most trivial provocations and the most banal repressions. They understood why the smallest incidents can lead, with astonishing speed, to a reopening of all questions. Specific, localized explanations tied to economic crises and political contexts never work, because the reason such events developed as they did was what the situationists said it was: people were bored, they were not free, they did not know how to say so. Given the chance, they would say so. People could not form a real image of freedom, and they would seize any opportunity that made the construction of such an image possible.

8

L eaving the 20th Century: The Incomplete Work of the Situationist International, edited and trans-lated by former British situationist Christopher Gray, published in the U.K. in 1974 and long out of print, was until Ken Knabb's book the best representation of situationist writing in English, and it was not good. Translations were messy and inaccurate, the selection of articles erratic and confusing, the commentary often mushy.*

With the exception of a good edition of *The Society of the Spectacle* put out by Black & Red of Detroit in 1977, other situationist work in English was far worse. A few pieces—"The Decline and Fall of the Spectacle-Commodity Economy" (on Watts), "On the Poverty of Student Life"

---

*I was wrong about *Leaving the 20th Century* (republished in 1998, in a stab at a facsimile edition, by Rebel Press, London). The illustrations, many of them orig-inal, are funny (one is the Jamie Reid collage of domesticity that in 1977 turned up on the sleeve to the Sex Pistols' "Holidays in the Sun"); the translations have a verve Knabb shies away from; the commentary is quick, passionate, and finally anguished.

(the S.I.'s most famous publication, which caused a scandal in France in 1966 and prefigured the May 1968 revolt), "The Beginning of an Era" (on May 1968)—appeared as smudgy, sometimes gruesomely typeset and translated pamphlets. Most were put out by the short-lived British or American sections of the S.I., or by small situationist-inspired groups in New York or Berkeley.

The situationist journal, and the situationist books as they were originally published in Paris, could not have been more different. Illustrated with photos, comics, reproductions of advertisements, drawings, and maps, *Internationale situationniste* had an elegant, straightforward design: flat, cool, and direct. It made a simple point: What we have written is meant seriously and should be read seriously.

The Situationist International Anthology does not present the complete text of the situationist journal, and it has no illustrations. But the translations are clear and readable—sometimes too literal, sometimes inspired. Entirely self-published, the anthology is a better job of bookmaking than most of the books published today by commercial houses. There are virtually no typos; it is well indexed, briefly but usefully annotated, and the design, binding, and printing are all first class.

In other words, Knabb has, unlike most other publishers of situationist writing in English, allowed it to speak with something like its original authority. One can follow the development of a group of writers which devoted itself to living up to one of its original prescriptions: "The task of an avant-garde is to keep abreast of reality."

The situationist journal was never copyrighted. Rather, it bore this legend: "All the texts published in *Internationale situationniste* may be freely reproduced, translated, or adapted, even without indication of origin." Knabb's book carries an equivalent notation.

9

The role of the Situationist International, its members wrote, was not to act as any sort of vanguard party. The situationists "had to know how to wait," and to be ready to disappear in a common festival of revolt. Their job was not to "build" the S.I., as the job of a Trotskyist or Bolshevik militant is to build his or her organization, trimming all thoughts and all pronouncements to that goal, careful not to offend anyone who might be seduced or recruited. Their job was to think and speak as clearly as possible— not to get people to listen to speeches, they said, but to get people to think for themselves.

Rather than expanding their group, the situationists worked to make it smaller, expelling careerist, backsliding, or art-as-politics (as opposed to politics-as-art) members almost from the day the group was formed. By the time of the May 1968 revolt, the Situationist International was composed mostly of Parisians hardly more numerous— perhaps less numerous—than those who walked the streets as the Lettrist International. Behind them they had 11 numbers of their journal, more than a decade of fitting theory to fragments of practice, and the scandals of Strasbourg and Nanterre, both of which gained them a far wider audience than they had ever had before. And so, in May, they made a difference. They defined the mood and the spirit of the event: Almost all of the most memorable graffiti from that explosion came, as inspiration or simply quotation, from situationist books and essays. "Those who talk about revolution and class struggle, without understanding what is subversive about love and positive in the refusal of constraints," ran one apparently spontaneous slogan, in fact a quote from Raoul Vaneigem, "such people have corpses in their mouths."

At the liberated Sorbonne and later in their own Council for Maintaining the Occupations, the situationists struggled against reformism, working to define the most radical possibilities of the May revolt— "[This] is now a revolutionary movement," read their "Address to All Workers" of May 30, 1968, "a movement which lacks nothing *but the consciousness of what it has already done* in order to triumph"—which meant, in the end, that the situationists would leave behind the most radical definition of the failure of that revolt. It was an event the situationists had constructed, in the pages of their journal, long before it took place. One can look back to January 1963 and read in *I.S. #8: "We will only organize the detonation."*

10

W hat to make of this strange mix of postsurrealist ideas about art, Marxian concepts of alienation, an attempt to recover a forgotten revolutionary tradition, millenarianism, and plain refusal of the world combined with a desire to smash it? Nothing, perhaps. The Situationist International cannot even be justified by piggy-backing it onto official history, onto May 1968, not because that revolt failed, but because it disappeared. If 300 books on May 1968 were published within a year of the event, as *I.S. #12* trumpeted, how many were published in the years to follow? If the situationist idea of general contestation was realized in May 1968, the idea also realized its limits. The theory of the exemplary act—and May was one great, complex, momentarily controlling exemplary act—may have gone as far as such a theory or such an act can go.

What one can make of the work the situationists left behind is perhaps this: Out of the goals and the perspectives they defined for themselves came a critique so strong it forces one to try to understand its sources and its shape, no matter how much of it one might see through. In an attack on the Situationist International published in 1978, Jean Barrot wrote that it had wound up "being used as literature." This is undoubtedly true, and it is as well a rather bizarre dismissal of the way in which people might use literature. "An author who teaches a writer nothing," Walter Benjamin wrote in "The Author as Producer," "teaches nobody anything. The determining factor is the exemplary character of a production that enables it, first, to lead other producers to this production, and secondly to present them with an improved apparatus for their use. And this apparatus is better to the degree that it leads consumers to production, in short that it is capable of making co-workers out of readers or spectators." The fact is that the writing in *The Situationist International Anthology* makes almost all present-day political and aesthetic thinking seem cowardly, self-protecting, careerist, and satisfied. The book is a means to the recovery of ambition.

May 1982

BANAL RETENTIVE

Andy Warhol's Romance of the Pose

By Guy Trebay

> THE ANDY WARHOL DIARIES
> *Edited by Pat Hackett*

Like his best art, Andy Warhol's diaries are full of surface information and tough to figure. They dare you to find them deep. After a life spent hustling for the spotlight with close personal friends like Liza and Liz and Halston and Mick, Warhol thoughtfully remembered them all from Beyond. The artist's bequest to his boldface buddies is a record of his innermost thoughts and theirs. The result is a thick, newsy volume that's either celebrity wallpaper or a Pop *Goncourt Journals*. Maybe both. Who else, as Suzy says, would have thought to record the man-keeping secrets of our major thinkers? "If you only have two minutes, drop everything and give him a blow job," Jerry Hall told Andy. "Keep a diary," Mae West once advised, "and someday it might keep you."

Without question *The Andy Warhol Diaries* is this summer's heavy reading. I weighed the book myself and it's over four pounds. In fact, the diary is a two-writer effort. Edited (or "redacted," to use an old *Interview* term) by Warhol's phone confidante Pat Hackett, it's a monument to the Blavatsky style—part dictation, part *re*-creation. Hackett was Warhol's secretary/stylus, skittering over the board while he telephonically gave her the words. As every *People* reader knows, the diaries were begun as a daily telephone account of the artist's activities, made to satisfy the IRS. With the constant notations of taxi fares and dinner tabs, they also satisfy Harold Nicolson's advice to the thorough diarist to remember what everything cost. Warhol remembers it all. The diaries started out as accountings and evolved into reckonings, but nobody expected that at the start.

Hackett met Warhol when she drifted down to the Factory from Barnard looking for part-time work. He hired her, sort of, by pointing to a desk. Warhol employees couldn't always count on remuneration: "volunteers" was the office word for trust-fund menials with no pressing need for a paycheck. Hackett stumbled into a relationship with Warhol the way most of his employees, stars, and friends did. Warhol seemed to have some powerful gravitational pull, a personal force field. One of the many unwholesome delights of *The Andy Warhol Diaries* is watching cosmic detritus get sucked into his strange orbit.

Early ads for the book have suggested that behind Warhol's platinum-wigged vacancy lay a knuckle-whacking moralist: He only *looked* as if no one was home. The artist is portrayed as a churchgoing Big Brother, always watching. The creepy implication is that the Pop jester never took his world seriously. While his companions snorted and screwed themselves to oblivion, he sneaked off to light votive candles and annihilate everyone on paper. If the marketing's too patly convenient—suggesting that what we secretly desire is a repudiation of the sex-drugs-and-disco decades—it's also pitched right for the times. The tease on *The Andy Warhol Diaries* is that the book offers the sin and the penance in one stop. It's a trendy notion, but Warhol's Weltanschauung makes things a trifle more complex.

In a nice, and possibly random, touch the photo section of the book opens with a picture of the Zavackys, the Czechoslovakian family of Julia Warhola, Andy's mom. Posed in their kerchiefs, mustaches, and rube finery, the Zavackys appear ready to set off on the great adventure: "Up from Steerage." They remind the reader what Warhol came from, more accurately than the usual inventions about his "coal miner" father (actually a construction worker) from McKeesport (actually Pittsburgh). In the whopping 807-page volume Warhol cites the Zavackys just once, and not by name, reminded of them by the onion dome churches in *The Deer Hunter*. But he doesn't need to dwell on his forebears since they hover like shades, embodied in the moralizing, shrewd, and unforgiving peasant who lopped the final vowel from his surname and hit it big.

Warhol's hardworking, penny-wise (and generous by turns) nature had deep Old Country roots. Even when he became the most famous artist in the world, he remained the child of immigrants and a first-generation working-class American. This helps explain his infatuation with surface and his success in Society: He lent himself as a kooky ornament to people who valued his tactful understanding that he'd never belong.

One of the enduring Warhol fictions casts him as a mooch. And it's true he loved a freebie. Like a crazed conventioneer, the diary Warhol swipes silver from the Concorde—working toward a complete set—accepts ludicrous invitations, even attends the opening of an escalator. With his tape recorder or Polaroid he brings back souvenirs. But Warhol paid his own way. Even in the druggy days of Max's Kansas City (not covered by the diary), it was Andy who picked up the check. Which doesn't mean he expected less than full value. He was a big tipper who got a kick out of handing employees pink slips. He had a solid prole sense of quid pro quo.

The '60s Warhol recorded in his earlier books—among the most accurate records of the time—starred the gargantuan, drugged personalities of his superstar friends: Viva, Brigid Berlin, Ondine, Jackie Curtis. His novel *a* and *The Philosophy of Andy Warhol (From A to B and Back Again)* are all slick finish or amphetamine rant. He left the tape running on a cast of talking heads who played themselves with manic, damaged brilliance. But by the time *The Andy Warhol Diaries* begin, the superstars have faded (most aren't dead yet), his films are in a vault, and the cast has changed.

From 1976 until his death, Warhol preferred to surround himself with consorts and gold diggers. There are really two diaries. One is thronged with celebrities. But beneath that glittering text lies a subsidiary world, populated by Warhol's steadies, a passel of attractive and ambitious vagrants without portfolio or evident talent—"artists" like Victor Hugo, the window dresser who kept Halston company; "models" like Barbara Allen, a beauty whose staggering romantic successes were accomplished despite mental limitations impossible to overstate. And Bianca Jagger, of course.

Jagger is one of the few characters who survives all the *Diary* years: She's a tenacious scenemaker. Over time, Jagger develops as something more than a cartoon celebrity in a marathon name-drop. There's a strange quality about her, pouting with Halston, pouting with Mick, pouting for the cameras, pneumatic mouth on labial cruise control. She's no Lily Bart, but somehow Bianca seems . . . better than her fate as a groupie/girlfriend/wife-of-fading-rockstar.

Warhol has no taste for the pathos of Jagger's trajectory from Nicaraguan nobody to celebrity nobody. He has no taste for pathos at all. He gets off on showing his friends with their pants around their ankles. He prefers that their embarrassments take place in public, as in this entry from December of 1978: "Marisa [Berenson] looked beautiful in silver, and Paul Jasmin was with her. She's finally leaving town. She's mad at Barbara Allen because Barbara was seeing her husband, Jim Randall, out in California, so Barbara wasn't invited. Steve [Rubell] told us that Warren [Beatty] had fucked Jackie O., that he talked about it. Bianca said that Warren had probably just made it up, that he made it up that he slept with *her*, Bianca, and that when she saw him in the Beverly Wilshire she screamed, 'Warren, I hear you say you're fucking me. How can you say that when it's not true?' "

There's an anecdote a minute in the diaries. They're thick on the ground. And if they don't render whole, authentic-sounding people, it's worth remembering that Warhol's friends were not entirely real. The famous "stars" he cultivated have egos so strained and distended they're like special-effects contraptions lurching from page to page. Baryshnikov as the Little Engine That Could. Attack of the Fifty Foot Liza.

Anyway, diaries aren't under obligation to render whole people. It's a miniaturist's skill, made for the slash, the wicked aside, the unflattering silhouette. Warhol becomes seductive the way Pepys or Henry (Chips) Channon or Cecil Beaton do, on the strength of his own greedy curiosity and sanguine optimism. Not to mention his gaga syntax, which becomes a form of addictive baby talk. "Oh, I read a great column in the *Times!*" he tells the diary in December of 1978. "It was something like 'Funky, Punky, and Junky,' and they had been talking about it at Tom Armstrong's—it was about 'silly people' and it (*laughs*) had me in it a lot. No mention of Steve Rubell, no Halston—just me, Marisa, Bianca, Truman, Lorna Luft—the silly people and the silly places. And later, at Halston's, Halston said he's glad he wasn't mentioned because he said (*imitates*) 'I'm! Not! Silly!' And then everyone started calling Bianca 'silly pussy, silly pussy.' And Marisa came over and when she heard about the 'silly' column she was upset to be 'silly.'" Maybe you had to be there.

Pat Hackett tells us that Warhol "mellowed" over the years. He outgrew "a cruel maddening way he had of provoking people to near hysteria." Still, he kept all the barbed conversational quirks of a '50s queen. In Warhol's "camp" lexicon gay men were "fairies," any "loud" woman could be a dyke, and hyperbole was the rule (especially when describing the male organ: Warhol's diary is the Home of the Whopper). In the early days of his fame, he trained himself to talk in unintellectual monosyllables because it made for a more "butch" presentation. When he slipped with a five-dollar word (never in public), he inevitably used the occasion to mock himself.

It was in Warhol's Pop nature to fetishize movie stars and objects and puppies, then exploit his woozy compulsion in art. He kept a tight rein on sentimentality, or exposed it to gamma rays that made it larger than life. Warhol's modus operandi, his "philosophy," was a stew of aesthetics and Czechoslovakian home truths. He disguised his politics (actively Democratic, although he only voted once in his life) and real opinions as credulous blather. He acted dumb. "Victor [Hugo] came by with his brother who's so good looking," he remarks one August Monday in 1983. "And Victor says his brother's cock is so big he used to hit the table with it at breakfast. I guess they were naked at breakfast, you know these South Americans. It takes years to get nervous and live in an uptight situation like civilization." How did people ever swallow the supposition that the real Warhol was a white-wigged idiot standing around saying, "Great"?

One of Warhol's better card tricks was to make it all look easy: He was careful to maintain his cool. And that wasn't always for the public's benefit. He worked hard to conceal creepy feelings like hurt and longing from himself. "[Producer] Jon [Gould] told me the other night that he liked *Popism,* but to Chris he said he didn't think Paramount could do it," Warhol writes in March of 1981. "But maybe eventually something will happen with it. Maybe it's too soon. Oh, and Jon said to me that he thought it was 'badly edited' so I don't know if he's good at reading."

This unexciting entry captures an essential Warhol. It replays one of his ancient ambitions, to be taken seriously (in Hollywood, of all places). And it displays his ego at work. Warhol knew the value of his talents, and could spot his own ephemeral garbage faster than anyone. Just as surely he knew what would last. Although he was a literary dunce (Joan Crawford's bio was a heavy tome), Warhol was "good at reading." And writing. With the exception of *a,* which was written and should be read on amphetamines, his books are skillful, composed in his own reedy ruthless voice. By the time he came to write them, his persona had achieved fictional proportions. Having invented Andy, there was little need to manufacture stories about him. Andy could follow Andy around and record Andy's adventures and Andy's nutty thoughts.

One problem with the diaries is their postmortem polish. (Another is the casual proofreading: Names are misspelled, luggage comes down a "shoot.") As the reader slogs through the years with Warhol, it becomes tougher to sustain belief in the method of straight dictation. Hackett has said the book was distilled from 20,000 pages and that she used a light editing hand. But anecdotes drift toward the Iowa Writers' Workshop as sentences start, "This was the day of . . ." Dialogue tags ("she groaned") stand out from the page. Hackett intrudes.

Still the book is great social history, with its lip-smacking tales of loveless, sexless marriages, its gimlet-eyed view of other people's success, and its rampant unclosetings (when he mentions how Tony Perkins once hired hustlers to come through his window and pretend to rob him, you can see the libel lawyers twist and squirm). And it's studded with gems of pure Warhol: "She was the nurse and he was Kaiser aluminum," he remarks. Or, "It was a Paloma Picasso day. Went to breakfast at Tiffany's for her." Or: "Ran into René Ricard who's the George Sanders of the Lower East Side, the Rex Reed of the art world—he was with some Puerto Rican boyfriend with a name like a cigarette."

The mellow Warhol was, if anything, even sharper in his ability to skewer with few words. "Decided to go to Peter Beard's party at Heartbreak," he writes of the socialite cocksman/photographer. "Peter was at the door showing slides. The usual. Africa. Cheryl [Tiegs] on a turkey. Barbara Allen on a turkey. Bloodstains. (Laughs.) You know."

By the mid-'80s, Warhol has absorbed many of his rich friends' daffy eccentricities. He becomes an unwitting caricature, extravagant and yet convinced he's being taken (often true), obsessed with his pets, with unreturned favors, social gaffes and horrors. (When his wig is snatched during a book-signing at Rizzoli, he can't even say the words; his editor does it for him.) He's increasingly snookered by crystal healers, acupuncturists, and pimple experts. And, as always, he pines for affection and sex—even after Jon Gould has moved into his 66th Street townhouse. New art stars have begun to upstage him, and Pop colleagues are selling higher at auction, a fact that obsesses a man whose lifelong fear was "going broke." Scarier still, he occasionally goes unrecognized on the street.

The drug scene dries up as his adventuress friends revert to type and scramble for the altar. And the "fairies" mysteriously begin to die off. Betrayal, disappointment, and the banality of aging erode the fun quotient. Always phobic about hospitals and illness, Warhol is nastily remote when friends contract "the gay cancer." These entries—almost any entry involving the physical difficulties of a friend—have a bald, ugly texture. Warhol was more sympathetic to animal distress than human. In one early entry he rails against his assistant Ronnie Cutrone for assassinating an ex-girlfriend's cats. Yet, later, when friends contract AIDS, Warhol refuses to sit near them at parties or share seats in a car. He begins to avoid restaurants where "fairies" prepare the food.

After 1983, the peppy atmosphere of Warhol World darkens. His long relationship with the decorator Jed Johnson fizzles out and his emotional shortcomings begin to redound nastily on himself. Johnson's desertion begins a string of "divorces." Bob Colacello (né Colaciello, as Warhol né Warhola likes to point out) quits the editorship of *Interview* to pursue moneyed Republicans. Halston sells his name to J.C. Penney. Steve Rubell is imprisoned for tax evasion. And with each cast change Warhol's life and the book become more banal. His schedule is still frenetic but the diary rhythm flattens. There's more time to kill.

Part of the problem is Warhol's new companions. Where he used to attract the most outlandish and beautiful people, he now settled for salaried companions and Social Register dregs like Cornelia Guest. These (sometimes titled) dullards had none of the crackling edge of his old drag queens or even his high-level hustlers. Warhol's "stupid" pose was no help with this crowd, who couldn't tell the difference. And the diary is forced to work harder on their behalf. Capering from party to party with the newly anointed "celebutantes" and "millionettes," Warhol found himself mentally slumming. It's in these sections that you begin to notice what's left out.

There are few entries about shopping or collecting, two of his major obsessions. And scant mention of work. Throughout the 11 years the book covers, Warhol was constantly turning out portraits, portfolios, new projects. But when "inspiration" crops up, the word seems like a sop tossed to the tax man, a joke.

The aging Warhol was still in demand, but he was less fun, more inward and cranky. "Cabbed up to 63rd Street ($8). . . . And Halston handed me a piece of paper in the shape of a boat and I was so thrilled. I knew it was the rent check for $40,000 [for Warhol's Montauk house]. So that made my evening. And since it was so rainy I didn't have any gifts with me so I wrote an I.O.U. to Halston and Victor and the niece: 'I.O.U. One Art' . . . So anyway I went home and I opened up the paper boat and instead of a check, it was just nothing—like 'Happy Birthday' or something. It wasn't a check and it should have been a check. All done up like a boat. It should have been a check." The reader cringes.

Like most people's, Warhol's holidays were anything but celebrations. For years, he celebrated Thanksgiving and Christmas at Halston's East 63rd Street house. The attempts at re-creating family are landmarks amid seasonless loops of fun. They arrest the narrative in a way that few other events seem to do. Perhaps it's because the touching gifts (often a dress for Andy), the Christmas trees, the roast turkey are the last thing you'd expect from a group of drugged publicity junkies. And somehow this makes them dear. The book doesn't end until Warhol's death in February of 1987, and the giddy pace never slackens. But for this reader, the diary hit an inadvertent conclusion when Halston called off all tomorrow's parties, leaving Andy without his little band. "Got up and it was Sunday," Warhol tells the diary on December 25, 1983. "Tried to dye my eyebrows and hair. I wasn't in the mood. Went to church. Got not too many phone calls. Actually none, I guess."

July 1989

LET'S GET PHYSICAL

By Vince Aletti

PHYSIQUE PICTORIAL (45 "CLASSIC STRAP ISSUES,"
1955 TO 1968)

*Pictorial is planned primarily as an art reference book and is widely
used in colleges and private art schools throughout the country. . . . Several
psychologists and psychiatrists have told us that books such as* Pictorial
*often have a highly beneficial effect on negative, withdrawn patients who
become inspired by the extrovert enthusiasm and exuberance of healthy,
happy athletes. It is our hope that everyone who sees* Pictorial *will become
a little more conscious of his own body—more willing to live the clean
wholesome life which makes bodies such as these possible.*

There were a number of magazines during the 1950s that made this sort
of claim before letting loose with page after page of photographs of
naked men in G-strings, but none was more earnest or more eccentric
than *Physique Pictorial*. Launched in 1951 and still publishing (available now by subscription only), *PP* is primarily an outlet for the work
of photographer Don Mizer, whose Los Angeles–based Athletic Model
Guild was the most prolific, entertaining, and idiosyncratic physique
photo studio of the '50s (AMG, sleazier these days, is also still in operation). Mizer approached his endless succession of sailors, Marines, construction workers, aspiring actors, gym instructors, boxers, students,
hustlers, and thieves with a combination of instinct, insight, and raw
enthusiasm. Though the images that resulted were sometimes magnificent kitsch, the best have a feverish vitality and obsessiveness that
allow Mizer to wrest souls—and some very compelling portraits—from
these glistening slabs of flesh.

But portraits, however vivacious, were hardly what customers of
physique photographers and their magazines were in the market for.
Operating behind the protective facades of Art and Health, *Physique
Pictorial* and its early contemporaries *Body Beautiful, Adonis, Vim, Gym,
Men and Art*, and *Physique Artistry* (their titles announced their good
intentions) provided nearly nude gay pin-ups at a time when this bor-

dered on outlaw journalism. Mizer was particularly conscious of his out-law status, so *Physique Pictorial* evolved into a bracingly incongruous mix of pecs and ass and angry, often hilarious, notes from the underground.

If he couldn't be truly provocative in his photography (there were too many legal taboos), Mizer stirred things up with the tiny-type editorials he squeezed into the bottom of almost every page. Under headings like "How Secure Is Freedom in America?," "Big Brother Is Still Eager To Control Your Life," and "The Progress of Art in a Nation of Filthy Minds," Mizer reported on rampaging censorship, police harassment, judicial corruption, and obscenity trials. He regularly urged his readers to join the ACLU and "fight for their privileges," even though he got letters calling him a Commie sympathizer and a crank. But he was a wonderful crank—full of advice (on what to do if arrested or called in by postal inspectors, how to avoid blackmailers and mail-order swindlers, how to detect syphillis) and opinions (on the "legalized murder" of Caryl Chessman, the Kinsey report, crotch-stuffing, body-building contests, Freudian symbols). Every issue was dense with his quirky footnotes.

Homosexuality, which was supposed to be far from everyone's minds, was handled a bit more cautiously, but Mizer usually got in a gibe at hetero intolerance and misinformation, then referred readers to the "very worthwhile material" in *One* and the *Mattachine Review*. Yet if readers turned to these gay pioneers for more inside facts, they probably returned to *Physique Pictorial* for bravado and beefcake. Mizer laid it all on thick, but with great charm and humor. Even if his photos started out to capture the classic body beautiful, he always brought his models down to earth. His casually intimate camera technique and the lovingly detailed descriptions that float across all the pictures give Mizer's work a sexy specificity few photographers can match. Half the fun of *PP* is its crazy pile-up of models' capsule bios—typically a jumble of measurements followed by a sentence like, "Tom is eager to be an actor and is currently attending dramatic school; works as a service station attendant." Other descriptions unfold into short stories: the boy who was killed in a barroom shooting, another who jumped bail on a gun possession charge; a drowning, a robbery, a studio brawl. But most of the blurbs are full of optimistic affection, even pride, as Mizer details the ephemeral passions of young lives ("swims, wrestles, worked as a grocery boy, wants to be a surfer"). Spiced up with countless splashy pages of physique art (including the first American publication of Tom of Finland), *Physique Pictorial* looks like a raunchy, furiously opinionated high school yearbook. Wish I'd gone there.

July 1986

CLOSE ENCOUNTERS

The Squandered Promise of Science Fiction

By Jonathan Lethem

In 1973 Thomas Pynchon's *Gravity's Rainbow* was awarded the Nebula, the highest honor available in the field once known as "science fiction"— a term now mostly forgotten. From our current perspective, the methods and approaches of the so-called "SF writers" seem so central to the literature of our century that the distinction has no value, and the historical fact of a separate genre is a footnote, of scholarly interest at best.

Notoriously shy, Pynchon sent beloved comedian Lenny Bruce to accept the award in his place. . . .

Sorry, just dreaming. In our world Bruce is dead, while Bob Hope lurches on. And though *Gravity's Rainbow* really was nominated for the 1973 Nebula, it was passed over for Arthur C. Clarke's *Rendezvous With Rama*, which commentator Carter Scholz rightly deemed "less a novel than a schematic diagram in prose." Pynchon's nomination now stands as a hidden tombstone marking the death of the hope that science fiction was about to merge with the mainstream.

That hope was born in the hearts of writers who, without any particular encouragement from the larger literary world, for a little while dragged the genre to the brink of respectability. The new-wave SF of the '60s and '70s was often word-drunk, applying modernist techniques willy-nilly to the old genre motifs, adding compensatory dollops of alienation and sexuality to characters who'd barely shed their slide rules. But the new wave also made possible books like Samuel Delany's *Dhalgren*, Philip K. Dick's *A Scanner Darkly*, Ursula LeGuin's *The Dispossessed*, and Thomas Disch's *334*, work to stand with the best American fiction of the 1970s—labels, categories, and genres aside. In a seizure of ambition, SF even flirted with renaming itself "speculative fabulation," a lit-crit term both pretentiously silly and dead right.

For what makes SF wonderful and complicated is that mix of *speculation* and *the fabulous:* SF is both think-fiction and dream-fiction. For the first 60-odd years of the century American fiction was deficient in exactly those qualities SF offered in abundance, however inelegantly.

While fabulists like Borges, Abe, Cortázar, and Calvino flourished abroad, a strain of literary puritanism quarantined imaginative and surreal writing from respectability here. Another typical reflex, that anti-intellectualism which dictates that novelists shouldn't pontificate, extrapolate, or theorize, only *show* and *feel*, meant the novel of ideas was for many years pretty much the exclusive domain of, um, Norman Mailer. What's more, a reluctance in the humanities to acknowledge the technocratic impulse that was transforming contemporary culture left certain themes untouched. For decades SF filled the gap, and during those decades its writers added characterization, ambiguity, and reflexivity, helping it evolve toward something like a literary maturity—or at least the ability to throw up an occasional masterpiece.

But a funny thing happened on the way to the revolution. In the '60s, just as SF's best writers began to beg the question of whether SF might be literature, American literary fiction began to open to the modes it had excluded. Writers like Donald Barthelme, Richard Brautigan, and Robert Coover restored the place of the imaginative and surreal, while others like Don DeLillo and Joseph McElroy began to contend with the emergent technoculture. William Burroughs and Thomas Pynchon did a little of both. The result was that the need to recognize SF's accomplishments dwindled away. Why seek in those gaudy paperbacks what was readily available in reputable packages? So what followed was mostly critical rejection, or indifference.

Meanwhile, on the other side of the genre-ghetto walls, a retrenchment was underway. Though the stakes aren't nearly as crucial, it's hard not to see SF's attempt at self-liberation as typical of other equality movements that peaked in political strength around the same time, then retreated into identity politics. Fearing the loss of a distinctive oppositional identity, and bitter over a lack of access to the ivory tower, SF took a step backward, away from its broadest literary aspirations. Not that SF of brilliance wasn't written in the years following, but with a few key exceptions it was overwhelmed on the shelves (and award ballots) by a reactionary SF as artistically dire as it was comfortingly familiar.

In the '80s, cyberpunk was taken as a sign of hope, for its verve, its polish, its sensory alertness to the way our conceptions of the future had changed. But even cyberpunk's best writers mostly peddled surprisingly macho and regressive fantasies of rebellion as transcendence—and verve and polish were thin meat for those who recalled the mature depths of the best of the new wave. Anyway, cyberpunk's best were quickly swamped themselves by gelled and pierced photocopies of adolescent power fantasies that were already very, very old.

Which brings us to today. Where, against all odds, SF deserving of greater attention from a literary readership is still written. Its relevance, though, since the collapse of the notion that SF should and would converge with literature, is unclear at best. SF's literary writers exist now in a twilight world, neither respectable nor commercially viable. Their work drowns in a sea of garbage in bookstores, while much of SF's promise is realized elsewhere by writers too savvy or oblivious to bother with its stigmatized identity. SF's failure to present its own best face, to win proper respect, was never so tragic as now, when its strengths are so routinely preempted. In a literary culture where Pynchon, DeLillo, Barthelme, Coover, Jeanette Winterson, Angela Carter, and Steve Erickson are ascendant powers, isn't the division meaningless?

B ut the *literary* traditions reinforcing that division are only part of the story.

Among the factors arrayed against acceptance of SF as serious writing, none is more plain to outsiders than this: The books are *so fucking ugly*. Worse, they're all ugly in the same way, so you can't distinguish those meant for grown-ups from those meant for 12-year-olds. Sadly enough, that confusion is intentional, and the explanation brings us back again to the mid-'70s.

It's now a commonplace in film criticism that George Lucas and Steven Spielberg together brought to a crashing halt the most progressive and interesting decade in American film since the '30s. What's eerie is that the same duo are the villains in SF's tragedy as well, though you might want to add a third name—J. R. R. Tolkien. The vast popular success of the imagery and archetypes purveyed by those three savants of children's literature expanded the market for "sci-fi"—a cartoonified, castrated, and deeply nostalgic version of the budding literature—a thousandfold. What had been a negligible, eccentric publishing niche, permitted to go its own harmless way, was now a potential cash cow. (Remember when *Star Trek* was resurrected overnight, a moribund TV cult suddenly at the center of popular culture?) As stakes rose, marketers encamped on the territory—for a handy comparision, recall the cloning of grunge rock after Nirvana. Books were produced to meet this vast, superficial new appetite—rotten books, millions of them—and fine books were repackaged to fit the paradigm. Out with the hippie-surrealist book jackets of the '60s, with their promise of grown-up abstractions and ambiguities. In with that leaden and literal style so perfectly abhorrent to the literary book buyer. The golden mean of an SF jacket since 1976 looks, well, exactly like the original poster for *Star Wars*. Men of the future were once again thinking with their swords—excuse me, *light sabers*. This passive sellout would make more sense if the typical writer of literary SF had actually made any money out of it. Instead, the act is still too often rewarded with wages resembling those of a poet—an untenured poet, that is.

Other obstacles to acceptance remain hidden in the culture of SF, ambushes on a road no one's taking. Along with being a literary genre or mode, SF is also an ideological site. Anyone who's visited is familiar with the home truths: that the colonization of space is desirable; that rationalism will prevail over superstition; that cyberspace has the potential to transform individual and collective consciousness. Tangling with this inheritance has resulted in work of genius—Barry Malzberg tarnishing the allure of astronautics, J. G. Ballard gleefully unraveling the presumption that technology extends from rationalism, James Tiptree, Jr. (née Alice Sheldon), replacing the body and its instincts in an all too disembodied discourse. But the pressure against heresy can be surprisingly strong, reflecting the emotional hunger for solidarity in marginalized groups. For SF can also function as a clubhouse, where members share the resentments of the excluded and a defensive fondness for stories which thrived in 12-year-old imaginations but shrivel on first contact with adult brains. In its unqualified love for its own junk stratum, SF may be as postmodern as Frederic Jameson's dreams, but it's also as sentimental about itself as an Elks lodge or a family.

Marginality, it should be said, isn't always the worst thing for artists. Silence, exile, and cunning remain a writer's allies, and despised genres have been a plentiful source of exile for generations of iconoclastic American fictioneers. And sure, hipster audiences always resent seeing their favorite cult item grow too popular. But an outsider art courts precious self-referentiality if it too strongly resists incorporation. The remnants of the jazz which refused the bebop transformation are those guys in pinstriped suits playing Dixieland, and the separate-but-unequal post-'70s SF field, preening over its lineage and fetishizing its rejection, sometimes sounds an awful lot like Dixieland—as refined, as calcified, as sweetly irrelevant.

If good writing is neglected because of genre boundaries, so it goes— good writing goes unread for lots of reasons. The shame is in what's left *unwritten*, in artists internalizing prejudice as crippling self-doubt. Great art mostly occurs when creators are encouraged to entertain the possibility of their relevance. Might a Phil Dick have learned to revise his first drafts instead of flinging them despairingly into the marketplace if *The Man in the High Castle* had been recognized by the literary critics of 1964? Might another five or 10 fledgling Phil Dicks have appeared shortly thereafter? We'll never know. And there are artistic costs on the other side of the breach as well. Consider Kurt Vonnegut, who in dodging the indignities of the SF label apparently renounced the iconographic fuel that fed his best work.

What would a less prejudiced model of SF's relation to the larger enterprise look like? Well, nobody likes to be labeled an experimental writer, yet experimental writing flourishes in quiet pockets of the literary landscape—and, however little read, is granted its place. When claims are made for the wider importance of this or that experimental writer—Dennis Cooper, say, or Mark Leyner—those claims aren't rebuffed on grounds that are, quite literally, *categorical*.

SF could ask this much: that its more hermetic or hardcore writers be respected for pleasing their small audience of devotees, that its rising stars be given a fair chance on the main stage. What's missing, too, is a Great Books theory of post-1970 SF: one which asserts a shelf of Disch, Ballard, Dick, LeGuin, Samuel Delany, Russell Hoban, Joanna Russ, Geoff Ryman, Christopher Priest, David Foster Wallace—plus books like Pamela Zoline's *The Heat Death of the Universe*, Walter Tevis's *Mockingbird*, D. G. Compton's *The Continuous Katherine Mortenhoe*, Lawrence Shainberg's *Memories of Amnesia*, Ted Mooney's *Easy Travel to Other Planets*, Margaret Atwood's *The Handmaid's Tale*, and Thomas Palmer's *Dream Science*—as the standard. Such a theory would also have to push a lot of the genre's self-enshrined but archaic "classics" onto the junk heap.

Tomorrow's readers, born in dystopian cities, educated on computers, and steeped in media recursions of SF iconography, won't notice if the novels they read are set in the future or the present. Savvy themselves, they won't care if certain characters babble technojargon and others don't. Some of those readers, though, will graduate from a craving for fictions that flatter and indulge their fantasies to that appetite for fictions that provoke, disturb, and complicate through a manipulation of those same narrative cravings. They'll learn to appreciate the difference, say, between Terry McMillan and Toni Morrison, between Tom Robbins and Thomas Pynchon, between Roger Zelazny and Samuel Delany—distinctions forever too elusive to be made in publishers' categories, or on booksellers' shelves.

Of course, short of a utopian reconfiguration of the publishing, bookselling, and reviewing apparatus, the barrier—though increasingly contested and absurd—will remain. Still, we can dream. The 1973 Nebula Award *should* have gone to *Gravity's Rainbow*, the 1977 award to DeLillo's *Ratner's Star*. Soon after, the notion of *science fiction* ought to have been gently and lovingly dismantled, and the writers dispersed: children's fantasists here, hardware-fetish thriller writers here, novelizers of films both real and imaginary here. Most important, a ragged handful of heroically enduring and ambitious speculative fabulators should have embarked for the rocky realms of midlist, out-of-category fiction. And there—don't wake me now, I'm fond of this one—they should have been welcomed.

April 1998

HERE COMES THE BRIBE

By Paul Berman

THE PENTAGON CATALOG:
ORDINARY PRODUCTS AT EXTRAORDINARY PRICES
Compiled by Christopher Cerf and Henry Beard

The Pentagon Catalog even looks like a schlock book. The cover says, "Buy this Catalog for Only $4.95 and Get this $2,043 Nut for FREE!"—with an arrow pointing to a genuine hardware nut sealed in plastic and impaled through the book.

The *Catalog* is a joke book based on a single joke: The Pentagon buys ordinary hardware for astronomical prices. The $243 pliers. The $2228 wrench. And here is the *Catalog* of these outrageous items, each properly defended for its gigantic price. The $640.09 toilet seat, for instance, whose price is justified because the seat can withstand earthquakes, acid clouds, and the test of portability.

Ho, ho, the Pentagon is full of dunderheads who waste our money. But the book does make one think of a brilliant comment by Eugene McCarthy, who said: It's not the fat in the Pentagon budget that worries me, it's the lean. Quite right. Let us raise, then, the whole issue of corruption. Are we really against corruption? Do we honestly think it so bad?

Lincoln Steffens asked this question in his classic *Education*. Steffens, the great turn-of-the-century muckraker, learned after many years of crusading that corruption served a function. It was the way government and business worked out a mutually profitable relation. Are you against the cooperation of government and business? The country would collapse tomorrow without it. And how is this cooperation established? Under the table, obviously.

One can say of corruption that in friends it is a vice, in enemies, a virtue. I would hate to elect some magnificent representative of my particular views and discover that he had sold out to the refrigerator lobby. But if an ideologue of the enemy camp should be elected, I will always be relieved to hear that the man or the woman can be bought. Someone who can be bought is obviously a human being, has normal motives, is free of fanaticism. The Ayatollah Khomeni cannot be bought. I fear him. Alfonse D'Amato may be somewhat different from Khomeni in this respect. I am glad. It is why an Alfonse is not an Ayatollah.

I spoke to a dear friend about this question, and he expressed himself volubly. "Corruption," he said, "is efficient, human, and democratic. It generates cooperation and good feeling. It smoothes edges, softens blows, unites the high and the low in a chain of productivity. It militates against wars and crusades. It is tolerant and kind.

"Corruption would never ban *Penthouse* from the supermarket, and if *Penthouse* is banned anyway, corruption will bring it back. Corruption is a virtue in the form of vice, generosity in the form of greed, decency in the form of the indecent. It is skepticism in the face of fanaticism, light in the face of dark. It is freedom, corruption is. It is the possibility of choice. It is rebellion against the tyranny of rules, eccentricity in a world of uniformity.

"It is"—and my friend grew heated—"the American Way. It is Western civilization. It is the banner of liberty against the hordes of—"

But I stopped him. He had gone too far.

I laughed over *The Pentagon Catalog*, yes I did. But I'm glad that the Pentagon paid $659.53 for an ordinary ashtray.

July 1986

THE NECRO FILES

Apocalypse Culture Falls Off the Edge

By Mark Dery

The way he tells it, Adam Parfrey—the Ron Popeil of fusion para-noia, pop Satanism, bad art, cannibal killers, Jews for Hitler, and fecal black magic (make that brown magic)—*had* to become America's most mondo publisher. Mainstream houses wouldn't touch the stuff he was drawn to—beyond-the-pale subject matter that makes the minds of most readers curl up like slugs on a hot griddle. "I couldn't really work for other people," he told *Salon*. "Like, 'Hey, I'll find another Chicken Soup book for ya!' I couldn't see myself doing that."

Since 1987, when he cofounded Amok Press, he's done it his way, beginning with *Apocalypse Culture*, his omnibus of crackpot scholarship, Spenglerian ravings about the decline of just about everything, and matter-of-fact interviews with an unrepentant necrophile, a connoisseur of child torture, and a devotee of "body play" who cinches his waist to a wasplike 14 inches. *Apocalypse Culture* reportedly has sold more than 55,000 copies.

It is a bona fide subcultural classic, widely credited with kick-starting alt.culture as we know it, from the zine revolution to the Gen-X vogue for body modification to serial-killer fandom to knowing paranoia in the ha-ha-only-serious *X-Files* mode (although my nominee for that dis-tinction would go to RE/Search books such as *Industrial Culture Hand-book* and *Modern Primitives*, avowed Parfrey influences).

Now, Parfrey has inflicted a sequel, *Apocalypse Culture II*, on an un-prepared world. Like its predecessor, *AC II* features conspiracy theory, right-wing fulminations, apologias for pedophilia, sympathetic portraits of psychopaths, and the true confessions of a necrophile, plus (at no extra charge!) fascist-flavored kiddie porn, John Hinckley, Jr.'s mash notes to Jodie Foster, the Aryan Nation's guide to deconstructing Don McLean's "American Pie," and a handy-dandy clip-'n'-save Necrocard ("I request that after my death A. my body be used for any type of sex-ual activity or B. gay only ❑ straight only ❑ I do not wish my body to be dismembered or disfigured during necrophiliac sex ❑").

No *Chicken Soup* here; *AC II* is a bottom-feeder's *Salmonella for the Soul*.

The question on every transgressophile's mind, of course, is: Does the sequel provide all the noxious delights of the first *AC*? The short answer is: No. It's a better book in almost every way, far broader in scope and more thoughtfully edited, not to mention more generously illustrated with eye-frying images: Shirley Temple in SS drag, hyperreal sex dolls with hermaphroditic genitals.

But millennial America's at once a far weirder, more niche-marketed place than it was in '87, when *Apocalypse Culture* introduced a new generation of overeducated lumpen to the perennial pleasures of tipping every sacred cow in sight. Necrophilia, pedophilia, dead-baby jokes, and sympathy for those old devils Uncle Adolf and Crazy Charlie just don't deliver the cattle-prod jolt they did before Jeffrey Dahmer, JonBenet Ramsey, Columbine, Waco, and most of all, the Web, which has proven hospitable to an algal bloom of sites like Spamgirl.com.

We've been there, pierced that. The escalation of subcultural hostilities and free-floating weirdness, in our age of extremes, has robbed all the old, reliable satanic verses—acts of "aesthetic terrorism," in Parfrey's words—of their power to outrage. So has the strip-mining and strip-malling of every fringe-culture ritual of resistance, virtually the moment it appears. There's a desperately insistent, methinks-thou-dost-protest-too-much quality to recent proclamations that the counterculture is alive and well, whether at the increasingly bobo-friendly Burning Man, in Ann Powers's *Weird Like Us: My Bohemian America*, or at Disinfo.con, the New York festival of transgression where a speaker declared, somewhat unconvincingly, "When they just buy the thing that we really believed in, that's them surrendering to us." (I get it! [*cue forehead slap*] So, like, when the Gap starts selling leather pants, it means that even the Gap has been infected with the, like, rebellion meme, right?) Ironically, Parfrey, in his role as pitchman on the pathological midway, has greatly accelerated this dynamic. The center is widening; the fringes cannot hold.

If he were simply a buck-hungry retailer of the unspeakable, he'd go down easier. But he insists on a more exalted status: that of a Luciferian Noam Chomsky, speaking the awful truths about The Conspiracy and the dictatorship of political correctness that the lapdog mainstream media dare not utter. Unfortunately, it's well-nigh impossible to reconcile his lofty claims with his mean-spirited "retard"-bashing, his seeming endorsement of wetbrained conspiracy theories about Waco, and his creepy coziness with neo-Nazis. The acknowledgment-page shout-outs to close friend Michael Moynihan, described in a *New Times* article as a "kind of fascist activist"; the inspirational quotes from Hitler and the

National Socialist Liberation Front poster in *AC I*; the ruminations on "democracy's deification of Victimhood," in *AC II*, by good buddy Boyd Rice, last seen in brownshirt attire, accessorized with a darling little Nazi knife, in James Ridgeway's study of white supremacists, *Blood in the Face*: I'm sensing a theme here. And I'm not the first: Former RE/Search publisher V. Vale told *New Times* reporter Scott Timberg, "Adam is a racist . . . and he's friends with a lot of racists. Here's why he publishes: purely to foment shock value and to celebrate himself. . . . He's just a typical privileged, stunted-growth, adolescent white male."

Parfrey stands unbowed in the face of such charges. "My articles and investigations take me far and wide, and I get friendly with SWAT teams, extreme right-wingers, and anarchist bomb-throwers," he writes, via e-mail. "To cull Boyd Rice out of a group of published friends and then do a guilt-by-association trip is sinister McCarthyism." He readily concedes that *AC I* and *AC II* "concern the extremes of human belief" but defends his refusal to render moral judgment with the disclaimer "I respect the human consciousness enough not to infantilize it by spelling out moral conclusions. I do admit that I like making people uncomfortable with nanny culture's ideas and expectations. . . . God help me, I'm a pot-smoking Green Party member."

Maybe, but from my sniper's perch on the new New Left, there are a lot of chinks in the pomo/boho argument that ethics is so over, already, and in the self-serving defense that blowing bong hits at the politically correct is bad-boy fun. Why should we infantilize ourselves by ceding all moral authority to neocon scolds like William Bennett or left-wing inquisitors like Andrea Dworkin? Moreover, chain-jerking the "nanny culture" doesn't have much intellectual frisson, at this point, for anyone besides the Don Imus fan and *New York Press*'s "Mugger." Parfrey's brighter than that, by far.

Sadly, Parfrey shows no sign of ranging beyond the traditional quarry of all 20th-century cultural vanguards. More's the pity, because he's got a deft, Mencken-esque way with the lacerating one-liner, and a nose for great stories: survivalist nutcake "Bo" Gritz's run for the White House; and the awesome Mr. Awesome, a beefcake legend in his own mind who stalks Parfrey's message machine with scary-funny ferocity. His dark, sardonic postcards from the abyss, in the *Apocalypse* books and (my personal favorite) *Cult Rapture*, are toxic good fun. In my dreams, he'll follow Clarice Starling's advice to Hannibal Lecter in *Silence of the Lambs* and point that "high-powered perception" at himself and all the unconsidered ideologies in his closet—train the philosophical crosshairs of his mordant wit, his withering irony, and his pitiless cynicism on his own forehead, and pull the trigger.

December 2000

F I V E

Brave New Wave: Spotlight on Emerging Writers

*V*LS always been addicted to discovering fresh blood. From precocious reviews of then barely-known novelists and poets like Dennis Cooper, A. M. Homes, Kathy Acker, and Sapphire to short fiction by soon-to-be-famous writers (Dorothy Allison's story "Bastard Out of Carolina," for instance, appeared in *VLS* in the mid-'80s), we've never hesitated to hail the new kids on the literary block.

Sometimes it's love at first sight. In his tender exaltation of Dennis Cooper's morally challenging debut *Closer*, Peter Schjeldahl seems surprised and relieved to find such a writer at work in the world. Jeff Yang encounters the spark of self-recognition in Chang-Rae Lee, whose work betrays the divided loyalties of an assimilated immigrant. Richard B. Woodward's 1997 celebration of Jonathan Lethem's third novel catches a writer poised on the threshold of wider recognition.

David Shields enumerates Nicholson Baker's virtues in comic, biting fragments, effectively giving him a leg-up into the pantheon.

Witnessing Kathy Acker's Don Quixote in drag as pregnant punk-ette, C. Carr can't help but admire the way the novelist fucks with language, sexuality, and the canon in one low blow. Katherine Dieckmann joins the burgeoning Lorrie Moore cult, thrilling at her skill for nailing female teendom, whereas Stacey D'Erasmo's reading of Mary Gaitskill's early work is more ambivalent, mirroring the characters' own mixed emotions and conflicted drives.

"I AIMED MY FEELINGS RIGHT AT HIM"

Dennis Cooper's Molten Miracle

By Peter Schjeldahl

SAFE

Dennis Cooper's *Safe* is a literary event of a kind not seen since the '60s, when American poetry lost its public role to rock songs and its private nerve to the collective imperatives of academics and coteries. By a 31-year-old Californian recently transplanted to New York, *Safe* is a work of ambitious scope, moral seriousness, and innovative style, the sort that galvanizes a literary generation. Like most poetry worth reading these days, it is also a work in prose—this being one of several grounds on which it will be misunderstood. Another is that it is a book of and about gayness—in a way Melville wrote of and about whaling, but a lot of people will let appearances deceive them.

No extenuation is required for these appearances, which include publication by a gay press (do beware the sappy jacket copy, however), a cover photograph of a young man apparently in orgasm, and a practically encyclopedic treatment of Los Angelean gay manners, mores, and sex practices. *Safe* begins this way: "Mark had just opened a beer when he noticed an ad in *The Advocate*. It asked for someone like him to write to 'a beautiful, blond, twenty-eight year old lawyer with very specific ideas of love-making.'" We're made to know, right off, where we are: in a promiscuous subculture with "very specific ideas," one of them being the absolute desirability of "someone like" Mark, the book's aptly named object/hero—a winsome, dissolute, mindless sometime hustler. But this is, in every sense, only the beginning.

A slim book so compactly written you could break your toe on it, *Safe* journeys from prosaic surfaces to lyrical depths, then back up again. Its construction—as symmetrical as a cyclone, holding a tumult of images and meanings in simultaneous suspension—is inexhaustibly subtle, packing special rewards for any number of rereadings. In three sections, each composed of jump-cut scenes and fragments, *Safe* works like an altarpiece triptych in which the sacred mystery of a madonna and child is flanked with bearded martyrs—or like a safety vault, forbiddingly encasing a core of treasure. The first and third sections are coldly, harshly satirical, and the middle one is a molten miracle.

The first, "Missing Men," conducts a bumper-car ride around the L.A. gay world, configured in the mental processes, acts, and activities—mostly in relation to Mark—of several men, including Rob, a self-seriously intense young writer who reads too many book reviews and is given to analyzing the semiotics of porn films. Rob is trying to write a novel about a melancholic young writer named Rick. Cooper has many surrogates in *Safe*, each distinct and each palpably some aspect, usually unflattering, of himself. So does Mark, whose narcissistic essence flows into many vessels, including mediated images: porn stars, a dead rock musician. In Cooper's post-everything L.A., identity is a hall of mirrors and scrims (images of reflective and translucent surfaces abound), garishly illuminated.

The third section, "Bad Thoughts," begins with Mark's funeral (his death is offstage and unexplained) and follows Doug—another writer, this one worldly-wise and spiritually burned out—through a period of desultory, sex-drenched mourning. It is a story about remembering and forgetting—mainly the latter. At the end, Doug surveys a drawerful of Polaroids of his former lovers: "He's had a pretty full life, he decides glancing over the pile, but not so full that the drawer can't be closed tight."

Safe, then, is about what happens—an enormous lot, which keeps happening and ramifying long afterward in the reader's mind—between the promise of a personals ad and the *memento mori* of a Polaroid, and between the opening of a beer and the closing of a drawer. At the heart of it all, in every way, is the central section, "My Mark," a contained explosion, like an underground nuclear test, of emotion and imagination. In it, an unnamed speaker, obsessed with Mark, explores and finally exorcises his obsession. The context is specifically gay, but the content—the art—breaks through to the universally human. Cooper's comprehension is rather frightening.

Like any good poem, "My Mark" is its own summary, a map coextensive with the territory it describes. Briefly, though: It begins with imagined, ruminative visions of Mark drunk and getting picked up, alone in his parents' house, and seen through the eyes of a wealthy john having sex with him. It segues into an account of the speaker's affair with Mark, an account leading to a relentless exposure of the speaker's feelings—intense, wrenching, slightly insane. Gradually the tone relaxes, becoming elegiac, a dying fall. The affair is over.

"My Mark" is without a trace of self-indulgence. It is a work of totally considered aesthetic artifice, of perfected and flattened, steam-rollered lyricism. It is also one of the bravest and most stirring things I have ever read about love, as well as one of the most challenging morally. It is a furiously principled act of clarity, of demystification, directed against what W. H. Auden called "the romantic lie in the brain," the engine of the everyday aesthetic projection that, investing a loved one with glory, extinguishes both loved and lover as persons.

Cooper owns this theme. He has addressed nothing else, essentially, from his earliest poems of romantic idolatry through his satires and shocking tales of sexual violence—most memorably, a delicately writ-ten, terrifying work about a mass murderer and his victims, "A Herd" (in Cooper's last book, *The Tenderness of the Wolves*). The murder varia-tion returns in "My Mark," bracketed and distanced by metaphors:

> There's an odor inside the body I can't figure out, unlike a crotch's, and worse than the ass's . . . I've read about it in novels: the madman poised over an innocent victim, his knife at the end of its trudge down the teenager's chest. . . . The murderer, thinking of rummaging inside the torso, is driven back by a frightening stink which writers leave in ob-scurity, stumped as to how to describe it, not having smelled it.
>
> Without it Mark's not complete, but it lies slightly out of my grasp . . . I mean the truth about anyone.

For Cooper, murder and necrophilia fulfill the logic of sexual love.

He abjures this logic, gazing into the abyss and turning away. Being out on the edge, looking back, gives him a startling perspective, a species of tender wisdom for which he has developed the perfect voice—deadpan tone and demotic diction adding up, in the ear, to a music of continual deflations, of truths hitting home.

> Mark . . . was, in part, a young man who happened to wind up with well balanced features, knew what to do with his eyes, and I exaggerated his power, as it was a time in my life when I needed to feel very strongly. Mark filled the bill. Seeing his face on first meeting, I was so speechless that friends had to turn me around and shake my shoulders. . . . I miss Mark. I aimed my feelings right at him. He moved back to Georgia, left no address or phone number, and was "lying nude in the dark listening to music" the last time I heard from him. I loved him. I should have said so less often. It got so his eyes wouldn't register that kind of input.

The precision and speed of Cooper's style—descending from the banal to the appalling with the celerity of a runaway elevator—make it often comic, though in a way so black that maybe only a god could laugh at it.

Mark's dad was once a hapless farm boy in Georgia. Mark was a crazy idea in his head—one more squabbling, lightly flushed blob indistinguishable from the rest of his first grade class. Mark sat in back by the windows because it was furthest from anyone, though he was told they would shatter and snow in his eyes when the bombs hit. He'd be found centuries later, crouched under beams which had beaned him, surrounding his head with stars.

In telling the truth—about the character, about himself, about the pathology of late 20th-century America—Cooper is efficient to the point of cruelty.

I fill a head with what I need to believe about it. It's a mirage created by beauty built flush to a quasi-emotion that I'm reading in at the moment of impact: its eyes on mine, mine glancing off for a second, then burrowing in. . . . [The head] eyes the reward of a power greater than loving, that stormy opinion which simply erupts in smudged irises, leaving this holiest look in its path. I want to slap it.

Literary art on this level is elating because, fully self-conscious, it vaporizes self-consciousness over the heat of a ruthless devotion to the real.

Sometime next morning Mark let his jeans be unbuttoned. It took thirty seconds. He watched his face in the skylight. He'll never forget how impressive he looked as long as he lives.

Though poetry, *Safe* is in prose because verse right now—as all poets who are honest with themselves must realize—is a reified medium, much as painting had become before its recent, postmodernist revitalization. Pretty soon there's going to be a mad race to appropriate old poetic crafts—for new reasons—and I expect that Cooper, already a skillful prosodist, will be in on that. (Obviously, I think the world of Cooper, who indicates by an acknowledgment on the copyright page that he somewhat returns the feeling—an acknowledgment that surprised, gratified, and, since I had already drafted this review, slightly appalled me.) Prose is further dictated now by the need to reinvest poetry with representational and communicative functions, to get it back into a closed circuit with the world: a schizoid world, in our day (as in *Safe*), of image and delirium, public squalor and private desolation. *Safe* is the first major work of a new, figurative American poetry, a prototype, I fervently hope, of great things to come.

June 1984

TEXT AND VIOLENCE
Kathy Acker Strikes Again

By C. Carr

DON QUIXOTE

Don Quixote is now a theoretical girl, a female character marching forth on the spindly legs of poststructuralism; that is, she can tell you what it means to be a cunt. Thus Kathy Acker updates another classic. Better known for her image as a big bad mouth than for her eight books, Acker's often labeled a "punk" writer—which is certainly to judge a book by its haircut.

In its cleverly concealed didacticism, her *Don Quixote* shares something with the original. Cervantes hoped that readers would learn to "abhor the false and foolish tales of chivalry" which had driven his knight-errant mad. The Quixote of yore believed every fiction and so perceived his shabby world as a landscape of monsters, enchantments, and lovesick princesses. Acker's Quixote believes nothing. She knows that she's roaming in a world of lies and fakes, that identity is itself an internalized fiction.

Even so, she has also gone mad, because she's about to have an abortion. As the girl-narrator puts it in an earlier Acker book, *Blood and Guts in High School*: "Abortions are the symbol, the outer image, of sexual relations in this world. Describing my own abortions is the only real way I can tell you about pain and fear ..." Her abortion gives Quixote "the most insane idea which any woman can think of. Which is to love." So this nothing-errant will tilt at love like the old Don at his windmill, for in the world of Acker's novels, there *is* no love. Certainly no romantic love.

In all her books, Acker is obsessed by her relationships to men and to (male) language. Failure may be inevitable, but she's compelled to keep trying. Failure, in fact, makes intellectual sense. She's part of that century-long tradition of writers—from dadaists to deconstructionists—who've railed at the limits of the word. And she's certainly absorbed poststructuralist theories about the death of the Author (of originality), the end of humanism, the impossibility of truth. As one of the girl-narrators in *Don Quixote* explains to a friend, these philosophies provided "a language with which I could speak about my work." And so Quixote does, for Acker deconstructs gender in this book as she never has before. A writer who feels more at home in the art world than in the literary one, Acker addresses the same issues of sexuality and representation that we see in the work of visual artists like Barbara Kruger, Sherrie Levine, and Cindy Sherman. I can't think of many other women novelists facing these tough questions so directly.

Sometimes, though, I'm more intrigued with the "project" than with the on-again off-again pleasures of an Acker text. *Quixote* is much like her other stuff in style. It refuses to behave like a good read. Sure, it has its Graphic Sex and Violence, but that doesn't make it fun. Narrators mutate, and narratives dangle or implode into filthy wacky little fragments. Acker almost always appropriates Great Novels or Great Dramas, though she generally throws out the plot. She wants the characters—or maybe just the title, as in her definitively post-Dickensian *Great Expectations*. The old novel is there like a ghost in the reader's mind. Just as the Great Artists or political figures who occasionally have roles (Kissinger, Genet, et al.) already carry symbolic baggage through our brains.

In her last book, *My Death, My Life, By Pier Paolo Pasolini*, she wrote dialogue for Hamlet, Romeo, Portia, and Banquo's Dead Body (among others) by way of solving the murder of Pasolini. Supposedly. In the last scene of *My Death, My Life*, she has Portia declare, "This is a message to you: This whole book isn't a message to you." Nor is the murder solved, or even referred to again after the introduction. Typically, Acker won't say what anything means, only that "language is more important than meaning." The reader enters a conundrum in her books. Often Acker's tone is so cynical, her content so contradictory, her structure so apparently haphazard that it's hard to tell where she is in the resulting chaos. She's a camouflaged writer creating the sort of work Barthes describes in *Image-Music-Text*: "a text is not a line of words releasing a single 'theological' meaning (the 'message' of the Author-God) but a multi-dimensional space in which a variety of writings, none of them original, blend and clash."

With no narrative-drug to hook us, no coherent voice to guide us, no emotional thread to pull us through it, Acker's text practically dares us to make something of it; when her play, *The Birth of a Poet*, created scandal at last year's Next Wave Festival, greeted nightly by catcalls and walk-outs, I felt the same atomizing vortex at work. Acker, set designer David Salle, composer Peter Gordon, and director Richard Foreman prepared their contributions without consulting each other, and the result pushed disintegration to the point where there seemed to be no there there.

Acker's books don't have living, breathing plots, but they have their motifs, their recurring nightmares; the mother dead by Suicide, the girl abandoned by her father (husband) (friend), the girl captured by white slavers or involved with a very old man, and, of course, the attraction born as much in hatred as in love. One problem I've always had with Acker's work is her refusal to move her girl-narrators out of their victim postures. They are despised, used, abused—and they take it, thinking this will get them love. ("If you beat me hard enough I'll never leave you and I'll do everything you say," narrator Janey Smith tells one of her lovers, President Carter, in *Blood and Guts in High School*—an all too typical declaration.) They never quite connect with the rage that could make them powerful. "Look what you did to me," they seem to say. But then, they are nothings. "Nothing matters so I can do what I want," they seem to say, as if nihilism bred spoiled brats.

Acker steps back from acting the victim in *Quixote*, however. The knight-narrator has moved to a whole new level of alienation, where she doesn't even believe the myth of her own masochism. For example, Don Quixote meets a handsome man who explains to her that "as soon as a woman loves, she's in danger. Why? Because the man for whom she'd do anything because he eats her up makes her almost die: Because she's the one who loves, not him, from not knowing whether or not he loves her, she becomes sick, yet she can't give him up."

This awkwardly phrased dilemma describes what the Acker heroine is usually up against. But here, Quixote replies, "Man. I don't accept your argument.... It isn't possible for your Culture to judge or explain my love."

In the middle section of the book, called "Other Texts," Don Quixote does not appear, having "died" at the end of Part One. (In Acker's writing, "death" often means that there's no hope of getting what you want—as it does here. Or death is death, "the one Absolute, the one thing know-able.") "Other Texts" turn out to be Ackered variations on the likes of Wedekind's *Lulu*, full of incidents that might have fit in earlier Acker books; a woman slitting her wrists as a man tells her "no man will ever love you"; a woman asking "how does my body feel pleasure?" and responding with what gives her boyfriend pleasure. But the entire section has been prefaced with a reminder that Quixote, being dead, can't speak. "All she could do was read male texts which weren't hers." Knowing this, she avoids being a victim, but won't succeed in becoming a victor either. Such behavior would emerge from some place where she's never been. She's in limbo, wandering through the shadows of New York and London and apparently through time as well, hoping to defeat the evil enchanters that prevent self-knowledge and make love impossible: poverty, alienation, fear, inability to act on desire, inability to feel. She understands herself to be picaresquing in a male, thus alien, land.

She decides that being part male may be the only way to go. So Quixote declares herself a "female-male or night-knight" after changing her names to "catheter" and "hackneyed"—long male names, as she puts it. And for perhaps the first time in an Acker novel, the narrator has a series of companions—her Sancho Panzas—instead of lovers. The first of these, Saint Simeon, disappears early on only to come back a few pages later as a talking dog. Together, knight and dog encounter a Leftist "who always had to explain the world to everyone," some monks who ask to be beaten, and the madam of a brothel, but as usual these are like incidents seen through gauze, told by a narrator more interested in her own mind than in making up some stories.

Mostly, Quixote philosophizes. On her abortion: "My wound is inside of me. It is the wound of lack of love. Since you can't see it, you say it isn't here." On how things have changed between men and women: "Today love is a condition of narcissism, because we've been taught possession or materialism rather than possessionless love. Those people in days of yore didn't have proper language, that is, correct Great Culture. They were just confused and loved out of contusion." On her personal quest: "Did she really have to be a male to love? What was a woman? Was a woman different from a man? What was this 'love' which, only having dreamt about, she was now turning around her total life to find?"

It's apparent from the language and scenarios in *Don Quixote* that Acker has found a brand of feminism she can live with—something wild and "post-Lacanian." Lacan's phallocentrism, like Freud's, dismissed women as impotent, defined by their "lack," defined by a whole vocabulary of negativity. In *Don Quixote*, the knight so aware of being "object," "mirror," and "endless hole" realizes that part of her problem is with definitions and who gets to define. "I wanted to find a meaning or myth or Language that was mine, rather than those which try to control me," Quixote reflects near the end of the book, knowing that she's failed. The post-Lacanian postfeminists assume that women have a different relationship than men do to both desire and language—a difference they are still struggling to understand, as Acker is. The new French feminists do not present themselves as a monolith. Their ideas vary and clash, and only outside France are they "the new French feminists." Some even object to the label "feminist" In terms of a "women's language," though, writers like Luce Irigaray and Hélène Cixous speculate on the breakdown of syntax, linear logic, and unity; on the end of mastery and authority. Cixous calls for "the emergence of a language 'close to the body.'"

Acker's female characters find their only truth in the body, in sexuality. "I want your cock inside me" becomes a first intimation of self-discovery for the nothings (cunts) who've been told what they are through the ladylike centuries. As one of her female dog-companions tells Quixote: "My physical sensations scare me because they confront me with a self when I have no self." This dog could easily be Quixote herself. The female narrators in Acker's texts always seem interchangeable, different names tagged to the sound of one voice raging—obscene, cynical, bewildered, and demanding to fuck.

Fourteen years ago Erica Jong created a sensation with her sexually aggressive heroine and repeated use of the word "fuck" in *Fear of Flying*, but the novel's bestseller achievements proved that "girls talk dirty" could be safely assimilated as just another Adult Novelty item. It was a fake subversive book. Acker's mocking chapbook, *HELLO I'M ERICA JONG* (excerpted from *Blood and Guts*), hints at the rage, terror, and irrationality *F of F* never attempted. "I'M RIPPING UP MY CLOTHES I'M RIPPING UP MY SKIN I HURT PAIN OH HURT ME PAIN AT THIS POINT IS GOOD ... ME ERICA JONG WHEE WOO WOO I am Erica Jong I am Erica Jong FUCK ME YOU CREEP ..." Four-letter words aren't even the issue, just the occasional springboard into a place words will never touch. As Acker tells us a number of times in *Don Quixote*, women don't know who they are; they've been taught who they are. Maybe down there at the "woo-woo" level, she'll have peeled enough layers back to find something unmediated by learned behavior.

But there are limits to what can be unlearned. In Acker's work, every connection with some possible love seems doomed. "I have certain characteristics from childhood traumas," writes Janey, in *Blood and Guts in High School*. "By *love* do I just mean satisfaction of the needs created by my characteristics?" In *Quixote*, one of the dog-companions tells a long convoluted tale about the beginnings of a relationship. The dog's neuroses and those of her lover seem to align in such a way that This Could Be Love (possibly). First the dog had resolved to be a lesbian because men treated her so badly, but "being with another woman was like being with no one, for there was no rejection or death." For the dog, sexuality was rejection. Finally she'd met a girlish man, De Franville, who saw her as a boyish woman, his mirror. De Franville had to control his lovers to make sure they didn't get too close, even though he despised control, while the woman (dog) could only love if she feared. One night De Franville went to a party dressed girlishly to attract the woman who had come dressed as a man (a Nazi captain, in fact). Because she wanted girls. Because she couldn't love them. Naturally, she and De Franville fell in love. From there on the dog who is telling this tale speaks sometimes as the woman (dog), sometimes as the man, but always refers to the other as she(he) or he(she): "De Franville knew damn well that she(he) needed anyone's correction. . . . What signifies and signified is that she(he) thought she(he) was nothing: she(he) was unable to love; everything had to be given to her(him) . . ." They fell immediately into an s/m relationship which allowed them the control and the rejection they needed, and "Don Quixote was disgusted that human heterosexuality had come to such an extreme end, even though the dog wasn't human, only female."

This master/slave dialectic recurs throughout the book and throughout Acker's work—the all-purpose metaphor for a society dependent on unequal power relations. "The only way Americans can now communicate is pain," the Angel of Death (Thomas Hobbes) announces to the Nixons while they're fucking. In Part Three, Don Quixote is doing battle with the Nixon administration. Apparently. It's sometimes hard to know what the hell is going on in a text this perversely dissociated. After many pages of the Angel lecturing on dualism, the dog-eat-dog of relationships, and so on, Acker suddenly tells us, "Don Quixote got rid of Nixon." She doesn't say how. The sentences refuse to build into a climax, the complicated ideas appear in Dick-and-Jane simplicity, and the ideas and events continue to contradict each other (because, says our narrator, contradiction is part of a dualistic world). I feel my mind slip over the opaque surface of it all. Is that, finally, the point? As Quixote put it to a character identified only as the old male creep, "Being female, I'm not used to points." And I have to remind myself, in my irritation, that when you're trying to make yourself from scratch, that opaque surface is like the thin ice you're crossing.

It's odd that someone who finds her only truth in desire seems to write less out of her emotions than her intellect—all those theories of posteverything. Sometimes I think they just get in her way. But then Acker questions her emotions too. What is it, anyway? And how connected to her consciousness? There is a pervasive sadness and longing in Acker's books. Sometimes, as she writes (at the end of *Great Expectations*) "wants go so deep there is no way of getting them out of the body, no surgery other than death." To me, this describes a desire beyond language that wipes out any narration or character or meaning in its path. *Don Quixote* ends with the death of God. Which I read as the death of the Author, since this God tells Quixote "there are no more new stories, no more tracks, no more memories: there is you knight." In the last few paragraphs, this Author-God—whom Quixote calls "my master"—sets the knight free, after asking her why she thinks She is Male. The knight then wakes up to the world before her, where she won't have an Author, a role, or a meaning. I found this moving—which "God" knows, might even be an inappropriate response to an Acker work. Certainly, for anyone who's always been an object, the goal is not to mean (or move) something, but to *be*.

March 1987

OF HUMAN BONDAGE
Mary Gaitskill's Rough Trade

By Stacey D'Erasmo

TWO GIRLS, FAT AND THIN
BAD BEHAVIOR

In Mary Gaitskill's first short-story collection, *Bad Behavior*, the theme was missed connections, and the leitmotif was prostitution. Like Alice Munro characters on the skids, Gaitskill's men and women were petty sex thieves endowed with sensitive psyches and ironic epiphanies: middle-aged men in love with young hookers who were also artists; Dexedrine-popping bookstore clerks who longed to wound delicate co-workers; secretaries who made the best of tawdry sexual harassment; young hooker-artists who discovered that they weren't quite as tough, or as liberated, as they imagined themselves to be. Gaitskill also displayed a lacerating gift for anthropology; she dissected low-rent boho pretensions even as she empathized with the confused aspirers to wildness who sported them.

The deeper question of *Bad Behavior*, however, was women's sexual and emotional survival. The quintessential Gaitskill heroine came on fragile, but was tough as painted nails underneath, a woman in control of her own masochism. In "A Romantic Weekend," Beth's tryst with a married sadist goes awry when he begins to discover that she is not as pliant, or as empty, as he had thought. He cannot figure out why she won't let him destroy her. During suitably savage lovemaking, he grows frustrated and resentful. "This exasperating girl . . . contained a tangible somethingness that she not only refused to expunge, but that seemed to willfully expand itself so that he banged into it with every attempt to invade her. . . . Why had she told him she was a masochist?" In "An Affair, Edited," the male protagonist remembers his "kinky" college girl-friend with longing, particularly her unshakable center. "'I am strong,' she said. Her eyes were serene. 'I'm stronger than anyone else I know.'"

The joke, more often than not, was that a woman can't even get beat up the way she wants to. Men, by and large, were disappointingly weak-willed and obtuse, skinny creatures hoarding their tiny libidos, too timid or withholding to go all the way with a woman who could obviously take it. Like the literary equivalent of Madonna, Gaitskill was clearly the ringmaster of the Last Tango on the Lower East Side scenarios she constructed. She, and her heroines, were figuratively on top even when they played at being on the bottom.

In *Two Girls, Fat and Thin*, Gaitskill's new novel, that "tangible somethingness" is still there, but it is far more battered, less sure of itself, and it has a past. The structure is intriguing: Two women, of different classes and temperaments, are drawn together when the thin one, Justine Shade, an office worker and sometime journalist, interviews the fat one, Dorothy Storm, about her involvement with Anna Granite, an Ayn Rand–like figure who founded a movement and philosophy called Definitism. Switching back and forth from Dorothy's first-person narrative to the third-person narrative of Justine, the novel is an extended flashback to the women's childhoods.

Technically messy as it is, *Two Girls* may not receive *Bad Behavior*'s widespread critical praise. It is sprawling and sometimes overwritten; adjectives and similes pile up, as if Gaitskill couldn't quite relinquish any because they were all her favorites. While neatness isn't everything, some judicious pruning would have taken the purple out of Gaitskill's basically innovative vision. A more grievous error is the odd, unreal quality of Dorothy Storm. Although she is the "I" of the book, the woman who speaks for herself, she feels more like an act of ventriloquism than a character with contours and edges. She is larger than life, both literally and figuratively, but instead of sharing the center of the novel with Justine, she seems to stand outside of it like a monument. In fiction (as in life), monumentalism has a way of dampening personality.

Gaitskill is writing about the ambiguous, inchoate dynamics between women, and the difficulty of cresting an authentic self in an oppressive and abusive culture. As these women circle around each other, *Persona*-style, they often seem more like the two poles of a single personality than separate worlds. On the surface, however, Justine and Dorothy are opposites. One thin, pretty, discreet, and ambitious; the other fat, asexual, a little crazy-looking, satisfied to be nothing grander than a word processor. Justine, as the flashbacks show, was a mean, popular girl in high school; Dorothy was a tormented, lonely one. As it turns out, however, the two women are intimately connected by their history of abuse, and their desperate strategies to survive it. Dorothy, molested by her father, and Justine, mauled by family friends, boyfriends, and cruel lovers, trigger in each other a complex reaction of memory and longing. (Why this should be so is never exactly clear; it seems to happen telepathically.)

If the novel had a moral, it would be that inside every thin woman is a fat woman dying to be set free. Dorothy, the culturally more despised, is revealed to be the stronger of the two; she does not suffer from the pervasive sense of emptiness and lack of self that afflicts Justine. The fact that she never has sex at all begins to seem noble compared to the dangerous liaisons in which Justine becomes entangled; Dorothy expresses her power not through cruelty and domination, but through an unyielding will to live—mostly embodied in the relentless, angry appetite she develops as a child: "candy bars, ice cream, cookies, sugar in wet spoonfuls from the bowl, Hershey's syrup drunk in gulps from the can, ReddiWip shot down my throat, icing in huge fingerfuls from other people's pieces of cake."

Her defense against her father's abuse is to escape into the lofty, definite world of Anna Granite. As Dorothy puts it, "I was deeply moved by the description of Asia Maconda and Frank Golanka, the proud outcasts moving through a crowd of resentful mediocrities, surrounded by the cold glow of their genius and grace. . . . When I read the words of Anna Granite, I visualized a man with a splendid chest standing stripped to the waist in the moonlit snow-covered field. He stood erect, arms loose at his sides, fists lightly balled, waiting in the dark for something he alone understood." In her fantasy life, Dorothy inverts the social order, putting herself regally, a splendid hero, at the pinnacle.

Justine, on the other hand, like the Sade heroine, is lost in a hellish landscape, flipping endlessly between victim and victimizer. At five, Justine is molested by a colleague of her father's. At seven, she orders "the Catholic boy who lived down the street to tie her to his swing set and pretend to brand her, as she had seen Brutus do to Olive Oyl on TV." At 12, she has a humiliating, quasi-sadistic sexual episode with a boy who has "the empty pretty eyes of a TV star"; soon after that, she ties up another girl and violates her with a toothbrush. At 16, she is raped by her boyfriend. As an adult she enters into a full-blown sadomasochistic relationship with a small-time sexual dictator.

Although the Dorothy character is compelling, an example of forbidden female empowerment, the raped and raping Justine is the novel's torn heart. Dorothy's pathology has a knowable cause, but Justine is as much a product of her culture as she is the victim of a single event. Gaitskill locates the source of Justine's sadomasochistic impulses not in her family, but in the games and plots of children and adolescents. Gaitskill is far and away at her best when she describes the *Lord of the Flies* pubescent milieu of Action, Illinois, the lower-middle-class suburb where Justine's nastiness first begins to flower.

The . . . classroom was filled with murderously aggressive boys and rigid girls with animal eyes who threw spitballs, punched each other, snarled, whispered, and stared one another down. And shadowing all

*these gestures and movements were declarations of dominance, of terri-
tory, the swift, blind play of power and weakness.*

Justine's adolescent world is complex, dangerous, and utterly different from what her relentlessly nice parents believe it is. It's a place
where a gang known as the D girls (Dody, Deidre, and Debby) terrorize
their classmates through a combination of sexual precocity and brute
force. Gaitskill's descriptions of the D girls are at adolescent eye level,
unsoftened by adult perspective:

> *[Dody was] a big raw-boned girl with large fleshy shoulders and hips,
> and big active hands and feet attached to long, confused arms and legs,
> multidirectional like rubber. Her eyes were extraordinary, huge and
> brown, shot with mad glowing strands of yellow and gold which, in con-
> junction with the tawny mass of hair sprawling frantic and uncontrolled
> on her head, gave her the look of a restless, fitful lioness.*

These girls are mythically wild, uncontrollable, and dominant; Justine remembers "the time Dody, humorously displaying her hugeness
and strength, picked up a scrawny fourth-grader by a fistful of hair and
swung her in a complete circle three times before letting the screaming
creature fly." Although their dominance mysteriously disappears in the
company of adolescent boys, these are the girls from whom Justine
learns about power and powerlessness.

In one sense, Gaitskill would have us believe that there is no specific
reason for Justine's preferences. She is the way she is because the world
is a mean, hard place with mean, hard people in it. Evil exists, and it
resists psychology. In another sense, however, there is a clear pattern:
She is raped, and she rapes in turn—but the victim is always female,
either herself or another girl. It is temptingly elegant to believe in Justine as a masochistic heroine, the love slave inside all of us. But Gaitskill
never subjects her male characters to narrative or any other kind of
punishment. They are cruel, they are petty, they disappoint, but they
almost always get away with it. They are sometimes (usually unwit-
tingly) exposed, but never consciously debased.

In this scenario, consciousness seems like the consolation prize, the
weapon that wounds offstage. It is not, generally speaking, the weapon
Gaitskill's men prefer. They tend to use their bodies, not their minds.
Two Girls, Fat and Thin breaks with this tradition at the very end, when
a male tormentor gets his comeuppance—at Dorothy's hands—and
Dorothy and Justine lie down together, tentatively. It is a fragile happy
ending, a place where many a novel could start: two women, alone in a
room together, talking.

February 1991

LUDD'S LABORS LOST

By David Shields

THE SIZE OF THOUGHTS: ESSAYS AND OTHER LUMBER
By Nicholson Baker

1. Following *Vox* and *The Fermata*, Nicholson Baker was becoming known to a wider reading public as, in a sense, the thinking person's pornographer (than which there are worse reputations); *The Size of Thoughts* reestablishes and repositions him, though, as what he has been all along: an utterly idiosyncratic, artistically adventurous, passionately intellectual writer.

2. This book has a great opening sentence: "If your life is like my life, there are within it brief stretches, usually a week to ten days long, when your mind achieves a polished and freestanding coherence." Baker thus not only flatters us that we think like (as well as) he does, but he also manages to introduce the major (very Nabokovian) theme of the book—the glory of human consciousness.

3. *The Size of Thoughts* also has a great closing sentence: "Books open, and then they close." This acute but not particularly tortured (strangely serene) self-consciousness is Baker's signature, and it is one of the many crucial (liberating) effects he has had on contemporary American writing.

4. The first page of the bound galley says, "He lives in Berkeley, California, with his wife and child." The last page of the bound galley says, "He is married with two children." This is exactly the kind of weird erratum in which Baker is interested and about which he can write at such length and so amusingly. Human error? Intentional?

5. Douglas Coupland. Sallie Tisdale. Daniel Harris. Kathy Acker. William Vollmann. Bernard Cooper. Nicholson Baker. Seven writers I'm particularly interested in these days, all of whom live on the West Coast (Baker's a relatively recent transplant to Berkeley) and whose interestingness derives, for me, principally from the ways in which they process information and write about how they process information. The West Coast seems somehow to give people the freedom to focus on informa-

tion and its conduits, its messengers; the East Coast, by contrast, is still to me so much about the old-fashioned minutiae of social strata.

6. Nabokov says somewhere that the essence of comedy—perhaps of all art—is that it makes large things seem small and it makes small things seem large. This is precisely what Baker does. In his cosmology, superhuman monumentality must always yield to the appealingly humdrum. Disarmingly disguised as a collection of essays, *The Size of Thoughts* is actually an ars poetica, Baker's defense (as if any defense were needed) of his aesthetic: an ode to the "transfiguration of the commonplace" through art: a jukebox of praise-songs for the discarded, the ignored, the overlooked—changes of mind ("I want each sequential change of mind in its true, knotted, clotted, viny multifariousness, with all of the colorful streams of intelligence still taped on and flapping in the wind"), small thoughts ("Large thoughts depend more heavily on small thoughts than you might think"), film projectionists, nail clippers ("A big clear drum of ninety-nine-cent Trim-brand clippers sitting near the drugstore's cash register like a bucket of freshly netted minnows is an almost irresistible sight"), nutty punctuation, American slang ("Real slang just happens"), the accumulation of residue gathered at the bottom of computer-screen pages, defunct library card catalogs ("the real reason to protect card catalogs is simply that they hold the irreplaceable intelligence of the librarians who worked on them"), the word "lumber," books themselves. Baker adores the ephemeral, the irretrievably lost, which art can rescue. He is a kind of literary Statue of Liberty: Give him our wretched refuse and he'll turn it into poetry.

7. I recently had a dream in which Baker and I were riding along in a Honda Accord. Baker was driving (of course). Updike was driving ahead of us. Baker suddenly turned to me and said, "You realize, don't you, that Updike's driving a Mercedes?" What is this dream about—the anxiety of affluence? Two WASPs and a Jew? No. It's about mechanical aptitude.

8. We read Baker. We read Updike and Nabokov. We may even read Proust. But what makes Baker so strangely eloquent—what torques his rhetorical register up so high—is the line of 19th- and 18th-century male meditators whom he reads extensively and with whom he clearly aligns himself: Gibbon, Mill, Newman, Pater, James, Burke, De Quincey, Carlyle, Ruskin, Johnson, inter alia.

9. Quibbles, qualifications? All the essays note the dates when they were written, and if the good news is that Baker keeps getting better, the bad news is that some of the older pieces—for instance, "Rarity" (1984)—seem at times rather arch and precious. Baker is so self-parodically narcissistic that he has difficulty praising anyone else; the passing mention of Alan Hollinghurst in *U & I* is more memorable than

the review of *The Folding Star* here. The essay on model airplanes failed to make that subject emerge with any clarity; but then cf. my dream about cars. A few of the shorter pieces tend to end somewhat anticlimactically. Regarding the nearly 150-page tour-de-farce "Lumber": it's the OED entry of all OED entries, the Nexis search of all Nexis searches, for the word "lumber"—especially the term "lumber-room"—as a metaphor for the brain; a meditation on the difference between a text-based world and an electronic-based world; an inquiry into the nature of literary legacy; a parody of *Pale Fire*; a paean to—what else?—incompleteness, tangentiality, contingency, but as Samuel Johnson said of *Paradise Lost*, no one ever wished it longer.

10. Still, "Lumber" contains a passage that gathers, for me, the entire book in its train:

> *So useful and welcome does the curiosity-shop model of literary activity become that by 1961, Muriel Spark could confidently assume, when she had a character in her book* The Prime of Miss Jean Brodie *write a treatise called "The Transfiguration of the Commonplace," that we would know pretty much what she was getting at. The commonplace was the entire arbitrarily window-framed world, the world of moral cliches, the world of cardboard-character types, the world of material junk, so familiar it was rejected and put in storage, and the transfigurer was the connoisseur-pawnbroker-auctioneeer who saw where he or she might tie a dangly hand-written price on a little white string, assigning value and ownership where there had been only oppressiveness and shopworn confusion.*

Tellingly, Baker then proceeds to excoriate Arthur Danto for appropriating "The Transfiguration of the Commonplace" as the title for his book on artists such as Duchamp and Warhol; their "smirking, loveless twentieth-century 'transfigurations'" are not what Baker is about at all. "Assigning value and ownership where there had been only oppressiveness and shopworn confusion": This is a precise blueprint for Baker's entire literary project, and it is the aesthetic principle toward which this particular book has, essay by essay, been driving.

11. My favorite passage in my favorite essay in the book, "Discards": "Why, then, did library administrators order the Berkeley subject catalog destroyed? Was it really just to have the space for eight study tables? Admittedly, eight study tables, incised with the inevitable obscene drawings, declarations of love, and reciprocal ethnic slurs, and populated with thirty or forty pre-midterm Psych 101 students making soft sighing noises with their pungent highlighters and burping like moss-gorged moose from time to time for comic effect, is a noble sight to

have in a library. But is it a reasonable trade-off?" It is almost too perfect that Nicholson Baker's initials are NB: n.b.: *nota bene:* note well. He notices things that no one else notices, and he articulates what he notices extraordinarily well. He writes heart-stopping sentences and he's hilarious—what more are we supposed to ask for?

May 1996

MORE MORE MOORE

By Katherine Dieckmann

> WHO WILL RUN THE FROG HOSPITAL?
> *By Lorrie Moore*

Lorrie Moore inspires a quivery reverence unlike any other writer I can
think of: those eminently crushable author photos only enhance a devotion inspired by her spooky command of language and deep understanding of two common states of being, embarrassment and grace. The cult
of Moore is not unlike the cult of Mitchell (Joni, that is); moodiness
and sentiment are savored, even encouraged.

Little surprise, then, that an homage to Mitchell appears in the
pages of Moore's latest novel, *Who Will Run the Frog Hospital?* Our narrator, Benoite-Marie Carr, nicknamed Berie, and her best and more
beautiful teenage girlfriend, Silsby Chausee (a/k/a Sils), sit in a bedroom in a far upstate New York town called Horsehearts circa 1972, listening to Joni "keening 'Little Green.'" Retrospectively, Berie muses:

> *Twenty years later at a cocktail party, I would watch an entire roomful
> of women, one by one and in bunches, begin to sing this song when it
> came on over the sound system. They quit conversations, touched people's
> arms, turned toward the corner stereo speakers and sang in a show of
> memory and surprise. All the women knew the words, every last one of
> them, and it shocked the men.*

This is pure Moore: Feelings unguarded and uncool leak out in some
codified social situation, revealing hidden bonds as well as crucial divisions. This is also pure Moore: "The thick pelts of our eyebrows
shrieked across our faces, some legacy of the Quebec fur trade. Hers
were faint and wispy, like an aerial shot of grain." There are many,
many other wonderful Mooreisms in *Who Will Run the Frog Hospital?*,
wry wisdoms galore to copy into journals and letters. So I regret to add
that unlike Moore's first novel, the daringly asymmetrical but cohesive
Anagrams, this second full-blown narrative doesn't quite hang.

Maybe Moore's mastery lies in the short story; her two collections,

Self Help and particularly *Like Life,* merit frequent rereading. Parts of *Who Will Run the Frog Hospital?* were synthesized in a *New Yorker* story called "Paris," which tracks grownup Berie and her husband Daniel on a miscommunication-prone trip to the city of imposed romance. The fragments worked far better in that linked state than as scattered interventions into the main story here: Berie's and Sils's coming of age.

Still, that narrative is so ripe, rich, and prickingly familiar that any reader—especially one who faced adolescence in the early 1970s, those days of Wrangler shorts, Eau de Love, and "Brandy (You're a Fine Girl)"—can ride out the jaunts overseas. *Who Will Run the Frog Hospital?* centers on the summer that 15-year-old Berie and Sils take jobs at a theme park called Storyland, where the donning of fairy-tale costumes prompts cig breaks and offhanded mutters of "What the fuck, babe."

Sils works as Cinderella, Berie as a cashier in a candy-stripe dress and straw hat, but the humiliations don't stop there. Sils is blessed with good looks, boyfriends, and boobs, while Berie is awkward, the perennial third wheel, and, as she puts it, "flat, my breasts two wiener-hued puffs." Moore takes a slightly glazed approach to the girls' teenworld, very much in accord with Berie's description of her childhood: "Liquid, like a song . . . just a space with some people in it." The story feels loose and ambling, even though its key events, including petty theft and abortion, form a clear trajectory.

Moore flawlessly renders the sensations of teendom, the manic swings, the thirst for savvy, the intimacies ("I knew her clothes by heart"), the sudden, scarring betrayals. Adolescence is in some ways ideal Moore terrain, with its devotion to song and slang, its regular emotional wallops. Despite the bumps, *Who Will Run the Frog Hospital?* is still primo Moore, proof positive that her habit-forming gifts remain, especially when it comes to rendering the female condition in all its sadness and hilarity:

> *I remember thinking that once there had been a time when women died of brain fevers caught from the prick of their hat pins, and that still, after all this time, it was hard being a girl, lugging around these bodies that were never right—wounds that needed fixing, heads that needed hats, corrections, corrections.*

November 1994

SECRET ASIAN MAN

Live and Let Dialect

By Jeff Yang

> NATIVE SPEAKER
> *By Chang-Rae Lee*

Let me take this moment to confess to sins of the first and worst order
for a writer: sins of language, my original sins. I was born in America
but English wasn't my first tongue, not even my second. I was raised to
toddlerhood in a three-room Brooklyn flat across from the hospital
where I was born and where my mother and father worked. I received
their native Chinese from an aunt who spoke little else, then frightened
my weary immigrant parents by mangling it with Spanish. To their
horror, I was experiencing multicultural meltdown, becoming a linguistic bastard. While my nanny-aunt was busy elsewhere, I'd been left to
sample the forbidden fruits of public broadcasting—*Villa Alegre, Carra-
scolendas*—and, *gracias al televisor*, was stumbling ever further from
their model of that good second-generational child who should be, must
be, reared as a *bi gok lang* (American) speaking *ying gi* (English).

They sent me to nursery school early, to root out the traces of my
parents' speech and of the polyglot electric box. Now I'm told that over
the phone I don't sound Asian, that I sound just like . . . embarrassed
pause, because in this day of recognized diversity, *American sounds
as American does*. So now I'm a speaker of English without portfolio: I
can't even successfully mimic the chingchong mockery of others speaking yellow. I'm stuck in basic broadcast.

Which leads to my second, conscious sin: becoming an accomplice to
the murder of my ancestral tongue, a language that could not be resurrected despite years of afterschool remedial classes and the best efforts
of my repentant parents. My Spanish is still better than my Chinese.

So reading Chang-Rae Lee's debut novel was like being handed a
confession to sign. I play the literary authority while hiding the suspicion that this name, this face, this carefully disciplined tongue will
someday betray me. And half hoping someone will remember that I

can't even read a Chinatown newspaper. Sorry, man. *Se habla* Asian American. Brother Lee too.

Which means we work the contradictions, and this is what we write: spools of cultural history looped and extended with spurious detail. Or immigrant fantasies embedding nuggets of remembered fact. Or ethnic Everyman metaphors that want to recount the story of our selves more surely than we would or could ourselves. All Asian-American stories, ultimately, are biocryptography—not fiction, not nonfiction, but unfiction, coded answers to the question: Who Am I?

Lee does have irony. He gives *Native Speaker* the disguise of a spy story, lending generic form to the spirit of cultural surveillance that inhabits most Asian-American literature. Though the form is only cosmetic: Lee knows full well (as you will, early on) that he won't deliver a thriller's payoff in blood, lead, and adrenaline. What Lee does is to take the bones of a so-American genre and build them into a work of tremendous grace and discomforting resonance.

Lee's protagonist, Henry Park, is a Korean-American man born to immigrant parents, raised in ivory suburban upstate New York, educated—overeducated—and then married and employed, both against the grain. His wife is a WASP speech therapist named Lelia, and their relationship has become broken and distant since the death of their son, Mitt, in a tragic accident.

Lelia's mourning over Mitt is raw and melodramatically American, open in a way that Henry finds he cannot match; this she correctly takes as a lack of feeling, or at least emotional truth, on his part. Their daily communication has shrunk into empty terminology. "We were hardly talking then," he says, "sitting down to our evening meal like boarders in a rooming house, reciting the usual, drawn-out exchanges of familiar news, bits of the day. When she asked after my latest assignment I answered that it was *sensitive* and *evolving* but going well, and after a pause Lelia said down to her cold plate, *Oh good it's the Henryspeak*."

If Henryspeak sounds disconcertingly like Company lingo—spook talk—that's no coincidence. Henry works as an ethnic intelligence expert, an identity-mole-for-hire. Working for Dennis Hoagland, a canny opportunist, he and his coworkers are assigned to get close to and observe their own, to speak their language and listen to their responses, reporting their secrets to unknown and invisible clients:

> *Each of us engaged our own kind, more or less. Foreign workers, immigrants, first-generationals, neo-Americans. I worked with Koreans, Pete with Japanese. We split up the rest, the Chinese, Laotians, Singaporans, Filipinos, the whole transplanted Pacific Rim . . . Hoagland had established the firm in the mid seventies, when another influx of*

*newcomers was arriving. He said he knew a growth industry when he
saw one; and there were no other firms with any ethnic coverage to
speak of.*

Henry is a very good agent. The same things that impair him as a
husband make him a perfect spy. A closeted identity is a necessary tool
in this field, and Henry's lifelong fear of appearing alien has been useful:

*If I may say this, I have always only ventured where I was invited or
otherwise welcomed. When I was a boy, I wouldn't join any school club
or organization before a member first approached me. I wouldn't eat or
sleep at a friend's house if it weren't prearranged . . . call me what you
will. An assimilist, a lackey. A duteous foreign-faced boy. I have already been whatever you can say or imagine, every version of the new-
comer who is always fearing and bitter and sad.*

Henry, friendly assimilist, cultural chameleon, has always been able
to get close to others without being touched himself. But his most
recent assignment has been a disastrous failure: Asked to investigate a
Filipino-American psychotherapist named Luzon, he instead finds himself offering up revelations, blending facts from his life with the faux
data of his cover. The loss of his son, his wife, his assembled artifacts of
assimilation, have been stripped away, and he is all too vulnerable.

John Kwang—Korean-American Queens councilman, potential may-
oral candidate and messiah apparent of the gorgeous mosaic—is Henry's
second and last chance. Hoagland plants Henry as a mole in the Kwang
campaign. It seems like a plum gig. Henry's long-disused ties of blood
and language make it easy for him to gain Kwang's trust. But Henry
himself is slowly seduced by this patriarch, this Moses out of Flushing,
in whom so many have invested immigrant hope. Kwang calls Henry by
his Korean name, weaves around him a cocoon of familiarity. By story's
end, Henry must make a painful choice: *Should he tell Kwang's secrets, or
should he keep them?* If he speaks, he will be returned to his former state
of cultural denial—the good agent-American, condemned to a voiceless
life. Silence, by contrast, might set him free.

Here as elsewhere, for Lee, "to speak or not to speak" and "to be or
not to be" have identical meanings. Language is pandemic, it infects
and pervades and mediates everything: Speech is culture, speech is
power, speech is sex. It's Lelia's crispness of tongue, her confidence
in lingua Americana, that first attracts Henry. "Even before I took
measure of her face and her manner," Henry muses, remembering
their original encounter, "I noticed how closely I was listening to her.
What I found was this: she could really speak. . . . Every letter had

a border. I watched her wide full mouth sweep through her sentences like a figure touring a dark house, flipping on spots and banks of perfectly drawn light."

In contrast with Lelia's lack of verbal inhibition, Henry is emotionally ingrown, mute. He attributes this to being brought up within his father's culture of silent endurance, where pain must be swallowed in public (before the whites) and can only be expressed in private in the secret speech of home, in the father tongue which Henry, at the hands of his American education, has lost. Henry notes that what remains is "all that too-ready devotion and honoring, and the chilly pitch of my blood, and then all that burning language that I once presumed useless, never uttered and never lived."

Having smothered that burning tongue beneath the English of his teachers and peers, he's left with a language stacked against him: "There isn't anything good to say to an average white boy to make him feel small. The talk somehow works in their favor, there's a shield in the language, there's no fair way for us to fight." So is it any wonder that when grown-up Henry speaks, it is with a dissociation that suggests that the syllables and images flowing from his mouth sluice around his being without touching it? They come from some external source, the pen of an unseen author, some primeval phrase book; they aren't native to his heart. Henry has become living proof that man can be an island, even an Alcatraz. What he *wishes he could say* lies trapped behind the seal of the Good, the Silent, the Model Minority.

The spy in the house of culture: Lee's device works on so many levels, none deeper than as an examination of the position of the immigrant, and particularly of the Asian immigrant. Since World War II, of course, Asians in America have faced suspicions of divided or imperfect loyalty. The internment of Japanese Americans and, more recently, allegations in the news of Chinese immigrants acting as sleeper spies: These are examples of how the foreignness of Asians is seen as running deep as blood. We are not only different from whites, but also blacks. Thus, too frequently, our survival in America's bicameral politics of race means adopting one or another alias, smiling and wearing camouflage.

I remember a late night with an Asian-American friend who'd been brought up midwestern; we were discussing Los Angeles's Museum of Tolerance, the identity theme park that had recently opened to mostly white, mostly uncritical acclaim. To enter its exhibit halls, you must pass through a set of doorways that damn you to self-definition, marked in cold letters WHITE and COLORED. Of course, we thought, this device would shock and "educate" only those for whom the recognition of this divide was not a fact of daily life, and how often is any person of color given a choice between these doors? And then we considered our own childhoods, marked by spot-moments of acceptance and rejection, by inane and desultory wranglings with identity.

"Which door would you've gone through?" my friend joked.

I thought for a moment before answering.

"In one, out the other, I think."

While I was being half facetious then, on another day I might have meant it—a more bitter or honest day. As Henry notes in *Speaker*, "It's still a black-and-white world."

"It seems so, Henry, doesn't it?" Kwang agrees. "Thirty years ago it certainly was. I remember walking these very streets as a young man, watching the crowds and demonstrations. I felt welcomed by the parades of young black men and women. . . . I tried to feel what they were feeling. How could I know? I had visited Louisiana and Texas and sat where I wished on buses, I drank from whatever fountain was nearest. No one ever said anything.

"Soon there will be more brown and yellow than black and white," Kwang says. "And yet the politics, especially minority politics, remain cast in terms that barely acknowledge us. . . . (I)f I don't receive the blessing of African-Americans, am I still a minority politician? Who is the heavy now? I'm afraid that the world isn't governed by fiends and saints but by ten thousand dim souls in between. I am one of them."

Dim souls—finless, featherless creatures of the gray world. In the binary of our race politics, Asians are regularly seen as double agents, outsiders and in-betweeners harboring an enigmatic personal agenda; more so now, when anti-immigrant hysteria has brought back the interrogator's hot lights and the loyalty oath. In post–Proposition 187 California, to be yellow or brown invites accusation. To be a nonnative speaker becomes a daily confession. "Traitor" and "spy" and "false speaker of language" have become identical; and now more than ever we are tongue-tied.

Like every politician, Kwang has skeletons hidden in his closets; unlike many, the powers that be won't allow him to keep them. Since he resolutely refuses to enter a door—WHITE or COLORED—Kwang will be swept off the stoop. This, Henry grows to realize, is the nature of his assignment. And so: Speak or be silent? The time comes when Henry is asked to call his loyalty, an identity to keep and be damned. It's to Lee's credit—or is it?—that Henry gets a third option, and a resolution of his *Who Am I?* is withheld. After all, there are no easy answers, and admission through whichever door comes at a price that Asian Americans—that no one—should have to pay.

March 1995

THE WIZARD OF ODD
Jonathan Lethem's Fantastic Fiction

By Richard B. Woodward

In the often somber, always disrespected genre of sci-fi fantasy, a field still dominated by vain predictive tales and time-honored myths about saber-wielding warrior kings and queens, Jonathan Lethem's is a fresh, brazen voice. He has seen the future, and it's a joke.

Conspicuously low-tech in his visions, more cerebral than swashbuckling, and as funny as he is paranoid, Lethem loves to cross-wire popular genres and watch the sparks fly. He can walk the walk in the sci-fi tradition, following the wayward, left-leaning path of Philip K. Dick and J. G. Ballard. But when he talks the talk, he can't help laughing. All of his books make fun of or undermine their own conventions. The literary roots of his family tree are sunk as deeply in Borges, Pynchon, Lewis Carroll, and Stanislaw Lem as they are in *Star Trek* or *The Foundation Trilogy*. And Lethem has talent to burn, an impression reinforced by his rapid pace of production (three novels and a book of stories in three years) and the snappiness of his prose.

His impressive debut, *Gun, With Occasional Music,* featured a race of genetically evolved talking animals, including a ditsy sheep named Dulcie and the unforgettable Joey Castle, a surly kangaroo who works as muscle for a mob boss, even though he has trouble holding a gun in his tiny paw. The story of a Raymond Chandler style P.I. on the case in cyberpunk San Francisco had the feverish energy of a young writer with a lot on his mind and little time to fuss over petty consistency of plotline. The dialogue shows an inspired sympathy with the give-and-take of hard-boiled patter. Joey Castle unknowingly mimics the snarling defensiveness of Wilmer in *The Maltese Falcon.* ("You think you can bluff your way through, flathead, but you're wrong. Not this one. You gotta call it quits.") And detective Conrad Metcalf insults the kangaroo with put-downs out of Sam Spade's or Philip Marlowe's bottomless store. ("I put my hands on the wheel so I wouldn't try to put them around his thick neck. 'Message received. Hop along, Cassidy.'")

Lethem's San Francisco is a brutal police state where cops send people away to the freezer if their karma cards run out. It's a world Philip K. Dick's characters might've called home, where everyone has a personal blend of state-sponsored narcotics—Acceptol, Avoidol, Addictol, Regrettol, or the deadly Forgettol.

The postapocalyptic world of *Amnesia Moon* was even more beholden to Dick. Amid the blasted remnants of America, a young man on the road to restore his shattered identity encounters a tribe of hippies called the McDonaldians. Holed up in a deserted fast-food restaurant, they "live to serve" burgers and fries, upholding the strict code of behavior learned from customer relations manuals left behind by the fleeing management. Featuring a mix of mind-warping drugs and zany satire, it's held together by a lonely quest to recover lost or stolen memories. "I will probably never write a book more influenced by one writer," says Lethem, who discovered Dick at the impressionable age of 14 and devoured everything he could find. "It's as if I were trying to write the influence out."

Even if traces of the California dreamer's witty paranoid style never entirely disappear from Lethem's work—and why should they?—the collection *The Wall of the Sky, The Wall of the Eye* signaled that he was moving on. For the first time, his characters were suited up in more or less realistic dress. Opening with a postcoital conversation in bed between an anxious young man and his accommodating, if puzzled, mate, the story "Five Fucks" becomes an allegory about the limits of communication.

> *"I feel different from other people. Really different. Yet whenever I have a conversation with a new person it turns into a discussion of things we have in common. Work, places, feelings. Whatever. It's the way people talk, I know, I share the blame, I do it too. But I want to stop and shout no, it's not like that, it's not the same for me. I feel different."*
>
> *"I understand what you mean."*
>
> *"That's not the right response."*
>
> *"I mean what the fuck are you talking about."*
>
> *"Right."*

As voluble and wised-up as Lethem's people can be, they often feel trapped by the language they are forced to speak. The reader of Lethem's work is never allowed to forget that fiction is, at some level, always metafiction.

As She Climbed Across the Table, Lethem's latest novel, plays with these linguistic high jinks on a higher wire. The conventions of a love story, in which needy boy chases capable girl, expose a more foolish heart than Lethem has heretofore revealed, while the preoccupations of postmodern literary theory have spurred him to write one of the cleverest satires of academia since *White Noise*. (Lethem admits that during the writing he was "drunk on DeLillo.")

The university physicists in *As She Climbed Across the Table* depart from traditional sci-fi types. Neither warped geniuses intent on blowing up the world nor heroes eager to save it, they are, instead, Swiftian seekers after exotic truths in cloud-cuckoo-land. The focus of their research—and the literal void at the heart of the plot—is an amazing new discovery: a small, invisible black hole that has appeared on one side of a room at the Lawrence Livermore Labs in Berkeley, and which the scientists have nicknamed "The Lack."

Imagine a romantic comedy about Stephen Hawking's cosmology and Jacques Lacan's psychoanalysis, told in the hangdog style of Albert Brooks, and you've begun to appreciate Lethem's enthusiastic urge to burst the boundaries of the genre while continuing to play by many of its rules.

Set in the hills around Berkeley, this love affair between two brainy malcontents is related by Philip Engstrand, professor of anthropology and author of a dissertation entitled "Theory as Neurosis in the Professional Scientist." Earnest and articulate, but engaged in pointless research ("my new work was irrelevant and strong"), he lives with the brilliant and beautiful young physicist, Alice Coombs.

More shy and less well-spoken than Philip, Alice finds an intellectual purpose outside the relationship, at first as a member and then as leader of the team studying The Lack. Lack turns out to exhibit more personality, however, than a typical electromagnetic field, expressing strong likes and dislikes. To test these parameters, Alice rolls a lab table up to Lack's "strike zone" and slides various objects toward the invisible maw of the void turned celebrity.

> *In the weeks that followed it was as impossible to avoid updates on Lack's tastes as it was to catch a glimpse of Alice. Lack had swallowed an argyle sock, ignored a package of self-adhesive tape. He disliked potassium, sodium, and pyrite, but liked anthracite. He ate light bulbs, but disdained aluminum foil . . . The lists in the campus paper, under the heading Lackwatch, served as a daily dose of found poetry: hole punch, rosin bag, cue ball.*

Sadly, for Alice, who falls hopelessly in love with her work, Lack also rejects her. Philip, now ardent and desperate to win back his beloved from a cunning rival, begins to stalk Alice. But the tactic backfires, repelling her—she goes home to her family—while drawing him ever closer to the bosom of Lack.

Combining the geometric elegance of farce—the romantic triangle of Philip, Alice, and Lack is worthy of Barthelme or DeVries—with Lethem's brand of loopy logic, *As She Climbed Across the Table* makes no sense as science even as it tingles the brain as fiction. Its themes lightly touch on the nature of desire, blindness and insight, jealousy and betrayal, the female void and the male phallus, shallowness and depth, the Self and the Other, as well as soft and hard science. Lethem claims that he never intended to send-up last year's *Social Text* fiasco, although in the character of the literary theorist De Tooth he has drawn a savage caricature of a pomo academic on the make.

As a thinker and stylist, Lethem is still a mockingbird. Generous to a fault in acknowledging debts to others, he may be the kind of writer whose voice imitates those writers he most admires at any given time. But in his giddy eagerness to test-fly weighty ideas from incompatible genres, Lethem is opening up blue sky for American fiction, heavily grounded in the middle-class and lowlife novel of diminished expectations. An experimental writer in the best sense of the word, he is rapidly evolving into his own previously uncatalogued species.

April 1997

Acknowledgments

Dozens of great minds have worked on *VLS* over the years, writing, editing, copyediting, fact-checking, designing, and illustrating decades worth of articles, including the ones in this collection. I'd like to thank them, and in particular M. Mark, who got *VLS* rolling in the first place

I'm grateful to current *VLS* editors Michael Miller and Lenora Todaro for their help with this anthology, as well as for their daily inspiration, hard work, and good humor. Interns Aaron Hamburger, Kristen Case, Alexis Sottile, Kicron Devlin, and Michele Henjum assisted me in pulling this collection together in any number of little ways. Judy Miszner, Don Forst, George Troyano, and Doug Simmons at the *Voice* supported the project and made it happen.

Thanks to agent Ira Silverberg, a long-time champion of *VLS*, and to Carrie Thornton, Philip Patrick, and Brian Belfiglio at Three Rivers Press.

Also thanks to David Schneiderman, Stacey D'Erasmo, Polly Shulman, Scott Malcomson, Gary Indiana, Geoffrey O'Brien, Laurie Muchnick, Dorothy Allison, Lynne Tillman, Lee Smith, Kimberly Hall, Jessica Bellucci, Samantha Hunt, Christa Ryan-Dwyer, Stacey Wakefield, Jen Gapay, and Hugh Garvey for their assistance.

Finally, thanks to Kieran and Simon Reynolds for nursing me through deadends and for putting up with my long hours and late nights hunched over old copies of *VLS*.

About the Contributors

VINCE ALETTI, a music critic and columnist for *Rolling Stone, Record World, Creem,* and *Fusion* during the '70s and early '80s, has in more recent years written about photography and photo books for *The Village Voice,* where he is currently the art editor, and for *Artforum.*

DOROTHY ALLISON is the author of the novels *Bastard Out of Carolina* and *Cavedweller* and the recipient of two Lambda awards.

HILTON ALS is a staff writer at *The New Yorker.*

PAUL BERMAN is the author of *A Tale of Two Utopias: The Political Journey of the Generation of 1968.* His was an often-heard voice at *The Village Voice* from 1978 until 1992.

MICHAEL BÉRUBÉ is the author of *Life As We Know It* and *Public Access: Literary Theory and American Cultural Politics.*

BLANCHE McCRARY BOYD, recipient of a Guggenheim Fellowship, is the author of the novels *The Revolution of Little Girls* and *Terminal Velocity* and a collection of essays which appeared in *The Village Voice* between 1979 and 1980, *The Redneck Way of Knowledge.*

C. CARR is a staff writer at *The Village Voice,* and the author of *On Edge: Performance at the End of the Twentieth Century.*

ERIK DAVIS, author of *Techgnosis: Myth, Magic + Mysticism in the Age of Information,* lives in San Francisco.

THULANI DAVIS is the author of the novels *1959* and *Maker of Saints,* as well as two volumes of poetry and the play *Miss Ruby's Blues.* She is a senior editor at *The Village Voice.*

STACEY D'ERASMO's debut novel, *Tea,* was published in 2000. A senior editor and critic at *The VLS* for seven years, D'Erasmo was also a recipient of a Walter Stegner fellowship.

MARK DERY edited *Flame Wars,* a seminal anthology of cybercrit, and is the author of *Escape Velocity: Cyberculture at the End of the Century.* His most recent book is *The Pyrotechnic Insanitarium: American Culture on the Brink.*

KATHERINE DIECKMANN is a writer-director living in New York. She is currently making a feature film about the 1960s all-girl band The Shaggs.

PAUL ELIE, an editor with Farrar, Straus & Giroux, is writing a group portrait of Flannery O'Connor, Thomas Merton, Walker Percy, and Dorothy Day.

HENRY LOUIS GATES, JR., is the chair of the Department of Afro-American Studies at Harvard University. His most recent book is *The African-American Century*, co-authored with Cornel West.

RICHARD GOLDSTEIN is an executive editor at *The Village Voice*, where he has written about popular culture, politics, and sexuality since 1966.

GARY INDIANA's *Salo, or The 120 Days of Sodom*, a book-length essay on Pasolini, was recently published in the Modern Classics series of the British Film Institute, and his fifth novel, *Depraved Indifference*, is forthcoming. He was a staff writer at *The Village Voice* for many years.

LISA JONES is the author of *Bulletproof Diva: Tales of Race, Sex, and Hair* and a former staff writer at *The Village Voice*.

WALTER KENDRICK is the author of *The Secret Museum: Pornography in Modern Culture* and was an editor at *VLS*.

JONATHAN LETHEM's novels include *Girl in Landscape* and *Motherless Brooklyn*, which won the National Book Critics Circle Award. He lives in Brooklyn and Toronto.

SCOTT MALCOMSON is the author of *One Drop of Blood: The American Misadventure of Race* and *Empire's Edge: Travels in Southeastern Europe, Turkey, and Central Asia*. He was formerly a senior editor at *The VLS*.

GREIL MARCUS is the author of *The Old, Weird America* (formerly *Invisible Republic*), *Lipstick Traces*, and *The Dustbin of History*. He lives in Berkeley, California.

ALBERT MOBILIO is a Whiting Writer's Award recipient. In 1998 he won the National Book Critics Circle Award for reviewing. His books of poetry include *Bendable Siege*, *The Geographics*, and *Me with Animal Towering*. He has written for *The VLS* since 1986.

RICK MOODY is the author of the novels *The Ice Storm* and *Purple America*, and two collections of stories, *Ring of Brightest Angels Around Heaven* and *Demonology*.

BHARATI MUKHERJEE's books include the novels *Leave It to Me* and *The Holder of the World*, and *The Middleman and Other Stories*, which won the National Book Critics Circle Award in 1988.

GEOFFREY O'BRIEN is the author of *Hardboiled America, The Phantom Empire, The Times Square Story*, and *The Browser's Ecstasy*. His poetry has been collected in *Floating City*, and a selection of his writing from *VLS* appears in *Bardic Deadlines: Reviewing Poetry, 1984–95*.

ANDREW O'HAGAN's novel *Our Fathers* was short-listed for the Booker Prize and the Whitbread Book Award. He lives in London.

PETER SCHJELDAHL was the chief art critic at *The Village Voice* for many years, before becoming art critic at *The New Yorker*.

DAVID SHIELDS's most recent book, *Black Planet: Facing Race During an NBA Season*, was a finalist for the National Book Critics Circle Award.

DARCEY STEINKE's most recent novel is *Jesus Saves*. She lives in Brooklyn with her daughter, Abbie.

GREG TATE, a staff writer for *The Village Voice* and a writer-at-large for *Vibe*, is the author of *Flyboy in the Buttermilk: Essays on Contemporary America*.

LYNNE TILLMAN's most recent novel, *No Lease on Life*, was a finalist for the National Book Critics Circle Award in 1988. *Bookstore: The Life and Times of Jeannette Watson and Books & Co.*, a cultural history and biography, was published in 1999.

GUY TREBAY's writing for *The Village Voice* won him many accolades, including a Deadline Club Front Page Award. He is currently a staff writer at the *New York Times*.

DAVID FOSTER WALLACE is the author of *Infinite Jest*, *Brief Interviews with Hideous Men*, and *A Supposedly Fun Thing I'll Never Do Again*.

MICHELE WALLACE is a professor of English, women's studies, and film at the City College of New York and the CUNY Graduate Center. She is also the author of *Black Macho and the Myth of the Superwoman*, *Invisibility Blues*, and *Black Popular Culture: A Project by Michele Wallace*.

MICHAEL WARNER is the author of *The Trouble with Normal: Sex, Politics and the Ethics of Queer* and is professor of English at Rutgers University.

EDMUND WHITE's books include *A Boy's Own Story*, *The Beautiful Room Is Empty*, *The Flâneur*, and biographies of Jean Genet and Marcel Proust.

ELLEN WILLIS's latest book is *Don't Think, Smile! Notes on a Decade of Denial*. She was an editor at *The Village Voice* for many years and now directs the Cultural Reporting and Criticism program in the department of journalism at New York University.

JOE WOOD was a senior editor at *The Village Voice* and at the New Press. He edited the book *Malcolm X: In Our Own Image*.

RICHARD B. WOODWARD is a writer and editor in New York City.

JEFF YANG is the publisher and founder of *A. Magazine* and author of *Eastern Standard Time: A Guide to Asian Influence in American Culture, From Astro Boy to Zen Buddhism*.

Permissions